P9-CLC-904

DEBATING
THE PRESIDENCY

Fourth Edition

CQ Press, an imprint of SAGE, is the leading publisher of books, periodicals, and electronic products on American government and international affairs. CQ Press consistently ranks among the top commercial publishers in terms of quality, as evidenced by the numerous awards its products have won over the years. CQ Press owes its existence to Nelson Poynter, former publisher of the *St. Petersburg Times*, and his wife Henrietta, with whom he founded Congressional Quarterly in 1945. Poynter established CQ with the mission of promoting democracy through education and in 1975 founded the Modern Media Institute, renamed The Poynter Institute for Media Studies after his death. The Poynter Institute (*www.poynter.org*) is a nonprofit organization dedicated to training journalists and media leaders.

In 2008, CQ Press was acquired by SAGE, a leading international publisher of journals, books, and electronic media for academic, educational, and professional markets. Since 1965, SAGE has helped inform and educate a global community of scholars, practitioners, researchers, and students spanning a wide range of subject areas, including business, humanities, social sciences, and science, technology, and medicine. A privately owned corporation, SAGE has offices in Los Angeles, London, New Delhi, and Singapore, in addition to the Washington DC office of CQ Press.

DEBATING
THE PRESIDENCY

Fourth Edition

Conflicting Perspectives on the American Executive

Richard J. Ellis
Willamette University

Michael Nelson
Rhodes College

Editors

Los Angeles | London | New Delhi
Singapore | Washington DC | Melbourne

FOR INFORMATION:

CQ Press
An Imprint of SAGE Publications, Inc.
2455 Teller Road
Thousand Oaks, California 91320
E-mail: order@sagepub.com

SAGE Publications Ltd.
1 Oliver's Yard
55 City Road
London EC1Y 1SP
United Kingdom

SAGE Publications India Pvt. Ltd.
B 1/I 1 Mohan Cooperative Industrial Area
Mathura Road, New Delhi 110 044
India

SAGE Publications Asia-Pacific Pte. Ltd.
3 Church Street
#10-04 Samsung Hub
Singapore 049483

Copyright © 2018 by CQ Press, an imprint of
SAGE Publications, Inc. CQ Press is a registered
trademark of Congressional Quarterly Inc.

All rights reserved. No part of this book may be
reproduced or utilized in any form or by any means,
electronic or mechanical, including photocopying,
recording, or by any information storage and retrieval
system, without permission in writing from the
publisher.

Printed in the United States of America.

ISBN: 978-1-5063-4448-5

This book is printed on acid-free paper.

Acquisitions Editor: Michael Kerns
eLearning Editor: John Scappini
Editorial Assistant: Zachary Hoskins
Production Editor: Olivia Weber-Stenis
Copy Editor: Talia Greenberg
Typesetter: Hurix Systems Pvt. Ltd.
Proofreader: Dennis W. Webb
Cover Designer: Candice Harman
Marketing Manager: Amy Whitaker

SUSTAINABLE FORESTRY INITIATIVE
Certified Sourcing
www.sfiprogram.org
SFI-01075

17 18 19 20 21 10 9 8 7 6 5 4 3 2 1

CONTENTS

PREFACE

Nearly half a century ago the political scientist Aaron Wildavsky published a hefty reader on the American presidency. He prefaced it with the observation that "the presidency is the most important political institution in American life" and noted the paradox that an institution of such overwhelming importance had been studied so little. "The eminence of the institution," Wildavsky wrote, "is matched only by the extraordinary neglect shown to it by political scientists. Compared to the hordes of researchers who regularly descend on Congress, local communities, and the most remote foreign principalities, there is an extraordinary dearth of students of the presidency, although scholars ritually swear that the presidency is where the action is before they go somewhere else to do their research."

Political scientists have come a long way since 1969, when Wildavsky's book was published. The presidency remains as central to national life now as it was then, and perhaps even more so. The state of scholarly research on the presidency today is unrecognizable compared with what it was nearly a half century ago. A rich array of new studies has reshaped our understanding of presidential history, presidential character, the executive office, and the presidency's relationship with the public, interest groups, parties, Congress, and the executive branch. Neglect is no longer a problem in the study of the presidency.

In addition, those who teach about the presidency no longer lack for good textbooks on the subject. A number of terrific books explain how the office has developed and how it works. Although students gain a great deal from reading these texts, even the best of them can inadvertently promote a passive learning experience. Textbooks convey what political scientists know, but the balance and impartiality that mark a good text can obscure the contentious nature of the scholarly enterprise. Sharp disagreements are often smoothed over in the writing.

The primary purpose of *Debating the Presidency* is to allow students to participate directly in the ongoing controversies swirling around the presidency and to judge for themselves which side is right. It is premised philosophically on our view of students as active learners to be engaged rather than as passive receptacles to be filled. The book is designed to promote a classroom experience in which students debate and discuss issues rather than simply listen to lectures.

Some issues, of course, lend themselves more readily to this kind of classroom debate. In our judgment, questions of a normative nature—asking not just what is, but what ought to be—are likely to foster the most engaging classroom discussions. So in selecting topics for debate, we generally eschewed narrow but important empirical questions of political science—such as whether the president receives greater support from Congress on foreign policy than on domestic issues—for broader questions that include empirical as well as normative components—such as whether the president has usurped the war power that rightfully belongs to Congress. We aim not only to teach students to think like political scientists but also to encourage them to think like democratic citizens.

Each of the fourteen issues selected for debate in this book's fourth edition poses questions on which thoughtful people differ, such as whether the president should be elected directly by the people or whether the president has too much power in the selection of judges. Scholars are trained to see both sides of an argument, but we invited our contributors to choose one side and defend it vigorously. Rather than provide balanced scholarly essays impartially presenting the strengths and weaknesses of each position, *Debating the Presidency* leaves the balancing and weighing of arguments and evidence to the reader.

Eleven debate resolutions have been retained from the third edition and, wherever appropriate, the essays have been revised to reflect recent scholarship and events. The new edition includes three new debate resolutions that we hope will ignite spirited classroom discussion on topics both timely and foundational. For this new edition we welcome six new authors: Jeffrey E. Cohen, Joel K. Goldstein, Gene Healy, Matthew R. Kerbel, Douglas L. Kriner, and Andrew Rudalevige.

In deciding which debate resolutions to retain and which to add, we were greatly assisted by advice we received from many instructors who adopted the previous edition of this book. Particularly helpful were the reviewers commissioned by CQ Press: Marilyn A. Davis, Spelman College; Sean Foreman, Barry University; Matthew Harrigan, Santa Clara University; Nicholas Higgins, Regent University; Charles Matzke, Central Michigan University Online; Henry B. Sirgo, McNeese State University; and Barry Tadlock, Ohio University. We are also deeply grateful to Charisse Kiino for her encouragement and guidance in developing this volume. Among the others who helped make the project a success were editorial assistants Zachary Hoskins and Raquel Christie, copy editor Talia Greenberg, and production editor Olivia Weber-Stenis. Our deepest thanks go to the contributors, not only for their essays but for their first-rate scholarship.

—*Richard J. Ellis and Michael Nelson*

CONTRIBUTORS

Terri Bimes (Ph.D., Yale University) is a lecturer in the Charles and Louise Travers Department of Political Science and assistant research director at the Institute of Governmental Studies. As a lecturer, she teaches courses on the presidency and the senior honor thesis writing seminar. Her past publications include articles on populism and presidential elections.

Andrew E. Busch is professor of government at Claremont McKenna College, where he teaches courses on American politics and government. He is the author or coauthor of more than a dozen books, including *Horses in Midstream: U.S. Midterm Elections and Their Consequences, 1894–1998* (1999); *Ronald Reagan and the Politics of Freedom* (2001); *The Front-Loading Problem in Presidential Nominations* (2004); *The Constitution on the Campaign Trail: The Surprising Political Career of America's Founding Document* (2007); and, most recently, *After Hope and Change: The 2012 Elections and American Politics* (post-midterm election revised version, 2015). He received his doctorate from the University of Virginia.

Jeffrey E. Cohen (Ph. D., University of Michigan, 1978) is a professor of political science at Fordham University. He specializes in American politics, especially the presidency, and has published articles on the presidency in journals such as the *American Political Science Review*, the *American Journal of Political Science*, and the *Journal of Politics*. He has published two books on the presidency and the news media, *The Presidency in an Era of 24-Hour News* (2008) and *Going Local: Presidential Leadership in the Post-Broadcast Age* (2010). *Going Local* won the 2011 Richard E. Neustadt Award from the Presidency Research Group of the American Political Science Association and the 2012 Goldsmith Award from the Joan Shorenstein Center on the Press, Politics, and Public Policy, John F. Kennedy School of Government, Harvard University. His most recent book is *Presidential Leadership in Public Opinion: Causes and Consequences* (2015).

Thomas E. Cronin is the McHugh Professor of American Institutions and Leadership at Colorado College and president emeritus at Whitman College. He is author, coauthor, or editor of more than a dozen books on American politics, including, as author, *On the Presidency* (2009) and *Imagining a Great Republic* (forthcoming); and, as coauthor, *The Paradoxes of the American Presidency* (5th ed., 2017) and *Leadership Matters* (2012). He is a past president of both the Presidency Research Group and the Western Political Science Association.

Matthew J. Dickinson is professor of political science at Middlebury College. His blog on presidential power can be found at http://blogs.middlebury.edu/presidentialpower. He is author of *Bitter Harvest: FDR, Presidential Power, and the Growth of the Presidential Branch* (1999); the coeditor of *Guardian of the Presidency: The Legacy of Richard E. Neustadt* (2007); and has published numerous articles on the presidency, Congress, and the executive branch. His current book manuscript, titled *The President and the White House Staff: People, Positions, and Processes, 1945–2012,* examines the growth of presidential staff in the post–World War II era.

George C. Edwards III is University Distinguished Professor of Political Science at Texas A&M University and holds the Jordan Chair in Presidential Studies. He has written or edited twenty-five books on American politics. He is also editor of *Presidential Studies Quarterly* and general editor of the *Oxford Handbook of American Politics* series. His recent books include *On Deaf Ears, Why the Electoral College Is Bad for America, The Strategic President, Overreach,* and *Predicting the Presidency.* Professor Edwards has served as president of the Presidency Research Group of the American Political Science Association, which has named its annual dissertation prize in his honor and awarded him its Career Service Award.

Richard J. Ellis is Mark O. Hatfield Professor of Politics at Willamette University. His recent books include *Judging the Boy Scouts of America: Gay Rights, Freedom of Association, and the* Dale *Case* (2014); *Debating Reform: Conflicting Perspectives on How to Fix the American Political System* (with Michael Nelson, 3rd ed., 2017); *Judging Executive Power: Sixteen Supreme Court Cases That Have Shaped the American Presidency* (2009); and *The Development of the American Presidency* (2nd ed., 2015). In 2008 he was named the Carnegie Foundation for Advancement of Teaching Oregon Professor of the Year.

Fred I. Greenstein is professor of politics emeritus at Princeton University. His books include *Children and Politics* (1965), *Personality and Politics* (1969), *The Hidden-Hand Presidency: Eisenhower as Leader* (1982), *How Presidents Test Reality* (with John P. Burke, 1989), *The Presidential Difference: Leadership Style from FDR to Barack Obama* (2009), *Inventing the Job of President: Leadership*

Style from George Washington to Andrew Jackson (2009), and *Presidents and the Dissolution of the Union: Leadership Style from Polk to Lincoln* (2013). He is a fellow of the American Academy of Arts and Sciences and past president of the International Society for Political Psychology. He received his doctorate from Yale University in 1960.

Joel K. Goldstein, the Vincent C. Immel Professor of Law at Saint Louis University School of Law, has written extensively about the presidency, vice presidency, presidential succession and inability, and constitutional law. He is best known for his work on the vice presidency, primarily his books *The White House Vice Presidency: The Path to Significance, Mondale to Biden* (Kansas, 2016) and *The Modern American Vice Presidency: The Transformation of a Political Institution* (1982). He has written numerous book chapters and articles in political science journals and law reviews. He is frequently interviewed regarding the subject by national and international media. He received his A.B. from Princeton University, his B.Phil. and D. Phil. in politics from Oxford University, which he attended as a Rhodes Scholar, and his J.D. from Harvard Law School.

Gene Healy is a vice president at the Cato Institute. His research interests include executive power and the role of the presidency as well as federalism and overcriminalization. He is the author of *False Idol: Barack Obama and the Continuing Cult of the Presidency* and *The Cult of the Presidency: America's Dangerous Devotion to Executive Power*, and is editor of *Go Directly to Jail: The Criminalization of Almost Everything*. Healy has appeared on PBS's *Newshour with Jim Lehrer* and NPR's *Talk of the Nation*, and his work has been published in the *Los Angeles Times*, the *New York Times*, the *Chicago Tribune*, the *Legal Times*, and elsewhere. Healy holds a BA from Georgetown University and a JD from the University of Chicago Law School.

William G. Howell is Sydney Stein Professor in American Politics at the University of Chicago. He has written widely on separation of powers issues and American political institutions, especially the presidency. He is the coauthor, with Terry Moe, of *Relic: How Our Constitution Undermines Effective Government— And Why We Need a More Powerful Presidency* (2016), which builds on the ideas laid out in their essay in this volume. His recent books include *The Wartime President* (2013), *Thinking about the Presidency* (2013), *While Dangers Gather: Congressional Checks on Presidential War Powers* (2007), and *Power without Persuasion: The Politics of Direct Presidential Action* (2003). His research also has appeared in numerous professional journals and edited volumes.

David Karol is associate professor of government and politics at the University of Maryland, College Park. He studies parties, interest groups, political institutions, and American political development. He is the author of *Party Position Change in American Politics: Coalition Management* (2009), coauthor of *The Party Decides: Presidential Nominations before and after Reform* (2008), and coeditor of *Nominating the President: Evolution and Revolution in 2008 and Beyond* (2009). His research has also appeared in several journals and edited volumes.

Nancy Kassop is professor in the department of political science and international relations at the State University of New York at New Paltz. She writes on issues of the presidency and law. Her articles have appeared in *Presidential Studies Quarterly* and in such edited volumes as *The Clinton Presidency and the Constitutional System* (2012) and *New Directions in the American Presidency* (2011). She has been a contributing scholar to The White House Transition Project (WHTP) for the 2000, 2008, and 2016 presidential transitions, is past president of the Presidency Research Group (now, Presidents and Executive Politics) of the American Political Science Association, and is currently a book review editor for *Presidential Studies Quarterly.*

Matthew R. Kerbel is professor and chair of the political science department at Villanova University. He has written or edited nine books about American politics and the media, including *If It Bleeds, It Leads: An Anatomy of Television News* (2000), *Netroots: Online Progressives and the Transformation of American Politics* (2009), and most recently, *Next Generation Netroots: Realignment and the Rise of the Internet Left* (with Chris Bowers, 2016). He began his career in radio and television news, including work as a news writer for the Public Broadcasting Service in New York, and is now the voice of the political blog WolvesAndSheep.com.

Douglas L. Kriner is associate professor of political science at Boston University. He has written four books, including most recently *Investigating the President: Congressional Checks on Presidential Power* (with Eric Schickler) and *The Particularistic President: Executive Branch Politics and Political Inequality* (with Andrew Reeves), which received the 2016 Richard E. Neustadt Award for the best book on the American presidency. *After the Rubicon: Congress, Presidents, and the Politics of Waging War* received the Lyndon Baines Johnson Foundation's D. B. Hardeman Award for the best book on Congress. His work has also appeared in the *American Political Science Review, American Journal of Political Science,* and *Journal of Politics,* among other outlets.

Burdett Loomis is professor of political science at the University of Kansas. He received his doctorate from the University of Wisconsin–Madison in 1974 and served as an American Political Science Association congressional fellow in 1975–1976 in the office of the then-representative Paul Simon, D-Ill. He was a guest scholar at the Brookings Institution in Washington, D.C., in 1984 and 2000 and served as the Australian-American Distinguished Chair of American Politics at Flinders University (Adelaide) in 2013. He has written or edited more than twenty-five books. His scholarship focuses on legislatures, interest groups, and policymaking. Among his books are *The New American Politician* (1988); *Time, Politics, and Policy: A Legislative Year* (1994); and *The Sound of Money* (coauthor, 1998). In addition, he has coedited nine editions of *Interest Group Politics*. He won a Kemper Teaching Award in 1996 and has lectured for the State Department in Brazil, the West Indies, Mexico, Malaysia, Singapore, China, Iraq, Nepal, Bangladesh, Brunei, and Indonesia. His current work focuses on political change in the 1960s and 1970s.

Nelson Lund is University Professor at the Antonin Scalia Law School at George Mason University, where he has served as vice dean and as coeditor of the *Supreme Court Economic Review.* Professor Lund served as law clerk for Judge Patrick E. Higginbotham of the U.S. Court of Appeals for the Fifth Circuit (1985–1986) and for Supreme Court Justice Sandra Day O'Connor (October Term, 1987). In addition to experience in the U.S. Department of Justice at the Office of the Solicitor General and at the Office of Legal Counsel, Lund served in the White House as associate counsel to the president from 1989 to 1992. He holds a doctorate in political science from Harvard University and a law degree from the University of Chicago, where he was executive editor of the *University of Chicago Law Review.*

John Anthony Maltese is the Albert Berry Saye Professor of American Government and Constitutional Law and interim associate dean of the School of Public and International Affairs at the University of Georgia. His books include *Spin Control: The White House Office of Communications and the Management of Presidential News* (1994), *The Selling of Supreme Court Nominees* (1998), *The Politics of the Presidency* (with Joseph A. Pika; 9th ed., 2016), and *Government Matters: American Democracy in Context* (with Pika and W. Phillips Shively; 2013). He was named Georgia Professor of the Year by the Carnegie Foundation for the Advancement of Teaching and the Council for the Advancement and Support of Education in 2004 and is a Josiah Meigs Distinguished Teaching Professor, the University of Georgia's highest teaching honor.

Terry M. Moe is the William Bennett Monroe Professor of Political Science and a senior fellow at the Hoover Institution. His scholarship includes work on political institutions, public bureaucracy, and the presidency. Among his articles are "The New Economics of Organization"; "The Politicized Presidency"; "The Politics of Bureaucratic Structure"; "Presidents, Institutions, and Theory"; "The Presidential Power of Unilateral Action" (with William Howell); "Power and Political Institutions"; and "The Revolution in Presidential Studies." He has also written on the politics of public education, including *Politics, Markets, and America's Schools* (with John E. Chubb) and *Special Interest: Teachers Unions and America's Public Schools.*

Michael Nelson is Fulmer Professor of Political Science at Rhodes College. He is also a senior fellow of the Miller Center of Public Affairs at the University of Virginia and a former editor of the *Washington Monthly.* His recent books include *Resilient America: Electing Nixon in 1968, Channeling Dissent, and Dividing Government* (2014); *The American Presidency: Origins and Development, 1776–2011* (with Sidney M. Milkis; 6th ed., 2012); *How the South Joined the Gambling Nation: The Politics of State Policy Innovation* (with John Mason; 2008), which won the Southern Political Science Association's V. O. Key Award for outstanding book on southern politics; *The Elections of 2012* (2013); and *The Presidency and the Political System* (10th ed., 2014). More than fifty of his articles have been reprinted in anthologies of political science, history, music, sports, and English composition.

David Nichols is an associate professor of political science at Baylor University. He is also a senior fellow of the Alexander Hamilton Institute for the Study of Western Civilization. He is the author of *The Myth of the Modern Presidency* (1994) as well as numerous articles on American politics, constitutional law, and politics and literature.

Richard M. Pious is the Adolph and Effie Ochs Professor at Barnard College and professor at the Graduate School of Arts and Sciences at Columbia University. His scholarly books include *The American Presidency* (1979), *The President, Congress, and the Constitution* (1984), *Why Presidents Fail* (2008), and a book of cases and materials, *The War on Terrorism and the Rule of Law* (2006). He has coauthored a widely used print and online reference work, *The Oxford Guide to the United States Government* (2001). Pious has lectured on war powers at the United States Military Academy at West Point, at universities in the United States and Canada, and at seminars in the Far East organized by the government of Taiwan; he has lectured on presidential power and the war on terrorism at Oxford University and the British Library. He has served as a consultant to the Foreign Ministry of Japan since 1994. Pious is on the editorial advisory board of *Presidential Studies Quarterly* and served on the foreign experts panel of the *Journal des Élections.*

Andrew Rudalevige is Thomas Brackett Reed Professor of Government at Bowdoin College. A contributor to the "Monkey Cage" blog on the *Washington Post* website, his current research deals with presidential management of the bureaucracy and unilateral executive actions. Rudalevige previously taught at Dickinson College and the University of East Anglia. He is the author of *Managing the President's Program* and *The New Imperial Presidency,* editor of volumes on the Bush and Obama presidencies, and coauthor of the textbook *The Politics of the Presidency.* In a former life he worked in state and local politics.

Byron E. Shafer is the Glenn B. and Cleone Orr Hawkins Chair of Political Science at the University of Wisconsin–Madison. He is the author, most recently, of *The American Political Pattern* (2016); *The American Political Landscape* (with Richard H. Spady; 2014); *The American Public Mind* (with William J. M. Claggett; 2010); and *The End of Southern Exceptionalism* (with Richard Johnston; 2006), winner of the V. O. Key Prize of the Southern Political Science Association and the Race and Ethnicity Prize of the American Political Science Association. Many of his article-length pieces are collected in *The Two Majorities and the Puzzle of Modern American Politics* (2003).

Peter M. Shane is the Jacob E. Davis and Jacob E. Davis II Chair in Law at the Ohio State University's Moritz College of Law and author of *Madison's Nightmare: Unchecked Executive Power and the Threat to American Democracy* (2009), among many other works. A graduate of Harvard College and Yale Law School, Shane clerked for Judge Alvin B. Rubin of the U.S. Court of Appeals for the Fifth Circuit. He served in the Justice Department's Office of Legal Counsel and as an assistant general counsel in the Office of Management and Budget before entering full-time teaching in 1981. He is an internationally recognized authority on constitutional and administrative law, with research interests in law and the American presidency; democratic theory; and cyberdemocracy— the use of new information technologies to expand public opportunities to participate meaningfully in government policymaking.

Stephen Skowronek is the Pelatiah Perit Professor of Political Science at Yale University. He is the author of, among other works, *Building a New American*

State: The Expansion of National Administrative Capacities, 1877–1920; The Politics Presidents Make: Leadership from John Adams to Bill Clinton; The Search for American Political Development (with Karen Orren); *and Presidential Leadership in Political Time: Reprise and Reappraisal.*

B. Dan Wood's research evaluates the relative responsiveness of American political institutions to democratic influence. Most recently he has focused on party polarization and its relation to political representation. However, past work has also considered the presidency, bureaucracies, Congress, the Supreme Court, the mass media, and public opinion. He has published *Party Polarization: The War Over Two Social Contracts* (2017); *Presidential Saber Rattling: Causes and Consequences* (2012); *The Myth of Presidential Representation* (2009; recipient of the 2010 Richard Neustadt Award); *The Politics of Economic Leadership: The Causes and Consequences of Presidential Rhetoric* (2007); and *Bureaucratic Dynamics: The Role of Bureaucracy in a Democracy* (1994). He has also published numerous articles in the *American Political Science Review, American Journal of Political Science,* and *Journal of Politics.* Wood teaches undergraduate courses in the presidency, public policy, and American political economy. He teaches graduate courses in mathematical modeling, econometrics, time series analysis, maximum likelihood, and limited dependent variables.

David A. Yalof is department head and professor of political science at the University of Connecticut. His first book, *Pursuit of Justices: Presidential Politics and the Selection of Supreme Court Nominees,* won the 1999 Richard E. Neustadt Award as the best book on the presidency from the American Political Science Association's Presidency Research Group. More recently, he authored *Prosecution among Friends: Presidents, Attorneys General, and Executive Branch Wrongdoing* (2012). He is also coauthor of *The First Amendment and the Media in the Court of Public Opinion* (2002) and *The Future of the First Amendment* (2008). Yalof is currently completing a manuscript that considers the Obamacare decision and the role that precedent plays on the Roberts Court.

1

RESOLVED, The framers of the Constitution would approve of the modern presidency

PRO: David Nichols

CON: Terri Bimes

Americans are supposedly a forward-looking people, devotees of progress who have scant respect for traditions or customs. But, at least when it comes to politics and government, Americans are, arguably, the most backward-looking people on the face of the Earth. What other nation spends so much time trying to decipher the intentions of people who lived more than two centuries ago? Few people in Great Britain, France, or Germany care about what politicians of the far-distant past would say about today's political debates. Nobody in England asks, "What would Pitt the Younger say?" Even fewer care what George III would say. But Americans care a great deal about what James Madison, Alexander Hamilton, and the other "founders" would say about the ways in which Americans order their political lives.

One reason why Americans care is that the United States, unlike Britain, has a written constitution that is a touchstone for how it resolves legal and political disputes. In deciding constitutional questions, federal and state judges regularly rely on the words of the framers to decipher the meaning of the Constitution. Politicians, too, frequently appeal to the framers to support their interpretations of what is and is not constitutional. Whether arguing about guns in the home, prayer in public schools, or filibusters in the Senate, Americans want to know what the framers had in mind when they wrote the Constitution.

The Constitutional Convention was conducted in the summer of 1787 behind closed doors—no cameras, no reporters, no observers. The fifty-five delegates were sworn to secrecy. One might think this secrecy would make it difficult for anyone to say today what the framers had in mind. But, fortunately, the convention was blessed with an energetic young member who was deter-mined to leave a detailed record of the proceedings. Every day that the con-vention was in session, Virginia's James Madison sat directly below the president's chair, facing the delegates and taking detailed notes of what they said. Every evening, he would write out the notes he had scribbled down dur-ing the day. It was a labor, he said, that almost killed him, yet it was also a labor that succeeded in bringing the framers' deliberations to life for subse-quent generations.

Even with Madison's heroic labors, the task of determining what the fram-ers intended remains difficult. To begin with, "the framers" were hardly a uni-fied group. They were a diverse collection of individuals with many different ideas and interests. Some were slaveholders; some abhorred slavery. Some were wealthy; some were of modest means. Some favored democracy; others feared the masses. Moreover, whose intent matters the most? Is it the intent of the fifty-five men who attended the convention or only of the thirty-nine who signed the document? Should the intent of the hundreds of delegates at the state ratifying conventions matter the most? Or should the intent as interpreted by the most articulate or the most prolific of the framers be accorded special importance? New York's Alexander Hamilton, who penned the essays in *The Federalist Papers* that focus on the presidency, is often read as the authorita-tive framer, but he missed well over half of the convention's proceedings.[1]

Complicating matters still further, the decisions reached in the convention often were not what any delegate or group of delegates intended. Many deci-sions were the product of compromise and bargaining. Such decisions might be defended and rationalized after the fact, but, as the political theorist Michael Walzer points out, they reflected, as political decisions often do, "the balance of forces, not the weight of arguments."[2]

David Nichols and Terri Bimes are well aware of the difficulties in ascertain-ing a single intent, but in their pro and con arguments they gamely try to reconstruct what the framers believed about the presidency. According to Nichols, the framers envisioned a strong and democratic executive. Although he does not ignore the undeniable differences between the presidency of 1787 and the presidency of today, Nichols argues that today's presidency is a natural outgrowth of the presidency created by the framers. Bimes's under-standing of the framers' intent is diametrically opposed. In crucial respects, she argues, the modern presidency is unrecognizable from the relatively weak office intended by the framers. They would neither recognize nor approve of the office that exists today. Short of bringing Madison, Hamilton, and the rest of the framers back from the grave, this is not a question that can be answered definitively. But it is a question that we cannot stop from asking.

PRO: David Nichols

The framers of the Constitution would approve of the modern presidency because, to a great extent, they created it. The essential elements of that presidency—executive discretion, legislative leadership, a substantial administrative apparatus directed by the president, and the president's role as popular leader[3]—originated in the institutional arrangements and incentives the framers established in Article II of the Constitution. Important changes in society and technology as well as in the size, scope, and purpose of government have occurred since the time of the founders, but these changes only accentuate the importance of a powerful, popular president to the successful operation of the U.S. constitutional system.

A common assumption among presidential scholars is that the Constitution, reflecting the founders' fear of monarchy, created a relatively weak chief executive—or, at most, provided a vague outline of the office that would only be filled in by history. The debates that surrounded the creation of the presidency reveal, however, a different and more complex picture.

The men who gathered in Philadelphia in the summer of 1787 had learned much about the problems of democratic government in the eleven years since the signing of the Declaration of Independence. Among other things, they had learned that overthrowing British rule was only the first step toward establishing a free and independent nation. Such a nation required a competent government, and the Articles of Confederation were inadequate to the task. The equal representation of the states in the Continental Congress, the requirement that major structural changes receive unanimous approval, and the inability of Congress to levy taxes were all important defects of the Articles, but perhaps their most fundamental flaw was the absence of a mechanism to enforce decisions of the national government. There was no national executive authority under the Articles, and from the beginning of the Constitutional Convention, most delegates agreed that an independent executive was essential to the success of a new constitution.

None of the delegates entered the convention with a definite plan for accomplishing this goal. Many were not fully aware of the enormity of the task, and even by the end of the convention most did not appreciate the originality and scope of their invention. The presidency evolved gradually over the course of three months of debate. This debate focused on specific practical problems involving the structure of the executive, and it occurred in the context of a host of other debates, not the least of which were states' rights and slavery. The creation of the presidency required compromise and improvisation. Through this process, however, a deeper and more complex understanding of executive power emerged, so that by the end of the process the framers were able to deliver a new institution to the world—the popular modern presidency.

The Virginia Plan provided the starting point for the debate on the executive. It called for the creation of a national executive that would be elected by the legislature for an undetermined number of years. The executive would receive a fixed salary, would be ineligible for reelection, would possess a general authority to execute the national laws, would enjoy the executive rights vested in Congress by the Articles of Confederation, and together with "a convenient number" of the national judiciary, would form a council of revision with the power to veto all laws subject to override by a vote of the legislature.[4]

This plan was only an outline—it did not even specify the number of executives. Edmund Randolph of Virginia wanted a plural executive, claiming that a unitary executive would be the "fetus of monarchy." Roger Sherman of Connecticut argued that, because the executive was to be a servant of the legislature, the legislature should be free to determine the number of executives it desired at any time. No other delegate, however, agreed with Sherman. Even Randolph stressed that the executive must be independent of the legislature.[5]

What powers would this independent executive possess? Article II does not present an extensive list of specific powers, but this has more to do with the framers' understanding of the character of executive power than with any desire to create a weak presidency. Article I begins, "All legislative Powers *herein granted* shall be vested in a Congress . . ." (emphasis added), whereas Article II begins, "The executive Power shall be vested in a President. . . ." Legislative powers could be enumerated in the Constitution, but the executive power could not be so easily delineated. The legislature makes laws or general rules, but the executive must implement these laws in an infinite number of possible circumstances. No rule can cover all cases, the framers realized. That is why an independent executive was needed.

The framers did, however, recognize that the president would need assistance. Some delegates suggested that the Constitution include a list of officers who would help the president carry out the law. They wanted there to be no doubt that the president was to be the head of the administrative offices of the government.[6] But their proposal was rejected because it might interfere with executive independence. It was feared that constitutionally created offices would undermine the unity of the executive branch. The president was to be the only constitutional officer responsible for the execution of the laws. The framers, then, created the structure of an executive branch under the direction of a president, leaving later presidents to expand it as the times required.

The framers' understanding of executive power is most apparent in two of the powers listed at the beginning of Article II, Section 2: the commander in chief power and the pardoning power. The commander in chief power involves the use of force, and the pardoning power involves the need for discretion. Together, these two provisions are a good description of executive power. Because of its many members, Congress is not suited to quick action, and because it makes laws that must apply to all citizens, it does not have the discretion to deal with particular circumstances. Force and discretion are the essence of executive power. Congress has often complained about the executive's unilateral use of force or discretion, but when President George Washington issued a Proclamation of Neutrality during the war between Great Britain and France in 1793, he understood the place of executive discretion in the Constitution; and when he led the militia in 1794 against an uprising by farmers in western Pennsylvania against a federal tax on liquor and distilled drinks (it was known as the Whiskey Rebellion), he understood the need for forceful action. The framers did not want the president to be a servant of Congress.

The framers also wanted the president to play an independent role in the legislative process. The Virginia Plan had called for the executive to share the veto power with the judiciary, but the convention delegates excluded judges because they feared such a scheme would undercut executive responsibility and independence. They wanted a president who could stand up to Congress and thereby play an active role in the legislative process.

The framers also specified that the president "shall from time to time give to the Congress Information of the State of the Union, and recommend to their Consideration such Measures as he shall judge necessary and expedient." The initial version of this provision began with the word *may* rather than *shall*. The change was made at the suggestion of Gouverneur Morris, a delegate from Pennsylvania who wanted to ensure that the president would play an active role in the legislative process. If recommending legislation were merely an option, a president might be reluctant to do so for fear of arousing the jealousy of the legislature. By making it mandatory, the framers enabled presidents to defend their actions as an obligation of their office.

Their constitutionally prescribed authority to help to set the agenda at the beginning of the legislative process together with their right to cast a veto at the end of that process have enabled presidents to exert tremendous legislative influence. Not all presidents have taken full advantage of this potential, but it exists because of the efforts of the framers.

Although they concede that the framers wanted an independent president, most scholars have concluded that the framers did not want a popularly elected one. Early in the Constitutional Convention, James Wilson of Pennsylvania called for the popular election of the president, claiming that it was necessary to guarantee executive independence from the legislature.[7] But during most of the convention, a majority of the delegates supported legislative election. Political scientist Charles Thach has argued that the preference for legislative election was based more on the fears of the small states than on any theory of executive power. The small states supported legislative selection because they thought it would give them more power than they would have in a direct popular election. They hoped to use their control of the Senate to veto any candidate whom they disapproved. However, when the delegates turned their attention to the specific mechanism for legislative election of the president, it became clear that a majority supported a joint vote of the House and the Senate. Because the influence of the small states would be greatly diminished in such an election, the small states became open to a compromise.[8]

The compromise was, of course, the Electoral College. The idea of an electoral college was first introduced on June 2 by James Wilson, who saw it as only a minor modification of his plan for a direct popular election. Recent commentators, however, often portray the Electoral College as a product of the framers' distrust of democracy. They go on to argue that if the framers distrusted democracy, they certainly would not approve of what is arguably the most important element of the modern presidency—popular leadership.

To be sure, some convention delegates did speak disparagingly of popular election. George Mason of Virginia said, "It would be as unnatural to refer the choice of a proper character for chief magistrate to the people, as it would be to refer a trial of colors to a blind man."[9] Roger Sherman of Connecticut said the people would be ill-informed, and South Carolinian Charles Cotesworth Pinckney complained that the people would be led by a few "active and designing men."[10] None of these delegates, however, supported the Electoral College; they were all proponents of legislative election. It was the delegates who defended the principle of popular election, such as James Madison, James Wilson, and Gouverneur Morris, who were the prime supporters of the Electoral College.

If these framers supported popular election, why then (apart from Wilson) did they not favor direct popular election? The reason was the need for compromise on two issues not directly related to executive power: federalism and slavery. Because the number of electors each state received in the Electoral College would be based on the number of representatives and senators from a state, the small states would have a little more weight in the Electoral College than they would in a direct popular election. The desire to protect the interests of their states, not distrust of democracy, motivated these delegates.

Madison also argued that the different election laws in the states made direct popular election virtually impossible.[11] Madison was gently reminding the delegates that direct popular election would reopen the question of slavery and potentially rip the convention apart.[12] The South wanted its entire slave population to count in apportioning seats in the House of Representatives, whereas the northern states argued that because the South did not recognize the rights of slaves as human beings, slaves should not count for purposes of apportionment. The Three-Fifths Compromise allowed the South to gain some representation in Congress based on its slave population, but no such compromise would be possible in a direct popular election of the president. Either the South would lose a substantial part of its power in the election because its slaves could not vote, or it would have to allow its slaves to vote. Neither option was acceptable to the South. The Electoral College, however, incorporated the Three-Fifths Compromise into the selection of the president because it based the number of electors for each state on the size of its congressional delegation.

One can debate the merits of the Three-Fifths Compromise, but its importance to the creation of the Electoral College cannot be ignored. The Electoral College represented the best approximation of direct popular election the framers could achieve, considering the political realities they faced. The framers who were the most influential in creating the Electoral College wanted a popular election; and in practice, that is what they got. Presidential electors have seldom exercised any independent judgment—and never in a way that affected the outcome of an election. The electors have been a conduit for, not a filter of, popular opinion.

The most far-sighted of the founders, Gouverneur Morris, understood the potential for popular leadership inherent in the constitutional presidency: "The Executive Magistrate should be the guardian of the people, even the lower classes, against Legislative tyranny, against the great and the wealthy who in the course of things will necessarily compose—the Legislative body. . . . The Executive therefore ought to be constituted as to be the great protector of the mass of the people."[13]

Morris also predicted the rise of political parties, explaining that two parties would soon form, one in support of the president and one in opposition. Not all of the framers were as prescient as Morris, and even he undoubtedly would find many aspects of modern American politics strange and disagreeable. But the framers were the first to see the need for a powerful, popularly elected executive in a modern republic, and they would certainly approve of the modern presidency they did so much to create.

CON: Terri Bimes

The job description of the modern president revolves around three central domestic roles: chief legislator, popular leader, and chief executive of the federal bureaucracy. Today, presidents are expected to offer extensive domestic legislative programs, which then become the basis for Congress's agenda. When President Dwight D. Eisenhower decided not to propose a legislative package in 1953, he was broadly criticized for falling short of the standard set by Presidents Franklin D. Roosevelt and Harry S. Truman. In pursuit of their programs, presidents now routinely barnstorm the country, delivering speeches to all manner of audiences. Indeed, "going public"—the strategy of rousing the people to put pressure on Congress to enact the president's priorities—has become a routine feature of the modern presidency.[14] Finally, modern presidents lead the immense federal bureaucracy, which provides the substantial resources needed to launch presidential initiatives independent of Congress. Within that bureaucracy, a "presidential branch" has emerged that is especially responsive to an administration's priorities. Signing statements, executive orders, and other mechanisms are increasingly being used to shape bureaucratic decision making. None of these three central roles of the modern presidency is spelled out in the Constitution. The framers would certainly be surprised at what they have wrought.

In fact, the Constitution says very little about executive power. The "vesting clause" of Article II states, "the executive Power shall be vested in a President of the United States of America." It is followed by a list of specific presidential powers. In the domestic policy realm, the most important are the duty to report on the State of the Union to Congress from time to time, to recommend "necessary and expedient" legislation to Congress, and to nominate officers to the various departments with the approval of the Senate. As spelled out in Article I, the president also is empowered to veto legislation, subject to override by a two-thirds majority of each chamber. This terse description of executive power constitutes the extent to which the Constitution gave the nation's first presidents formal guidance on domestic policymaking.

This scarcity of guidance is not surprising, however. The debates at the Constitutional Convention focused more on how presidents would be selected than on the proper scope of presidential power. This emphasis likely reflected the delegates' view that the legislature would be the most powerful branch of government, at least in domestic policymaking. As noted in *Federalist* No. 51 by James Madison, "the legislative authority necessarily predominates" in a republic.[15] The legislative branch enjoyed two critical advantages: its close ties to the people and its authority to make laws. Thus the most important question of executive design was how to provide a mode of election that ensured some independence from Congress, while still leaving the president accountable to the public. The obvious answer—popular election—was advocated by a handful of the founders—notably James Wilson and Gouverneur Morris—but it was widely regarded as impractical. In the view of most of the founders, the people would be unable to judge candidates for the presidency and would have trouble agreeing on a single candidate. Election of the president by the legislature was repeatedly, if controversially, approved by the Constitutional Convention, but this plan foundered upon a basic dilemma: unless the president was ineligible for reelection, legislative selection would give presidents a strong incentive to defer to congressional whims in the hope of securing another term. Yet limiting each president to a single term was inadvisable because reelection was regarded as a vital incentive for good behavior by the president.

The Electoral College emerged as the solution: it gave the president a power base independent of Congress, while providing a measure of accountability. Although several of the founders expected the ultimate selection of the president to often end up in the hands of the House of Representatives (the Constitution-mandated solution when a single candidate failed to obtain a majority in the Electoral College), this mode of election afforded at least a partial barrier to legislative domination of the president. The Electoral College also solved the dispute between large and small states by granting each state a number of electors equal to its representatives and senators.

The president's role as popular leader was not at stake in these debates. By delegating the decision on how electors would be chosen to each state legislature, the framers neither precluded nor required a substantial role for ordinary voters in selecting the president. In the first presidential election in 1788, the state legislatures divided equally on the issue of how popular the presidential vote should be. Six states (Delaware, Maryland, Massachusetts, New Hampshire, Pennsylvania, and Virginia) opted for various sorts of direct popular election of electors, and five states (Connecticut, Georgia, New Jersey, New York, and South Carolina) opted for legislative appointment of electors.[16] Thus the framers' endorsement of the Electoral College cannot be interpreted as a stamp of approval for modern popular presidential leadership.

It is highly unlikely that even the two main supporters of popular election, Gouverneur Morris and James Wilson, envisioned the president going out on the hustings to rally voter support. Instead, Morris and Wilson conceived of the president as a "patriot king"—that is, as a leader who would rise above politics and not engage in aggressive popular leadership appeals. Morris described the president as the "guardian of the people" and the "great protector of the people" against legislative tyranny.[17] Wilson, in his defense of the executive at the Pennsylvania convention held to consider ratification of the Constitution, contended that the president would "watch over the whole with paternal care and affection."[18] Meanwhile, throughout *The Federalist Papers*, Hamilton and Madison described campaigning as the "art" of flattering prejudice and distracting people from their true interests.[19] In *Federalist* No. 10, for example, Madison argued that a large republic would make it more difficult for "unworthy candidates to practice with success the vicious arts by which elections are too often carried."[20] In *Federalist* No. 71, Hamilton lamented that, although "the arts of men" can delude the people, the executive would be their "guardian," rescuing them from the "fatal consequences of their own mistakes."[21] The president would not respond to "every sudden breeze of passion," but instead would take a more reflective view of the public good. In short, these framers portrayed the executive as a trustee who exercises his own judgment rather than as a delegate who slavishly follows the opinions of the people.

Most of the framers supported a more limited conception of executive power than did Morris, Wilson, and Hamilton. Certainly, many of the convention delegates would have been uncomfortable with the notion of the president as a guardian protecting the public interest against legislative excesses. Distrust of executive power still ran deep in a nation that had only recently fought a war against the British king. But there was no disagreement among the framers that the role of Congress was to initiate legislation and that presidents would not actively cultivate mass support in order to pressure Congress to cater to their priorities. The supporters and opponents of a strong executive agreed on this much.

Although the framers anticipated a more direct role for the president in leading the executive branch, their conception of presidential administrative leadership was limited when judged by the standards of the modern presidency. At first, convention delegates granted the power to make appointments—one of the president's most important tools in controlling the bureaucracy—to the Senate. But toward the end of the convention that idea fell by the wayside, in part because the Senate now represented states rather than population. The convention voted instead to give the power of appointment to the president, preserving an important role for the Senate in providing "advice and consent." As historian Jack N. Rakove has noted, "The growth of the presidency owed more to doubts about the Senate than to the enthusiasm with which Hamilton, Morris, and Wilson endorsed the virtues of energetic administration."[22] In *Federalist* No. 51, Madison clarified why the president and the Senate were linked in this manner, explaining that the "qualified connection between this weaker department [the executive] and the weaker branch of the stronger department [the Senate]" would enable "the latter . . . to support the constitutional rights of the former, without being too much detached from the rights of its own department."[23] The presidency needed the support of the Senate because otherwise it would lack the firmness to withstand the initiatives of the House, the more popular legislative branch.[24]

In summary, the framers anticipated a division of powers in which Congress would be the leading legislative force and the president would provide a limited check. The House would be the branch closest to the people, and as such would have a critical advantage in battles with the president. As a trustee for the nation, the president would not be entirely divorced from the people, nor would he wield public opinion as a weapon in institutional or policy battles. Even in the area of administration, where the president had the appointment power, the framers expected close consultation and cooperation with the Senate to be the norm.

The modern presidency has overturned each of these expectations. Strains in the founders' model could be seen even in the conduct of the first presidents, but for the most part George Washington and his immediate successors sought to abide by the model of the restrained patriot king.[25] Washington played a vital role in defining appropriate presidential behavior, helping to resolve some of the ambiguities left by the framers. In many ways, Washington was the republican embodiment of a patriot king. His two tours of the country as president were not the modern-day campaign swings in which presidents kiss babies and shake hands.[26] Rather, great formality and aloofness marked these affairs. Washington also stuck to a script devoid of comment on public policy issues, and his remarks were strictly ceremonial. The most common criticism of the tours was that they were "monarchical" in nature—more befitting a king than an elected president. Partly as a result of such criticism, Washington's successors generally did not go out on tour and assiduously avoided monarchical gestures. Above all, the first generation of presidents generally steered clear of explicit appeals to the public to support their policies.

In the capital, Washington often entertained public visitors, but these events, or "levees" as they were called, resembled his tours of the country. Washington stood at the fireplace and greeted each visitor with a bow. After making some brief remarks, he then resumed his place in front of the fireplace and each visitor then bowed to the president as he or she left the room.[27] By holding these levees, Washington acknowledged that it was important for the president to be accessible to the public. At the same time, the regal choreography of the event imposed a respectful distance between the president and the people.

Even Washington's one bold public appeal, which appeared in his Farewell Address, showed the vitality of the patriot leadership model. In the address,

Washington dealt with the rise of political parties—entities that are crucial to the operation of the modern presidency but were disparaged by the framers. Even though by the end of his administration Washington had cast his lot with the Hamiltonian Federalists and against the Jeffersonian Republicans, he used this stance of nonpartisanship to attack those who opposed his administration's foreign policy. He warned Americans about a "small but artful and enterprising minority of the community" who sought to replace the "delegated will of the nation" with the "will of party."[28] The fact that Washington attacked the Jeffersonian Republicans in the language of nonpartisanship reveals the power of the patriot king model in the early republic. It is also noteworthy that Washington waited until he was leaving office to launch an explicitly political attack in an address that is now widely regarded as a "campaign document."[29] Only then could he offer such criticisms without appearing to promote his own self-interest.[30]

The early presidents were also circumscribed in how they practiced legislative leadership. The president was expected to leave most of the initiative and maneuvering of the legislative process to Congress. Even when the president and his allies lobbied for legislation, they used "hidden-hand" leadership techniques that were consistent with the norm that made it unacceptable for the president to aggressively push his program through Congress.[31] Thomas Jefferson, for example, drafted bills behind the scenes and had members of Congress introduce them as their own. He also quietly appointed floor leaders to be his personal lieutenants in Congress, directed cabinet members to act as political liaisons with Congress, lobbied members of both parties at White House dinners, and anonymously penned editorials supporting his administration's policies in the official government newspaper.[32] The Federalists attacked Jefferson for his backstage dominance of Congress, but Jefferson's public deference to the legislature limited the damage.

Finally, in part because the federal bureaucracy was so small, the president's administrative role was limited in the early republic. The general expectation was that departments would be staffed by people chosen for their good character and that they would serve during good behavior. Even Jefferson, who took office after the acrimonious election of 1800, did not purge many Federalists from the bureaucracy. John Quincy Adams, one of the last presidents to adhere to this character-based norm when staffing the bureaucracy, promised in his inaugural address to base his appointments on "talent and virtue alone."[33] With the election of Andrew Jackson in 1828 came an avowedly partisan approach to administration. Bureaucratic appointments would now be distributed on the basis of party loyalty and service. But this partisan approach did not necessarily empower the White House. Instead, presidents became brokers, forced to respond to the aggressive patronage demands of state and local party organizations. Not until the twentieth century did presidents begin to build an extensive bureaucratic apparatus that they could control, the Executive Office of the President. The rise of presidential administration has been a relatively recent process, not something foreordained by the Constitution.[34]

In general, then, the most important features of the modern presidency were neither anticipated nor desired by the founders. They did not want or expect the president to become the chief legislator, setting much of Congress's agenda. Nor did they want or expect the president to be a public opinion leader, aggressively rallying the people to the administration's side in battles with the legislative branch. Nor, finally, did they desire or anticipate that the president would become the leader of an extensive administrative apparatus. These elements of the modern presidency, which took shape over many decades, have created an office that neither the founders nor early presidents would recognize, let alone embrace.

NOTES

INTRO

1. *The Federalist Papers* were originally published as a series of eighty-five newspaper articles (under the pseudonym "Publius") intended to explain the thinking that led to the Constitution and to persuade Americans to adopt it as the cornerstone of the new nation. The essays were written by James Madison, Alexander Hamilton, and John Jay.
2. Michael Walzer, *Politics and Passion: Toward a More Egalitarian Liberalism* (New Haven, CT: Yale University Press, 2004), 96.

PRO

3. For the classic description of the modern presidency, see Fred I. Greenstein, "Change and Continuity in the Modern Presidency," in *The New American Political System*, ed. Anthony King (Washington, DC: American Enterprise Institute, 1978), 243–44.
4. Max Farrand, ed., *The Records of the Federal Convention of 1787*, 4 vols. (New Haven, CT: Yale University Press, 1966), 1:21.
5. Ibid., 1:65–6.
6. Ibid., 2:342.
7. Ibid., 1:68–9.
8. Charles Thach, *The Creation of the Presidency, 1775–1789* (Baltimore: Johns Hopkins University Press, 1969), 101–03.
9. Farrand, *Records of the Federal Convention of 1787*, 2:31.
10. Ibid., 2:29, 230.
11. Ibid., 1:111.

12. See Donald L. Robinson, *"To the Best of My Ability": The Presidency and the Constitution* (New York: Norton, 1987), 82–3.
13. Farrand, *Records of the Federal Convention of 1787,* 2:52.

CON

14. Samuel Kernell, *Going Public: New Strategies of Leadership,* 3rd ed. (Washington, DC: CQ Press, 1997).
15. *The Federalist Papers,* No. 51 (New York: Penguin Books, 1961), 322.
16. North Carolina and Rhode Island had not ratified the Constitution by the time of the first presidential election and could not participate. See *Selecting the President: From 1789 to 1996* (Washington, DC: Congressional Quarterly, 1997), 4.
17. Max Farrand, ed., *The Records of the Federal Convention of 1787,* 4 vols. (New Haven, CT: Yale University Press, 1966), 2:52.
18. Jonathan Elliot, ed., *The Debates in the Several State Conventions on the Adoption of the Federal Constitution* (New York: Burt Franklin, 1888), 2:448.
19. *Federalist Papers,* No. 71, 432.
20. *Federalist Papers,* No. 10, 82.
21. *Federalist Papers,* No. 71, 432.
22. Jack N. Rakove, *Original Meanings: Politics and Ideas in the Making of the Constitution* (New York: Knopf, 1996), 267.
23. *Federalist Papers,* No. 51, 323.
24. Rakove, *Original Meanings,* 281.
25. Ralph Ketcham, *Presidents above Party: The First American Presidency, 1789–1829* (Chapel Hill: University of North Carolina Press, 1984), 4.
26. In addition to these two tours, President Washington visited Rhode Island upon its admittance to statehood.
27. As described in Stanley Elkins and Eric McKitrick, *The Age of Federalism* (New York: Oxford University Press, 1993), 49–50.
28. George Washington, "Farewell Address," September 17, 1796, in *A Compilation of the Messages and Papers of the Presidents* (New York: Bureau of National Literature, 1897), 214.
29. Elkins and McKitrick, *Age of Federalism,* 494.
30. Garry Wills, *Cincinnatus: George Washington and the Enlightenment* (Garden City, NY: Doubleday, 1984), 88–89.
31. Fred I. Greenstein, *The Hidden-Hand Presidency: Eisenhower as Leader* (New York: Basic Books, 1982); Robert M. Johnstone Jr., *Jefferson and the Presidency: Leadership in the Young Republic* (Ithaca, NY: Cornell University Press, 1978).
32. James Sterling Young, *The Washington Community, 1800–1828* (New York: Columbia University Press, 1966), 162–63; Mel Laracey, *Presidents and the People: The Partisan Story of Going Public* (College Station: Texas A&M Press, 2002).
33. John Quincy Adams, "Inaugural Address," March 4, 1825.
34. Terry Moe, "The Politicized Presidency," in *The New Direction in American Politics,* ed. John E. Chubb and Paul E. Peterson (Washington, DC: Brookings, 1985), 235–71.

RESOLVED, The unitary executive is a myth

PRO: Richard J. Ellis

CON: Saikrishna Prakash

In 1988 in *Morrison v. Olson*, the U.S. Supreme Court heard a challenge to the constitutionality of the Office of the Independent Counsel (OIC), which was created by Congress in 1978.[1] Born out of a belief—forged in the experience of the Watergate scandal—that the executive branch could not be trusted to investigate its own wrongdoing, the Office of the Independent Counsel was designed to be independent of the president and the attorney general so that the investigation and prosecution of high administration officials could be carried out without fear or favor. Congress stipulated that an independent counsel would be selected by a panel of three federal judges and could only be removed from office by the president for "good cause." The Reagan administration challenged the independent counsel law in court, arguing that prosecution was a purely executive function and therefore the president should be free to dismiss an independent counsel for any reason.

Eight justices brushed aside the administration's argument, reasoning that allowing the executive branch to remove an independent counsel for "good cause" preserved the executive's ability to "perform his constitutionally assigned duties" of seeing that the laws are faithfully executed. The Court's newest justice disagreed, however. Antonin Scalia excoriated the Court for declaring "open season upon the President's removal power for all executive officers." Scalia argued that the independent counsel statute was not merely unwise—a position that both parties ultimately accepted when they let the statute expire in 1999—but also that it was unconstitutional. According to Scalia, the text of the Constitution is unambiguous: all executive powers are vested in the president. Faithful adherence to the text of the Constitution, Scalia maintained, required the Court to strike down any legislative restriction on the president's power to remove officials exercising executive powers. At stake, Scalia argued, was the integrity of the "unitary executive" established by the framers of the Constitution.

At the time, few if any Americans would have even recognized the term *unitary executive.* But the term had deep meaning for the Reagan Justice Department. Under the leadership of Attorney General Edwin Meese III, a cadre of conservative lawyers was devising a constitutional theory and legal strategy that could enable the Reagan administration to gain control over the independent regulatory agencies that were seen as impeding the administration's agenda of deregulating business. Speaking before the Federal Bar Association in 1985, Meese signaled the administration's intent: "federal agencies performing executive functions are themselves properly agents of the executive. They are not 'quasi' this or 'independent' that." Meese argued that any statutory restrictions on a president's removal power are unconstitutional, and that indeed "the entire system of independent agencies may be unconstitutional."[2] Meese did not use the term, but this was precisely what Scalia meant by the "unitary executive."

The administration's challenge to the independent counsel statute was the opening gambit in a calculated effort to get the courts to accept the unitary executive thesis and to roll back the regulatory state. At the D.C. Circuit Court of Appeals the administration was spectacularly successful. Reagan appointee Laurence Silberman not only struck down the independent counsel statute but affirmed that "the doctrine of the unitary executive" is "central to the government instituted by the Constitution."[3] After the Supreme Court's emphatic 8–1 reversal of Silberman, however, Solicitor General Charles Fried, who argued the case before the Court, pronounced the unitary executive thesis "dead."[4]

Fried turned out to be dead wrong. If anything, conservatives' attachment to the unitary executive grew stronger in subsequent years. Although Reagan rarely used the term *unitary executive,* his successor, George Herbert Walker Bush, invoked it more often. But it was during the administration of George W. Bush that the term *unitary executive* became part of the public conversation. George W. Bush and his top aides relentlessly invoked the unitary executive to justify presidential power. Whereas Bush the father mentioned the unitary executive in only five signing statements (about 2 percent of the total number of statements he issued when signing a bill), Bush the son referenced it in close to seventy signing statements (well over 40 percent of his signing statements). It is worth noting, however, that neither George W. Bush's predecessor, Bill Clinton, nor his successor, Barack Obama, used the term even once.

Far from being dead, then, the important—if often partisan—debate over the unitary executive continues to invoke strong convictions on both sides. One side, exemplified by Richard J. Ellis, insists that the unitary executive is a myth that distorts the framers' understanding of the Constitution. The other side, articulated by Saikrishna Prakash, maintains that the unitary executive is, as Silberman put it, "central to the government instituted by the Constitution." Whether myth or not, the unitary executive doctrine will likely be debated by politicians, courts, and citizens for decades to come.

PRO: Richard J. Ellis

Partisanship and political ideology have never lain far from debates about presidential power. From the 1930s through the 1960s, progressive Democrats championed a robust presidency, while conservative Republicans sounded cries of alarm or at least notes of skepticism. Progressives looked to the president to transcend the power of parochial interests and to combat powerful special interests. Only a strong president, they believed, could overcome the tremendous centrifugal force exerted by a constitutional system that endlessly divided and checked power.[5] By the 1980s, with Republican Ronald Reagan ensconced in the White House and Democrats seemingly in permanent control of the House of Representatives, the roles were reversed. Progressives now warned of the imperial presidency, while conservatives sang the virtues of a powerful presidency.[6]

Both progressive and conservative advocates of a presidency-centric political system have invented history and propagated myths to suit their political aspirations. The liberal narrative relied heavily on the myths that presidential elections bestow policy mandates and that a president's words express an authentic "voice of the people."[7] Conservatives exploited these fictions as well—most notably after Reagan's election in 1980—but they also created new myths that departed dramatically from the progressive storyline of presidential development as "the work of the people breaking through the constitutional form."[8] Whereas progressives had located the sources of presidential power outside the Constitution, conservatives—specifically, conservative lawyers— insisted that broad, unilateral presidential powers could be located in "the text, structure, and ratification history of the Constitution."[9]

Writing in 1960, political scientist and liberal Democrat Richard Neustadt famously advised presidents not to rely on the formal powers of the Constitution.[10] Instead, presidents needed to master the art of persuasion, as Franklin Delano Roosevelt allegedly had done.[11] Beginning with Reagan and culminating with President George W. Bush, conservative lawyers offered very different advice, premised on a very different myth. They counseled conservative presidents to trust less in personal persuasion than in the inherent executive power that Article II of the Constitution vests in the president.

Personal persuasion was too dependent on bargaining and compromise and the willingness of other actors to acquiesce to the president's wishes. In contrast, the Constitution, properly interpreted, gives the president power that no political opponents could take away or diminish. This is the myth at the heart of the conservative theory of presidential power that flourished during the presidency of George W. Bush.

Conservative constitutional mythmaking took two forms. The first myth was that in wartime the Constitution, particularly the commander in chief clause, endows the president with virtually unlimited powers to keep the nation safe. So long as there is a "war on terror," according to this legal fiction, the president is not required to abide by laws that compromise the president's power to conduct electronic surveillance or carry out interrogations of enemy combatants, including bans on torture. The second myth—the myth of the unitary executive—was that the Constitution at all times gives the president absolute control over the executive branch. Under this theory, Congress has no constitutional right to prevent the president from firing executive branch officials or from ordering subordinates to follow the president's dictates. Statutes that restricted the president's power to remove or control agents of the executive branch were not textbook instances of "checks and balances" but were instead unconstitutional encroachments on presidential power.

To describe the doctrine of the unitary executive as a myth is not to deny the indisputable fact that there is only one president—what Alexander Hamilton, in *Federalist* No. 70, famously called "unity in the executive." On that question there is no debate, though many of the delegates at the Constitutional Convention—at least a quarter of them—did prefer a plural executive.[12] Unity in the executive, however, is a far different thing than a unitary executive. In fact, as a logical matter, the two ideas are completely independent. From the perspective of the unitary executive doctrine, it should not matter whether there is one president or three presidents. Either way, Congress is proscribed by the Constitution from interfering with the functioning of the executive branch.[13]

It is worth accenting at the outset that labeling the unitary executive doctrine as a myth does not commit one to the proposition that Congress should, as a practical matter, micromanage the executive branch. There are good, pragmatic reasons in many, maybe even most, instances why Congress should give the president wide latitude in administering and executing the laws. But the Constitution does not forbid Congress from "meddling" in the executive branch any more than it commands Congress to keep the president on a short leash.

Advocates of the unitary executive doctrine reject the pragmatic argument for executive discretion because it requires them to accept Neustadt's classic formulation of the American political system as "a government of separated institutions sharing powers."[14] To grant this premise is to allow that presidential power is ultimately the power to persuade, and that Congress can legitimately constrain the president's exercise of executive power.

This is not merely an abstract or theoretical debate. The unitary executive doctrine, at its heart and in its origins, is an assault on the regulatory state that has existed for more than a century. At stake are the legitimacy and independence of all the myriad "independent agencies" that regulate economic activity, such as the Board of Governors of the Federal Reserve System (1913), the Securities and Exchange Commission (1934), the National Labor Relations Board (1935), and the Commodity Futures Trading Commission (1975). Congress has generally made these agencies independent of presidential control by providing agency heads with fixed terms and specifying that they cannot be fired without cause. According to the unitary executive doctrine, such limits on a president's ability to direct the bureaucracy are unconstitutional. By vesting executive power in the president, this theory holds, the Constitution forbids Congress from insulating administrative agencies from presidential control.[15]

What is the evidence that the Constitution establishes a unitary executive? The answer is, precious little—so little that the unitary executive can only be regarded as a myth. It is admittedly a simple, seductive construct with "a beautiful symmetry" and a seemingly "perfect logic."[16] If (1) the president is the chief executive, and (2) the president alone is vested with the executive power, then surely it must follow that (3) the legislature has no say in how the executive branch is run, except where the Constitution explicitly grants the legislature that power. The only problem with this syllogism is that there is no evidence that the framers understood the Constitution in this way.

The unitary executive thesis rests principally on two clauses in Article II: the vesting clause ("The executive power shall be vested in a President of the United States of America") and the faithful execution clause (the president "shall take care that the laws be faithfully executed"). It strains credulity that, in commanding the president to take care that the laws be faithfully executed, the framers intended to empower the president to defy Congress. The clause, as Peter Shane points out, is "derived from the ban on the executive suspension of statutes that appears in the English bill of rights and clearly implies the faithful execution of Congress's will, not the President's."[17]

What about the vesting clause? The opening sentence of Article II announces that there will be a single president ("unity in the executive," in Hamilton's language), but the further claim that it posits a unitary executive is without foundation. Neither those who wrote nor those who ratified the Constitution understood discretionary executive power as the power to set public policy. That was Congress's job, subject of course to the president's veto. Administration could be "good or ill" (again to quote Hamilton), but the metric of good administration was efficiency, honesty, and neutral competence, not compliance with the president's policy preferences.[18]

There is also the inconvenient matter of another "vesting clause" in Article II, which states, "Congress may by Law vest the Appointment of such inferior Officers, as they think proper, in the President alone, in the Courts of Law, or in the Heads of Departments." In this clause, the Constitution leaves it entirely up to Congress to decide ("as they think proper") whether "inferior officers" (that is, those government officers that the Constitution does not require to be approved with the advice and consent of the Senate) should be appointed by the president or department heads or the courts.[19] If the framers had intended to create a unitary executive, they would not have included this clause.

Indeed, if the framers were intent on creating a unitary executive, they were guilty of constitutional malfeasance since nowhere did they even mention the president's removal power. Even more striking, the subject never came up at the Constitutional Convention in Philadelphia. If the framers—even if only some of them—had in mind a unitary executive, one would think they would at least have discussed removal at some point during the nearly four months they argued over the making of a new constitution.

Perhaps this silence was because everybody assumed that the president had the removal power, since it was self-evidently part of the executive power that was vested in the president in the opening sentence of Article II. But this interpretation runs into the embarrassing problem of *Federalist* No. 77, also written by Hamilton. No framer of the Constitution was a more enthusiastic advocate of presidential prerogative. Yet in *Federalist* No. 77, published May 28, 1788, Hamilton explicitly rejected the idea that the Constitution endowed the president with the sole power to remove executive officers. Instead, he listed as one of the virtues of the Constitution the fact that the "the consent of [the Senate] would be necessary to displace as well as to appoint . . . officers of the government."[20] Some have interpreted Hamilton's statement as either a disingenuous attempt to sell the new Constitution or as a poorly thought-out remark that he subsequently repudiated. However, as political scientist Jeremy Bailey has shown, Hamilton's vision of a restrained removal power was perfectly consistent with his understanding of robust executive power.[21]

Hamilton valued "unity" in the executive—one president rather than several—because he believed it was an essential part of "energy" in the executive. Unity was necessary for the executive to act decisively, swiftly, and sometimes secretly. Unity also ensured that presidents would be held accountable for their actions. But Hamilton also valued stability in the executive branch.

Frequent turnover in the executive, he feared, would lead to a neglect of longer-term projects.[22]

In *Federalist* No. 72, Hamilton favored allowing the president to be eligible for reelection precisely because it would minimize administrative disruption. There is, he stressed, an "intimate connection between the duration of the executive magistrate in office and the stability of the system of administration." If presidents changed constantly, and with them the "men who fill the subordinate stations," then there would be a "ruinous mutability in the administration of the government."

Similarly, in *Federalist* No. 77, Hamilton defended the Senate's involvement in appointments and removals on the ground that then "a change of the Chief Magistrate . . . would not occasion so violent or so general a revolution in the officers of the government as might be expected, if he were the sole disposer of offices." Requiring the Senate—which "from the greater permanency of its own composition, will in all probability be less subject to inconstancy than any other member of the government"—to consent to removals, in short, would make it more likely that these removals would be based on competence and integrity rather than political ideology or personal whim. An unrestrained use of the removal power, in Hamilton's view, thus would undermine administrative stability and expertise, which are as central to an energetic executive as is executive unity. Presidential control over the executive branch (the unitary executive) thus could actually sap energy from the executive by politicizing the neutral competence that is so essential to good public administration.

Prevented from enlisting Hamilton in the unitary executive cause, advocates of the unitary executive often invoke instead "the great debate of 1789" to support the notion that the framers intended the Constitution to bestow on the president the unilateral power to remove any executive officer for any reason. It is true that the first Congress (1) included many who had been delegates at the Constitutional Convention (eight in the House and ten in the Senate) and (2) decided to vest the removal of department heads in the president. But it is not true that the congressional debate demonstrates that the framers intended the Constitution to grant the president an unlimited power to remove executive officers. In fact, the debate shows nearly the opposite.[23]

First, it is important to recall the context for this "great debate." It began in the House of Representatives on May 19, 1789, when Virginia congressman James Madison introduced a motion to establish the Department of Foreign Affairs (soon to be renamed the Department of State), headed by a secretary who would "be removable by the president." (The Constitution did not establish any executive departments, leaving that task to Congress.) The debate that ensued was not over the president's power to control or remove "inferior" executive officers. Instead, it centered on the question of the proper relationship between the president and the department head (what the Constitution refers to as "the principal officer"). Madison rightly worried that requiring the Senate to consent to the removal of a department head would fatally weaken the executive's independence and thereby undermine the Constitution's checks and balances.

Second, Madison's motion was incredibly contentious—hence the "great debate" that ensued. The fierce debate belies the suggestion that the Constitution's silence on executive branch removals is evidence that it was widely understood that the removal power is an inherent part of executive power. Instead, the great debate of 1789 suggests that it is far more likely that the framers avoided taking up the question of removal because they believed it would be divisive and difficult to obtain agreement.

Third, careful examination of the congressional debate and voting that ensued after Madison introduced his resolution shows that only a minority in the House maintained that the Constitution vests the president with the inherent power to remove a department head. As Charles Thach showed more than ninety years ago, the House was divided essentially into three blocs. One bloc, the largest of the three (about 40 percent), opposed Madison's resolution because they insisted that a department head should only be removable with the advice and consent of the Senate, since the Senate's advice and consent were necessary to the appointment. Otherwise, a unilateral power to remove would undo the constraints that the Constitution had carefully placed on the president's appointment power. A second bloc (about 30 percent) agreed that the Constitution does not give the president the power to unilaterally remove officers, but they supported Madison's resolution because they thought it prudent for Congress to allow the president to remove a department head. A third bloc (about 30 percent) believed that the Constitution implicitly vests the president with the power to remove a department head. Only two of the eight House members who were delegates at the Constitutional Convention voted with this third bloc.[24]

The final language approved by the House specified that a chief clerk should assume the duties of department head "whenever the said principal officer shall be removed from office by the President of the United States, or in any other case of vacancy." When the legislation was taken up in the Senate, gadfly William Maclay proposed to strike out "by the President of the United States." Maclay was a bit of an hysteric about executive power, but his amendment attracted surprisingly strong support from even reliable Federalists who supported the Washington administration. Four of those who backed Maclay's amendment had signed the Constitution, including Connecticut's widely respected William Samuel Johnson, who chaired the five-person Committee of Style that polished the Constitution into its final form. Only through a furious last-ditch lobbying campaign did the Washington administration manage to engineer a deadlocked vote and avoid an embarrassing defeat on the amendment.[25]

The unitary executive thesis looks even more implausible if we look at the statute creating the Treasury Department, the only domestic executive department set up by the nation's first Congress (the other two departments created in 1789 were the Department of Foreign Affairs and the Department of War). The legislation establishing the Treasury Department required the department head to submit to Congress "plans for the improvement and management of the revenue, and the support of the public credit." This language did alarm some in Congress, but their objection was not that requiring the Treasury secretary to "digest and prepare plans" for Congress violated a unitary executive. Instead, the objection was that it encroached on legislative autonomy. In any event, the wording was endorsed by a "great majority" of those in Congress.[26]

One person who certainly had no objection to the wording—and may even had a hand in drafting it—was Alexander Hamilton, who virtually everyone believed (correctly, as it turned out) would be named the first secretary of the Treasury. Hamilton was an ardent admirer of the British political system—"the best in the world," he called it in his June 18, 1787, speech at the convention. What made the British system effective, in Hamilton's view, was not only that the nation was symbolically united in its attachment to a monarch but that the executive and legislative powers were knitted together through the great ministers of state, particularly the prime minister, who served both as a leader in Parliament and as the chancellor of the Exchequer. Hamilton envisioned himself, as historian Forrest McDonald puts it, as "Sir Robert Walpole to Washington's George II." That is, Washington would be the symbolic unifying force that commanded the nation's love and respect, while Hamilton would be the government's prime minister, directing the new nation's economic policies. This is hardly a vision to warm the hearts of proponents of the unitary executive.[27]

In sum, as a reading of the original intent of the Constitution's framers, the unitary executive doctrine is a myth. However, even if we are right to reject the effort to make the framers into apostles of the unitary executive, there still remains the question of whether as a political or pragmatic matter—as opposed to a constitutional one—something very like a unitary executive is preferable to a messier pluralist vision. That is, regardless of what the Constitution dictates, are we better off with the president as (in George W. Bush's oft-quoted phrase) *the decider?* After all, presidents are elected and their subordinates are not. Doesn't democratic accountability, not to mention administrative efficiency, require that the president be able to direct the actions of subordinates and remove them when they do not comply with the president's wishes?

The idea is appealing, but it rests on an unproven assumption that insulating agencies or officials from presidential desires will lead to decisions that adhere less closely to the law, the preferences of a majority of the people, the public interest, or all three. Two examples from George W. Bush's administration should give us reason to doubt that the assumption is warranted: "Firegate" and Hurricane Katrina.

In 2006, Bush fired nine federal district attorneys. A central premise of the unitary executive thesis is that presidential control is necessary to ensure the "uniform execution of the laws" across the nation. But the firings had nothing to do with a concern for ensuring that the law was enforced the same way in different jurisdictions. Instead, the firings were motivated purely by politics: the desire to dispense patronage to supporters and to punish attorneys who had resisted political pressure to pursue legally weak voter fraud cases. Far from trying to achieve uniform execution of the laws, the White House used its removal power to try to enforce federal law more aggressively in some parts of the country (electorally competitive, "battleground" states) than others. The White House's aim was to advance Republican political interests; the federal attorneys, adhering to the norms and rules of the legal profession, were trying to "take care" that the laws were faithfully executed.[28]

Hurricane Katrina struck the Gulf Coast in 2005, killing nearly 2,000 people and causing more than $100 billion in damage. The Bush administration and the Federal Emergency Management Agency (FEMA) were widely criticized for their slow and inept response to the disaster. Yet from the unitary executive perspective, FEMA is a model agency since it possesses an extraordinarily high number of political appointees—a number that increased by 50 percent under Bush. More political appointees, according to the logic of the unitary executive, should mean more accountability and responsiveness to the president's agenda. Yet, as political scientist David Lewis has shown, not only was politicization of the agency directly responsible for the agency's incompetent response to Hurricane Katrina, but the increase in political appointees under Bush was driven not by a desire to make bureaucracy more responsive but instead by the old-fashioned desire to reward supporters and campaign workers with patronages.[29]

Let us not be bedazzled by the beguiling myth of a "unitary executive" or trust in the beneficence of the president. Instead, we should recognize that, in a pluralist system, administrative accountability and effectiveness are achieved in multiple ways, including through professional norms and policy expertise, congressional committees and oversight, the courts, and the media.[30] The pluralist vision is admittedly messy, but then reality generally is messier than myth. The pluralist recognizes that Article II vests executive power in a president but doubts that the powers were intended to be hermetically sealed within the different branches of government. As Madison emphasized in *Federalist No. 47*, "The three great departments of power should be separate and distinct," but that does "not mean that these departments ought to have no partial agency in, or no control over, the acts of each other." On this reading, the Constitution's aim is not an elegant or simple governmental structure but a complex system of checks and balances that are designed to curb the abuse or accumulation of power. The purpose of the Constitution, as Supreme Court Justice Louis Brandeis wrote in 1925, "was not to avoid friction but, by means of the inevitable friction incident to the distribution of the governmental powers among three departments, to save the people from autocracy."[31]

CON: Saikrishna Prakash

Unitary executive has become a bogeyman, something of an accomplishment for a phrase coined by scholars. If a member of the commentariat believes that a president is grasping, lawless, or imperial, the pundit often will finger the administration's supposed embrace of the theory of the unitary executive. The concept is said to be relevant to, among other things, disputes about executive privilege, signing statements, and adherence to laws the president believes are unconstitutional. In each area, the theory supposedly insists that the Constitution grants presidents tremendous, perhaps limitless, authority. In other words, executive unity supposedly sanctions executive license.

In fact, the unitary executive theory has more humble roots and a more modest reach. Properly understood, the theory has nothing to do with executive privilege or signing statements. Rather, it asserts that the Constitution's vesting of the "executive power" in one person has significant consequences for control of the civilian executive branch.

The theory has descriptive and normative elements. The descriptive features can be summed up in five simple principles, all grounded in readings of the original Constitution. First, the Constitution grants the president the "executive power," subject to considerable constraints (e.g., the president cannot create offices, unilaterally appoint to high offices, and fund executive agencies). Second, this grant makes the president, in the words of Alexander Hamilton, the "constitutional executor" of the law, meaning that the president has constitutional authority to execute any federal law personally. Third, the president may direct others charged with executing federal law, issuing general orders, or intervening in specific cases. The president has such power because, when others execute federal law, they help exercise *his* constitutional power over execution. As James Madison said in Congress in 1789, "If any power whatsoever is in its nature Executive, it is the power of appointing, overseeing, and controlling those who execute the laws." Fourth, the president may remove federal executives at will. Because such officers help implement the president's executive power, the chief executive may determine that some are unfit to serve as assistants. Finally, Congress has no constitutional power to divest or redirect the president's executive power. Hence it cannot create independent agencies or autonomous executive officers.

The benefits of a unitary executive are many. To begin with, "Decision, activity, secrecy, and dispatch" result from unity in the executive, said Alexander Hamilton, writing as "Publius" in *Federalist* No. 70. When one person decides what should be done, decisions can be made rapidly and implemented vigorously. In contrast, when the executive's apex is plural—for example, an executive council—deliberations may be protracted or inconclusive, and the losing coalition may try to obstruct the implementation of the collective decision.

Unity also conduces to accountability. As compared to a plural executive, where assigning responsibility is often difficult, a unitary executive naturally draws the public's attention. Because the president decides (or may decide) all executive matters and may direct officers, the president is properly responsible for the executive branch and its decisions.

Finally, the president's superintending authority ensures that someone can coordinate policies across the executive departments. When disputes arise about what ought to be done, the president can resolve them and do so in ways that ensure that the administrative departments do not act at cross-purposes, with one agency barreling toward one goal and another erecting obstacles to its attainment.

Some may recoil at this portrayal of the president, wondering whether the theory of the unitary executive regards the president as something of a monarch. All agree that the Constitution's presidency bears little resemblance to an absolute monarchy. Yet given the president's extensive powers, including authorities typically wielded by monarchs (such as the pardon and veto powers), no one should be surprised that the presidency resembles a limited monarchy in many respects. The similarities were not lost on people in the eighteenth century. After beholding the Constitution for the first time, people with vastly different sensibilities, including Thomas Jefferson and John Adams, regarded it as ushering in a regal presidency. To some extent they were right. The founders created a "republican monarch."

Many moderns fail to see the semblance to monarchy because they mistakenly suppose that what the founders wished to avoid at all costs was anything approaching a monarch. This reads the Constitution as if it had been written in 1776. Yet between 1776 and 1787 there was a sea change in opinion. Many leading thinkers came to believe that what the nation needed was a powerful executive. Several founders supposed that America's post-independence dalliance with weak executives had handicapped the states and the nation.

In 1776 and 1777, framers of the state constitutions had been extraordinarily suspicious of executive authority, creating executives that were, in the estimation of James Madison, generally no more than "cyphers." The state governors typically had limited appointment powers, were dependent on the legislature for election, served but a single year, and had no veto power. In several cases, fear of executive unity led to the creation of a plural executive in the form of an executive council, with executive authority exercised via majority vote.

At the national level, the Continental Congress served as a plural chief executive, appointing, directing, and removing executive department heads. Experience quickly revealed the folly of a plural executive. Whereas the proper exercise of executive power was said to require energy and decision, a plural, deliberate, and part-time executive could only function at a glacial, halting pace. Congress experimented with various administrative structures, including the creation of departments headed by secretaries. But these reforms proved inadequate. The root problem—a ponderous, distracted, and unstable chief executive in the form of Congress—could not be addressed with mere tinkering.

Surveying the scene in 1787, several delegates to the Philadelphia Convention openly pushed for a single, powerful chief executive on the theory that the executive branch needed vigor. Others protested, preferring a triumvirate on the ground that unity in the executive was a "foetus" of monarchy. After the idea of a triumvirate quickly faded, some sought an executive council to check the unitary executive's actions. If the British king had his councilors, why shouldn't the American president have a few as well? Although the Senate serves as a council of sorts on appointments and treaties, the framers never established a generic executive council. Delegates feared that such a council would enervate the executive and shield the president from responsibility. Decisions would be contested and much belated. If difficulties surfaced after decisions had been made, the president might blame the council and the council might fault the president. The public would have no way of umpiring such disputes, and accountability would suffer. The Constitution, as adopted, ensured that the president could seek advice from executive officers (via the "opinions clause"), but that the chief executive, vested with the executive power, would be responsible for the measures taken.

During the ratification debates, people commonly read Article II as empowering the president to superintend the executive branch. Alexander Hamilton spoke of executive officers as the president's "assistants" and "deputies" and subject to the president's "superintendence." Future Supreme Court justice James Wilson said that when the executive power rests with "one person, who is to direct all the subordinate officers of that department; is there not reason to expect, in his plans and conduct, promptitude, activity, firmness, consistency, and energy?" Other Federalists said that if the president gave wrong instructions to subordinates, people could seek legal redress, a claim premised on the president's power to direct officers. Even Anti-Federalists spoke of the president's power to command executive officers. As the Federal Farmer put it, "a single man seems to be peculiarly well circumstanced to superintend the execution of laws with discernment and decision, with promptitude and uniformity."

After the new government commenced, Congress had to recreate the executive departments and consider the implications of the unitary executive. Many in the House of Representatives, including James Madison, thought the president had a constitutional power to direct and remove executive officers in what would become the three great departments—Foreign Affairs (later State), War, and Treasury. Such members of Congress derived the power to direct and remove officers from the grant of executive power and believed the clause was a crucial means by which the president could fulfill the duty to ensure faithful execution of the laws. Others denied these claims, arguing that the grant of executive power ceded nothing more than the powers specifically listed elsewhere in Article II and insisting that the Senate had a role in removal. After months of back and forth, the Madisonians prevailed. No statute conveyed the president a power to remove. Rather, the acts creating all three departments discussed what would happen when the president removed a secretary, thereby implying that the Constitution itself granted the president the authority to remove. This language was purposely designed to make clear that Congress had concluded that the president had a constitutional power to remove, and by implication a power to direct, executive officers.

This was precisely how others at the time understood the three acts. When Congress created other officers, its legislators recognized that the president could remove them as well. As Thomas Jefferson said in 1793, the department and officers were "instituted to relieve the President from the details of execution." Even before Congress acted in 1789, the new president had come to these conclusions on his own. Upon assuming office, George Washington immediately began directing the entities formerly under the sole control of the Continental Congress, including the secretary of foreign affairs, the postmaster general, and the Board of Treasury. His direction lacked any statutory warrant. These commands were appropriate because Washington correctly saw himself as the font of law execution authority, and therefore empowered to direct executive officers as they implemented the law. As he explained on one occasion, "The impossibility that one man should be able to perform all the great business of the State, I take to have been the reason for instituting the great Departments, and appointing officers therein, to assist the Supreme Magistrate in discharging the duties of his trust." The first president evidently believed that the departments and their officers existed to help him exercise his powers and satisfy his duties. They were not free agents.

Washington continued in this view after the creation of officers and departments under the new Constitution. He directed ambassadors, tax collectors, the attorney general, district attorneys, and numerous other federal executives. There was no statutory warrant for issuing any of these commands. He even directed state governors in their execution of federal laws because they were helping to implement his power to over those laws. Undergirding his commands to federal officers was the threat of removal. Indeed, the commissions he issued invariably mentioned that they held their offices at his "pleasure," language that reflected his view that these officers were his instruments and tools. He periodically acted on this belief, unilaterally removing various federal executives.

Years later, Thomas Jefferson described the benefits of a "singular executive," as borne out by the Washington administration. Washington had the wisdom and information of his secretaries at his disposal and ensured a "unity of action and direction" in the executive departments, recounted Jefferson. Despite severe disagreements within the administration, the president heard from all and "decided the course to be pursued and kept the government steadily in it." A plural executive, said Jefferson, would have yielded less accountability and more discord, indecision, and inaction.

Over time, the consensus about the unitary executive disintegrated because of partisanship, legitimate concerns about a spoils system, and anxieties about a domineering executive. When Andrew Jackson's Treasury secretary refused his order to withdraw federal deposits from the Bank of the United States, Jackson fired him and found a more compliant instrument in Roger Taney. The Senate, dominated by Whigs, censured Jackson's actions as contrary to the law and the Constitution. Later still, Andrew Johnson unilaterally ousted his war secretary, a removal that on some accounts violated a recent federal statute requiring the Senate's consent. The House impeached, and the Senate came within one vote of removing Johnson from office.

Eventually, the Supreme Court waded into the fray, issuing opinions difficult to reconcile. In *Myers v. United States* (1926), the Court said the president had an illimitable constitutional power to remove all those appointed with the Senate's consent. Later, in *Humphrey's Executor v. United States* (1935), the Court said that Congress could constrain the president's power to remove quasi-judicial and quasi-legislative officers, two categories never mentioned in the Constitution. In the late 1980s *Morrison v. Olson* (1988) declared that removal restrictions were permissible with respect to all officers so long as the president enjoyed enough authority to exercise constitutional powers and satisfy constitutional duties. Because the Court never identified what would satisfy this rather unclear standard, we have only a hazy sense of how far Congress may go in insulating departments and officers from presidential direction.

Based in part on such Court decisions, in practice we have had both a unitary executive *and* plural executive councils for a century or so. As to the executive departments—Defense, State, Treasury, Justice, and all those whose heads form the president's cabinet—we have a unitary executive of the sort that dates back to the Washington administration. The measures of these departments are seen as the president's policies, and the chief executive directs their execution of federal law and their exercises of discretion. The cost-benefit rules established by executive order and overseen by the Office of Management and Budget are perhaps the most conspicuous example of presidential control. The significant officers in these traditional departments typically resign when the president asks them to do so and almost invariably resign when a new president comes into office. How far presidents intrude into particular executive departments turns on their policy agendas and their desire to allow their deputies to wield expertise. But few doubt the president's legal authority to direct these departments.

Alongside these remnants of the original constitutional structure are dozens of specialized executive councils. The so-called independent agencies—including the Securities and Exchange Commission (SEC), the Federal Election Commission (FEC), the Federal Reserve, and the Federal Communications Commission (FCC)—are headed by panels of commissioners who direct their agencies via majority votes. In their functions, the independent agencies mirror the executive departments—they make rules, enforce federal laws, and adjudicate violations. What makes the independent agencies different is that many regard them as unconnected to the executive.

Sometimes a federal statute will declare that an agency is "independent." Other times, observers infer independence from the multimember nature of these councils and the fact that the statutes restrict presidential removal. Finally, sometimes the assertion of independence reflects nothing more than conventional wisdom that the agency is supposed to be free of presidential control, a convention that incoming presidents typically accept. For instance, the statutes creating the SEC never declare that the commission is to be independent. Nor does any other federal law limit the president's ability to remove SEC commissioners. Yet many suppose that the SEC is an independent agency and that the president may remove its commissioners only "for cause."

The independent agencies are unconstitutional, or so the theory of the unitary executive instructs. These agencies—the SEC, the FEC, the FCC, and so forth—execute federal laws as they create interstitial rules, judge violations of them, and bring civil prosecutions. As such, they implement the president's executive power. The president, as "constitutional executor," has a constitutional power to superintend the execution of these laws, just as the president may direct the execution of laws committed to the Treasury or the Commerce Departments. Neither the necessary and proper clause nor anything else in the Constitution grants Congress the power to parcel out the president's executive power among various officers and agencies. Congress can no more subdivide and redirect the executive power than it may split and strip away the president's powers to make treaties or pardon offenders. Congress only has such power when the Constitution explicitly grants it. With respect to inferior officers, for instance, the appointments clause specifically allows Congress to vest appointment authority in others. No analogous clause authorizes Congress to deprive the president of the "executive power" and vest it elsewhere.

The arguments for the constitutionality of independent agencies have no stopping point. If Congress can insulate civil prosecutions from presidential supervisions (as is the case now) and if the independent prosecutor statute was constitutional (as *Morrison v. Olson* held), the consequences are startling. Every prosecutor in the Department of Justice, including all U.S. attorneys, could enjoy "for cause" protections, thereby granting them independence from the president. Indeed, the Congress could make the Department of Justice wholly independent of the president. More generally, current Supreme Court case law makes it possible for Congress to wrest loose all executive departments (other than Defense and State) from the president's orbit and refashion them into independent agencies.

Apart from their constitutional infirmities, independent agencies are less than ideal as a matter of governmental structure, for the very reasons the founders supposed. With such agencies, there is far less coordination, far more opacity, and rather little responsibility. Because each plural executive council executes separate areas of federal law, these councils typically do not coordinate with either the president or each other. At least when the Continental Congress served as a plural chief executive, there was a chance that it could coordinate across all executive agencies. That sort of harmonization is rather unlikely in a world in which Congress has carved up the unitary executive into different subject-matter fiefdoms.

Moreover, when these plural executives take measures, the public finds it difficult to assign responsibility, as almost all commissioners are relatively anonymous. While a commission may be at fault for some rule or prosecution, exactly which commissioners are to blame is difficult to determine. And the proliferation of personnel and agencies with responsibility for different areas of federal law makes it impossible to hold individuals accountable. In a world where many Americans have difficulty identifying who serves as vice president, precious few can identify the members of even powerful independent agencies, like the FCC or the SEC. While the electorate is naturally drawn to a single person, they cannot be bothered with keeping track of a hundred commissioners, much less discerning which are to blame for particular blunders or oversights.

The independent agency concept has such a tight grip on modern thought and practice that it has staved off any meaningful presidential supervision of independent agencies. While the president could theoretically monitor these plural councils and remove commissioners for cause (because the underlying statutes typically provide as much), the executive branch often knows relatively little of what transpires in the independent agencies. The independent agencies generally do not report to the president, and the president rarely requests opinions or facts from them. Instead, presidents and their minions seem to have accepted the idea of independent agencies to such an extent that they rarely consider if a commissioner has given cause for removal. Put another way, the independent agencies are more autonomous than their statutes demand because the executive has turned a blind eye toward them. By failing to superintend the execution of these laws, modern presidents have not only ceded their power to execute federal law, they have violated their obligation to take care that the laws are being faithfully executed. A duty that requires watchfulness cannot be satisfied by a persistent presidential indifference.

The independent agencies should be integrated into the executive branch, with presidents superintending them just as they do the various executive departments. We ought to return to the presidency's early days, when responsible chief executives routinely directed executive branch officers regarding prosecutions, investigations, and law execution more generally, and when no set of federal laws were walled off from the constitutional executor of federal laws.

Reform would be easy. With respect to the independent agencies, the Supreme Court could eliminate the "for cause" restrictions on presidential removal on the ground that they are unconstitutional and make clear in its opinions that presidential direction of the FEC, SEC, FCC, and so forth is entirely appropriate. The reformed agencies could continue to be structured as commissions, for the theory of the unitary executive does not require unitary heads of departments or agencies. Executive commissions are fine so long as the president may superintend and remove the commissioners that compose them.

Presidents have a part to play. At a minimum, they ought to monitor the independent agencies and remove commissioners who have been remiss in their duties or have misread their statutes—that is, remove commissioners for "cause." Going further, presidents ought to attempt to direct the independent agencies—say, by requiring them to engage in cost-benefit analysis when they come up with rules and by reviewing their civil prosecutions. Should commissioners fail to heed directions, presidents ought to remove them. Before the courts, presidents ought to consistently repudiate the idea of independent agencies and urge the courts to do so as well.

The unitary executive is no panacea, for scandals would not disappear. As history proves, presidents are quite capable of abusing power. But that is the point. The powers assigned by Article II properly rest with the president, as does the responsibility. Fortunately, the public can readily perceive who is to blame for the misuse of those powers. Contrast this with a system no less prone to abuses, where it is impossible to say who should be held accountable.

In sum, we ought to end the failed experiment with a "fourth branch of government" and revert to the original constitutional design, where power to execute the laws and responsibility for their execution rest with the president. Only a single accountable person, like the president, may direct the execution of federal laws "with discernment and decision, with promptitude and uniformity." When it comes to law execution, the buck stops with the president.

NOTES

INTRO

1. The reader interested in the case should read Kevin M. Stack, "The Story of *Morrison v. Olson:* The Independent Counsel and Independent Agencies in Watergate's Wake," in Christopher H. Schroeder and Curtis A. Bradley, eds., *Presidential Power Stories* (New York: Foundation Press, 2009), 401–46.

2. Steven G. Calabresi and Christopher S. Yoo, *The Unitary Executive: Presidential Power from Washington to Bush* (New Haven, CT: Yale University Press, 2008), 381.

3. *In re Sealed Case* 838 F.2d 476.
4. Charles Fried, *Order and Law: Arguing the Reagan Revolution—A Firsthand Account* (New York: Simon and Schuster, 1991), 167.

PRO

5. See, for instance, Harold J. Laski, *The American Presidency: An Interpretation* (New York: Harper and Brothers, 1940), and Grant McConnell, *The Modern Presidency* (New York: St. Martin's Press, 1967). I discuss the progressive vision in more depth in Richard J. Ellis, *The Development of the American Presidency* (New York: Routledge, 2015; 2nd ed.), 13–16. Also see Stephen Skowronek, "The Conservative Insurgency and Presidential Power: A Developmental Perspective on the Unitary Executive," *Harvard Law Review* (2009): 2070–2103, esp. 2083–92.
6. Compare Arthur M. Schlesinger Jr., *The Imperial Presidency* (Boston: Houghton Mifflin, 1973), with L. Gordon Crovitz and Jeremy Rabkin, eds., *The Fettered Presidency* (Washington, DC: American Enterprise Institute, 1989).
7. On the myth of the presidential mandate, see Robert A. Dahl, "Myth of the Presidential Mandate," *Political Science Quarterly* 105 (Autumn 1990): 355–72; and Richard J. Ellis and Stephen Kirk, "Presidential Mandates in the Nineteenth Century: Conceptual Change and Institutional Development," *Studies in American Political Development* 9 (Spring 1995): 117–86. Also see B. Dan Wood, *The Myth of Presidential Representation* (New York: Cambridge University Press, 2009).
8. Henry Jones Ford, *The Rise and Growth of American Politics* (New York: Macmillan, 1898), 292–93.
9. John Yoo, quoted in Skowronek, "The Conservative Insurgency and Presidential Power," 2093.
10. Skowronek, "The Conservative Insurgency and Presidential Power," 2092; Richard E. Neustadt, *Presidential Power: The Politics of Leadership* (New York: Wiley, 1960).
11. On the mythical persuasive powers attributed to FDR as well as the "Great Communicator" Ronald Reagan, see George C. Edwards III, *The Strategic President: Persuasion and Opportunity in Presidential Leadership* (Princeton, NJ: Princeton University Press, 2009). Also see Ellis, *Development of the American Presidency,* 123–28, 187–93.
12. Ellis, *Development of the American Presidency,* 3, 47.
13. The same point is made somewhat differently in Peter M. Shane, *Madison's Nightmare: How Executive Power Threatens American Democracy* (Chicago, IL: University of Chicago Press, 2009), 32.
14. Neustadt, *Presidential Power,* 33.
15. Ellis, *Development of the American Presidency,* 447–54.
16. Charles Fried, *Order and Law: Arguing the Reagan Revolution—A Firsthand Account* (New York: Simon and Schuster, 1991), 171. Fried concedes that the unitary executive vision, however appealing, "is not literally required by the words of the Constitution.

Nor did the framers' intent compel this view" (170). On Fried's distrust of the young "revolutionaries" in the Reagan Justice Department who pushed the "unitary executive" doctrine, see Ellis, *Development of the American Presidency,* 448.

17. Shane, *Madison's Nightmare,* 37.

18. The "good or ill" quote is from *Federalist* No. 68. Also see Shane, *Madison's Nightmare,* 38.

19. According to Madison's notes, Madison was the only person at the convention to speak against this clause, and his objection was that it did "not go far enough" because "Superior officers below heads of Departments ought in some cases to have the appointment of the lesser offices" (Richard J. Ellis, ed., *Founding the American Presidency* [Lanham, MD: Rowman and Littlefield, 1999], 197).

20. Hamilton was not the only prominent Federalist to make this argument. Six months before Hamilton penned *Federalist* No. 77, Tench Coxe made the same claim at the Pennsylvania ratifying convention. Upon Congress's creation of the Treasury Department in 1789, Coxe became assistant secretary of the Treasury; Hamilton, of course, was secretary of the Treasury.

21. See Jeremy Bailey, "The New Unitary Executive and Democratic Theory: The Problem of Alexander Hamilton," *American Political Science Review* 102 (November 2008): 453–65.

22. Ibid., 459–61.

23. A detailed summary and analysis of the debate can be found in Ellis, *Development of the American Presidency,* 414–18.

24. Ellis, *Development of the American Presidency,* 417, 460–61nn14, 18; Charles C. Thach, *The Creation of the Presidency, 1775–1789* (Baltimore: Johns Hopkins University Press, 1969; originally published 1923), 154.

25. Ellis, *Development of the American Presidency,* 417–18. Amazingly, this "great debate" was adduced in 1926 by Chief Justice (and former president) William Howard Taft to justify striking down as unconstitutional an 1876 statute—signed into law by President Ulysses S. Grant—that required Senate consent for the removal of postmasters. Champions of the unitary executive hail Taft's opinion as "masterful and scholarly" (Steven G. Calabresi and Christopher S. Yoo, *The Unitary Executive: Presidential Power from Washington to Bush* [New Haven, CT: Yale University Press, 2008], 248), but in truth the opinion is the sort of potted history that only legal advocates could love. That Taft's opinion is considered "one of the cornerstones of unitary executive scholarship" (ibid., 248) should be warning enough of the weakness of the foundations upon which conservative lawyers have built the unitary executive doctrine. For a critical analysis of Taft's opinion in *Myers v. United States,* 272 U.S. 52 (1926), and a capsule summary of the devastating dissenting opinions, especially those by Louis Brandeis and Felix Frankfurter, see Ellis, *Development of the American Presidency,* 440–42.

26. Ellis, *Development of the American Presidency,* 151; Shane, *Madison's Nightmare,* 38–9.

27. Ellis, *Development of the American Presidency,* 152. Forrest McDonald, *The American Presidency: An Intellectual History* (Lawrence: University Press of Kansas, 1994), 228. Also see Forrest McDonald, *Alexander Hamilton: A Biography* (New York: Norton, 1982), 125–26.
28. For a fuller discussion of Firegate and its connection to the unitary executive, see Ellis, *Development of the American Presidency,* 454–58. The quote is from Chief Justice Taft's opinion in *Myers.*
29. David E. Lewis, *The Politics of Presidential Appointments: Political Control and Bureaucratic Performance* (Princeton, NJ: Princeton University Press, 2008).
30. See Shane, *Madison's Nightmare.*
31. The quotation is from Brandeis's dissent in *Myers.*

RESOLVED, Political parties should nominate candidates for the presidency through a national primary

PRO: Michael Nelson

CON: Andrew E. Busch

Americans celebrate that the United States has had the same constitution for nearly its entire history: more than two centuries and counting. No other democracy in the world can make the same claim. But constitutional stability does not mean the nation has undergone no fundamental institutional changes. Indeed, some American institutions have been characterized by almost perpetual change. Nowhere is this truer than with elections—specifically, the ways in which political parties nominate presidential candidates.

The framers were smart men, but they did not foresee the rise of political parties. They anticipated that the Electoral College would both nominate and select presidential candidates. Yet almost as soon as the Constitution went into effect, it became clear that this system would not work. Groups with common interests and values must be able to come together and agree on a candidate. If they are unable to do so, their votes will be spread among too many candidates, and they will lose the election to those groups that agree to direct all their votes toward a single candidate.

The first nominating process centered in Congress. Each party's members of Congress got together and decided who would be their party's nominee. But almost as soon as the congressional caucus system emerged, it began to attract criticism. That criticism intensified when the Federalist Party went into decline, leaving the Jeffersonian Republicans as the only national party. Nomination became equivalent to election. Critics complained that "King Caucus" was undemocratic because it was conducted by just a few individuals behind closed doors. Moreover, they argued that legislators had no business nominating presidential candidates.

In 1824 the congressional caucus system fell apart. Dissatisfaction with the caucus's choice, Secretary of the Treasury William H. Crawford, propelled state legislatures to nominate their own favorite-son candidates, including John Quincy Adams of Massachusetts, Henry Clay of Kentucky, and Andrew Jackson of Tennessee—all Democratic-Republicans. The result was a fractured general election in which the winner of the popular vote—Jackson—failed to receive a majority of the electoral vote and the election was sent to the House of Representatives. Clay then threw his support to Adams, and Adams prevailed on the first ballot. Three days later, Adams chose Clay to be his secretary of state, igniting charges that the new president had made a "corrupt bargain" with Clay. The outrage was aimed not only at Adams and Clay but also at the nominating system that had made the election of Adams possible.

The congressional caucus system was soon replaced by national nominating conventions. In 1831 and 1832 the National Republicans (soon to become the Whigs) and the Democrats followed the lead of the Anti-Masons in holding national nominating conventions made up of delegates from every state. Although more inclusive than the congressional caucus system, the conventions were made up of delegates selected by the state parties, not by popular vote. The conventions were often long, contentious affairs, especially those in the Democratic Party, which required its presidential nominee to receive at least a two-thirds vote of the delegates (this requirement remained in place until 1936). In 1924 the Democrats met for eighteen days and endured 103 ballots before nominating John W. Davis, who was promptly thrashed in the general election by the Republican nominee, Calvin Coolidge.

In the early twentieth century, the national convention system came under attack for being undemocratic and corrupt. Reform was in the air again—this time in the call for presidential primaries that would enable voters to have a direct say in selecting the parties' nominees. In the 1912 election, twelve states, including California, Illinois, Massachusetts, New Jersey, Ohio, and Pennsylvania, held primaries. Former president Theodore Roosevelt's challenge of President William Howard Taft for the Republican nomination generated intense excitement. In virtually every primary state, Roosevelt defeated Taft, including Taft's home state of Ohio. Although Taft won the nomination anyway, because his allies controlled the convention, his victory was an empty one. In the general election, Taft received only 23 percent of the popular vote and 1.5 percent of the electoral vote. He finished a distant third behind the winner, Democrat Woodrow Wilson, and Roosevelt, who ran at the head of the Progressive Party.

Unlike the 1824 election, the 1912 election did not transform the way presidential elections were conducted. Despite calls by prominent national figures, including President Wilson, for a national primary, the parties decided to retain the national nominating convention. Primaries were still held, but as late as the 1960s they remained a subordinate part of the nominating process. A primary occasionally played an important role in demonstrating a candidate's strength—in 1948, for example, Thomas E. Dewey's victory over Harold E. Stassen in the Oregon primary helped to secure Dewey the Republican nomination. Still, winning primaries was no guarantee of victory. In 1952, for example, Adlai E. Stevenson II did not enter a single primary, and yet he secured the Democratic Party's nomination anyway, besting Estes Kefauver, who had received two-thirds of the votes cast in Democratic primaries.

Not until 1972 did primaries become the linchpin of the nominating process. As primary voters displaced party officials in selecting the parties' presidential nominees, the national convention ceased to be the theater in which the nominating process played itself out. This transformation led to yet more change. After the triumph of the largely unknown Democratic nominee, former governor Jimmy Carter, in 1976, and his defeat by another former governor, Republican Ronald Reagan, in 1980, Democrats changed their rules to ensure that around one-seventh of convention delegates (dubbed "superdelegates") would be state governors and members of Congress and the Democratic National Committee.

A more consequential change has been that states, jockeying for advantage in the selection process, have advanced the dates of their primaries and caucuses to earlier in the election year, creating the "front-loading" that Michael Nelson and Andrew E. Busch discuss. Both Nelson and Busch agree that front-loading is a problem. They disagree, however, about what should be done about it. Nelson favors a national primary; Busch opposes such a plan. It is difficult to say whether a national primary is in the nation's future, but one thing is certain: the nominating process will continue to change, sometimes dramatically and often unexpectedly.

PRO: Michael Nelson

How about this for an idea? Because we Americans have to elect a president every fourth November, let's choose the Democratic and Republican nominees seven or eight months earlier, in March or April, when most voters aren't paying much attention. Let's start the process in two small, rural, nearly all-white states—Iowa and New Hampshire would be perfect—and give them the power to weed out all but a few candidates from each party. Then, before we've had a chance to learn much about even these few, let's get as many other states into the game as we can in the next several weeks. And because there's no real way to keep score in such an accelerated and far-flung contest, let's trust the news media to decide who's winning, who's losing, and who isn't even worth paying attention to. Then, after we know who the nominees are, let's sit back and relax for nearly half a year—until August or September, when the final campaign begins. If during that time we learn things about one or both major-party candidates that make us want to change our minds and nominate someone else, let's stick with them anyway.

Bad idea, right? Considering the stakes—the choice of the two finalists for the most powerful job in the world—no one ever would adopt such an approach if given the choice. And, the truth is, no one ever did. The current system for nominating presidential candidates is one that the United States stumbled into.

It happened like this. In the early 1970s, both parties decided that every state's delegates to the presidential nominating conventions should be chosen through a process in which the rank-and-file members of each party—and in many states, even independent voters and members of the other party—can participate. In practice, that meant choosing the delegates through either primaries or caucuses. (In a primary, one votes by secret ballot; in a caucus, one attends a meeting and votes openly.) New Hampshire, which began holding the first primary of the election year in 1952, when primaries were unimportant, then found itself in the privileged position of holding the first primary when primaries were very important. Iowa quickly jumped to the head of a different line, becoming the earliest caucus state and voting even before New Hampshire.

Both states have reaped the harvest of going first ever since. Nearly all the candidates campaign endlessly in Iowa and New Hampshire, promising their voters the moon (or, in cornfield-laden Iowa's case, ethanol subsidies) and infusing their economies with huge doses of campaign spending. The news media also camp out for months in Iowa and New Hampshire and, depending on how scholars do the counting, devote between one-fourth and three-fourths of their coverage of the entire nominating process to these two small states.[1] A candidate who does not win Iowa or New Hampshire has hardly any chance of being nominated, and candidates who do not finish in the top three are finished period, regardless of how popular they may be elsewhere in the country.

Iowa and New Hampshire deserve credit for quickly figuring out what most other states realized only slowly: the earlier a state votes, the more influence it has in the nominating process and the more benefits it derives.[2] Succumbing to "New Hampshire envy,"[3] nearly every state soon advanced its primary or caucus to as close to the start of the year as possible, a process called "front-loading." In the 1976 election, the second held under the reformed nominating system, only 10 percent of delegates were chosen by March 2. By 2008, some 70 percent were.[4] Rules tinkering by the GOP slowed the process down a little starting in 2012, but even so a majority of delegates are selected while the snow is still melting in many states.

Faced with the current mess, some thoughtful observers have wanted to try to undo the reforms of the early 1970s and revive the nominating process that existed during most of the nineteenth and twentieth centuries. "Under the old system," wrote *Washington Post* columnist David Broder, "running for president involved taking a few months off from your public office in the election year to present your credentials largely to political peers—other officeholders, party leaders, leaders of allied interest groups—and then persuade them that you were best qualified to carry the party banner." As it happened, argued political scientist Jeane Kirkpatrick, the qualities those "political peers" were looking for were the very qualities that made for good presidents: "the ability to deal with diverse groups, ability to work out compromises and develop consensus, and the ability to impress people who have watched a candidate over many years."[5]

All this may sound good, but, unfortunately, nostalgia more than history marks these and similar accounts of the prereform system. Writing in the late nineteenth century, James Bryce noted in his classic book *The American Commonwealth* that party professionals indeed had a talent for choosing electable candidates. But he also felt compelled to explain "Why Great Men Are Not Chosen President" in terms of that very talent: "It must be remembered that the merits of a President are one thing and those of a candidate another thing. . . . It will be a misfortune to the party, as well as to the country, if the candidate elected should prove a bad President. But it is a greater misfortune to the party that it should be beaten in the impending election, for the evil of losing national patronage will have come four years sooner."[6]

The indifference of party professionals to nominating good presidents extended to an occasional inability to weed out dangerous ones. Of the presidents beginning with William Howard Taft who were analyzed by James David Barber in his 1972 study *The Presidential Character,* four of the eleven who were nominated under the old rules (Woodrow Wilson, Herbert C. Hoover, Lyndon B. Johnson, and Richard Nixon) fell into the category of "active-negatives"—that is, persons who tended to turn political crises into personal crises and "persevere in a disastrous policy." Only three of the eleven—Franklin D. Roosevelt, Harry S. Truman, and John F. Kennedy—qualified as "active-positives," or leaders with "personal strengths specially attuned to the presidency." The other four presidents were mediocre—or in Barber's terminology, "passive"—presidents.[7] So much for the party professionals' much-vaunted talent for peer review.

Even the party pros' ability to choose electable candidates may have been overstated. Bryce wrote at a time of unusually close electoral competition. But in the twentieth century, twelve of the eighteen presidential elections held before the reforms of the early 1970s took effect were landslides in which the loser won less than half as many electoral votes as the winner. At least one set of party pros in each of these elections must have poorly judged their candidate's electability. In all, then, the good old days of the past were no better than the bad new days of the present, at least when it comes to nominating candidates for president.

Fortunately, Americans are not bound by either the past or the present—they can shape the future. In designing a new presidential nominating process, two criteria should be foremost in our thinking: simplicity and clarity.

To be sure, complexity in a political system need not mean that it is undemocratic, just as simplicity and clarity alone do not guarantee a democratic process. For example, a lottery drawing would be a clear, simple—and awful—method for nominating a presidential candidate. The Constitution, by contrast, is a complex system of "separated institutions sharing powers," in which citizens exercise limited authority, chiefly by voting in elections.[8]

In the design of the presidential nominating process, however, Americans are squarely in the center of that domain in which citizens get to exercise their limited authority, and that is where simplicity and clarity come in. As Henry Mayo argued in *Introduction to Democratic Theory,* "If [the] purpose of the election is to be carried out—to enable the voter to share in political power—the voter's job must not be made difficult and confusing for him. It ought, on the contrary, to be made as simple as the electoral machinery can be devised to make it."[9] In other words, whenever the Constitution opens the door to citizens, walking through it should be a straightforward process.

Federalism, like complexity, is another vital constitutional principle that is irrelevant to the presidential nominating process. The states not only are constitutionally sovereign in their own domain but also are embedded in Congress, where the people are represented in both the House of Representatives and Senate according to where they live. Although the president, uniquely among elected officials, is meant to represent the entire country, federalism is even woven into the Electoral College, in which presidential candidates seek electoral votes state by state. Federalism does not need to be entrenched in the nominating process as well.

The best way to remedy the problems with the current nominating process and replace it with one that is clear and simple (as well as democratic and practical) is to create a national primary.

Here is how a national primary could work. Any candidate trying to get on the Republican or Democratic national primary ballot would have until June of the election year to round up valid signatures equal in number to 1 percent of the turnout in the most recent presidential election (around 1.3 million in 2016). Each party's rank-and-file supporters would be eligible to vote for their party's nominee. The primary itself would be held on the first Tuesday in August—that is, voters across the country would all go to the polls on the same day. If none of a party's candidates receives 50 percent of the vote, a runoff election between the top two candidates would be held three weeks later. The national party conventions would meet soon afterward to approve the vice presidential candidates, write party rules, adopt their platforms, and hear the nominees' acceptance speeches.

Most of the specific elements of this proposal are subject to tinkering. Perhaps independent voters could be eligible to vote in the primary of their choice. The 1 percent requirement could be a little higher or lower, so long as it is high enough to screen out frivolous candidates but not so high as to screen out serious ones. A further variation could make the 1 percent rule mandatory in a minimum number of states as well as nationwide. The date of the primary could be a little earlier than August. Forty percent could be defined as sufficient for victory. The conventions could take a different form. Because none of these variations would alter the essential nature of the national primary, any or all of them would be fine.

The national primary is not a far-fetched idea. It has a distinguished pedigree: both Theodore Roosevelt and Woodrow Wilson promoted it a century ago. Since then, through reforms of state election laws, direct primaries have become the way Americans nominate almost every candidate for elective office in the country except president. Virtually every U.S. senator, member of the House of Representatives, and governor had to win a primary election to become the nominee of his or her party. It is hard to imagine an idea riper for extension to the presidency or more thoroughly road-tested at the federal, state, and local levels than the national primary.

Apart from its intrinsic democratic virtues and its deep resonance in the American experience, what beneficial effects would flow from the adoption of a national primary? First and foremost, every vote would count equally. No longer would the ballots of a relatively few New Hampshirites, now so crucial in determining who can be president, count infinitely more than the votes of the millions of people in states whose primaries are held after the nominating contest is essentially over. As a consequence, voter turnout would rise substantially. In recent elections, the turnout rate in the New Hampshire primary has been double that in the rest of the country.[10] Why the disparity? Because the people of New Hampshire know that their votes will directly affect the choice of the major-party nominees for president, and in most years the people of most other states know that their votes will not. If everyone is allowed to vote on the same day, everyone will feel the same connection between their vote and the outcome that New Hampshirites do now. Moving the date of the national primary to August, several months closer to the November election than is the current round of crucial primaries, would mean that people would be asked to vote when they are paying attention to the election, not before—another spur not just to higher turnout, but also to a more informed electorate.

An additional beneficial effect of the national primary is that it would reduce the scorekeeping role of the news media. The national primary is its own scoreboard. When the votes are counted on primary night, everyone can see who won. Public opinion polls would continue to measure how the candidates are doing before primary day, but journalists no longer would be called on to determine as well as to report on the status of the race—a role journalists themselves are uncomfortable performing.

Yet another benefit of the national primary would be a shift in the candidates' focus from the local issues that preoccupy Iowa and New Hampshire to the national issues that presidents must confront. Today, candidates for president have little incentive to address, for example, the concerns of racial minorities or the residents of big cities (neither of whom are found in Iowa and New Hampshire) and lots of incentive to defend agricultural subsidies in rural Iowa and the deductibility of property taxes in high-property-tax New Hampshire. If presidential candidates are forced to compete nationwide, then national—that is, presidential—issues will rise to the fore, as they should.

Finally, adopting the national primary would mean that the American people would have the presidential nominating process they want. Since the Gallup Poll began asking voters in 1952 what they think of the national primary, they have endorsed it every time by margins ranging from two to one to six to one. Democrats, Republicans, and independents consistently support the idea, as do the people of every age, income, race, sex, region, religion, and educational level.[11] The national primary would not have to prove itself to voters, because its legitimacy has been preapproved.

The case for a national primary is strong, but what about the case against? One common objection is that only established political figures would have a chance to be nominated, because only they would be able to raise the vast amounts of money needed to wage a nationwide campaign. To the extent that this is true, would it be any different than the current system? After all, for more than a quarter-century every major-party nominee for president has begun the election year as either the front-runner or a top-tier candidate.[12] But *is* this still true? As a freshman senator from Illinois, Barack Obama, showed in 2008 and Sen. Bernie Sanders from tiny Vermont showed in 2016, it is now possible for a political outsider to raise tremendous sums of money through the Internet, as long as he or she is saying things that strike a powerful chord with a great many people. Twitter, Facebook, YouTube, and cable news enabled a number of poorly funded Republicans to wage credible campaigns for their party's nomination in 2012. Donald Trump revealed another possibility—spending one's own money and making oneself endlessly available to cable news programs and social media—in 2016.

Another objection is that by making Iowa and New Hampshire no more influential than their combined 1.4 percent of the nation's population warrants, a national primary would remove from the nominating process the kind of face-to-face scrutiny by voters (so-called retail politics) that presidential candidates must now undergo to compete successfully in those two states. That is a reasonable objection if one believes that Iowans and New Hampshirites are uniquely qualified to serve as the screening and selection committee for the rest of the country. There is good reason to doubt that they are, however, especially considering that these states do not represent the country in anything close to its variety and also that they have a record of imposing locally major but nationally minor policy litmus tests on candidates.

A final objection to the national primary is that it would undermine the political parties. This tired wheeze was raised by defenders of the old nominating process when the reforms of the 1970s mandated that delegates be chosen through state caucuses and primaries—in complete disregard of the fact that the strongest party organizations in the country (for example, the Daley machine in Chicago, the Crump machine in Memphis, and the Byrd machine in Virginia) happily coexisted with primary elections for decades. Since the 1970s, the two major parties, which had been in steep decline during the 1960s, have grown stronger in government, in the electorate, and as organizations.

In summary, the front-loaded, Iowa and New Hampshire–centric presidential nominating process is broken. Either the federal government, through simple legislation, or the two national parties, by requiring states to participate in the national primary or forfeit their say in the choice of the nominees, has the power to fix it.[13] Other proposed remedies—regional primaries, for example, in which the states of each region would vote on a different first Tuesday between February and June—are inadequate. Whichever region got to go first would have the same distorting power in the choice of presidential nominees as Iowa and New Hampshire do now. The truth is that because more and more states are cramming their primaries into the same few early weeks of the election year, the country has already drifted into a kind of de facto national primary, but a lousy one. It is time to have a good one.

CON: Andrew E. Busch

The idea of a national primary election to choose presidential party nominees is almost as old as the primary itself. The 1912 Progressive Party platform demanded "nation-wide preferential primaries for candidates for the presidency." One year later, President Woodrow Wilson endorsed the idea in his first State of the Union message to Congress.[14]

Since then, the national primary has garnered considerable support, chiefly because of its appeal as a simpler form of democracy. It is clean, straightforward, and majoritarian—or so it would seem. In more recent years, some have also advocated a national primary as a means of combating the flaws in the modern "front-loaded" primary system—that is, one in which the state primaries and caucuses are disproportionately crammed together early in the primary season. In national opinion polls, at least two-thirds of Americans typically say they would prefer a national primary to the current system.

Yet despite its seductive appeal, the national primary is a bad idea. Upon closer examination, its supposed advantages prove to be largely illusory, and its disadvantages are serious indeed.

THE VIRTUE OF SIMPLICITY?

Much of the argument for a national primary lies in its alleged simplicity, but should simplicity be the driving motivation behind reform of the nominating system?

The genius of the American political system lies in its complexity. Separation of powers, checks and balances, bicameralism, and federalism all represent a deliberate embrace of complexity, as does the very idea, outlined in *Federalist* No. 10, of a large republic filled with contending and balancing "factions." When it comes to presidential selection, the Electoral College was adopted by the framers, and is defended today by its supporters, precisely because its complexity allows for a tempered democracy and a balance between large and small states. It is, as such, emblematic of the "Compound Republic" extolled by James Madison in *Federalist* No. 39—a republic whose complicated structure does not fit neatly into the category of a unitary national government or of a confederation of states, but does succeed in meeting the needs of a diverse nation.

America's previous experiments with simplicity in presidential nominations have not turned out well. By far the most straightforward system for party nomination was the congressional caucus, in which congressional members of each party met to select their presidential nominee. From 1800 to 1824, the congressional caucus was a model of simplicity, but that benefit was rapidly outweighed by various defects, including insufficient representation of party voters in the caucus and the potential for a breakdown in separation of powers brought on by Congress's involvement in selecting presidential nominees. In 1824 the system collapsed due to the conflicts among political factions that shattered its simple frame.

The congressional caucus was quickly replaced by the national convention system, a nominating mechanism that relied on local and state party meetings to supply, through a circuitous route, delegates to the convention. It was highly decentralized, depending on the actions and calculations of dozens of local party leaders and hundreds of delegates. This complex system served the nation well for the better part of a century before progressive reformers inadvertently added even more complexity by superimposing primaries in some states on top of the traditional convention system. The convention system and the "mixed" system that supplanted it were both more complicated than the congressional caucus system and more democratic. Thus, there is no evidence that simplicity is inherently better.

Just as the congressional caucus threatened separation of powers, the national primary threatens to undermine central features of the complex and balanced American political system. It would weaken federalism by reducing the importance of states in the selection process, reduce deliberation within the nominating process, and strengthen the presidency by adding power to the president's claim of possessing an unmediated popular mandate. In an era featuring the rise of what scholar Andrew Rudalevige has called "The New

Imperial Presidency," it is far from clear that we should be seeking to enhance the president's position further.[15] Moreover, the national primary can prevail only if the public is persuaded that simplicity is preferable to subtlety—a success that could have the side effect of lowering Americans' resistance to other reforms that seek to dismantle other, more central manifestations of the complex American system (such as the Electoral College). As French political observer Alexis de Tocqueville argued long ago in *Democracy in America,* the seeking of simplicity and uniformity often drives a political centralization that, over time, can unbalance and degrade America's polity and even threaten its liberty.

NOT AS SIMPLE AS IT SEEMS

In addition to the symbolic damage it might do to federalism, the notion of limited presidential power, and popular respect for the nuances of the American system, a national primary would probably not deliver on its promise to simplify American democracy. Instead, in the name of simplicity, the nation would just trade one set of complexities for another—and it is hardly obvious that the trade would be a good one.

For example, there is a potential conflict between the simplicity of the plan and its democratic nature. Nomination races often feature more than two candidates, and so the winners of early primaries frequently finish with less than 50 percent of the primary votes. In a national primary, should a plurality (more votes than those won by any of the opponents) be enough for a candidate to be declared a victor? Or must the winner win an outright majority (more than half of the votes)? A plurality rule diminishes the democratic element of the plan, making it possible for an extreme candidate who has intense but narrow support to win the nomination in a multicandidate field. To an extent, the GOP race of 2016 showed that this can also happen in the current system, but even then, as candidates dropped out, a leader was eventually able to build a majority (albeit later than usual). On the other hand, a runoff between the top two candidates would guarantee that someone wins a majority, but would introduce a second election, thereby diminishing the plan's simplicity. Experience has also shown that runoff elections almost invariably draw fewer voters—often many fewer—sometimes bringing into question the validity of the results.[16]

To avoid the problems inherent in multicandidate fields, some students of the electoral process have suggested introducing novel and complicated forms of voting, such as approval voting or cumulative voting. In such schemes, voters would vote for all the candidates they find acceptable, indicate their preferred ordering of all candidates, or allocate multiple votes in whatever proportions they wish. None of these experimental voting methods has ever been tried on a national scale in the United States, and they are certainly not simple.

There is also the question of whether the "national primary" would really be a single, unified national election or whether it would consist of fifty-one separate primaries held on the same day. Most national primary proposals follow the first course, but in the latter case there would still be delegates and a convention. And there would be little opportunity, as there is now, for a multicandidate field to "shake out," increasing the likelihood that a convention would be split and deadlocked among numerous contenders and dominated by unseemly deal making. Again, such an outcome is not impossible in the current system, and was a real possibility for several months in 2016, but has not actually happened for decades. Although many political scientists and news correspondents might welcome the return of the "brokered" convention, it is not clear who in the modern era of fractured parties would have the power to broker it. More to the point, however interesting the spectacle might prove, it is the last thing that supporters of the national primary have in mind.

FRONT-LOADING REDUX

Proponents of a national primary have recently argued that such a reform is needed because of the increased front-loading of the primary process since the 1980s. However, the nation's experience with front-loading actually supplies some of the strongest arguments against the national primary.

Front-loading is a phenomenon that has been driven predominantly by the independent decisions of a large number of states to move their primary elections forward in the primary calendar. "Meaningful" primaries—primaries whose results could actually have an impact on the outcome of the nomination race—were once spread out over three months or more. By contrast, in 2004 the meaningful primary season began in Iowa on January 19 and ended on March 7, only six weeks later; the decisive portion of the 2008 Republican nominating contest lasted from January 3 through February 5, a period of only five weeks.

The front-loading of presidential primaries has been almost universally decried, including by the officials who pushed their states' primaries up. Critics have focused on four central shortcomings of the front-loaded system.[17] First, it is clear that front-loading has enhanced the importance of the so-called invisible primary—that is, the jockeying among candidates and the preparatory work that takes place in the year or more before the real primaries begin.

In 2008 only one candidate in either party who won even one primary had raised less than $37 million by January 1. In 2012 Republican Mitt Romney had raised $56.3 million by January 1; Rick Santorum, having raised a mere $2 million before the primaries started, won a handful of contests but did not have the resources to capitalize. Altogether, in most years, political insiders have regained most of the advantage that they allegedly had before the Democratic Party undertook reforms in 1970 that sought to open up and democratize the nominating process.[18]

Second, because the meaningful primary season often ends so soon after it begins, voters have fewer opportunities for second thoughts or careful deliberation. In the aftermath of the 2004 general election, some Democrats argued that the front-loaded system that sped John Kerry's nomination failed to allow sufficient examination of Kerry's strengths and weaknesses as a nominee.[19] Likewise, John McCain's 2008 victory in all but name by February 5 left Republican voters little opportunity for rethinking their choice.

Third, as the state primaries begin to come fast and furious, candidates no longer have time for the "retail" (face-to-face) politicking they cultivated in small states like Iowa and New Hampshire. Instead, they engage in a wholesale "tarmac campaign" in which they flit from one big-city airport to another, while relying mostly on expensive and superficial television ads to reach mass audiences.

Finally, once one candidate has amassed enough convention delegate votes to capture the nomination (or to drive serious opponents from the field), all later presidential primaries are rendered moot. In most recent years, roughly half of the states have had no meaningful participation in the presidential nominating process, and the contests in those states, compared with those held earlier, see a marked decline in voter turnout. If the later primaries do not matter, the incentive to vote is significantly reduced.

So, why not adopt a national primary to address these problems?

The first and lesser answer is that it has become apparent since 2008 that front-loading and short contests are not inevitable and can be addressed by means short of the radical reform represented by a national primary. The extended 2008 Democratic nomination contest, in which Barack Obama fought Hillary Rodham Clinton tooth and nail for five months before prevailing in early June; the 2012 GOP contest, which Mitt Romney did not nail down until late April; and both parties' hard-fought 2016 races demonstrated that the current system is capable of breaking out of some of the problems associated with front-loading. Among other things, the parties have deliberately engineered a modest back-loading through rules changes, and the rise of Super PACs after 2010 has enabled some candidates to remain viable contestants for longer periods of time. (Increasing the individual contribution limit for presidential campaigns could have a similar effect.) As some nomination contests began to last longer, states noticed the benefits of going later and moved their contests back.

More to the point, the national primary would actually worsen all but one of the problems associated with front-loading. The irrelevance of later primaries would end, because everyone would vote at once. Modest Iowa and tiny New Hampshire could not start a stampede toward a candidate, and no state would be left out of the decision. In every other respect, a national primary— no matter how it is arranged—is sure to drastically worsen the problems that most analysts associate with front-loading. Indeed, the national primary would represent, in essence, front-loading taken to its extreme.

If there is a high entry fee for the invisible primary now, that fee will only go up in a national primary. As the stakes of primary day rise, the price of playing will rise as well. To participate in a one-day national election, candidates will have to run national campaigns from the beginning. They will have to raise more money—all of it up front. And candidates will not be able to take advantage of an early surprise win in a small state to raise more money via the Internet, as John McCain did in the 2000 Republican primaries. The higher campaign costs will discourage some potential candidates from running, and more of those who do enter the race will withdraw before the primary voters have a chance to render a verdict. Long-shot candidates will have even less chance of overtaking the leader than they do in the current system. If there is a runoff provision, fund-raising will become even more important, because candidates who advance will have to finance not one but two hugely expensive national primary campaigns.

If there is too little retail politicking in the front-loaded system after Iowa and New Hampshire, there would be virtually *no* retail politicking in a national primary system. The entire race would revolve around a costly and impersonal mass media effort, with little chance for the candidates to come face-to-face with the voters. No state would vote after the nominees have been selected, but many states and regions would be ignored in the rush of wholesale politics. Many issues of local significance that now receive at least some attention may be shunted to the side entirely.

Finally, if voters in today's front-loaded system often have little opportunity to change their minds or to gather and reflect on new information produced in earlier primaries, a national primary decided by a plurality vote would allow for no second thoughts at all. A national primary with a runoff would be a bit better, but the second thoughts would be limited to the top two candidates.

In short, to the extent that front-loading is the problem, a national primary is most definitely not the solution. Indeed, a national primary will only exacerbate the pathologies of a front-loaded system.

THE PROBLEM OF ENACTMENT

An additional reason to oppose a national primary is the difficulty of establishing it through legitimate means. Almost all supporters of a national primary seem to assume that such a reform could be implemented by federal legislation. However, there are ample reasons to doubt this assumption.

The Constitution gives no outright authority to the federal government to intervene in the presidential nominating process. Only three provisions of the Constitution deal explicitly with elections for federal office. Two of the three (in Article II, Section 1) allocate between the states and Congress the powers related to the selection of presidential electors; Congress is given only the right to determine the "time" of such selections. The third (in Article I, Section 4) provides that "[t]he Times, Places, and Manner of holding Elections for Senators and Representatives, shall be prescribed in each State by the legislature thereof; but the Congress may at any time by Law make or alter such regulations, except as to the Places of chusing Senators."

Strictly speaking, then, the presidential nominating process for the parties is outside the Constitution—that is, in literal terms no constitutional provision touches nominations. Less strictly speaking, in "spirit" the Constitution treats congressional control of congressional elections more favorably than it does congressional control over presidential selection processes, which are placed mostly under the supervision of state governments.

A handful of Supreme Court cases have permitted federal legislation affecting presidential elections beyond what a strict reading of the Constitution would seem to allow—for example, some rulings have upheld campaign finance regulations for both presidential and congressional elections. Some would go even further. Justice Hugo Black's opinion in *Oregon v. Mitchell* (1970) argued that the power of Congress to regulate presidential elections was equal to its power to regulate congressional elections. The Court, however, has never concurred with Black's solitary view.

Indeed, two recent lines of Supreme Court interpretation have moved in the opposite direction. In one of these strands, the Court has increasingly held over the last four decades that the political parties are substantially private associations with considerable power to set their own nomination procedures.[20] This line of reasoning would limit both federal and state legislative interference in party affairs, at least in theory; all actual cases have involved state legislation. The second strand, evident especially since the mid-1990s, has reasserted the rights of the states against federal domination on the basis of the Tenth Amendment and a narrower reading of the enumerated powers of Congress.[21] Both strands have worked to limit, not expand, federal legislative powers that might be used to impose a national primary. Thus, both the text of the Constitution and recent judicial interpretations of that text give little reason to assume that the federal government possesses the authority to pass legislation establishing a national primary.[22] A constitutional amendment could solve this problem, but amendments are not easily ratified.

In contrast, the national parties would seem to possess the legal authority to seek such a reform, but primaries are actually established by state law. The national parties can refuse to seat delegates selected in a manner contrary to party rules, but they cannot force state legislatures to change primary dates. Although there were exceptions in both parties in 2008, the parties are typically reluctant to follow through on threats to deny seating to state delegations.[23] Refusing to seat state delegations is one of only a very few enforcement tools available to the parties, but it is too blunt an instrument to be used frequently. The more radical a proposed change—and a national primary is radical—the more unlikely it is that the national parties will be able to compel compliance. They may possess the authority, but they may not possess the power.

WHAT KIND OF CANDIDATE?

Finally, one of the most crucial considerations in the evaluation of any electoral system is what kind of candidates it will produce. Successful candidacies for party nomination are, of course, the result of a variety of factors, only one of which is the system in which the candidates compete. And it is entirely possible that the same candidate can succeed, perhaps to different degrees, in two different systems. Nevertheless, it is always the responsibility of reformers to give serious thought to this question. Given what we know, it is possible to offer an educated guess regarding what sort of candidates would be advantaged by the move to a national primary:

- Candidates who have very deep pockets, especially wealthy candidates who can self-finance

- Well-known and charismatic celebrities who can dominate the national media—today's version of those feared by the founders as "brilliant appearances of genius and patriotism, which, like transient meteors, sometimes mislead as well as dazzle"[24]

- Candidates whose support is deeply concentrated regionally

In contrast, in the current system, candidates must win in many places, just as in the Electoral College. We have long taken for granted, even ignored, that in this respect the nominating system is synchronized with the general election system. It is an interesting question what sort of dislocation might result from selecting nominees in a manner that potentially contradicts one of the most important goals (and achievements) of the general election system—namely, requiring a broad geographical coalition from winners. Moreover, campaigns in the current system can acquire resources somewhat more gradually, and, because they are ultimately nominated by delegates meeting in convention, usually benefit from immersing themselves in local politics and mastering organizational details.

None of these observations is absolute. Donald Trump succeeded in the current system as a charismatic celebrity (many would say demagogue) whose campaign was notably inept at mastering organizational details and local politics. It is no secret that the current system has already gone far along the plebiscitary path that the national primary would complete. However, with a national primary, one might anticipate that we would see many more Donald Trumps, a troubling prospect to many Americans across the political spectrum.

CONCLUSION

In summary, the national primary should be rejected. It offers a simplicity that is both illusory and undesirable. Although it would solve one problem associated with primary front-loading—the loss of meaningful participation by states that vote too late in the primary calendar—it would exacerbate the other problems. Indeed, a national primary would produce the most front-loaded schedule imaginable, with everything riding on a single day's contest. There is no obvious way to bring about the reform, as the federal government likely does not have the authority to impose it and the parties have the authority but probably not the power. Not least, it is reasonable to fear that the national primary would more frequently elevate charismatic, potentially demagogic, characters, or could lead to unanticipated outcomes as a key principle of the nominating system is decoupled from the general election system. Despite the good intentions of the proponents of the national primary, the nation can do better.

NOTES

PRO

1. Barry C. Burden, "The Nominations: Technology, Money, and Transferable Momentum," in *The Elections of 2004,* ed. Michael Nelson (Washington, DC: CQ Press, 2005), 19.

2. States receive more attention from the candidates and the media when they advance the dates of their primaries. See Andrew E. Busch and William G. Mayer, "The Front-Loading Problem," in *The Making of the Presidential Candidates, 2004,* ed. William G. Mayer (Lanham, MD: Rowman & Littlefield, 2004), 11–12.

3. Ibid., 9.

4. Barry C. Burden, "The Nominations: Rules, Strategies, and Uncertainty," in *The Elections of 2008,* ed. Michael Nelson (Washington, DC: CQ Press, 2010), 25.

5. Broder and Kirkpatrick are quoted in Michael Nelson, "The Presidential Nominating System: Problems and Prescriptions," in *What Role for Government? Lessons from Policy Research,* ed. Richard J. Zeckhauser and Derek Leebaert (Durham, NC: Duke University Press, 1983), 42–3.

6. James Bryce, *The American Commonwealth* (New York: Putnam's, 1959), 28–9.

7. James David Barber, *The Presidential Character: Predicting Performance in the White House* (Englewood Cliffs, NJ: Prentice-Hall, 1972).

8. The phrase is from Richard E. Neustadt, *Presidential Power* (New York: Wiley, 1960).

9. Henry Mayo, *Introduction to Democratic Theory* (New York: Oxford University Press, 1960), 73.

10. Busch and Mayer, "Front-Loading Problem," 33.

11. Nelson, "Presidential Nominating System," 50; Stephen J. Wayne, *The Road to the White House 2004: The Politics of Presidential Elections,* 7th ed. (Belmont, CA: Wadsworth, 2004), 311–12.

12. Busch and Mayer, "Front-Loading Problem," 23.

13. The Supreme Court, which has already confirmed Congress's authority to govern campaign finance through legislation, would hardly blanch at a national primary law. As for the national parties, the Court has regularly endorsed their authority to establish their own rules.

CON

14. Arthur S. Link, ed., *The Papers of Woodrow Wilson,* vol. 29 (Princeton, NJ: Princeton University Press, 1979), 7.

15. Andrew Rudalevige, *The New Imperial Presidency: Renewing Presidential Power after Watergate* (Ann Arbor: University of Michigan Press, 2008).

16. See Stephen G. Wright, "Voter Turnout in Runoff Elections," *Journal of Politics* 51 (May 1989): 385–96; and Charles S. Bullock III and Loch K. Johnson, *Runoff Elections in the United States* (Chapel Hill: University of North Carolina Press, 1992), chap. 6.

17. For a detailed critique of front-loading, see William G. Mayer and Andrew E. Busch, *The Front-Loading Problem in Presidential Nominations* (Washington, DC: Brookings, 2004), esp. chap. 4.

18. See Marty Cohen, David Karol, Hans Noel, and John Zaller, *The Party Decides: Presidential Nominations before and after Reform* (Chicago, IL: University of Chicago Press, 2008).

19. See Emily Goodin, "Enough Blame to Share," *National Journal* (December 4, 2004): 3630.

20. See, for example, *Cousins v. Wigoda,* 419 U.S. 477 (1975); *Republican Party of Connecticut v. Tashjian,* 479 U.S. 208 (1986); and *March Fong Eu v. San Francisco County Democratic Central Committee,* 489 U.S. 214 (1989).

21. See *New York v. United States,* 488 U.S. 1041 (1992); *United States v. Lopez,* 514 U.S. 549 (1995); *Printz v. United States,* 521 U.S. 898 (1997); *United States v. Morrison,* 529 U.S. 598 (2000); and *National Federation of Independent Business v. Sebelius,* 567 U. S. ____ (2012). The enumerated powers of Congress are those listed in Article I, Section 8, of the Constitution defining the extent and limits of congressional authority. The Tenth Amendment specifies that "[t]he powers not delegated to the United States by the Constitution, nor prohibited by it to the States, are reserved to the States respectively or to the people."

22. See William G. Mayer and Andrew E. Busch, "Can the Federal Government Reform the Presidential Nomination Process?" *Election Law Journal* 3, no. 4 (2004): 613–25.

23. Democrats initially voted to deny delegates to Florida and Michigan when the two states scheduled their primaries earlier than party rules allowed, although the delegates were ultimately restored at the convention in a gesture of party unity. For the same reason, Republicans refused to seat half of the delegates from Florida, Michigan, and three other states.

24. John Jay, *Federalist* No. 64.

RESOLVED, The president should be elected directly by the people

PRO: Burdett Loomis

CON: Byron E. Shafer

No issue vexed the delegates to the Constitutional Convention more than how the president should be chosen. A few wanted the president to be elected directly by the people. Quite a few more (but, in the end, not a majority) preferred that Congress elect the president. Other ideas included having the governors of the states or a small group of randomly selected members of Congress make the choice. After going around and around on this question, the delegates created a committee to come up with a solution that all of them could live with. The committee's proposal—the Electoral College— accomplished that goal. Offered to the convention on September 4, it was adopted with only minor modifications two days later.

Further tinkering took place in 1804, when the Twelfth Amendment stipulated that each elector must vote separately for president and vice president instead of voting (as the Constitution originally provided) for two candidates for president. Since then, more amendments have been introduced in Congress to replace or overhaul the Electoral College than to change any other feature of the Constitution—about five hundred. But the only one to be enacted was the Twenty-third Amendment, which left the Electoral College intact but enfranchised voters in the District of Columbia to participate in the election.

How does the Electoral College work? To begin with, each state is assigned a number of electors equal to its number of representatives and senators in Congress. Currently, for example, California has fifty-five electoral votes, and several small states have the minimum number of three, corresponding to the one representative and two senators that a state gets no matter how few people live there. With the adoption of the Twenty-third Amendment in 1961, the District of Columbia received three electors. The Constitution leaves it up to each state to decide how its electors will be chosen and its electoral votes allocated. In practice, all of the states entrust this decision to the people. Except in Maine and Nebraska, where each congressional district chooses an elector, the candidate who receives the most popular votes in the state wins all of its electors, a system known as winner-take-all.

To be elected president or vice president, a candidate must receive more than half of all the electoral votes in the country—currently, at least 270 out of 538. If no candidate does so, the House of Representatives elects the president from the top three electoral vote recipients, with each state delegation in the House casting a single vote until one of the candidates receives a majority. Meanwhile, the Senate chooses the vice president from the top two vice presidential candidates, with each senator assigned one vote. The House has been called on to elect the president twice: in 1800, when it chose Thomas Jefferson over Aaron Burr, and in 1824, when it chose John Quincy Adams over Andrew Jackson. The latter was a highly controversial decision because Jackson had outpaced Adams in both the popular vote and the electoral vote. Although it has been a long time since the House had to act, every time a serious third-party candidate enters the race against the Republican and Democratic nominees, the possibility arises that none of them will secure an electoral vote majority and the House will once again be called on to elect the president.

A more frequent occurrence, although still a relatively rare one, is for the candidate who receives the most votes from the people to lose the election because the other candidate receives a majority of electoral votes. This is what happened in 1876, in 1888, and most recently in 2000, when Democrat Al Gore received a half million more popular votes than his Republican rival, George W. Bush, but Bush prevailed in the Electoral College by a vote of 271–266. By contrast, in every election from 1892 to 1996 (and again in 2004, 2008, and 2012) the Electoral College "magnified" the victory of the popular vote winner—that is, the winner received a larger percentage of electoral votes than of popular votes.

The Electoral College has ardent defenders, including Byron E. Shafer. But as the many attempts to repeal it indicate, the Electoral College also has its critics. In the early 1950s, Congress seriously considered modifying the Electoral College by adopting a proportional system in which each state's electoral votes would be awarded in proportion to the popular vote each candidate received in the state. More recently, the leading alternative to the Electoral College has been direct election by the people. This is the idea championed by Burdett Loomis.

PRO: Burdett Loomis

Ilive in Lawrence, Kansas, home of the University of Kansas and part of the last "blue" county for well over five hundred miles to the west. More prosaically, Kansas is a Republican state, even though the GOP's two major factions have energized state politics with their bloody feuds. When presidential elections roll around, however, Kansans are reliably "red," voting by large margins for every Republican nominee in the past forty years (60 percent for Mitt Romney in 2012).

In 1979 I moved to Kansas from Illinois, and earlier I had lived in Wisconsin and Pennsylvania. In all these states the race for president meant candidate visits, lots of advertising, and a real sense of competition. But not here, where both the Democratic and Republican presidential campaigns studiously avoid the state, knowing full well that Kansas's six electoral votes will almost certainly end up in the Republican column. This winner-take-all element of presidential elections, state by state, means that most Americans are written off in the process, because only a handful of states enjoy competitive contests.

Since 1980 I have cast a Kansas ballot in each election for the Democratic presidential candidate. For all the difference it has made, I may as well have voted for the Libertarian candidate, the Socialist Workers' nominee, or the Man in the Moon. In this country's most important election, my vote, along with those of my fellow Kansas Democrats, counts for nothing.

The contrast with Colorado, our western neighbor, is stark because of that state's increasingly competitive partisan makeup. Colorado voters get to participate actively in the presidential election. It's great. Candidates fly in, have press conferences, and tend to any number of local and state issues. They raise money and spend lots of it on television advertising. Both parties seek to win every possible vote in Colorado, and its citizens benefit from a vigorous campaign, fought in every corner of the state.

Strangely enough, most Kansas Republicans are irrelevant to the presidential campaign. Aside from a few top fund-raisers, the rank and file are simply expected to deliver the state's six electoral votes and contribute some money to a candidate who will continually fly over Kansas's airspace but never land. All of this would be bad enough if Kansas were somehow an oddity in presidential politics. But it is not; in fact, Kansas is far closer to the norm than is Colorado, because most states are not competitive and are thus ignored by presidential campaigns.

To summarize, because of the nature of contemporary presidential politics under the rules of the Electoral College, most Americans are effectively disenfranchised in choosing the president, whose actions affect all of them. Simply put, that is just not fair.

As a student of American politics, I certainly understand and even celebrate the importance of the nation's political institutions. Moreover, as a political scientist, I recognize that institutions affect elections and policy decisions, and that institutional rules are never neutral. But I have a hard time appreciating a system in which the deck is stacked, over and over again, so that my vote for president does not count.

Although I am a Democrat in a GOP stronghold, this is no partisan argument. Indeed, a Massachusetts Republican might well offer the same complaint. But my argument is both personal and general, lodged on behalf of the minority-party voters in the thirty-plus states that are uncompetitive in any given presidential election. Unlike most other statewide electoral contests in Kansas, the presidential race is finished before it even starts. Indeed, even in a year (2016) when outsider Republican candidates have made a strong showing, no serious observer thinks that Democrats have any chance in the Land of Oz.

So what? Should Americans condemn the Electoral College because most state races are not competitive? After all, presidential elections have been vigorously contested and competitive at the national level for more than two centuries. Even if every voter is not treated equally or fairly, the system has worked reasonably well, producing legitimate winners for 225 years, despite disagreements that once rose to the level of a civil war. It is an argument worth addressing, and so I will now abandon, for the time being at least, the frustrating stories of Kansas and other similarly situated states. But I will return to them later, because in the end the most profound critique of the Electoral College rests on its failure to give each citizen an equal voice in selecting the nation's president.

THE ELECTORAL COLLEGE AS A CONTINUING POLITICAL EXPERIMENT

The Electoral College is the institutional mechanism used to select the president of the United States. Like the legislative and judicial branches, the executive branch was conceived by the framers in their dual roles as political philosophers and practicing politicians. Although the framers' debates about the nature of the Constitution and the subsequent debates over its ratification reveal many of the core theoretical underpinnings of the U.S. system, the framers were political reformers who were seeking institutional solutions to actual problems of governance.[1]

Although the framers seriously considered allowing Congress to select the president, they decided that any such process would have given lawmakers too much power while rendering the executive less strong and independent. At the same time, direct election of the chief executive was rejected, largely for practical reasons rather than because of an aversion to direct democracy. To be sure, some delegates to the Constitutional Convention rejected the idea of direct election because they feared placing too much power in citizens' hands. More of the framers, however, found direct election impractical because of the difficulties of communicating effectively and knowledgeably across the entire nation.[2]

As for the Electoral College, during the battle over ratifying the Constitution, New York delegate Alexander Hamilton argued that it had escaped serious scrutiny at the convention.[3] In fact, it was an amalgam of various compromises, including the number of electors to be assigned to each state, the counting of slaves as three-fifths of a person for the purpose of calculating voting population, and the mediation of direct elections through the state-by-state selection of electors. The Electoral College, then, is more a product of political necessity than of overriding principle. The framers also proved to be poor prognosticators when it came to the Electoral College. They anticipated that electors would exercise judgment in voting for candidates, and they gave no consideration to the possibility that political parties—specifically, two parties—would come to dominate the process. Rather, the framers foresaw eminent men being chosen as electors and then selecting a highly qualified president.

But their expectations about the Electoral College proved wrong on almost every count. Political parties, both in their emerging form of the early 1800s and in their more mature manifestations that appeared in the Jacksonian era, proved capable of holding electors to their pledges to support the parties' choices for president and vice president. The role of electors as independent intermediaries vanished almost as soon as the first real contest for the presidency was waged, in 1796.

By 1836 the role of the Electoral College had become well defined. Voters selected electors pledged to candidates who ran for president under party labels. In large part because each state adopted a "winner-take-all" rule for presidential (and most other) elections, only two major parties emerged.

Although the politics of presidential nominations and campaigns has changed greatly since the early 1800s, the basic features of the Electoral College have not. So there the Electoral College sits, an eighteenth-century institution conceived in political compromise and largely unchanged for two hundred years. Yet during those many years Congress has evolved, as has the presidency and the Supreme Court. Why, then, do Americans return every four years to a jury-rigged system that discriminates against millions of American voters and raises profound questions over the legitimacy of its results?

THE ELECTORAL COLLEGE: A SUCCESSFUL FAILURE

If twenty-first-century Americans designed a system to select their chief executive, two values would likely emerge as especially important: equality and transparency. Each vote should count the same, and all citizens should understand easily how the process works. Over the course of U.S. history, those values have become part of the fabric of the democratic process. Today, almost no one is denied access to the polls, and in almost all elections—whether for governor or school board or on referenda—each vote counts the same. Likewise, the reforms of the twentieth century, from the Australian ballot to primary elections to campaign finance reporting rules, have increased the transparency of the electoral process. Irregularities may remain, but the values of equality and transparency are essentially honored in how Americans conduct their elections—with one major exception: the Electoral College. Here, the votes of individual citizens in different states do not count the same. And despite legions of newspaper stories that purport to explain the Electoral College every four years, it remains notoriously misunderstood, in large part because Americans vote simultaneously for a presidential candidate *and* the slate of electors who formally cast their votes for president a month after the November general election.

So, in two major ways the Electoral College falls short. But these are just the first two counts in a long indictment. Before turning to some of these other problematic features of the Electoral College, let's flesh out the equality issue a bit more.

Many critics of the Electoral College complain about the numerical inequalities among the states or about how the institution counts some votes differently from others. Many of these related concerns flow from the disparities produced by giving each state a number of electors equal to its congressional delegation. Delaware thus receives three electoral votes, while California gets fifty-five. At first blush, Delaware and the six other states with a single House member seem to be getting away with murder. After all, their electoral votes are triple the number they would receive if population (reflected in the number of House seats) were the sole criterion. At the same time, the Senate "bonus" barely changes California's electoral total; the two extra electors pale in comparison with the state's fifty-three House members.

But Delaware's citizens understand that they do not have nearly the clout held by Californians. Under the winner-take-all rule, all fifty-five of California's electors go to the candidate who carries the state; Delaware's prize is tiny by comparison. Thus, even with their extra electors, small states remain at a disadvantage. Moreover, anyone wanting to look at real inequality in the U.S. political system need look no further than the U.S. Senate, which is among the most unrepresentative major legislative bodies in the world. The inequalities of the Electoral College pale before those of the Senate.

Ironically, the core inequity of the Electoral College involves neither the largest nor the smallest states but the handful of truly competitive states (about fifteen or so in the past few elections but fewer than ten in 2012). Not only do these states—such as Florida, Iowa, Virginia, Ohio, Pennsylvania, and Wisconsin, as well as Colorado—receive the lion's share of the campaigns' attention, but the value of each vote in these states is magnified by the fact that the entire presidential election could well be decided by a relatively small number of votes in a single state.[4]

That said, the gravest defect of the Electoral College is that the candidate who receives the most popular votes can lose the election. Before the 2000 election, the last time this situation unambiguously arose was in 1888, when Republican Benjamin Harrison defeated the Democratic incumbent president, Grover Cleveland, despite the fact that Cleveland received more popular votes.[5] Prior to the 2000 election, then, defenders of the Electoral College could have argued that the institution, while perhaps flawed, had generally proved a success. At the same time, skeptics could look at the narrow elections of 1916, 1948, 1960, 1968, and 1976 and express wonderment that the system did not produce more presidents who won the electoral vote while losing the popular count.

The 2000 election brought the flaws of the Electoral College into full view. Republican George W. Bush received fewer popular votes than Democrat Al Gore, yet Bush won the electoral vote count by five votes. In the popular vote, Gore had a narrow but clear national plurality of more than five hundred thousand votes. A direct popular election would have awarded him the presidency, but the Electoral College—with a razor-thin margin for Bush in Florida—created a constitutional crisis and elected the candidate who lost the popular vote count.

Unfortunately, the defects of the Electoral College were obscured in the shuffle of postelection court battles and vote counting in Florida. But the simple truth remains that the popular vote count was far less ambiguous than was the result of the Electoral College, save for the Supreme Court's late and highly questionable intervention on Bush's behalf. Moreover, the popular vote results would have stood as a more legitimate result in the eyes of the voters than either the electoral vote count or the Supreme Court's decision.

Despite some initial calls for electoral reform after the 2000 contest, the wind soon went out of reformers' sails, and elections since then have been conducted in the same manner as the 2000 election, with candidates focusing on the ten to fifteen states that were in play. A Kansan or even a Californian had no more role to play in 2008 or 2012 than in 2000. Still, the Bush–Kerry contest in 2004 again demonstrated the potential for an Electoral College "mistake" because Bush, despite winning the national popular vote by three million votes, had only a 119,000-vote margin (of almost three million cast) in Ohio, a state essential to his victory. With a shift of sixty thousand votes, Democrat John Kerry could easily have become the second consecutive chief executive who lost the popular vote, in which case concrete, bipartisan concerns about presidential legitimacy would certainly have surfaced.[6]

So far, I have focused on actual problems with the Electoral College. Its dysfunctional nature comes into even sharper focus when one considers what happens when no candidate receives a majority of the electoral vote and the election requires resolution by the House of Representatives, where *each state receives one vote*. This situation arose in both 1800 and 1824, but never in the modern two-party era. There have, however, been a lot of near misses, most notably in 1948, when "Dixiecrat" candidate Strom Thurmond won thirty-nine electoral votes in the South, and in 1968, when American Independent Party candidate George C. Wallace won forty-six electoral votes. In a closer election, either might have been in a position to determine the winner by negotiating an Electoral College deal with one of the major-party candidates. Many states have sought to avoid such deal making by binding electors to candidates, but most constitutional scholars agree that the courts would not uphold such laws.[7]

Governments in parliamentary systems often come into existence through this kind of negotiation, but the United States does not have such a system. Americans can scarcely anticipate the possible implications of politicking for the Electoral College vote, but the preparations for negotiations that third-party candidate H. Ross Perot made in 1992 and the actions of both the Bush and Gore camps in 2000 are reminders of the potential for a backroom deal to decide the presidency.

And what if the deal making fails and the Electoral College does not produce a majority for any candidate? As noted earlier, the House of Representatives decides who will be president; each state delegation receives one vote, with a majority (twenty-six) required for victory. Anyone who finds the Electoral College unrepresentative would become apoplectic at the patent unfairness of such a decision-making process. California would have a voice equal to that of Delaware. Indeed, California, which has more House members (fifty-three) than the smallest twenty-one states together (fifty), could be outvoted twenty-one to one. To be sure, small states would probably not vote as a bloc, but that does not make the process any more equitable.

The inequities of the "one state–one vote" rule pale in comparison with the political machinations it invites. Consider the following scenario: the Democratic candidate receives 260 (of the 270 necessary) electoral votes and wins fifty million popular votes; the Republican candidate wins 230 electoral votes and forty-five million popular votes; and a third-party candidate receives forty-eight electoral votes and thirty-five million popular votes. Republicans control the House delegations in twenty-seven states, Democrats in twenty, and three are equally divided. The Republican candidate won the popular vote in four Democratic states, while the Democrat prevailed in six GOP states. Would Republican House members toe the party line, elect a president who received only about 36 percent of the popular vote, and risk their seats in the next elections, especially in districts where the Democratic presidential candidate won? Would the third-party candidate try to throw his or her support to one of the major-party nominees? And on and on. This, too, is the Electoral College system at work.

DUMP THE ELECTORAL COLLEGE

A short essay cannot fully explore the many problems posed by the Electoral College. But excellent alternatives are available that rely on a direct popular vote. A pure plurality vote election might be the cleanest alternative, but other systems, including a runoff between the top two candidates, would also count every vote equally and produce a clear winner more often than the Electoral College, with its myriad possibilities for breaking down.[8]

In any event, the Electoral College should go. And I could then cast my vote in Kansas, certain that it counted just as much as if I were in Ohio or Nevada or any other of the so-called battleground states. We in the Sunflower State might even see a few ads, a lot of tweets, and maybe presidential candidates in the flesh. It probably won't happen, but it should.

CON: Byron E. Shafer

"Is there any other point to which you would wish to draw my attention?"

"To the curious incident of the dog in the night-time."

"The dog did nothing in the night-time."

"That was the curious incident," remarked Sherlock Holmes.

—Arthur Conan Doyle, *Silver Blaze*

Isolating the systemic contribution of the Electoral College to American politics has never been a simple task. The College is, after all, only one part of a matrix of institutions that help to select American presidents, just as the presidency is only one of the major institutions whose interaction shapes the processes of American government. Worse yet, in that long stretch between 1888 and 2000 when the Electoral College did nothing—superficially—but confirm the winner of the popular vote as the next president, the argument on both sides had to be about things that did not happen or were not happening—that is, about dogs that did not bark. Yet the basic arguments remain straightforward enough, while the strategic politics surrounding them has changed substantially in our time, a fact that further justifies returning to the debate.

The last time the Electoral College received sustained scholarly attention, during the late 1960s and early 1970s, it was as part of a larger debate about institutional reform. The essence of that discussion involved participatory versus representative democracy and reached into every institutional theater: political parties, Congress, the bureaucracy, and, by way of the Electoral College, the presidency as well.

- Proponents of reform focused on procedural fairness. They argued against the "distorting" effect of the Electoral College on the popular will, quite apart from the ultimate risk of electing the wrong contender, and against an institutional barrier to the direct registration of the public will, distorted or not.

- Opponents of reform focused instead on behavioral effects. They countered that the Electoral College had to be judged in the full context of the institutional structure of American government and that, when it was, the College contributed important countervailing influences to *other* distortions.

Both sides used the same basic data in pursuit of these arguments. Proponents argued that the campaign, both the activities and the positions of the presidential contenders, was being heavily influenced—distorted—by the Electoral College. What these proponents correctly saw was that candidates attended to the competitive states, where a small shift in the popular vote could swing a large bloc of electors. In the process, candidates did *not* go to states where the partisan outcome was obvious and thus did not stimulate participation and turnout in these neglected areas.

Opponents accepted the diagnosis but disagreed with the conclusion. They focused on the identity of these competitive states, which tended to be larger and more socially diverse. In practice, Republicans had to reach out to the northeastern industrial states plus California rather than to their guaranteed base in the Midwest and Rocky Mountains. Conversely, Democrats had to reach out to the same northeastern industrial states plus California rather than to *their* guaranteed base in the South. Ideological liberalism, coupled with energy and innovation, were thereby fostered within both parties, compensating for other conservatizing elements in the Constitution.

Opponents won the debate in the sense that reform of the Electoral College did not proceed, though it was not necessarily their arguments that carried the day. The small and less competitive states were often most actively opposed to reform. They focused on the fact that they were overrepresented within the Electoral College, because every state gets two electoral votes for their two senators regardless of population, rather than on the fact that the big states gained leverage by being more competitive. And the larger and more competitive states often supported reform, despite the concrete benefits of the status quo, because they were the home of many ideologically committed reformers.

Flash forward to 2000. Proponents of Electoral College reform heard their clarion call. The Electoral College, not the popular vote, determined the outcome. The "wrong candidate" won. Members of the general public were, however, unimpressed. The winner in the Electoral College was the "right candidate" by definition. That is, after all, how presidents have been chosen since adoption of the Constitution itself. By the time George W. Bush took the oath of office, ten weeks later, even the elite argument had receded so that no one stopped to look seriously at the changed context within which the College operated. We need to do that here.

Nothing approaching the ultimate impact of the Electoral College on the election of 2000 has occurred since, yet there is a lesser strategic impact that reliably recurs. To wit: in the new environment for electoral politics, the candidate who is running behind in the polls reliably shifts to an "Electoral College strategy," concentrating resources in the hope that the short end of a popular vote tally might still deliver an electoral vote win. This was the story of Democrat John Kerry in 2004, Republican John McCain in 2008, and Republican Mitt Romney in 2012. Because this particular strategy has not yet succeeded, we can do no more than point to the way that it is nevertheless reliably tried.

On the other hand, if we refocus the argument on two *other* things that the Electoral College does accomplish, in every year and across time, it should be possible to weigh the alternatives intelligently. At the extreme, it ought to be possible to see whether these contributions are sufficient to compensate even for the occasional year when the Electoral College does not award the presidency to the contender with a plurality of the popular vote. One of these key contributions is the way that the College conduces toward ongoing *majority formation*. The other is the way that it encourages what has become known as *retail politics*. The two together are the nub of the argument for the Electoral College in our time.

CONDUCING TOWARD MAJORITIES

The leading "curious incident" in the presidential contest of 2000 was evident and controversial. The popular vote winner and the electoral vote winner were not one and the same. Yet a second major "curious incident" was latent and ironic. The Electoral College kept pumping away as a device for majority formation in the usual manner despite that controversial outcome. In other words, the surface influence of the Electoral College on the way we form presidential majorities was exercised in the usual way during the 2000 campaign, through its hostility toward third parties and independent candidacies. Ralph Nader, Green Party candidate for president, bore the brunt of this effect, though he appeared to bear its burden lightly. During the campaign, the Electoral College produced the usual argument against supporting Nader: if a third contender cannot win, then voting for that person will always benefit the major-party candidate you like least.

Democrats hammered this theme in televised campaign ads, most especially in the state of Florida. And in fact, as Election Day approached, the stated intention of voting for Nader did decline, and it declined most in those states where the outcome was apparently closest—states where the strategic argument was most true. Afterward, in an election close enough that a myriad of factors could be argued to have been sufficient to alter the outcome, the Nader vote in Florida certainly qualified. Had the Electoral College managed to repress that vote even further, Al Gore would actually have become president.[9] It was the *interaction* of the Nader vote and the Electoral College that made George W. Bush president instead.

Yet this still grossly understates the majority-forcing aspect of the Electoral College. For in fact, the College is regularly shaping not just the fortunes but the very *field* of presidential candidates. And here, the question of how American politics would handle the shaping of this field, if we imagine doing away with the Electoral College, becomes critical to the argument—and critical to the functioning of American democracy. For the Electoral College is not just repressing the vote for announced third candidates for president, its evident surface impact. It is also powerfully reinforcing the definitiveness of the processes by which the two *major-party candidates* are selected. In the long run, this deeper process (another dog that does not bark) may be far more consequential.

At a minimum, the Electoral College reinforces the dynamic under which, by the time a national party convention confirms a major-party candidate for president, the battle within that party is over, and the other candidates who sought its nomination withdraw from the field. Because of the College, all they could do alternatively is to launch a quixotic independent bid for the presidency, thereby guaranteeing victory for the other major-party candidate, probably while terminating any further political career of their own. The combination of their vote plus that of their party's anointed nominee might be larger than the (single) vote for the nominee of the other party, but the latter would almost surely be larger than either of these (split) alternative votes.

The moment the Electoral College is gone, however, this dynamic is drastically altered. At a minimum, aggrieved candidates for major-party nominations would no longer *need* to withdraw. Depending on the actual arrangements for aggregating popular votes by some means other than the Electoral College (about which, more below), they might actually argue that they were making a further contribution to democratic choice. And losing candidates are reliably aggrieved. Some always believe that their positions have been distorted by opponents or the press. Some always conclude that they have lost only because other contenders had unfair resource advantages. Some always have supporters who desire—and in some sense deserve—to continue the crusade.

Fanciful? Recent campaigns suggest not. For example, it is not difficult to imagine even the 2000 contest with all four main contenders—George W. Bush, John McCain, Al Gore, and Bill Bradley—continuing on to the general election. McCain and Bradley were certainly injured by the regular party establishment and its main organized interests, in a manner for which they could not easily compensate. Indeed, it is not that difficult to imagine the nominating contests of 1992, with the senior George Bush and Bill Clinton still as major-party nominees, but with Pat Buchanan not dropping out, with Jesse Jackson entering—he certainly wanted to—and, of course, with H. Ross Perot staying in.

These counterfactual fantasies help to underline some very real facts about the general operation of the Electoral College. At a minimum, they emphasize how important the new rules of presidential election would be in the *absence* of the College. Would the general public demand a majority of the popular vote in order to affirm a president? Possibly not—we do not demand it now—though note that this is precisely because we have an alternative majority-forcing device in the form of the Electoral College. We could easily enough demand a similar majority, and we might well have to do so, once the Electoral College was gone. This would almost certainly require some sort of runoff. Indeed, strict application of this majority standard means that there would have had to be runoffs not just in 1992 and 2000 but even in 1996—and all those are without the encouragement to additional candidacies that the absence of the Electoral College would provide.

Most reform arguments instead proceed on the theory that the winner of the plurality vote would become president. Yet this is a safe assumption only within a system that is already powerfully constrained by the Electoral College. That is, it assumes that: (1) the two parties will be creating the two main candidates, (2) this selection process will simultaneously be repressing major partisan alternatives, and (3) the coronation of these two main alternatives will then deter independent candidacies. Yet these parties guarantee their two major-party nominees and deter third (fourth, etc.) alternatives *by way of the Electoral College*. Both proponents and opponents agree that the existence of the College shapes the field of candidates and their electoral strategies. Surely, removing the College would likewise (re)shape them.

And here the alternatives become less fanciful. Surely, there will often be presidential contenders who might expect to draw a substantial portion of their support from partisan independents plus loyalists of the opposite party. The current system is nevertheless stacked against them, all but forcing them to run within a party. A direct vote system is what they need, to encourage them to run directly for president instead. Surely, there will likewise—nearly always—be presidential contenders who could expect to rally a major social group. The current system encourages them not to, since they cannot win a nominating majority with such a strategy, while they would be drawing their preferred group *away* from influence on the actual winner. Again, a direct vote system is what they need, as a device for rallying their group and then attempting to trade its influence.

Yet if more than two serious contenders actually ran in the general election, year in and year out, would we still be willing to elect the plurality winner? The answer morphs very quickly into a question about how large a plurality the public would require. Would you tolerate a candidate as president, for example, who had "won" with 27 percent of the vote? Twenty-three percent? Nineteen percent? The moment we establish a system in which, say, 30 percent of the vote might win, we encourage any candidate who might hope to attain that total to run as an independent rather than seek the Democratic or Republican nomination. The moment we address this problem by having a second round of voting—a runoff—we encourage *every* candidate to enter the first round rather than be content with an internal party process under which all but one would be eliminated early.

In the face of these alternative rules, how fissiparous is American society? That is, how many candidates can it "naturally" support? If you believe that it is quite diverse—socially diverse, economically diverse, geographically diverse, ideologically diverse—the answer is in principle "many." With the presidency, the two-party system as buttressed by the Electoral College works against such a multiplication of candidacies. In its absence, at a minimum, the strategic calculations of many potential candidates would be altered. Yet the chain of impacts would likely go on and on. A presidency that is either "balkanized" by major ongoing social divisions, each with its own designated candidate, or "unified" by superficially repudiating those divisions and thus obscuring candidate attachments, will be a weakened institution: either devoid of mandate or devoid of program.

ENCOURAGING RETAIL POLITICS

We are not, however, reduced to *imagining* that the interaction of social change with institutional rules might alter the character of politics. For in our time, the combination of the Electoral College as the central institution for presidential elections with the changing nature of American society has already transformed the character of presidential politicking. This impact is widely recognized, though the role of the Electoral College in creating it is less so. Nevertheless, this impact is yet another reason one might—or here, might not—desire to see the College continue to perform its major roles. For what the Electoral College has done, when imposed upon partisan shifts in the states and localities, is to restore what is known as "retail politics" to the presidential campaign.

This is a terminology more commonly recognized at the nominating stage. We say that the opening contests—Iowa, New Hampshire, maybe South Carolina, sometimes one or two others—feature a retail politics in which candidates meet voters face to face in their localities. After this opening phase, we switch to "wholesale politics," the politics of the tarmac, in which candidates are flown from airport to airport delivering set speeches while the bulk of the campaign switches to televised advertising. There are proponents and opponents of this system as well, and it is true that we emphasize these early contests in small places at the cost of later and larger ones. But both proponents and opponents recognize that the country has designed a nominating process privileging retail over wholesale politics at the start.

This was long thought to be part of the impact of the Electoral College too, forcing candidates to address individual states on the way to the general election. In recent decades, much of this effect appeared to go away, replaced by fully national campaigns—retail campaigns, tarmac campaigns, media campaigns. Now, as evidenced by 2000 and all the elections that have followed, the old effect is back with a vengeance. For the general election, the two major contenders focus on a small set of what are widely recognized as "battleground states," and they do so on a scale that is radically scaled down from that of only a few years ago. No one can deny that many states are thereby ignored. But neither can one deny that both the focus and the character of campaigns have changed.

How did this come about? Short answer: through the impact of partisan shifts *as funneled through the Electoral College.* In truth, what was previously viewed as a national campaign was in part illusory, resulting from the fact that the Electoral College focused the campaign on the bigger and more socially diverse states. If you have to worry about California, New York, Pennsylvania, and Illinois, the result will *seem* like a national campaign. More to the practical point, it will inevitably be wholesale politics. You cannot campaign in California as you would in Wisconsin; scale alone forbids it. But if, as in 2004 and its successors, you have to worry instead about Wisconsin, Iowa, Minnesota, New Hampshire, and New Mexico—even throwing in Florida and Ohio—the story is different. The fact that you are campaigning within states is no longer hidden. The retail character of that campaign is likewise evident.

The result is not as self-evidently virtuous as the majority-forcing impact of the Electoral College, and the effect of removing the College is thereby not as self-evidently disastrous. But the point here is a different one. What needs emphasis is that the choice between having an Electoral College or not is inherently a choice between one vision of politics and another. It is not between one set of rules and "no rules." It is not between one impact and "no impact." The choice is instead between majority-forcing and minority-inducing strictures. It is between incentives toward retail and wholesale politicking. It is between one set of institutionalized "distortions" and another. In such a world, anyone who opposes the Electoral College without specifying a (detailed!) alternative and then elaborating the consequences cold-bloodedly is irresponsible at best, dishonest and pernicious at worst.

A BITE WITH NO BARK?

The charm of 2012, by these lights, was that it put most such issues to sleep. President Barack Obama was renominated without opposition. The Republicans were hardly going to run several candidates against him within the Electoral College. Yet one needs to go back only to the election of 2008 to see the power of the way that the Electoral College was nevertheless functioning, as it had in 2000 and every bit as forcefully—though no one appeared to notice, much less complain. Barack Obama rather than George W. Bush was the beneficiary this time, because 2008 was the kind of election that would most plausibly have spawned multiple candidates under reformed arrangements, encouraging some contenders to undertake an independent candidacy while encouraging others to fight for a major-party nomination but then continue on to the general election.

To help make this hidden impact explicit, consider the candidate array of 2008 as it began to emerge. Begin with those who obviously did feel encouraged to seek major-party nominations, especially John McCain, Mike Huckabee, and Mitt Romney among Republicans, along with Barack Obama and Hillary Clinton among Democrats. Then consider their strategic alternatives in the absence of the Electoral College, once the process of delegate selection had concluded:

- For the Republicans, their party was left with a maverick nominee, John McCain, who had been an intermittent thorn in the side of the regular party for years. Said the other way around, the active base of the Republican Party was left without a candidate. The Electoral College nevertheless made this the end of their line. In its absence, this active base would have been free to continue the search for a champion. Indeed, under reformed arrangements, major losing contenders like Fred Thompson might have been better advised to delay entry and wait for just such an appeal from the regular party, making them into heroes rather than spoilers in the process.

- For the Democrats, the situation was opposite, but the result was the same. For them, the candidate who had received the most total votes toward a nomination, Hillary Clinton, was actually defeated. In the absence of the Electoral College, and even more so if it had been replaced by a two-stage runoff process, she would thus have had to think seriously about continuing on. Indeed, even if she had been privately disinclined, she would have had to deal with an outraged campaign whose active members believed that she, not Barack Obama, would ultimately emerge from a multicandidate opener and a two-candidate runoff.

And at that point, the floodgates would open. Other candidates who had not seriously considered the run for a major-party nomination would have been encouraged to consider running for president as independents. The two most obvious examples stayed out in 2008, despite evident indications of interest. In the absence of the Electoral College but in the presence of *four* presidential candidates for the general election, the strategic environment would have been aligned with—not against—their inclinations:

- Michael Bloomberg, mayor of New York City, had thought seriously about just such a run, to the point of establishing a shadow campaign charged with developing themes, issues, and strategies. Like H. Ross Perot before him, Bloomberg was sufficiently wealthy that he could have funded such an effort out of his own pocket. Like Perot, his incipient theme was "a plague on both your (partisan) houses."

- Jesse Jackson, who had run for the Democratic nomination twice before, was volcanically—even scatologically—angry at the prospect that Barack Obama would become the premier champion of black America. If he never looked like the ultimate winner, Jackson had the name recognition and activist connections to enter as an explicit spoiler, in hopes that his first-round support—even 2 or 3 percent would do—could be traded at the second round of the general election.

Would these candidates ever actually have responded to their personal siren songs? If they had, what would the ultimate vote actually have looked like, in round one but also in the new round two? No one knows the answers, but it hardly matters, for these are the wrong questions. Instead, ask yourself how sure you are that none of this would have come to pass. Then ask yourself how many times it would have to happen before it was a common—even expected—occurrence. And once you have done all that, ask yourself whether American politics would work better by your lights with fragmented candidacies and/or nonmajoritarian presidents.

Let me say the same thing differently. The fact that the existing dogs do not normally bark does not mean that they are not standing by the gate, protecting the commonwealth. If they are slain by accident, no less than if they are slain deliberately, the majoritarian process in American politics—a politics riddled with nonmajoritarian elements in its institutions and in its society—can hardly be said to have been reinforced. If that process is weakened, it is hard to see how government would become either more effective or more responsive. Holmes knew how to make the proper deduction.

NOTES

PRO

1. John P. Roche, "The Founding Fathers: A Reform Caucus in Action," *American Political Science Review* 55 (September 1961).
2. George C. Edwards III, *Why the Electoral College Is Bad for America* (New Haven, CT: Yale University Press, 2004), 81.

3. Ibid., 80. For an enlightening musical discourse on one key flaw in the original design of the Electoral College, listen to "The Election of 1800" on the soundtrack of the Broadway musical *Hamilton*.

4. The importance of battleground states was nicely captured by the *New York Times*' Nate Silver in his blog, fivethirtyeight.com, where he offered daily updates on which states were most likely to swing the election and which had the biggest electoral payoffs for the candidates' "investment" of their funds.

5. Some think that a true count of the votes in the 1960 election would have given Richard Nixon more popular votes than John F. Kennedy, but the only count available shows Kennedy receiving more popular votes than Nixon. See Edwards, *Why the Electoral College Is Bad for America*, chap. 3.

6. In 2004 the Harris Poll conducted a survey with the extremely large sample size of almost seven thousand voters. In the survey, 64 percent of respondents expressed support for a popular vote to choose the president, while just 22 percent expressed opposition. See http://harrisinteractive.com (accessed April 12, 2005).

7. William Ross, "'Faithless Electors': The Wild Card," http://www.jurist.law.pitt.edu/election/electionross4.htm

8. Fair Vote advocates have devised an arguably constitutional plan to produce a popular-vote winner without amending the Constitution. This is how it would work: "Under the National Popular Vote bill, all of the state's electoral votes would be awarded to the presidential candidate who receives the most popular votes in all 50 states and the District of Columbia" (http://www.fairvote.org/nationalpopular-vote). This plan would be implemented once states with a majority of electoral votes approved the plan. As of 2015, ten states plus the District of Columbia with 165 votes have done so. The National Popular Vote scheme has received increasing support, but having enough states adopt its compact remains a long shot—and even then it would face a difficult court battle.

CON

9. In the same way—a wonderful ultimate irony—it is possible to argue that in the absence of the Electoral College, those Gore voters who preferred Nader would have voted for him, such that George W. Bush would have been the popular vote winner too. But this leads on to a kind of analytic madness.

RESOLVED, The Twenty-second Amendment should be repealed

PRO: David Karol

CON: Thomas E. Cronin

How many four-year terms should a president be allowed to serve? From 1789 to 1951, the Constitution's answer to that question was: as many as the president chooses to seek and the voters choose to grant—in other words, an unrestricted number of terms. With the addition of the Twenty-second Amendment to the Constitution in 1951, the answer changed: no more than two.

The belief that the president should always be eligible for reelection was important to the delegates at the Constitutional Convention. Throughout most of their deliberations, they maintained that the president should be elected by Congress to a seven-year term. A necessary corollary to this provision, they believed, was that the president could only serve one term. Otherwise, presidents would spend all their time conniving to get reelected by, in effect, bribing members of Congress with political patronage and illegitimate favors.

As they deliberated further, however, confining the president to one term struck most of the delegates as a bad idea, so much so that they jettisoned the provision for election by Congress and created the Electoral College. Reeligibility would allow the country to keep good presidents in office and give every president what Pennsylvania delegate Gouverneur Morris called "the great motive to good behavior, the hope of being rewarded by a reappointment." More ominously, Morris warned, "Shut the Civil road to Glory & and he may be compelled to seek it by the sword."

Once the Constitution was ratified and took effect, the absence of term limits became in practice a two-term limit. George Washington, who retired at the end of his second term, is often credited with inventing this tradition. In truth, Washington meant to do no such thing. He stepped down because he longed for the "shade of retirement" and also because he thought it was important for the country to learn that the new Constitution would work just as well without him as with him. The real inventor of the two-term tradition was the third president, Thomas Jefferson, who thought that the lack of a term limit on the president would lead to a kind of elective monarchy.

The two-term tradition endured until Franklin D. Roosevelt broke it by being elected to a third term in 1940 and a fourth term in 1944. Indeed, two-thirds of FDR's predecessors actually served one term or less. Some presidents, including Andrew Jackson, even argued for a constitutional amendment that would confine the president to one term but lengthen it to six years. The best argument for this proposal was that it would free presidents from all concerns about getting reelected while giving them time to see their initiatives through to completion. The best argument against it was that with the single six-year term the country would have a president it liked for two years less than it does now and a president it disliked for two years more.

The single six-year term still has adherents, but it was a different proposal that garnered the support of the nation after FDR's record-breaking tenure in office. Enacted in 1951, the Twenty-second Amendment stipulates, "No person shall be elected to the office of the President more than twice." An exception applies to presidents who succeed to the office less than halfway through their predecessor's term, as Gerald R. Ford did when Richard Nixon resigned nineteen months into his second term in August 1974. These presidents may be elected only once.

Politically, the enactment of the Twenty-second Amendment expressed the conservative backlash against FDR that followed his death in 1945. Every Republican in Congress voted for the amendment in 1947, along with many Southern Democrats. Liberal Democrats from the North opposed it. The amendment remained controversial when it was sent to the states for ratification. It required an unusually long period (nearly four years—a record at the time) to be approved by the same coalition of Republican and Southern Democratic state legislatures.

Controversial at its birth, the two-term limit has remained so ever since. Three of the presidents who have bumped up against the limit by serving two terms—Dwight D. Eisenhower, Ronald Reagan, and Bill Clinton—have favored repealing or amending it; Clinton suggested that a president should be able to serve a third term, but only after some reasonable interval out of office. David Karol agrees that the Twenty-second Amendment was a short-sighted mistake and should be repealed, while Thomas E. Cronin defends the amendment as a sensible addition to the Constitution.

PRO: David Karol

The simplest case against the Twenty-second Amendment is that it is undemocratic. If voters think that an individual who has already served two terms in the White House is the best candidate for the next four years, then their wishes should be respected. Although the undemocratic aspect of the amendment is its most offensive feature, there is also reason to believe that it makes presidents less effective without curbing their abuses of power.

The Twenty-second Amendment is based on a fundamental mistrust of the democratic process. Admittedly, the presidential term limit is far from the only antimajoritarian provision of the Constitution.[1] Because majority rule is not the only value dear to Americans, some of the Constitution's deviations from it can still be justified. The Bill of Rights and the post–Civil War civil rights amendments protect fundamental liberties of individuals whose religious practices or political speech may be abhorrent to the majority, and they ensure minorities equal protection. Other constitutional provisions, including the separation of powers and bicameralism, encourage deliberation and promote stability by impeding policy changes that lack broad support. Still other aspects of the Constitution protect federalism, a value important to the founders, if not always to later generations.

Yet, although all of these values have some weight against the claims of majority rule, the Twenty-second Amendment promotes none of them. It does not protect individual liberties or minority rights. Nor does it encourage deliberation, stabilize policymaking, or preserve federalism.

Moreover, American values have long been more democratic than those of the founders, to whom "the people" meant white, propertied males. As a result, with the glaring exception of the Twenty-second Amendment, constitutional reforms affecting the electoral process have consistently moved toward greater democracy. Constitutional amendments mandated the direct election of senators; granted electoral votes to the District of Columbia; guaranteed voting rights to African Americans, women, and young adults; outlawed the poll tax; and shortened the lame-duck period in which officials no longer accountable to voters can govern.[2] In considering these reforms, Americans had to choose between the founders' careful design and their own growing preference for democratic values.

By contrast, the question of the Twenty-second Amendment's repeal does *not* force us to choose between the founders' design and democratic values, since that amendment uniquely overturned the considered judgment of the founders at the same time that it restricted voters' rights.

We know from James Madison's notes that the delegates to the Constitutional Convention considered and ultimately rejected a term limit for the chief
executive. Early in the convention, a majority did support a single seven-year
term for the president. Yet delegates favored a single term at a time when they
were planning to have Congress elect the president and feared that a chief
executive who knew his reelection was in the hands of the legislature would not
be sufficiently independent of it. Later, the delegates accepted a committee
proposal that created an Electoral College to choose the president. Having
removed presidential election from Congress, the committee decided to make
presidents eligible for reelection. Several delegates saw preserving the president's "reeligibility" as an important advantage of the Electoral College.[3]

Why did many of the founders think it was useful for a president to be reeli-
gible? It is notable that the opponents of term limits did not ground their
arguments on a naive or optimistic view of human nature and took seriously
concerns about tyranny. For Gouverneur Morris, the most vociferous opponent of term limits at the convention, barring the president from seeking
reelection "tended to destroy the great motive to good behavior, the hope of
being rewarded by a re-appointment. It was saying to him, make hay while the
sun shines."[4] Morris worried that a term-limited president might be corrupt or
tempted to create a crisis or stage a coup to remain in office.

In *Federalist* No. 72 Alexander Hamilton defended the Constitution's lack of
a presidential term limit. Hamilton built on Morris's arguments, noting that
such a limit would reduce presidents' incentive to perform well, especially to
undertake projects that would have no immediate reputational payoff and
whose success would depend on their successors' actions. Hamilton also noted
that the country would be depriving itself of experienced leadership and might
be unable to select the person best suited to deal with a pressing problem. Term
limits might also require turnover in the presidency during a war or other
crisis, and in general would lead to unhelpful policy instability.

Supporters of the Twenty-second Amendment make several claims. They
assert that George Washington believed two terms were sufficient for a president and that Jefferson agreed, and that their examples convinced Americans
of the wisdom of this view. Therefore, some have contended, the amendment
merely codifies what had been an entrenched norm dating from the days of the
first president until it was recklessly cast aside in 1940. Yet scholars have shown
that the two-term tradition prior to the second reelection of Franklin
D. Roosevelt was both less venerable and more tenuous than advocates of the
Twenty second Amendment claim. Washington did indeed retire when he
could have won a third term. Yet Washington's own explanation for this decision was *not* that he believed that presidents should serve no more than eight

years. In correspondence with Lafayette, Washington questioned the value of term limits.[5] Rather, the first president claimed to want to show that the new political system did not depend on any individual. Washington also said he was exhausted and eager to return to private life.

It was only starting with Thomas Jefferson's renunciation of a third term and his dubious interpretation of the motives underlying Washington's decision that the two-term norm began to gain currency.[6] Until 1940 no president had served more than two terms, and many thought this was proper. Some presidents even tried to establish a norm that a president should only serve one term.[7]

Yet, in practice, many Americans were not wedded to the notion that presidents could serve only two terms. In 1880 former president Ulysses S. Grant sought a third term and won much support, despite having already served from 1869 through 1877. Grant led on the first thirty-four ballots at the 1880 Republican National Convention before a compromise dark-horse candidate was selected.[8] Similarly, in 1912 former president Theodore Roosevelt, who had served more than seven years after succeeding the assassinated William McKinley, won almost all the Republican primaries only to be denied the nomination by the party machine that preferred President William Howard Taft. A defiant Roosevelt went on to run the most successful third-party campaign in history as the candidate of the Progressive Party. Running as the "Bull Moose" candidate, Roosevelt outpolled Taft and carried several states. Clearly, in the late nineteenth and early twentieth centuries, many Americans did not object to a president serving more than two terms. And in 1940 and 1944, Franklin D. Roosevelt won his third and fourth terms by solid margins.

If the founders rejected term limits for the chief executive and many voters in both parties favored presidential candidates who sought more than two terms, why was the Twenty-second Amendment adopted? As historian Henry Steele Commager argued and President Ronald Reagan later agreed, "There is simply no denying that in many ways the two term limit 'was imposed as posthumous vengeance on Franklin D. Roosevelt.'"[9] In the Eightieth Congress, the first one with a GOP majority since the beginning of the Great Depression, the Twenty-second Amendment won unanimous support from Republicans as well as the backing of some Southern Democrats who had fallen out of sympathy with Roosevelt's New Deal policies. FDR's political opponents, temporarily in the majority, made sure that no one else would repeat his feat.

Yet if partisanship indisputably motivated the adoption of the amendment, it should play no role in consideration about repealing it. It is not merely that a constitution ought to transcend partisan concerns, but from a more practical standpoint, we simply cannot know which party will be advantaged by repeal in coming decades. The Twenty-second Amendment was a Republican initiative. Yet it did not affect a Democratic president who was in good enough physical and political shape to aspire to a third term until Bill Clinton left office almost fifty years after the amendment came into force. By contrast, Dwight D. Eisenhower, a Republican, might have secured a third term in 1960 had he sought one. And despite his advanced age, Republican Ronald Reagan might have won a third term had he desired it in 1988.

A more valid concern raised by advocates of the Twenty-second Amendment is excessive presidential power. Charges that FDR had been or verged on becoming "a dictator" were partisan hyperbole, but the power of the presidency vis-à-vis Congress and the broader society did increase greatly during Roosevelt's time in office and subsequently. Given this unmistakable trend, concerns about presidential abuse of power are reasonable, but term limits are not the answer.

Generally, presidential power is greatest and the risk of abuse most serious in the fields of national security, foreign policy, and law enforcement. Yet the growth of the so-called imperial presidency largely postdates the Twenty-second Amendment. The actions that led Congress to enact the War Powers Resolution in 1973 were taken mostly by term-limited presidents.[10] The only president forced to resign over abuse of power, Richard Nixon, was term limited, as was George W. Bush, who made many assertions of presidential power that remain controversial.

It still might be argued that presidential abuses of power would be even worse were it not for the Twenty-second Amendment, since "power corrupts" over time. Yet this contention is undermined by a review of the record. Many of the most widely criticized presidential actions in recent decades were undertaken in presidents' first terms. Lyndon B. Johnson's misleading of the public over the Gulf of Tonkin incident, which led to an escalation of U.S. involvement in Vietnam, occurred in his first term. The secret bombing of Cambodia as well as the Watergate break-in and much of the ensuing cover-up took place during Richard Nixon's first term. Similarly, many of George W. Bush's most controversial actions in the realms of national security and civil liberties occurred during his first term. We do not want presidents to conduct unaccountable foreign policies, to undermine civil liberties, or to use law enforcement agencies for partisan or personal vendettas. Yet there is little evidence that term limits address these problems.

Although the consequences of repealing the Twenty-second Amendment are inevitably uncertain, examining evidence from other political systems both in the United States and around the world can help us reach a more informed judgment of the merits of presidential term limits. Presidents are term limited in many countries that lack long traditions of stable democracy, including much of Latin America and Africa. In Russia, where democratic traditions and values are weak, a two-term limit achieves little; although he stepped down from the presidency in 2008, Vladimir Putin continued to dominate politics via a hand-picked successor, Dmitry Medvedev, who appointed him prime minister. Putin was then reelected to the presidency as soon as he was eligible in 2012, reappointing Medvedev (who did not seek a second term) to the prime ministership. Despite trading titles back and forth, Putin never really lost power. Similarly, the example of Hugo Chávez in Venezuela shows that, faced with a popular leader with authoritarian tendencies, term limits might be eliminated. It is the least dangerous leaders in the most stable democracies who are most affected by term limits.

In long-standing democracies more comparable with the United States, many chief executives have served for more than eight years since the ratification of the Twenty-second Amendment in 1951 without those countries devolving into tyrannies. In the United Kingdom, Margaret Thatcher was prime minister from 1979 to 1990, and Tony Blair from 1997 to 2007. In Canada, Pierre Trudeau was prime minister from 1968 to 1979 and again from 1980 to 1984, and Jean Chrétien held that office from 1993 to 2003. In Australia, Robert Menzies was prime minister from 1949 to 1967, as was John Howard from 1996 to 2007. In New Zealand, Keith Holyoake was prime minister from 1960 to 1972. In the Netherlands, Ruud Lubbers was prime minister from 1982 to 1994. In Spain, which only returned to democratic rule in the 1970s, Felipe González was prime minister from 1982 to 1997. In the democratic postwar Federal Republic of Germany that arose after the defeat of the Nazis, Konrad Adenauer was chancellor from 1949 to 1963, and Helmut Kohl served from 1982 to 1998. Angela Merkel has been the German chancellor since 2005. All these examples are drawn from parliamentary systems, but in France Charles de Gaulle was president from 1958 to 1969, François Mitterrand served from 1981 to 1995, and Jacques Chirac from 1995 to 2007.[11]

We can also find examples of polities that function well absent term limits without venturing abroad. The American office most analogous to the presidency is the governorship. So it is notable that the lifetime, two-term limit that the Twenty-second Amendment imposes is more restrictive than the rules that exist in a majority of states. Lifetime bans after two terms equivalent to the federal restriction are in force in only eight states. Twenty-eight states limit the number of consecutive terms a governor can serve, generally to two, but permit a subsequent return to office after a specified period of time. The remaining fourteen states still do not limit governors' terms at all.

The states have been called the "laboratories of democracy," and the diversity of arrangements concerning governors' terms allows us to draw some inferences about the effect of term limits on chief executives. Given concerns about power corrupting over time, it is notable that little correlation is evident between corruption and gubernatorial term limits. Louisiana, a state with a tradition of corrupt governors, has long had term limits, while good-government Minnesota does not. Illinois governors are notorious and the state lacks term limits, but the record of governors in neighboring Wisconsin and Iowa is far better and neither state limits the terms of its chief executive.[12] A systematic study finds no significant relationship between states' term limits for governors and rates of corruption in state government.[13]

Yet if there is no evidence suggesting the Twenty-second Amendment limits abuse of power and corruption, there is reason to believe it does reduce the political and administrative effectiveness of chief executives. Despite a persistent notion that presidents could somehow do a better job if they did not have to worry about reelection, there is little evidence supporting this view. Lame-duck presidents are less successful than first-term ones in getting Congress to enact legislation they support.[14] Presidents also have difficulty retaining staff as turnover increases in their lame-duck terms.[15] Staff members believe that a lame-duck administration, especially in its last two years, is unlikely to achieve much and are tempted to leave office and cash in on their experience. Similarly, it is harder for presidents to attract replacements of the same high caliber because individuals are less attracted to serving in an administration that is clearly on its way out. These are costs of term limits. Even presidents who ultimately decline to seek a third term might be more effective during their second administration were their lame-duck status not certain from the outset. Americans want a president who does not abuse the office, not one who cannot exercise its powers effectively.

Ending presidential term limits may have one downside. Sidney Milkis and Michael Nelson argue that the "Twenty-second Amendment has strengthened the vice presidency by allowing vice presidents to campaign for the presidency during the second term of an administration without competing with the sitting president." These scholars contend "the Twenty-second Amendment gives second-term presidents a stake in the success of their vice presidents, which is the closest to vindication and continuity they will achieve."[16] As the vice presidency has come to be seen as a stepping-stone to the presidency, it has attracted more able politicians who have been given more responsibilities that prepare them for a possible ascension to the Oval Office.

The strengthening of the vice presidency is a positive trend that repeal of the Twenty-second Amendment could counteract. Yet it is doubtful that repeal would lead to the wholesale deinstitutionalization of the vice presidency, which now includes a large staff, a residence, Secret Service protection, and a seat on the National Security Council. In any case, this modest benefit is far outweighed by the costs the Twenty-second Amendment imposes on voters and the reduction in presidential effectiveness it produces.

None of this is to suggest that we need presidents in perpetuity. For most chief executives, Thomas E. Cronin is surely right that "eight years is enough."[17] Starting with John Adams in 1800, voters have often decided that one term was enough and evicted presidents from the White House. History suggests that even absent the Twenty-second Amendment, many reelected presidents would still not be in physical or emotional shape or retain sufficient political support to secure a third term.

Yet there was an exceptional case earlier in our history, when in the midst of a crisis voters decided a chief executive should serve more than two terms. Many decades later he is widely considered one of our greatest presidents. Who is to say another such crisis and another such leader may not one day emerge? There is no reason to tie voters' hands. The historical record does not justify the extreme distrust of the electorate that the Twenty-second Amendment embodies. While voters' knowledge and attention spans are quite limited, they do react predictably, rewarding leaders who preside over "peace, prosperity, and probity" and punishing those who do not.[18]

The Twenty-second Amendment is the only revision to the U.S. Constitution that reduces the ability of voters to influence their government. It restricts voters' choice of presidential candidates by ruling out those individuals about whom voters know the most. It is the residue of a spasm of vindictive partisanship. It reduces presidents' effectiveness as leaders and administrators without curbing their abuses of power. Alexander Hamilton said it best in 1787: "There is an excess of refinement in the idea of disabling the people to continue in office men who had entitled themselves, in their opinion, to approbation and confidence; the advantages of which are at best speculative and equivocal, and are overbalanced by disadvantages far more certain and decisive."[19] The Twenty-second Amendment should be repealed.

CON: Thomas E. Cronin

The Twenty-second Amendment to the U.S. Constitution should be retained. It became part of the Constitution on February 27, 1951, after 70 percent of those voting in Congress approved it and the requisite thirty-six state legislatures ratified it; a handful of additional legislatures ratified it shortly thereafter. The amendment had broad support among the public and the press, including the *New York Times*. President Harry S. Truman did not oppose it. Polls have consistently found more than two-thirds of the American people favor retaining it, and this support has increased in the past generation.[20]

Among the members of Congress to vote in favor of the Twenty-second Amendment was a young John F. Kennedy, D-Mass. Asked about this amendment in 1962, when he was president, Kennedy reaffirmed his belief that two terms were enough for any president. Former president Bill Clinton, who left little doubt about wishing he could have run for a third term, agreed: "We have it for good reasons." When people are too long in power, Clinton explained, political sclerosis sets in.[21]

The principle of a two-term limit has a rich heritage in this country.

Thomas Jefferson, several other founders, and most of the leading Anti-Federalists favored term limits for the newly proposed U.S. presidency.[22] Term limits were proposed and approved in at least four of the state constitutional ratification conventions, most notably at New York's State Convention in 1788. Democratic icon President Andrew Jackson embraced term limits. The idea was supported in Democratic and Republican national party platforms at various times in the nineteenth century, including the populist-leaning Democratic Party platform of 1896. Progressive Republican Robert M. La Follette, R-Wis., introduced a two-term limit measure in 1927, and his U.S. Senate colleagues approved it on a bipartisan 56–26 vote. La Follette's resolution, which was similar to many that had been previously introduced in Congress, declared that "it is the sense of the Senate that the precedent established by Washington and other Presidents of the United States in retiring from the Presidential office after their second term has become by universal concurrence, a part of our republican system of government, and that any departure from this time-honored custom would be unwise, unpatriotic and fraught with peril to our free institutions."[23]

The Twenty-second Amendment affirms the wisdom in La Follette's warning. There are a number of compelling reasons for retaining the amendment, but here are the four most important.

First, the Twenty-second Amendment codifies the long-standing American commitment to the principle of rotation in office and helps to protect against the abuse of power.

Ours is a rich tradition of citizen-leaders premised on the belief that a robust constitutional republic needs regularly to generate new, capable, and responsible civic servant-leaders. The widely accepted Twenty-second Amendment allows a citizen to serve four or eight years in one of the world's most demanding and consequential political positions, while protecting the country from potential abuses of power that might come from officeholders who over-stay their welcome.

The United States has been blessed with many good presidents, but we have also unfortunately had presidents and presidential advisers who have lied to us, misled us, or covered up corruption. Today's presidency is a place of great pow-ers, more responsibilities, and even more temptations. Calvin Coolidge put it well in his presidential autobiography when he warned, "It is difficult for men in high office to avoid the malady of self-delusion. They are always surrounded by worshippers. They are consistently . . . assured of their greatness." Coolidge understood that presidents live in an "artificial atmosphere of adulation and exaltation which sooner or later impairs their judgment" and puts them "in grave danger of becoming careless and arrogant."[24]

The rotation principle institutionalized in the Twenty-second Amendment is a check against the ultimate type of corruption—the arrogance that an indi-vidual leader is indispensable. It was precisely this assumption of indispens-ability that led Venezuela's Hugo Chávez to campaign for the end of term limits in his country and Robert Mugabe in Zimbabwe to rig his staying in office; it also led to the antics of dictator Ferdinand Marcos in the Philippines, to Sukarnoism in Indonesia, and to the schemes of countless other authoritarian "saviors." History teaches that the longer leaders are in office, the greater the tendency toward isolation, stagnation, hubris, and abuse of power.[25]

A study of comparative government contends that presidential term limits have become a defining feature of constitutional democracies. Why is this so? "First," explains Gideon Maltz, "because of manifold incumbency advantages, a long-serving president can all too easily cease to face any real danger of evic-tion from office." In addition, "a long tenure leads to a dangerous accumulation of power in the president's hands, and also a greater arrogance and tendency to abuse it."[26]

We can learn the same lesson by looking closer to home, at many of the big-city mayors who have stayed for third, fourth, and fifth terms. In Boston, Chicago, Detroit, Kansas City, Newark, Providence, Syracuse, and Washington, D.C., for example, multiterm mayors and their associates, especially during their later terms, have often been less responsive, less accountable, and more tempted to become arrogant and corrupt than in their first or even second terms.

The negative impact of the Twenty-second Amendment—namely, that it would prevent us from reelecting a great president for a third term—would come into play rarely, perhaps once in a century. Yet the amendment is there, like the option of impeachment, to ensure respect for republican principles, prac-tices, and processes, and to guard against an unfettered accumulation of power.

Second, national security and economic issues have resulted in a strengthened national government, especially the presidency and the executive branch.

The U.S. president holds powers today unimaginable even in 1951, when the Twenty-second Amendment was adopted. The twenty-first-century president presides over a massive military machine with cyber and drone technologies easily employed at a moment's notice by the commander in chief. Nuclear weapons, covert operations, satellite intelligence, extraordinary rendition policies, extraordinary data mining, and hundreds of U.S. military bases in as many as seventy nations have reshaped and expanded the powers of the presidency beyond anything the framers of the Constitution could have imagined.

We might not like it—and the framers certainly did not intend it—but the White House has become the world's "911." This does not mean presidents always get their way. But presidential responsibilities have grown so large that the American people and the U.S. Congress increasingly turn to presidents for leadership, often delegating wide discretion to them. In the post–September 11, 2001, presidency-centric system, the Twenty-second Amendment becomes an even more indispensable check on presidential power.

Third, presidents have a vast power of appointment, the effects of which often outlast their two terms.

Imagine the consequence on the judicial system if, over three or four terms, a president could appoint the entire Supreme Court as well as a majority of the federal lower-court judges. Indeed, Franklin D. Roosevelt, who wanted to pack the Supreme Court in 1937, actually did appoint all nine Supreme Court justices before he died in 1945. President George W. Bush, in less than eight years, appointed nearly half of the judges in federal district courts around the country. Americans do not want a president who, by packing the judiciary, can in effect control two of our three independent branches of government.

An independent judiciary is necessary for ensuring executive power accountability. Important Supreme Court rulings like *New York Times v. U.S.* (1971), *U.S. v. Nixon* (1974), *Hamdan v. Rumsfeld* (2006), and *Boumediene v. Bush* (2008) might not have occurred without an independent judiciary.

The expansion in the role of administrative and regulatory agencies has made presidential appointive powers increasingly significant. Presidents appoint, subject to Senate confirmation, members of the powerful Federal Reserve Board for fourteen-year terms. They also appoint members to crucial regulatory boards, such as the Securities and Exchange Commission and Federal Communications Commission—these for seven-year terms.

Absent the Twenty-second Amendment, the president's appointive power, combined with the president's influence over appropriations, tax benefits, and federal bailouts, can perpetuate one person's or one party's dominance.

Finally, the two-term limit is healthy for our two-party system and for democracy.

It helps prevent political stagnation and encourages new ideas and new leaders on the national stage. The two parties are rejuvenated by the challenge of nurturing, recruiting, and nominating a new team of national leaders at least every eight years. In this sense, this amendment helps prevent the hardening of political arteries. Change every eight years adds a degree of freshness and new energy—elements our Madisonian system of checks and balances can usually use. A "country is better off if you have new blood and new ideas," said President Barack Obama in support of the Twenty-second Amendment. He believed he was a pretty good president, "but I know that somebody with new energy and new insights will be good" for the country.[27]

FOUR REBUTTALS

Those who advocate repeal of the Twenty-second Amendment are not without plausible talking points. Here are their chief worries and the appropriate rebuttals.

First, repeal proponents contend the ban on third presidential terms diminishes a voter's right to select their preferred candidate for president. Moreover, they note, the passage of the Twenty-second Amendment was mainly a retrospective vendetta against Franklin D. Roosevelt.

True, there were both partisanship and paternalism in the campaign to adopt the Twenty-second Amendment. Republicans feared another popular Democrat serving another three or four terms. Proponents of the amendment recognized that it might occasionally prevent voters (presumably for their own good) from choosing someone they believed might be the best candidate. Yet most people in Congress, the state legislatures, and the country understood term limits as a trade-off for the protection of liberty and as a price they were willing to pay for enforcing the democratic principle of rotation in office.

Americans continue to believe that it is a trade-off worth making. A 2003 Fox News/Opinion Dynamics Corporation poll found only 20 percent supported changing the Twenty-second Amendment, while 75 percent opposed repealing it. The poll revealed, too, that this issue has ceased to be partisan, with Democrats and Republicans equally opposed to altering the two-term limit.[28]

The citizens of New York also weighed in on their preferences for term limits. New York's billionaire mayor, Michael Bloomberg, persuaded the New York City Council in late 2008 to approve a law extending term limits from two to three terms for both the mayor and city council members. Although

Bloomberg was reelected and was generally well regarded as mayor, a 2012 *New York Times* poll found that over 70 percent of New Yorkers surveyed nonetheless believed the two-term limit should not have been amended. Only about one in five New Yorkers thought terms limits were a bad idea.[29]

Ever since James Madison, scholars have understood that there is an intrinsic tension in a constitutional democracy because the people are sovereign and yet need to be checked. That's why we have a Bill of Rights, federalism, and three branches of government. It is in this sense, too, that the Twenty-second Amendment is a safeguard.

Public opinion favoring a two-term tradition for elected executives plainly reflects both the public's fondness for the idea of rotation in office as well as an ingrained fear that power held for too long may encourage officials to lose touch with the concerns of average voters and may breed abuse of power.

Second, repeal proponents suggest that the Twenty-second Amendment encourages lame-duck second terms.

Second terms are always a challenge. But this was the case well before the passage of this amendment. Madison, Grant, Cleveland, Wilson, and Truman, all of whom preceded the Twenty-second Amendment, had troubled second terms.

Contrary to the conventional wisdom, post–Twenty-second Amendment presidents can have productive second terms.[30] In their second terms, Eisenhower helped implement the landmark legislation creating the national highway system, Reagan helped to enact a major tax reform and conducted strategic diplomacy that many people believed helped end the Cold War, and Clinton balanced the budget and presided over a sustained period of job creation and economic growth. Both Reagan and Clinton also enjoyed higher public approval ratings in their second terms than in their first terms. In short, recent presidents, in spite of being term limited, have had notable successes in second terms.

The less happy second terms of Nixon and George W. Bush had little to do with their being limited to two terms. Nixon was brought down by the Watergate scandal that stemmed from misdeeds in his first term and his 1972 reelection campaign, and Bush grew unpopular because of a war he started in his first term. They floundered in their second terms, less because they were lame ducks than because of a number of ill-advised decisions in their first terms.

Third, advocates of repeal, echoing Hamilton's famous argument in *Federalist* No. 72, contend that the opportunity to stand for reelection for third terms promotes accountability. As Hamilton put it, "one ill effect" of a limit on the president's terms "would be a diminution of the inducements to good behavior."

The quasi-monarchical Hamilton was prescient on many things, yet on this he exaggerated. There are in fact plenty of inducements to good behavior or excellence in a second term. Second-term presidents still want to pass legislation to ensure their priorities will continue and succeed after their eight years are completed. And second-term presidents want their policies and their party to succeed because their place in history depends on this success. Presidents who fail us in their second terms risk being impeached, shamed in the polls, or condemned as ineffective.

Fourth, proponents of repeal contend that someday we may need that tried and tested, wise and experienced leader to continue as our president. The ban on third terms, they argue, could deny us a proven leader in times of crisis.

Political scientist Larry Sabato has an appropriate riposte to this canard: "America benefited from Roosevelt's strong hand as we semi-secretly prepared to enter war, but it is very possible that the impressive, internationalist Republican nominee Wendell Willkie or an able Democrat of Roosevelt's stripe could have led the country well, had either been elected in 1940." Adds Sabato, "if we can credibly suggest that a presidential giant like FDR was replaceable, then any president is."[31] France's Charles de Gaulle once reminded us "the cemeteries of the world are filled with people once deemed irreplaceable."

If a president of the ability, agility, and savvy of a Washington, a Lincoln, or an FDR were available at the end of a second term and if the nation were facing dire emergencies, such as Pearl Harbor, the Cuban missile crisis, or September 11, 2001, the wisdom and counsel of the former president can still be tapped. Former presidents can be retained as senior counselors, roving ambassadors, or cabinet members without portfolios, in order to take advantage of their experience and expertise. We might recall the example of John Quincy Adams, who after he finished his presidency served admirably in the U.S. House of Representatives for seventeen years. Former president Jimmy Carter won a Nobel Peace Prize for post–White House humanitarian leadership, and former president Bill Clinton won similar acclaim for humanitarian fund-raising achievements.

AN "AUXILIARY PRECAUTION"

Americans want an energetic and effective presidency yet understandably fear the potential abuse of power. Political scientist Michael Korzi, in a prizewinning history of presidential term limits, concludes that the Twenty-second Amendment strikes a pragmatic balance between our need for "leadership and our suspicions of the temptations of power" and "the democratic rights of the people and the growing powers of the office."[32]

Americans have unreasonably high expectations for presidents yet do not view the presidency as a career job with tenure. Rather, they see the office as a temporary honor to be exercised with Lincoln-like humility. Eight years should be ample time for a president and administration to launch major policy changes. If such policies are valued, needed, and accepted by majorities of Americans, they will likely be honored and continued by succeeding presidents.

This amendment is, in many ways, the "constitutionalizing" of the two-term tradition—a tradition broken by just one president. The amendment can be viewed as a modern "auxiliary precaution" in the finest sense of James Madison's phrase in *The Federalist Papers*. It is a practical, if imperfect, compromise between the need for Hamiltonian energy and continuity on the one hand and republican and democratic principles on the other.[33]

The United States has been fortunate. Our founding leaders, George Washington and Thomas Jefferson especially, refused to succumb to a "cult of indispensability." Other national liberation leaders (such as Mao Zedong, Fidel Castro, Robert Mugabe, Kim Il-Sung, or Muammar Gaddafi) viewed themselves as indispensable and deserving life tenure.

Unaccountable royal governors and an out-of-touch monarch helped foment our American Revolution. Today's enlarged presidency has become, for understandable and generally valid reasons, a far more powerful institution than was ever imagined back in 1787. Most of this growth in executive power cannot, and should not, be reversed, which makes the Twenty-second Amendment needed. John F. Kennedy was right: two terms are plenty for any human being.[34]

NOTES

PRO

1. For a useful summary, see Robert A. Dahl, *How Democratic Is the American Constitution?* (New Haven, CT: Yale University Press, 2001). Calling presidential elections "majoritarian" and "democratic" requires acknowledgment that owing to the Electoral College—another problematic aspect of the Constitution—the candidate with the most popular support may not be elected. Yet this has rarely happened.
2. Even the Twelfth Amendment may be seen as a democratizing move, because in cases when no candidate secured a majority of electoral votes Congress was henceforth required to hew more closely to the people's wishes by choosing from among the top three finishers rather than the top five candidates.

3. Yale Law School, "Notes on the Debates in the Federal Convention of 1787," Madison Debates, September 4, 1787, Avalon Project, Yale Law School, http://avalon.law.yale.edu/18th_century/debates_904.asp

4. "Notes on the Debates," Madison Debates, July 17, 1787, and July 19, 1787.

5. Bruce G. Peabody, "George Washington, Presidential Term Limits, and the Problem of Reluctant Political Leadership," *Presidential Studies Quarterly* 31 (2001): 439–53.

6. Ibid.

7. Ibid.

8. Kenneth D. Ackerman, *The Dark Horse: The Surprise Election and Political Murder of President James A. Garfield* (Cambridge, MA: Da Capo Press, 2003).

9. Ronald W. Reagan, "Restoring the Presidency," in *Restoring the Presidency: Reconsidering the Twenty-second Amendment* (Washington, DC: National Legal Center for the Public Interest, 1990), 4.

10. Gordon Silverstein, *Imbalance of Powers: Constitutional Interpretation and the Making of American Foreign Policy* (New York: Oxford University Press, 1996).

11. France has recently established term limits for its presidents, but they are much less severe than the American version. A French president may now serve two successive five-year terms and then is again eligible after sitting out five years.

12. See *The Book of the States 2007* (Lexington, KY: Council of State Governments, 2007), Table 4.9, "Constitutional and Statutory Provisions for the Number of Consecutive Terms of Elected State Officials."

13. James E. Alt and David Dreyer Lassen, "The Political Economy of Institutions and Corruption in American States," *Journal of Theoretical Politics* 15 (2003): 341–65.

14. Andrew W. Barrett and Matthew Eshbaugh-Soha, "Presidential Success on the Substance of Legislation," *Political Research Quarterly* 60 (2007): 100–12.

15. Matthew J. Dickinson and Kathryn Dunn Tenpas, "Explaining Increasing Turnover Rates among Presidential Advisers, 1929–1997," *Journal of Politics* 64 (2002): 434–48.

16. Sidney M. Milkis and Michael Nelson, *The American Presidency: Origins and Development, 1776–2007,* 5th ed. (Washington, DC: CQ Press, 2008).

17. Thomas E. Cronin, "Two Cheers for the Twenty-second Amendment," *Christian Science Monitor,* February 23, 1987.

18. For three studies decades apart illustrating this point, see V. O. Key Jr., *The Responsible Electorate: Rationality in Presidential Voting* (Cambridge, MA: Harvard University Press, 1966); Morris P. Fiorina, *Retrospective Voting in American National Elections* (New Haven, CT: Yale University Press, 1981); and Douglas A. Hibbs Jr., "Bread and Peace Voting in U.S. Presidential Elections," *Public Choice* 104 (2000): 149–80.

19. Alexander Hamilton, *The Federalist Papers,* No. 72, http://thomas.loc.gov/home/histdox/fed_72.html

CON

20. Roper Center for Public Opinion Research Archive, cited in Kathleen Weldon, "The Public and the 22nd Amendment: Third Terms and Lame Ducks," *Huffpost Pollster*, September 12, 2015, p. 2.
21. Bill Clinton interview on *CNN: Piers Morgan Live*, September 25, 2012. On this occasion, as in earlier interviews, Clinton indicated his interest in modifying the amendment so only consecutive third terms would be prohibited. See Michael J. Korzi, *Presidential Term Limits in American History* (College Station, TX: Texas A&M University Press, 2011), 124.
22. Jefferson initially supported a single seven-year term, but he eventually embraced the notion of service for eight years with the public's right to remove a president at the end of four years. He admired Washington's precedent, intentionally followed it, and hoped it would become tradition. Early in his second term, Jefferson presciently wrote, "Perhaps it may beget a disposition to establish it by an amendment of the Constitution." Jefferson to John Taylor of Caroline, quoted in Jon Meacham, *Thomas Jefferson: The Art of Power* (New York: Random House, 2012), 409.
23. Robert M. La Follette, quoted in *The Congressional Digest* (January 1947): 16.
24. Calvin Coolidge, *The Autobiography of Calvin Coolidge* (New York: Cosmopolitan Book Corporation, 1929), 241.
25. Hugo Chávez's story is a classic illustration of this tendency. He was well intentioned and a gifted, empathetic politician. During his first campaign, he pledged to serve for just one term. But he soon linked the success of his "revolution" with his remaining in power. He fought to abolish term limits, won two more reelections, and before his death "bellowed to rallies" of his loyalists that he might serve another twenty or thirty years. See the splendid biography by Rory Carroll, *Comandante: Hugo Chávez's Venezuela* (New York: Penguin, 2013), esp. 271.
26. Gideon Maltz, "The Case for Presidential Term Limits," *Journal of Democracy* 18 (January 2007): 131.
27. Remarks by President Obama to the People of Africa, Mandela Hall, Addis Ababa, Ethiopia, July 28, 2015, https://www.whitehouse.gov/the-press-office/2015/07/28/remarks-president-obama-people-africa. The president later quipped in a speech at the University of Nebraska–Omaha that even apart from the constitutional prohibition he couldn't run again because if he did, "Michelle would kill me." Remarks by the President at the University of Nebraska–Omaha, January 13, 2016, https://www.whitehouse.gov/the-press-office/2016/01/13/remarks-president-university-nebraska-omaha
28. Fox News/Opinion Dynamics Poll, June 5, 2003. Retrieved from iPoll Databank, The Roper Center for Public Opinion Research, University of Connecticut, www.ropercenter.uconn.edu/data_access/ipoll/ipoll.html
29. Michael M. Grynbaum and Marjorie Connelly, "Good Grade for Mayor; Regret over His 3rd Term," *New York Times*, August 20, 2012. The poll was conducted August

10–15, 2012; see http://www.nytimes.com/interactive/2012/08/22/ nyregion/22nyc-poll.html?ref=nyregion

30. James R. Hedtke, *Lame Duck Presidents—Myth or Reality* (Lewiston, NY: Edwin Mellen Press, 2002).

31. Larry Sabato, *A More Perfect Constitution* (New York: Walker, 2007), 87.

32. Korzi, *Presidential Term Limits*, 170.

33. I do not favor term limits for state and national legislators for reasons I have explained elsewhere. I do not believe that favoring the Twenty-second Amendment and opposing legislative term limits is inconsistent. See Thomas E. Cronin, "Term Limits—A Symptom, Not a Cure," *New York Times*, December 23, 1990, E11.

34. I thank Elliot Mamet for research assistance.

RESOLVED, The new media have brought the president closer to the people

PRO: Matthew R. Kerbel

CON: Jeffrey E. Cohen

William McKinley was a media pioneer. Who knew? As historian David Greenberg records in *Republic of Spin: An Inside History of the American Presidency*, McKinley was a presidential candidate in 1896 when "motion pictures were just escaping the vaudeville booths and amusement arcades and arriving in urban theaters." A few weeks before the election, moviegoers began seeing a newsreel called "Major McKinley at Home." "It was as if the governor had literally ambled into the theater," Greenberg records. "The crowd cheered; some called for the apparition to speak."

McKinley was far from a natural on the silver screen, but his successor as president, Theodore Roosevelt, was right at home. Movie audiences grew accustomed to seeing newsreels not just of the athletic, hyperactive TR but also of his young children (the first to be raised in the White House since Abraham Lincoln's sons). Concerns arose among critics who saw the new medium as trivializing politics and government. In 1920, for example, Democratic vice presidential candidate Franklin D. Roosevelt said, "Carefully rehearsed moving picture films do not necessarily convey the truth." But he and other ambitious politicians soon got with the program, realizing that to reach voters, you must meet them where they are.

Newsreels exemplify a recurring pattern in the history of the presidency: the periodic rise of a new entertainment-centered mass medium, its grudging and awkward adoption by the president who is in office at the time, and then its mastery by subsequent presidents.

Take radio. In 1920 hardly anyone had one. By 1930 almost everyone did: big, ornate pieces of furniture that became the new centerpiece of American living rooms. Early in the decade, President Warren G. Harding broadcast a few speeches to crowds, but he always focused on the live audience. His successor, Calvin Coolidge, seized on the new medium. Confessing that "I can't make an engaging, arousing, or oratorical speech to a crowd," Coolidge discovered that "I have a good radio voice and now I can get my messages across."

A few years later FDR famously mastered radio with his relaxed, seemingly informal (but actually well-rehearsed) fireside chats. "The president likes to think of his audience as being a few people around his fireside," said press aide Stephen Early—which is exactly what his audience was, only times tens of millions in number and in their own homes, not FDR's. Many people today think Roosevelt delivered about a chat per week. Instead, he did just two or three per year. Roosevelt realized that when people turned on the radio to hear him they were in effect allowing him into their homes. He knew better than to wear out his welcome.

TV saturated the country as thoroughly during the 1950s as radio had during the 1920s. Repeating the cycle, Dwight D. Eisenhower, the first president elected in the television age, was okay, even smearing on makeup to cut the glare from his bald head. But it took John F. Kennedy to make the pictures as pleasing as the words were persuasive. JFK was the first president to broadcast his press conferences live, which seemed brave and daring even though there was seldom a question he and his staff hadn't anticipated or an answer he hadn't rehearsed.

As with radio and television, the online world moved from the margins of American life to its center in about a decade, from roughly 1995 to 2005. Barack Obama was the first national politician to make masterful use of the new medium through his Obama for America (OFA) campaign website in 2008. OFA became Organizing for America when he assumed office, but it never really took off in its postelection incarnation. Some future president undoubtedly will turn the Internet from a useful tool for campaigning into one that works just as well for governing. But in doing so, that president will have to take full account of the fact that social media are interactive, not unidirectional, from leader to led as in the past.

Even in the current phase of transition from novelty to familiarity to mastery, a serious question arises about the new media: Have they brought presidents and the people closer to each other or farther apart? Matthew R. Kerbel argues the case for increasing closeness. Jeffrey E. Cohen contends that the new media actually have made the president a more remote figure to most Americans.

PRO: Matthew R. Kerbel

President Obama celebrated his fifty-fourth birthday in August 2015 and Americans across the country celebrated with him—on Twitter.[1] They tweeted pictures of the president with balloons, confetti, and party hats, and sent heartfelt wishes like they would to relatives or friends. The hashtag #44turns54 is filled with so many personal comments and expressions of well-being that it's easy to forget there once was a time when the president was a distant and unapproachable figure. That was before the Internet and social media revolutions broke down barriers and afforded ordinary individuals the opportunity to engage in virtual relationships with virtually anyone.

President Obama—the first president of the social media age—maintained a strong and carefully cultivated Internet presence, and as social media increasingly defined our interpersonal relationships, the president used them to draw closer to the people. Television may have brought presidents into our living rooms and made them accessible figures by saturating us with their likeness and words, but television is an "old" medium that communicates messages from single individuals to massive numbers of people. At best, television created the illusion of proximity to the president, an image of familiarity crafted on the president's terms. In contrast, the "new media," with their decentralized platform, permit a wide range of interactions that can easily start with ordinary people. And when we initiate the engagement we develop a deeper and more enduring bond.

Television is built on a parallel architecture to radio and newspapers in that an elite group of gatekeepers crafts and disseminates a message to a mass audience. Skillful practitioners of the art of broadcasting, including successful past presidents, managed how they were presented on television in order to shape a positive image of themselves for the mass public. Long before Bill Clinton played the saxophone on late-night TV, before Ronald Reagan packaged his likeness with the Statue of Liberty and the American flag, John F. Kennedy honed a young, vigorous television image and Dwight D. Eisenhower marketed himself through television advertising as a heroic figure with homespun roots by carefully combining thematic messaging with iconic images.[2] Presidents during this period would "go public" to market their major legislative plans over the heads of Congress,[3] using television as a key resource in a strategy designed to shape the public agenda. When successful, these efforts at media outreach could move public opinion. But television-age presidents did not have the tools to reach out to and connect with individual constituents.

Far from being an ideal medium for building relationships, television is implicated in facilitating a range of attitudes and behaviors associated with disconnection from the political process. Political scientist Robert Putnam documented a decline in social capital, or the collective benefits derived from interpersonal connections, during the period of television's peak influence from the 1960s through the rise of the Internet at the turn of the century, which he suggests was aggravated by the central role of television in people's lives.[4] Social capital is key to a virtuous cycle where strong relationships engender trust and cooperation, leading to greater public engagement and support for political institutions and individuals like the president.

The elements of this cycle were notably absent in the television age, a time of decreased political participation and diminished support for government. Regardless of how favorably presidents may have presented themselves in their scripted appearances, television news coverage dwelled on the negative, portraying presidential actions as self-serving, scheming, and informed by the base motivation of holding onto power and position. The result was widespread cynicism about presidents and the political process.[5]

Evidence abounds of the weakening of political bonds during this period. By 1992, at the height of television's influence and just before the Internet revolution, the American National Election Study found rampant cynicism and political disengagement. Supermajorities expressed the sentiment that public officials do not care about the concerns of individual citizens and that government is not run for the benefit of society. Fully half felt their elected officials were corrupt.[6]

Even if television is not to be blamed for these attitudes—and it is certainly too convenient to blame television for every social ill—there is little evidence of the sort of engagement between the president and the public that we would expect to find if television-age presidents had successfully built bonds with the public. Television programming, with its frenetic pace and innate preference for trouble and turmoil, is a poor vehicle for promoting positive partnerships between presidents and the public. Skilled presidents may have figured out how to use television to move aggregate opinion in their direction for fixed periods of time, but by no means did this reflect greater closeness or proximity to individuals. Perhaps it's not coincidental that of the presidents who served between 1964 and 2000, only Ronald Reagan and Bill Clinton left office with their approval on the upswing. The electorate discarded the other five.

But the Internet is different. It is built on an architecture designed to facilitate relationships. Its "many-to-many" design permits what television-age presidents could only dream about: the chance to microtarget messages to small or specific groups and inspire people to initiate their own, personalized contacts with the White House. While the Internet supports top-down communication like television, it also permits bottom-up and many-to-many contacts that shift the locus of communication to the general public. This is particularly true with social media, where anyone can initiate political outreach in 140 characters, and it has transformed how presidents interact with the public.

You can trace this transformation to the 2008 campaign, where candidate Obama and a nexus of young, Internet-savvy advisers understood the defining nature of personalized communication in the Internet age[7] and were able to develop tools to empower supporters to create their own campaign experience. The hub was the candidate's official social network, my.barackobama.com (or, to campaign officials, simply MyBO). The site was a gateway that permitted voters to take the campaign into their own hands by building their own networks with other supporters.[8] Its decentralized nature and easy, intuitive functionality personalized the Obama experience on a mass scale in a manner only possible on the Internet. Users responded by reaching out to others in their social networks to convince them to become Obama supporters, exchange information about the candidate, raise money, and even plan campaign events.[9]

The top-down complement to MyBO, perfected to a high art in 2012, was a deep investment in microtargeting supporters, reaching them through social media, e-mail, and even text messages to cultivate relationships, initiate conversations, and call to action on behalf of the candidate.[10] This enabled the candidate to invert the traditional campaign model, in which a small group of paid staffers performed the vast majority of campaign functions, in favor of a community involvement model in which massive numbers of unpaid volunteers each contributed small amounts of their time to the cause of electing the candidate.[11] The campaign benefited from a motivated nationwide army of supporters, while supporters became personally invested in the campaign.

Obama nurtured these virtual connections after he took office, bringing the campaign's social media skills to the White House. "I am Barack Obama, President of the United States—AMA," read the message on the social media website Reddit one day in August 2012.[12] "AMA" is an acronym for "ask me anything." People did, with the president dutifully responding to a cascade of questions for half an hour and triggering a discussion that continued for days.[13] Obama is the first president to have a YouTube channel.[14] He has a presence on Google Plus, Instagram, BuzzFeed, Tumbler, and Pinterest. With over 3,600,000 Facebook followers and 6,260,000 Twitter followers, his social media outreach is objectively generating an enormous public response.

The Obama administration used these connections to engage citizens in the political process on behalf of his policy agenda. Social media outreach helped to mobilize support for the 2009 stimulus package, the Supreme Court nomination of Sonya Sotomayor, and the Affordable Care Act.[15] Over 200,000 people pledged to prevent sexual assault on college campuses in response to a White House social media campaign.[16] In 2015 the fourteen-person White House Office of Digital Strategy was larger than the Office of the Press Secretary in the George W. Bush administration.[17]

Presidential contacts are effective because of the power the Internet gives individuals to engage one another and initiate social action, even if it is on behalf of the administration's agenda. Social media are about cultivating relationships, something the Obama campaign understood well. "The relationship that Obama built with individual supporters and between them was the unique part," said Joe Rospars, the campaign's primary digital strategist. "Our [social media] tools were sort of the glue for the relationships."[18] Added Thomas Gensemer, managing partner at Rospars's media technology firm Blue State Digital, people "expect a conversation, a two-way relationship that is a give and take."[19] The open nature of the Internet strengthens these relationships by breaking down barriers between politicians and citizens.[20]

Social networks also serve as "trust filters" where people can rely on interpersonal connections to evaluate information and decide whether it should be believed or set aside.[21] Having personal networks to verify information enables people to navigate a hypersaturated media environment, ultimately permitting ordinary individuals to act as gatekeepers for others in their networks—a role once limited to television producers and newspaper editors. As in any relationship, trust is the prerequisite for successful engagement.[22] Once trust is established, presidents are in a position to influence the behaviors of those who open their networks to them, and through their gatekeeping role the recipients of presidential contacts can amplify that influence.

The collective result of the trust developed through social networks is the creation of social capital, deepening and tightening community connections through the power to link directly to others in a manner unseen during the television age,[23] evident through increased political and civic participation. Once believed to be the exclusive product of face-to-face encounters, social capital is now understood to be associated with virtual networks as people spend more time connected to one another online.[24] This beneficial effect can extend to personalized communication between political figures like the president and individuals who are predisposed to social engagement.[25]

It is hardly automatic that all future presidents will have the understanding and skill to use social media to form bonds with the public. President Obama and his advisers had a keen understanding of how social media work and were able to employ them impressively, recognizing the value of reaching people through emotional appeals that communicated enthusiasm and even humor.[26] It would not be difficult to imagine other presidents with a less intuitive feel for online communication having difficulty using social media in a way that feels as natural. Likewise, not all presidents will have the impulse to allow others to play an important role in their communication strategy. Effective social media connections require ordinary citizens to feel empowered to act on their own, and that could spell difficulty for a president not secure enough to relinquish top-down control of the media.

Additionally, not everyone will be interested in engaging with the president through social networks. In an era marked by intense partisanship, it would not be surprising if the White House disproportionately reaches those who are predisposed to support the president. But there should also be no question that the Internet and social media give the president a multitude of options for connecting with the public that were not available only a few years ago, and that the nature of those connections is profoundly richer than what was possible in the television age.

The new media have undoubtedly brought the president closer to the people. They can strengthen relationships around political engagement. They can generate social capital. And they can create a bond with the president strong enough to inspire voting, involvement in a policy campaign, and countless tweeted birthday cards.

CON: Jeffrey E. Cohen

Americans now enjoy easier and more varied access to information and news about politics, government, and the presidency than ever before. Three cable television networks, MSNBC, CNN, and Fox News, offer round-the-clock news; interested viewers can tune into news whenever they want. People can also receive information about politics from television programs that blend political satire with commentary and news, such as *Saturday Night Live*, the *Daily Show* and the *Colbert Report*.[27] The Internet offers an even greater diversity of news sources. All the major newspapers publish online editions, available to anyone, anywhere, at any time. There are also Internet-only news sites like Politico, the Daily Beast, and the Huffington Post, as well as less formal news and information sources such as blogs. The rise of social media, like Facebook and Twitter, allows greater flexibility in accessing and sharing information, two-way interaction, and collaboration in the production of content, including news.

Presidents, too, increasingly employ a variety of means to communicate with citizens. The combination of jet-airplane technology and broadcasting allows presidents easy travel around the nation and the globe. They can speak to targeted groups or the entire nation from almost anywhere. More recently, the Internet has become an important communication tool for political campaigns and the presidency. Campaigns use the Internet to generate interest in and provide information on the candidate, to solicit donations, and to locate and mobilize potential campaign workers and voters. The presidency has established a formal governmental Internet page, WhiteHouse.gov, which offers information about the president and the administration, including positions on issues, texts and videos of speeches, a portal to other government agencies, and even a way to submit questions and comments to the White House. President Barack Obama built his own nongovernmental webpage, https://www.barackobama.com/, where people could learn about the administration, volunteer to actively support the president on specific issues, and buy T-shirts and other products proclaiming support for Obama and his policy initiatives.

With myriad ways for communication between the president and voters, one would think that the president and the public are closer now than they have ever been. But this is not the case. Citizens are more distant now from the president, and presidents have a harder time reaching voters than was the case in the 1960s and 1970s, before the creation of cable television—the first of the new media. Why, if there are so many ways for voters and presidents to communicate and learn about each other, are voters and the president more distant now than they were forty years ago, before the advent of the new media?

Two Eras of Communication: Broadcasting and the New Media

To address the question of the closeness between the president and the public, it is useful to divide the years since 1960 into two broad eras, the *Broadcast Era* (1960–1980) and the *New Media Era* (1980–present).[28] During the Broadcast Era, the most important news sources for most voters were the evening news broadcasts from three major television networks (ABC, CBS, and NBC). Each broadcasted their major news program during the dinner hour, they competed with one another for viewers, and their programs covered essentially the same news stories. If someone wanted to watch television during the dinner hour, which many appeared to want to do, practically the only viewing choice one had was a news program. Consequently, voters, no matter their interest in news and politics, were exposed to a lot of news about politics and government.

Moreover, there was a similarity in news across most of the major news organizations, whether television or newspapers. The *New York Times,* the *Washington Post,* and a few other sources set the news agenda, especially with regard to national and international events, for most news organizations. To keep from offending viewers and readers of different political orientations and to generate as large an audience as possible, news reporting in this era primarily described the president's activities, with much less commentary and analysis than is now so common for news reporting.

The era of new media began with two major developments—VHS (and, later, DVDs) and cable television. A defining characteristic of the era of new media is that people have much more choice about what to watch than they did during the Broadcast Era. For example, technologies, like VHS and DVDs, allow people to record a television show or rent a movie, to be watched whenever they desire. Cable television offered viewing choices, from sports, to music videos, to reruns of television programs, to movies that competed with the dinner hour news broadcasts of the three networks. The audience for network news broadcasts declined as many viewers flocked to these entertainment programs that cable offered. Most people, it appears, prefer entertainment to news. Cable television also offered around-the-clock dedicated news networks (CNN, Fox, MSNBC), but they have quite small viewerships. In 2014 their combined prime-time audience was only 2.8 million, and they might be best described as niche networks catering to an audience hungry for news.[29] To try to stem the loss of viewers, who preferred entertainment to news, the big three television networks decreased the amount of hard news—that is, news on politics, government, and economics—and increased the amount of soft news— that is, human interest stories, often concerning entertainment, popular arts, and lifestyle.[30]

Since the advent of cable television, there have been other major new media developments, primarily the Internet, and more recently, social media. But like cable, these newer new media resemble cable in being primarily human interest media. Despite the possibility of accessing news-on-demand from a variety of sources, news acquisition is not the top or even a highly ranked activity among those using the Internet or social media. For instance, in 2013 the *New York Times,* the most trafficked dedicated news site on the Internet, ranked thirty-first overall, but received only 7 percent as many visits as Facebook.[31]

Still, Internet access is nearly ubiquitous in the United States. In 2014 approximately 87 percent of the population had Internet access,[32] and nearly two-thirds owned a smartphone.[33] According to a study by the Pew Research Center, in 2015 approximately 63 percent of both Facebook and Twitter users said they got some news from those social media platforms.[34] This means that about 40 percent and 13 percent of the population receive some news from Facebook and Twitter, respectively—quite large numbers. How has the spread of these technologies affected the relationship between voters and the president?

Trends in the Closeness of the President and the Public

There are several ways to think about the closeness between the president and the public. One is to look at policy agreement, but there will always be some policy disagreement between the president and a significant number of voters.[35] Instead, let us think of the presidency as the primary political institution for most voters. For a large number of voters, the only political leader they can name is the president, and many lack basic knowledge or understanding of our admittedly complex system of separation of powers and checks and balances.[36] Large numbers of voters look to the president for leadership, especially in troubling times. To fulfill this leadership expectation, presidents must be able to get their message to the public—that is, voters must pay some attention to presidential communications, and they must be able to make sense of them.

Declining News Coverage of the President

Presidents communicate with the public through two means—either directly, by giving prime-time national addresses, or indirectly, through the coverage they receive from the news media. Through both of these means, presidents convey information to the public, educating them on the important issues of the day. Since presidents cannot give national addresses frequently, the news is especially important for continual day-in–day-out communication from the president to the voters. If the president does not receive sufficient news coverage, it becomes more difficult for the public to learn about the many issues and policies being debated. Moreover, if presidents do not receive much news coverage, the public will not look upon them as being particularly strong or important.

But how much news coverage does the president receive? It is difficult to compare the amount of news coverage that the president has received over time because of the evolution of communication—from broadcasting, to cable television, to the Internet, to social media. Still, we can look at news coverage for one news source that has remained important in both the Broadcast and New Media Eras, the *New York Times*.

As noted above, the *Times* is the most prestigious news organization, irrespective of medium, and it still sets much of the news agenda for most news organizations—that is, other news organizations tend to follow the lead of the *Times* in deciding what is newsworthy, especially for national and international news. Figure 6-1 plots the average number of stories per day that appeared on the front page, which is usually reserved for what news editors consider the most important news. There is an unmistakable decline in the amount of presidential news. In the 1950s through the 1960s, presidents received about 3.0 front-page news stories per day, compared to about 1.5 in the 2000s. This decline partially reflects the decrease in the number of front-page stories. But there is a similar trend if we look at the entire newspaper. In the early 1970s, there were about 15 articles per day on the president in the entire paper, compared to about 8–9 in the 2000s. There is much less news coverage on the president today than there was forty years ago. If there is so much less news coverage of the president now than in the past, it is hard to argue that the relationship between the president and the public is closer.

Figure 6-1

Average Daily Number of Front-Page News Stories on the President in the *New York Times*, 1953–2010

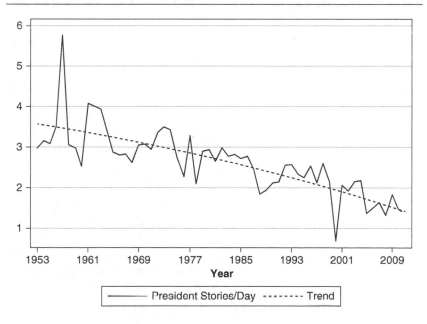

Source: ProQuest Historical Newspapers Archive.

Declining Audience for Presidential Speeches

Instead of trying to track the overall volume of news, which may be impossible to do, we can ask how much attention people pay to the president. The State of the Union Address (SOTU) is the most important speech presidents give. They do it once a year, and in the address presidents outline their policy agenda for the upcoming year. How many people watch the SOTU?

The A. C. Nielsen company has been tracking the ratings of television broadcasts since the 1950s, and it has done the same for the State of the Union Address since 1969. Figure 6-2 plots the rating for the SOTU since 1969. Each rating point can be thought of as the percentage of households with televisions that watch a program. As nearly every household in the United States has a television, a ratings point is approximately the percentage of households.[37]

There is an unmistakable and dramatic decline in the ratings for the president's State of the Union Address. In the early 1970s, nearly one-half of households watched the speech. By the 2000s, barely 20 to 25 percent did so. The audience for

Figure 6-2

Trend in Ratings for the President's State of the Union Address, 1969–2015

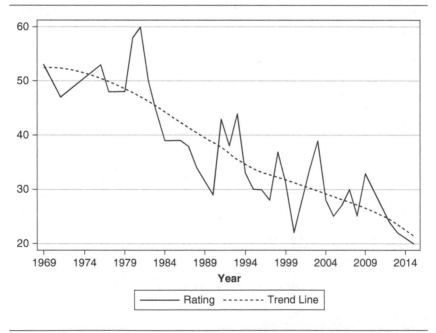

Source: A. C. Nielsen.

the president's speech *on broadcast television* has declined by one-half. But people do not have to watch the speech when it is being broadcast. They can stream it on platforms like YouTube, when it is most convenient for them. In 2015 the Obama administration was aware of the falloff in the number of people who watch the SOTU. For a month prior to the address, the administration publicized the outlines and initiatives the president would discuss, and it heavily used new media like YouTube, Facebook, Medium, Vine, LinkedIn, and Twitter to get the message out, especially to those who traditionally do not pay much attention to news about politics and government.[38] Table 6-1 lists the number of views of the president's SOTU on the official White House YouTube channel from 2010 through 2015. The 2015 YouTube audience rose greatly over that of the previous two years, at nearly 1.9 million, but this is a small number given the vast size of the United States. As each ratings point is equivalent to approximately 1,156,000 households currently, the YouTube audience would add about 1.5 ratings points, perhaps bringing the rating to about 21–22; this is still well shy of the levels reached decades ago.[39] Even with a determined campaign by the White House to boost attention to the SOTU through social media, the effort still produced an audience woefully small compared to that during the Broadcast Era.

Moreover, in the New Media Era, the audience for the president's address is composed primarily of those who agree with the president and are of the same

Table 6-1

Number of Views of the State of the Union Address on the Official White House YouTube Channel (whitehouse.gov)

Year	Number
2009	470,014 (on C-SPAN)
2010	500,249
2011	926,077
2012	2,772,567
2013	378,919
2014	525,535
2015	1,860,373
2016	613,432

Source: YouTube, as of September 9, 2016.

party. Opposition party identifiers and those generally uninterested in news and politics pay little attention to the address. This differs from the Broadcast Era, when the audience for the address represented a broader cross section of American society.[40]

Declining Levels of Political Knowledge

A knowledgeable citizenry is crucial for the functioning of a democracy, as the founders, in particular Thomas Jefferson, acknowledged and advocated.[41] The news media—in fact, all forms of communication among people—were considered central in the role of informing the citizenry about what its leaders were doing, such as their policies. One promise of the new media is to increase and ease access to relevant information about politics, government, and the presidency. A more knowledgeable citizenry will be closer to the president, if only because a citizenry that lacks the requisite knowledge of politics and government cannot hold the White House accountable or communicate its needs and aspirations to the president.

For each election cycle since the early 1950s, the American National Election Studies has polled nationally representative samples of Americans, asking a variety of questions, including some that tap into their basic knowledge and understanding of politics and government. One question that has been repeated numerous times asks voters whether they know which party holds the majority in the House of Representatives. This is a useful question for measuring basic political knowledge, as it is a fundamental fact about our political system's constitutional structure.

Since only the Democrats or Republicans could hold the House majority, we would expect that if everyone merely guessed, one-half would get the answer right. Fifty percent, thus, should serve as a baseline for making comparisons over time and assessing the knowledge level of voters. Moreover, as educational levels have risen over the last fifty years, we should expect larger percentages of voters correctly answering this question over time. Figure 6-3 plots the percentage correct from 1960 through 2012.

Although there is some volatility from election to election, the figure shows a steady decrease in knowledge over time. Whereas about 65 percent correctly identified the House majority party in the 1960s, only 50 percent could do so in the 2000s—not much better than guessing. Moreover, this decline has been occurring while educational levels have risen. This trend, like the ones discussed above, suggest a distancing between the president and the public.

Figure 6-3

Percentage of Voters Who Correctly Identify the Party Controlling the House of Representatives, 1960–2012

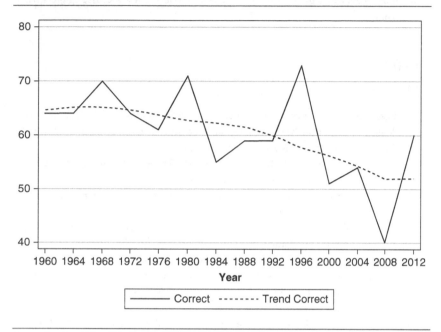

Year

——— Correct   ------- Trend Correct

Source: American National Election Studies, 1960–2012.

Conclusion

At a minimum, a close relationship requires a sufficient degree of interaction and knowledge by the two parties about each other. One would think that the new media, with their ease and convenience of use, would have helped bring the president and the public closer together. But that does not seem to be the case. There is less news about the president than during the Broadcast Era, which means that voters will learn less about what the president does. In addition, voters seem to pay less attention to news and major presidential events, like the State of the Union Address, now than during the Broadcast Era. Perhaps most important, despite rising educational levels, voters in the New Media Era are in general less knowledgeable about politics and government than during the Broadcast Era.

This distancing between the president and voters is not merely a function of the arrival of the new media. Polarization and decreasing civility in modern politics probably also play a role. But the choices the new media offer citizens have led many to spend their time in nonpolitical activities. Thus, there is considerable political disengagement in the New Media Era. It is hard to call the relationship between presidents and citizens close if they are disengaged from each other.

NOTES

PRO

1. Elise Viebeck, "#44turns54: Twitter celebrates Obama's Birthday," *Washington Post*, August 4, 2015, https://www.washingtonpost.com/news/powerpost/wp/2015/08/04/44turns54-twitter-celebrates-obamas-birthday/
2. Edwin Diamond and Stephen Bates, *The Spot: The Rise of Political Advertising on Television* (Cambridge, MA: MIT Press, 1988).
3. Samuel Kernell, *Going Public: New Strategies of Presidential Leadership* (Washington, DC: CQ Press, 2007).
4. Robert D. Putnam, *Bowling Alone: The Collapse and Revival of American Community* (New York: Simon and Schuster, 2000).
5. Joseph N. Cappella and Kathleen Hall Jamieson, *Spiral of Cynicism: The Press and the Public Good* (New York: Oxford University Press, 1997). See also Joseph N. Cappella, "Cynicism and Social Trust in the New Media Environment," *Journal of Communication* (March 2002): 229–41.
6. Warren E. Miller, Donald R. Kinder, and Steven J. Rosenstone, *American National Election Study, 1992* (Ann Arbor, MI: Inter-University Consortium for Political and Social Research, 1993).
7. W. Lance Bennett, "The Personalization of Politics: Political Identity, Social Media, and Changing Patterns of Participation," *Annals of the American Academy of Political and Social Science* 664 (November 2012): 20–39.
8. Rahaf Harfoush, *Yes We Did: An Inside Look at How Social Media Built the Obama Brand* (Berkeley, CA: New Riders, 2009), 74.
9. Ibid.
10. Emma Svensson, Spiro Kiousis, and Jesper Stromback, "Creating a Win-Win Situation? Relationship Cultivation and the Use of Social Media in the 2012 Campaign." In John Allen Hendricks and Dan Schill (eds.), *Presidential Campaigning and Social Media: An Analysis of the 2012 Campaign* (New York: Oxford University Press, 2015), 28–43. See also Bruce Bimber, "Digital Media in the Obama Campaigns of 2008 and 2012: Adaptation to the Personalized Political Communication Environment," *Journal of Information Technology and Politics* 11 (2014): 130–150.
11. Auren Hoffman, "It Takes Tech to Elect a President," *Bloomberg Business*, August 25, 2008, http://www.bloomberg.com/bw/stories/2008-08-25/it-takes-tech-to-elect-a-presidentbusinessweek-business-news-stock-market-and-financial-advice

12. Tom Price, "Social Media and Politics," *CQ Researcher* 22 (October 2012): 867–74.

13. Ibid.

14. Harfoush, *Yes We Did,* 183.

15. Derrick L. Cogburn and Fatima K. Espinoza-Vasquez, "From Networked Nominee to Networked Nation: Examining the Impact of Web 2.0 and Social Media on Political Participation and Civic Engagement in the 2008 Obama Campaign," *Journal of Political Marketing* 10 (2011): 189–213.

16. Juliet Eilperin, "Here's How the First President of the Social Media Age Has Chosen to Connect with Americans," *Washington Post,* May 26, 2015, https://www .washingtonpost.com/news/politics/wp/2015/05/26/heres-how-the-first-president-of-the-social-media-age-has-chosen-to-connect-with-americans/

17. Ibid.

18. Victoria Chang. "Obama and the Power of Social Media and Technology," *The European Business Review* (May–June 2010): 16–21.

19. David Carr, "How Obama Tapped into Social Networks' Power," *New York Times,* November 9, 2008, http://www.nytimes.com/2008/11/10/business/media/10carr .html?_r=1

20. Annie Hellweg, "Social Media Sites of Politicians Influence Their Perception by Constituents," *The Elon Journal of Undergraduate Research in Communications* 2, no. 1 (Spring 2011): 22–36.

21. Darrell M. West, "Ten Ways Social Media Can Improve Campaign Engagement and Reinvigorate American Democracy," Brookings.edu, June 28, 2011, http:// www.brookings.edu/research/opinions/2011/06/28-social-media-west

22. Ibid.

23. Howard Rheingold, "Using Participatory Media and Public Voice to Encourage Civic Engagement." In W. Lance Bennett (ed.), *Civic Life Online: Learning How Digital Media Can Engage Youth* (Cambridge, MA: MIT Press, 2008), 97–118.

24. Jason Gainous and Kevin M. Wagner, *Tweeting to Power: The Social Media Revolution in American Politics* (New York: Oxford University Press, 2014), 96–98.

25. Eun-Ju Lee and Soo Youn Oh, "To Personalize or Depersonalize? When and How Politicians' Personalized Tweets Affect the Public's Reactions," *Journal of Communication* 62 (2012): 932–49.

26. Porismita Borah, "Facebook Use in the 2012 USA Presidential Campaign: Obama vs. Romney." In Bogdan Pătrut and Monica Pătrut (eds.), *Social Media in Politics: Case Studies on the Political Power of Social Media* (Cham, Switzerland: Springer International Publishing, 2014), 201–11.

CON

27. As of this writing, Jon Stewart has left *The Daily Show,* now hosted by Trevor Noah, and Stephen Colbert moved on to become host of *The Late Show* on CBS. Research indicates that viewers learn from programs like these. See Josy Baumgartner and Jonathan S. Morris, "The *Daily Show* Effect: Candidate Evaluations, Efficacy, and American Youth," *American Politics Research* 34, no. 3 (2006): 341–67.

28. Matthew A. Baum and Samuel Kernell, "Has Cable Ended the Golden Age of Presidential Television?" *American Political Science Review* 93, no. 1 (1999): 99–114; and Jeffrey E. Cohen, *The Presidency in the Era of 24-Hour News* (Princeton, NJ: Princeton University Press, 2008).

29. Pew Research Center, "State of the News Media 2015," http://www.journalism .org/2015/04/29/cable-news-fact-sheet/

30. Carsten Reinemann, James Stanyer, Sebastian Scherr, and Guido Legnante, "Hard and Soft News: A Review of Concepts, Operationalizations and Key Findings," *Journalism* 13, no. 2 (2012): 221–39.

31. Moz, https://moz.com/top500 (accessed August 27, 2015).

32. Internet Live Stats, Internet Users by Country (2016), http://www.internetlivestats .com/internet-users-by-country/

33. Pew Research Center, "Mobile Technology Fact Sheet," http://www.pewinternet .org/fact-sheets/mobile-technology-fact-sheet/

34. Pew Research Center, "The Evolving Role of News on Twitter and Facebook," http://www.journalism.org/2015/07/14/the-evolving-role-of-news-on-twitter-and-facebook/. In 2015 about 73 percent and 23 percent of Internet users had a Facebook or Twitter account. With 87 percent of the population having Internet access, this means that 63 percent and 20 percent of the population had Facebook and Twitter accounts. Multiplying these percentages by the 63 percent who say they get some news from Facebook or Twitter produces the 40 percent and 13 percent for the population.

35. B. Dan Wood, *The Myth of Presidential Representation* (New York: Cambridge University Press, 2009).

36. Michael X. Delli Carpini and Scott Keeter, *What Americans Know about Politics and Why It Matters* (New Haven, CT: Yale University Press, 1997).

37. See Baum and Kernell, "Has Cable Ended the Golden Age of Presidential Television?"

38. Michael D. Shear, "Obama's Social Media Team Tries to Widen Audience for State of the Union Address," *New York Times,* January 19, 2015, A14, http://www .nytimes.com/2015/01/20/us/politics/doing-more-than-putting-an-annual-address-into-140-characters.html?_r=0

39. In fact, slightly less than 600,000 people subscribe to the WhiteHouse.gov YouTube channel.

40. Samuel Kernell and Laurie L. Rice, "Cable and the Partisan Polarization of the President's Audience," *Presidential Studies Quarterly* 41, no. 4 (2011): 693–711.

41. Delli Carpini and Keeter, *What Americans Know about Politics and Why It Matters.*

7

RESOLVED, Presidential success and failure have more to do with political time than with a president's character and leadership qualities

PRO: Stephen Skowronek

CON: Fred I. Greenstein

Only the most resolute historical determinist would deny that individuals make a difference in history. And yet just as surely, many things are beyond any individual's control. Conditions not of people's own making structure their choices, shape their decisions, and affect their chances for success. On this much all can agree. But truisms are no substitute for political analysis. Can scholars do better at specifying the conditions under which individual attributes matter in politics?

One of the most influential efforts to do better was James David Barber's 1972 landmark study, *The Presidential Character: Predicting Performance in the White House.*[1] Barber insisted that character matters a great deal, but the book's originality lay in its effort to categorize character types and to use those types to predict presidential performance.

Character, for Barber, was "the way the President orients himself to life." Barber identified two key dimensions of character: (1) a president's activity level in office and (2) whether the president "gives the impression he enjoys his political life." Those who are active and enjoy their political life are "active-positive" presidents. Such presidents have high self-esteem and an ability to draw flexibly on different styles of leadership, depending on the situation and the president's goals. These are the presidents who are most likely to be successful. Those most likely to fail spectacularly are the "active-negative" presidents, who compensate for low self-esteem with compulsive activity. Active-negative presidents, according to Barber, work hard with little sense of enjoyment. Because their political actions are animated by personal demons, they become personally invested in policies. When those policies falter, they are likely to feel personally threatened and are thus reluctant to make concessions or corrections. Persevering rigidly in a failed policy is the hallmark of the active-negative president.

Barber's prediction that Richard Nixon's active-negative character would cause his downfall gave his ideas a celebrity status rarely achieved by political science theories. *Time* magazine featured Barber's theory, and some presidential candidates put the book on their reading lists (Jimmy Carter claimed to have read it twice). Political scientists greeted Barber's work with more skepticism, asking searching questions about its validity. Do the measures of activity level and attitude toward the job correspond with the psychodynamic patterns and personality needs that Barber identifies? Was Nixon's self-destruction really a product of psychological rigidification? Was Herbert Hoover's rigidification a result of character or of ideology? Where is the line between principled adherence to one's views and unhealthy rigidity? And can that distinction be made without involving one's own political values?

Whether Barber's theory is useful or not, he deserves credit for understanding that, if individual attributes are to predict performance, the infinite variety of human behaviors must be reduced to a manageable number of types. If every president is viewed as entirely unique, then one can never hope to learn from the past. Prediction requires theory, which, in turn, requires simplification.

Stephen Skowronek's seminal 1993 book *The Politics Presidents Make* has the same sort of theoretical ambitions that animated Barber's *Presidential Character*.[2] Like Barber, Skowronek generates a fourfold typology from two dimensions. But whereas Barber's aim was a theory of character, Skowronek's is a theory of political regimes. Barber hoped to generalize about individuals. Skowronek wants to simplify the types of situations presidents face.

Skowronek identifies two crucial situational dimensions: (1) whether the president is affiliated with the dominant regime or governing coalition and (2) whether the regime is resilient or vulnerable. A president's chance of success, Skowronek argues, depends on the president's place in "political time"—that is, in the cycle of regime formation and decay. A president affiliated with a regime that is vulnerable—think of Herbert Hoover or Jimmy Carter, both of whom were saddled with faltering economies—has little prospect for success. Although the failure of such presidents is not predetermined, the political deck is stacked against them. By contrast, presidents who come to power opposed to a vulnerable regime—think of Franklin D. Roosevelt and Ronald Reagan, Hoover's and Carter's successors, respectively—are in the best position to remake the political order. Their success is not guaranteed, but they have greater opportunities for success than most presidents do. Personal qualities still matter, but according to Skowronek, success and failure are often attributed wrongly to character and skill when the credit or blame really belongs to the situation the president faced.

In his widely read *The Presidential Difference,* Fred I. Greenstein resolutely defends the importance of understanding a president's personal attributes: political and communication skills, organizational capacity, cognitive style, as well as emotional intelligence.[3] Unlike Skowronek (and Barber), Greenstein shuns simplifying typologies. The result is a less parsimonious theory, but readers can decide whether it is a less useful way of understanding or even predicting presidential performance. The debate between Skowronek and Greenstein prompts us to ask not only how much individual attributes matter but also how scholars of the presidency should build theories that enable us to apply the lessons of presidencies past to the prospects for presidencies yet to come. This is not merely an academic question; the nation's ability to elect successful presidents in the future may depend on the answer.

PRO: Stephen Skowronek

When presidents succeed, people are inclined to laud the special talents and skills they brought to the office; when things go wrong, they look for personal missteps and character flaws. There is something comforting in these judgments, for they sustain confidence in the office of the presidency no matter what the experience of the particular incumbent holding power at the moment. So long as performance is tied to the personal attributes of the individual president, success is always a possibility; it awaits only the right combination of character and skill. So long as the presidency is a true test of the person, its incumbents are free to become as great as they can be.

Much of what is written about the presidency reinforces these conceits. Typically, analysis of presidential leadership begins by describing an office that all presidents have shared, a position defined by constitutional arrangements that have undergone remarkably little change since 1789. To this is added the trappings of modernity—new governing responsibilities imposed on the office in the wake of the Great Depression and World War II and new resources made available to it. These responsibilities and resources distinguish the leadership situation shared by all presidents after Franklin D. Roosevelt from that of all their predecessors. Setting things up this way, the analysis holds the demands and capacities of the office constant and presents leadership as a problem of how best to apply the resources of the modern presidency to the responsibilities of the modern presidency. In effect, each modern incumbent becomes a new source of insight into what attributes of character and skill work best, what strategies are most effective, and what it takes to measure up.

In fact, however, the political demands on incumbents and the leadership capacities of the office of the presidency vary considerably from one administration to the next, and much of what is taken to be evidence of personal flaws and leadership skills can be accounted for by paying closer attention to the particular relationships established between the presidency and the political system by each incumbent in turn. To see how, we first need a clear idea of these changing relationships, and that, in turn, entails thinking about presidential history a bit differently. Rather than set the modern presidents apart from the premoderns to treat them as a separate and coherent group, we will need to compare them individually with counterparts in earlier periods. By making better use of the whole history of presidential leadership, we can better assess the contextual conditions under which great leaders typically arise and identify the limitations on leadership possibilities imposed by less fortuitous circumstances.

The alternative history I have in mind charts change in American politics through the recurring establishment and disintegration of relatively durable political regimes. This regime-based structure of American political history has been widely observed by political scientists and historians alike. It demarcates the rise and decline of Federalist nationalism between 1789 and 1800, of Jeffersonian democracy between 1800 and 1828, of Jacksonian democracy between 1828 and 1860, of Republican nationalism between 1860 and 1932, and of New Deal liberalism between 1932 and 1980. Each of these regimes can be identified with the empowerment of an insurgent political coalition whose reconstruction of basic governing arrangements endured through various subsequent configurations of party power. Just as America's fragmented constitutional system has made sweeping political change rare and difficult to achieve, it has worked similarly to perpetuate the ideological and programmatic commitments of the few insurgencies that have succeeded. To this extent, at least, the regime structure of American political history may be considered a by-product of the constitutional structure of American government. It is manifest today in the persistence of the conservative regime ushered in by Ronald Reagan in 1980.

Looking over the course of each of these regimes suggests a number of typically structured relationships between the presidency and the political system, and thinking about the modern presidents in these terms places each of them in a unique analytic relationship with the presidents of the past. I do not want to suggest that regime formation and decay are processes external to presidential leadership; on the contrary, I intend to show that the active intervention of presidents at various stages in these processes has driven them forward. What I am suggesting is that we try to understand the political demands and challenges of presidential leadership as variables mediated by the generation and degeneration of these political orderings, and that we reverse the standard analytic procedure by holding personality and skill constant and examining the typical political effects of presidential action in the differently structured political contexts characteristic of the U.S. constitutional system.

THE POLITICAL STRUCTURES OF PRESIDENTIAL LEADERSHIP

Each regime begins with the rise to power of a new political coalition out to construct and legitimize alternative governing arrangements and to recast relations between state and society in ways advantageous to its members. These coalitions will then attempt to extend their claims on power by elaborating and modifying their basic agendas in ways that are responsive to new political demands and changes in the nation at large. Once they are established, however, coalition interests can have an enervating effect on the governing capacities of these regimes. An immediate and constant problem is posed by conflicts of interest within the dominant coalition. The danger here is that attempts to elaborate the coalition's political agenda in ways responsive to new governing conditions will focus a sectarian struggle, weaken regime support through factional disaffection, and open new avenues to power for the political opposition. A longer-range and ultimately more devastating problem is posed by changes in the nation at large that throw into question the dominant coalition's most basic commitments of ideology and interest. The danger here is that the entire political regime will be called into question as an inadequate governing instrument and then repudiated wholesale in a nationwide crisis of political legitimacy.

Considering the history of the presidency in this light, two systemic relationships stand out as especially significant for an analysis of the politics of leadership. The first is the president's affiliation with the political complex of interests, institutions, and ideas that dominated state/society relations before coming into office. The second is the current standing of these governmental arrangements in the nation at large. These relationships are always highly nuanced, but the basic variations are easily discerned, and when it comes to explaining outcomes, they do a good deal of the work. For the sake of simplicity, the leadership problem can be conceptualized by referring to those institutions with which political regimes are invariably identified in the United States—namely, the political parties. With the use of this shorthand, the leadership problem confronting each president can be framed by the answers to two simple questions: Is the president affiliated with the political party that has defined the government's basic commitments of ideology and interest? Are the governmental commitments of that party vulnerable to direct repudiation as failed and irrelevant responses to the problems of the day?

Answers to these questions specify four typical opportunity structures for the exercise of political leadership by a president. In the first, the basic governmental commitments of the previously dominant political party are vulnerable to direct repudiation, and the president is associated with the opposition to them (the politics of reconstruction). In the second, the basic governmental commitments of the previously dominant political party are again on the line, but this time the president is politically affiliated with them (the politics of disjunction). In the third, the governmental commitments of the previously dominant political party still appear timely and politically resilient, but the president is linked with the political opposition to them (the politics of preemption). In the fourth, the governmental commitments of the previously dominant political party again appear to hold out robust solutions to the problems of the day, and the president is affiliated with them (the politics of articulation).

These four opportunity structures are represented in Table 7-1, with the "previously dominant political party" designated as the "regime party" for easy reference. Each of these structures defines a different institutional relationship between the presidency and the political system; each engages the president in a different type of politics; and each defines a different kind of leadership challenge. These differences are summarized in the four cells of the table. Any discussion of the table must be prefaced, however, by two points of clarification. First, the table is a schematic presentation of pure types that are only more or less closely approximated in history. In the discussion that follows, the presidents that best fit each type are grouped together. The objective is to highlight the distinctive problems and dynamics of political action that adhere to leadership in these situations and, by implication, to reconsider the problems and prospects faced by contemporary presidents. The procedure radically

Table 7-1

The Political Structures of Presidential Leadership

		Presidents' Political Identity	
		Opposed	*Affiliated*
Regime Party Commitments	Vulnerable	Politics of reconstruction	Politics of disjunction
	Resilient	Politics of preemption	Politics of articulation

delimits the play of personality and skill in determining leadership outcomes, but in doing so, it may allow a more precise determination of their significance. The second point is that this typology does not provide an independent explanation of the historical patterns on which it draws. There is no accounting here for whether a regime affiliate or a regime opponent will actually be elected (or otherwise come into office), nor for when, in the course of the nation's development, a regime's basic governmental commitments will be called into question. My purpose is to reorganize the analysis of the politics of leadership by cutting into political history at certain typical junctures. It is to suggest the rather blunt ways in which political structure has delimited the political capacities of the presidency and informed the impact of presidential action on the political system as a whole.

Politics of Reconstruction

The *politics of reconstruction* has been most closely approximated in the administrations of Thomas Jefferson, Andrew Jackson, Abraham Lincoln, Franklin D. Roosevelt, and Ronald Reagan. Each led a political insurgency and rose to power on the heels of an electoral upheaval in political control of the institutions of the federal government. More specifically, their victories were driven by a nationwide crisis of political legitimacy—a tide of discontent with the established order of things potent enough to dislodge a long-established majority party from its dominant position in Congress as well as the presidency. With political obligations to the past severed in this way, these presidents were thrust beyond the old regime into a political interregnum in which they were directly engaged in a systemic recasting of the government's basic commitments of ideology and interest. It is in these circumstances and apparently only in these circumstances that presidents are free to do what all political leaders seek to do: redefine legitimate national government in their own terms.

These presidents are widely regarded as the most effective of all political leaders in presidential history, but what is less well appreciated is that they shared the same basic relationship to the political system at large. They are all known as great communicators, but this seems to have less to do with any common training or shared skill than with the fact that they all had the same basic message to communicate. Each was able to repudiate received commitments of ideology and interest outright; to indict them forthrightly as failed and illegitimate responses to the problems of the day; and to identify their leadership with a new beginning, with the salvation of the nation from political bankruptcy.

More important, however, is what the performance of leaders in this situation can say about the structured capacities of the presidency as a political institution. Order-shattering elections do not themselves shape the future, but they vastly expand the president's capacities to break prior governmental commitments and to orchestrate a political reordering of state/society relations. It is significant in this regard that none of the presidents who reconstructed the terms and conditions of legitimate national government had much success in actually resolving the tangible problems that gave rise to the nationwide crisis of political legitimacy in the first place. Jefferson's embargo policy proved to be a total failure in dealing with the international crisis of the opening years of the nineteenth century; Jackson's attempt to deal with the long-festering problem of national banking precipitated an economic panic and ultimately exacerbated a devastating depression in the late 1830s; Lincoln's proposed solution to the sectional conflict of the 1850s plunged the nation into a civil war; and Roosevelt's New Deal failed to pull the nation out of the Great Depression of the 1930s. But what these presidents could do that their predecessors could not was define for themselves the significance of the events they oversaw and secure the legitimacy of the new governing commitments they brought to power. Released from the burden of upholding the integrity of the old regime, these presidents were not restricted in their leadership to mere problem solving. Unaffiliated with the old regime, they reformulated the nation's political agenda as a direct response to the manifest failures of the immediate past, presented their solutions as the only alternative to national ruin, and galvanized political support for a government that eyed an entirely new set of possibilities.

The leadership opportunities afforded by this kind of political breakthrough are duly matched by its characteristic political challenges. In penetrating to the core of the political system and forthrightly reordering relations between state and society, these presidents ultimately found it imperative to try to secure a governmental infrastructure capable of perpetuating their cause. The shape of the new regime came to depend on the way party lines were recast and on how institutional relationships within the government were reorganized. Reconstructive presidents are all great party builders, and each is engaged in rooting out the residual institutional supports for the politics of the past. Court battles, bank wars, a real civil war—great confrontations that dislodged entire frameworks of governing—are the special province of the reconstructive leader, and they can be counted on to forge new forms of opposition as well as support. Reconstructive leaders pass to their successors a political system that is not only reconfigured in its basic commitments of ideology and interest but also newly constricted in its potential for independent action.

Politics of Disjunction

The *politics of disjunction* has been most closely approximated in the administrations of John Adams, John Quincy Adams, Franklin Pierce, James Buchanan, Herbert Hoover, and Jimmy Carter. With due regard for the reputations of these men for political incompetence, it is evident in identifying them as a group that they shared what is an impossible leadership situation. Rather than orchestrating a political breakthrough in state/society relations, these presidents were compelled to cope with the breakdown of those relations. Their affiliation with the old regime at a time when its basic commitments of ideology and interest were being called into question severely limited their ability to control the meaning of their own actions, and this limitation ultimately turned their office into the focal point of a nationwide crisis of political legitimacy. This situation imparts to the president a consuming preoccupation with a political challenge that is really a prerequisite of leadership—that is, establishing political credibility.

Each of the major historical episodes in the politics of disjunction has been foreshadowed by a long-festering identity crisis within the old majority party itself. But the distinctiveness of this juncture goes beyond these simmering tensions within the ranks; it lies in changes within the nation itself that obscure the regime's relevance as an instrument of governance and cloud its legitimacy as caretaker of the national interest. The Adamses, Pierce, Buchanan, Hoover, and Carter are notable for their open recognition of the vulnerabilities of the establishments with which they were affiliated; each promised to solve national problems in a way that would repair and rehabilitate the old order. But solving the nation's problems is a hard test for any president, and in this situation, in which they had little else to offer, presidents find themselves in especially difficult straits. Actions that challenge established commitments in the name of rehabilitation and repair are likely to isolate the president from natural political allies, and actions that reach out to allies and affirm established commitments are likely to provide insurgents with proof positive that the president has nothing new to offer, that the incumbent is really nothing more than a symptom of the problems of the day.

Invariably, these presidents drive forward the crisis of legitimacy they came into office to forestall. Unable to control the meaning of their own actions, they find their actions defined by others. They become the leading symbols of systemic political failure and regime bankruptcy and provide the reconstructive leaders their essential premise. Certainly, it is no accident that the presidents who have set the standards of political incompetence in American political history are succeeded by presidents who set the standards of political mastery. This recurrent coupling of dismal failure with towering success suggests that the contingent political relationship between the presidency and the political system is far more telling of leadership prospects than the contingencies of personality and skill.

Politics of Preemption

The *politics of preemption* has engaged a large number of presidents. Some of the more aggressive leaders among them are John Tyler, Andrew Johnson, Grover Cleveland, Woodrow Wilson, Richard Nixon, and Bill Clinton. The men in this grouping stand out as wild cards in American political history. As their experiences indicate, the politics of leadership in this situation is especially volatile and perhaps least susceptible to generalization. Tyler was purged from the ranks of the party that elected him; Wilson took a disastrous plunge from the commanding heights of world leadership during World War I into the political abyss; and Andrew Johnson and Nixon were crippled by impeachment proceedings. Of all the presidents who might be grouped in this category, only Dwight D. Eisenhower finished a second term without suffering a precipitous reversal of political fortune, but this exception is itself suggestive, for Eisenhower alone kept whatever intentions he might have had for altering the shape of national politics well hidden.

As leader of the opposition to a regime that still claims formidable political, ideological, and institutional support, the president interrupts the working agenda of national politics and intrudes into the establishment as an alien power. The opportunity for creative political leadership in this situation comes from the independence these presidents enjoy by virtue of their opposition stance. However, so long as the incumbent is unable to issue a forthright repudiation of established commitments, declaring them bankrupt and illegitimate as solutions to the problems of the day, opposition leadership is limited in its reconstructive power. Short of authority to redefine legitimate national government, preemptive leaders exploit their relative freedom from received political definitions. They disavow orthodoxies of all kinds. They offer hybrid political alternatives. Their attraction lies in their unabashedly mongrel appeal, their free mixing of different, seemingly contradictory political commitments.

As a practical matter, preempting the political discourse of an established regime means simultaneously carrying the support of its stalwart opponents, avoiding a frontal attack on the orthodoxy they oppose, and offering disaffected interests normally affiliated with the dominant coalition a modification of the regime's agenda that they will find more attractive. Floating free of established commitments, preemptive leaders look for and play upon latent interest cleavages and factional discontent within the ranks of the regime's traditional supporters. Though these opportunities are not hard to identify, the political terrain to be negotiated in exploiting them is treacherous. Testing both the tolerance of stalwart opponents and the resilience of establishment allies, preemptive leaders provoke the defenders of regime norms to assault the president's highly personalized, seemingly normless political manipulations.

Compared with presidents caught in a politics of disjunction, preemptive leaders have a much greater opportunity to establish and exploit their political independence; all preemptive leaders who were elected to office in the first instance were reelected to second terms. The danger for presidents in this situation is not that they will get caught in a systemic rejection of regime norms, per se, but that they will find themselves the object of a relentless campaign of character assassination, the effect of which would be to confirm those norms. Compared with a president engaged in the politics of reconstruction, these leaders do not cut into national politics deeply enough to create durable political alternatives, and personal political isolation is the ever-present danger. Preemptive leadership is, in fact, historically unique in its propensity to provoke impeachment proceedings. Probing alternative lines of political cleavage, these presidents may well anticipate future party-building strategies, but they are more effective at disrupting the established political regime than at replacing it.

Politics of Articulation

The *politics of articulation* has engaged the largest number of presidents; in contemporary politics George H. W. Bush and his son George W. Bush both fit the bill. Although it may be no more "normal" a situation than any other, this situation does pinpoint the distinctive problems of political leadership that arise when relations between the incumbent and established regime commitments are the most consonant. Here, the presidency is the font of political orthodoxy, and the president is the minister to the faithful. The leadership posture is wholly affirmative; the opportunity at hand is to service coalition interests, to deliver on outstanding political commitments on the regime's agenda, and to update these commitments to accord with the times. The corresponding challenge is to uphold definitions, to affirm established norms, to maintain a sense of regime coherence and integrity in changing times, and to mitigate and manage the factional ruptures within the ranks of the regime's traditional supporters that inevitably accompany alterations in the status quo ante. These challenges have been met in various ways and with varying degrees of skill, but a look at the record suggests that the political effects are pretty much the same.

Consider the most impressive of the bunch. In each of America's major political regimes, there has been one particular episode in orthodox innovation that stands out for its programmatic accomplishments. In the Jeffersonian era, it was the administration of James Monroe; in the Jacksonian era, the administration of James Polk; in the Republican era, the administration of Theodore Roosevelt; in the era of New Deal liberalism, the administration of Lyndon B. Johnson. These administrations were not only pivotal in the course of each regime's development but also emblematic of the problems this situation poses for presidential leadership. These men exercised power in what were, for all appearances, especially propitious circumstances for orthodox innovation. At the outset of each presidency, a long-established regime party was affirmed in its control of the entire national government, and the national posture was so strong at home and abroad that it left no excuses for not finally delivering on long-heralded regime promises. Each president thus set full sail at a time when it was possible to think about completing the unfinished business of national politics, realizing the regime's vision of the United States, and finally turning the party of orthodoxy into a consensual party of the nation. To that end, each in fact enacted a full and programmatic policy package.

But just as surely as a leadership project of culmination and completion suggests a great leap into the promised land, it accentuates the underlying problem of definition, of upholding fundamental commitments in some coherent fashion and having old allies see the new arrangements as the legitimate expression of their ideals. Each of America's great orthodox innovators found his administration mired in the dilemmas of reconciling old commitments with the expansive political possibilities at hand. Leading a regime at the apex of its projection of national power and purpose, each was beset by a political implosion of conflicting expectations. By pushing ahead with the received business of national politics and embellishing its commitments, these presidents fomented deep schisms within their own ranks; by making real changes in governing commitments, they undercut their own ability to speak for the party faithful. While most fully articulating his regime as a system of national government, each of these presidents was charged with a betrayal of the faith, and each pulled the regime into an accelerated sectarian struggle over the true meaning of orthodoxy. These presidencies were not undermined by the assaults of their nominal political opponents but by the disaffection of their ostensible allies.

CHARACTER AND SKILL IN CONTEXT

Presidential success, in summary, is determined at least as much by systemic factors as by presidential character, decision-making styles, or political skills. It is hard to make it to the presidency without a modicum of political competence. The stark variations lie in the political challenges presidents face in the office. These shift abruptly from one presidency to the next. If this analysis is correct, any evaluation of the importance of a president's personal attributes and skills in leadership must be rendered with great caution.

Take Bill Clinton. Setting Clinton's experience against that of other preemptive presidents recasts understanding of both the typical and extraordinary aspects of his leadership. Although the convulsive character of the Clinton administration stands out among recent presidencies, it fits a recurrent pattern of extraordinary volatility in pursuit of a third way. Independence is the watchword of preemptive leadership, and in exercising this independence preemptive leaders provoke intense political struggles in which their own personal codes of conduct take center stage. Other presidents may be judged incompetent or misguided; these presidents have been attacked as moral degenerates, congenitally incapable of rising above nihilism and manipulation.

When the attraction of "third-way politics" under Woodrow Wilson and Richard Nixon became evident, opponents labeled them "Shifty Tom" (Wilson's first name was Thomas) and "Tricky Dick." When the same became evident under Clinton, his opponents saddled him with the label "Slick Willy." These characterizations are all of a type—a political type, not a personality type. They are characteristic of the personalization of politics that occurs when an opposition leader seeks to preempt established conceptions of the political alternatives and to substitute a third way. Determined to sustain their contention that Clinton's "New Democratic Party" was really a ploy masking a rearguard defense of liberalism, Republicans deftly transposed the question of ideology into a question of character. Character flaws offered an explanation for Clinton's repeated forays onto conservative ground; they accounted for his use of the presidency to mask his party's true leanings and selectively incorporate his opponents' most attractive positions. As Clinton challenged received definitions of liberal and conservative, of Democrat and Republican, and of left, right, and center, opponents compiled evidence from his personal life to suggest that he really had no standards at all, that he was wholly lacking in principles. By casting Clinton as a man who never cared much for the truth, who had proven incapable of standing by any commitment, and who had no higher purpose than his own self-indulgence, opponents found a way to preserve the truth that they wished to promote—namely, that Democrats remained a desperate party of discredited ideas and debased leadership, while the Republicans remained the only legitimate exponents of national solutions.

Consider, too, the leadership of George W. Bush. As indicated, Bush came to power as an orthodox innovator; his political challenge was to redeem long-standing conservative commitments while at the same time updating the conservative agenda with politically attractive proposals addressed to the changing problems of the day. Plausible counterparts in other periods include James Monroe, James Polk, Theodore Roosevelt, and Lyndon Johnson. The pattern is clear. Each of these presidents moved forward aggressively with their updated versions of the orthodox agenda, and all of them ended up shattering the political foundations on which their accomplishments were to rest. Bush's leadership proved true to form. He advanced simultaneously on a variety of fronts—tax cuts, the turn to Iraq, deregulation, a new prescription drug benefit—and ultimately he left conservative government overextended, at cross-purposes, and tumbling into disarray. Before we dub these results a personal failure or a failure of political skill, we might want to think carefully about whether any president regardless of skill has solved the riddle of orthodox innovation.

Barack Obama came to power as an opposition leader at a time when long-standing commitments of ideology and interest had been exposed as failed and barren of new solutions to the problems of the day. Historically speaking, these have been the most auspicious of circumstances for political leadership in the American presidency. Certainly, Obama began his term better positioned politically than any president since Ronald Reagan, and like Reagan, Obama spoke of seizing the moment to change the nation's trajectory. But notwithstanding some extraordinary breakthroughs, an Obama reconstruction has failed to materialize.

On its face, this would seem to be an especially good case for the primacy of personality and individual skill. The deviation from type needs to be explained, and a large presidential persona is ready at hand to help. But was Obama too much of a policy wonk or too much of a crowd pleaser? Was he overly invested in bipartisanship or too much the partisan? Did he lack the common touch or was he all style? Did he intrude on congressional sensibilities or was he too aloof? Did he need to be more of a "people person" or did he need to take charge? Perhaps it was just that he was black. There are arguments on all sides.

Before we wade into this morass, we might want to reflect on just how much of a deviation this case really was, for it would appear on inspection that Obama pursued a reconstructive course rather intently. To observe that political reconstruction only occurs in certain circumstances is not to say that the circumstances facilitate a presidential cakewalk. On the contrary, as the apparatus of government becomes more complex and interdependent, we should expect that the challenge of reconstruction will become more imposing and that our reconstructive leaders will become more encumbered. Obama fought true to form to put the classic elements of a political transformation into play. He tried at every turn to cross the line between a momentary political preemption and a more decisive departure. Clinton was rebuffed on health care, and he backed away from economic regulation; Obama advanced on both fronts. The president pressed ahead even after his opponents broke his party's control of Congress in 2010. He did not blur the differences between their agenda and his, as Clinton so deftly did. Instead, he chose issues for his second term—immigration, gun control, climate change, gay rights—that would sharpen differences, consolidate a reliable majority, and stigmatize his opponents as being hopelessly out of touch with the true state of the nation. Recognizing the impediments to enacting legislation, the president played the long game, setting sights on a more systemic and durable change, one that might isolate the conservative establishment and eventually break its hold over the political commitments of the national government.

Obama left a nation hanging between preemption and reconstruction, making it nearly impossible to determine whose commitments were established and whose were vulnerable. The 2016 election campaign opened against that backdrop, with the political context indeterminate and the reconstruction up for grabs. The stakes were well understood by both sides, and at this writing, the leading characters approach pure types. There are Republicans and Democrats preaching radical reconstruction; and there are Republicans and Democrats pitching orthodox innovation. The former are frenzied in their repudiation of "the establishment"; the latter are struggling to defend prior affiliations. It remains to be seen who will bring clarity to this curious moment of confusion in political time.

CON: Fred I. Greenstein

The President is at liberty, both in law and conscience, to be as big a man as he can. His capacity will set the limit.

—Woodrow Wilson, 1908

From George Washington's decision to buy time for the new nation by signing the less-than-ideal Jay Treaty with Great Britain in 1795 to George W. Bush's order of a military intervention in Iraq in 2003, the matter of who happens to be president of the United States has often been of critical importance. The most telling illustration of the difference a White House occupant can make comes from the nuclear age. In October 1962, President John F. Kennedy learned that the Soviet Union had secretly installed in Cuba ballistic missiles that were capable of striking much of the United States. His advisers were split between those who favored using peaceful means to induce the Soviets to withdraw their missiles and those who called for an immediate air strike on the missile sites, an act that almost certainly would have triggered a nuclear war. If Kennedy had chosen a violent option, the result could have been catastrophic.

The impact of personal qualities on presidential job performance is a variable, not a constant. Some political contexts point so compellingly toward a particular course of action that virtually any president would react to them in the same manner. It is difficult to conceive of a White House incumbent who would not have responded militarily to the September 11, 2001, attacks on the World Trade Center and Pentagon. Other contexts leave wide latitude for personal attributes to have an effect. It was not preordained that Bush would order an invasion of Iraq. If Al Gore had been elected in 2000, it is unlikely that he would have taken that action.

Few time periods offer a better target of opportunity for studying the difference a president makes than the early republic. The first presidents served at a time when it was up to them to give meaning to the Constitution's sketchy description of their responsibilities. As a result, the conduct of the presidency was strongly influenced by the personal qualities of the incumbent chief executive. I begin by considering the first three presidents—George

Washington, John Adams, and Thomas Jefferson—and conclude by considering the sixth and seventh presidents—John Quincy Adams and Andrew Jackson.[4]

THE FOUNDATIONAL PRESIDENCY OF GEORGE WASHINGTON

George Washington had already been acclaimed throughout the British colonies for his exploits in the French and Indian War two decades before the United States declared its independence. Such was the esteem in which Washington was held that he was unanimously elected to high positions four times—commander in chief of the Continental Army in 1775, president of the convention that framed the Constitution in 1787, and for two terms as chief executive in 1789 and 1792.

Washington was acutely aware that his every presidential action was likely to establish a precedent. Shortly after his inauguration on April 30, 1789, he consulted with his associates on protocol and other matters. Pointing out that "many things which appear of little importance in themselves . . . may have great and durable consequences from their having been established at the commencement of a new general Government," he asked whether it would be "advantageous to the interests of the Union" for him to tour the states "in order to become acquainted with their principal Characters and internal Circumstances, as well as to be more accessible to numbers of well-informed persons, who might give him useful informations and advices on political subjects." He decided that he would do so.

In the late summer of 1789, Congress established the organs of the new government. But before then, there was a development that cast doubt on whether Washington or Vice President John Adams would be in charge of those bodies. In mid-June, Washington became ill from a large and painful growth that had developed on his thigh. He ran a high fever, and it was feared that he would die. He gradually recovered, however, and in October departed on a twenty-eight-day tour of New England. This and his later tour of the southern states helped impart his towering prestige to the new nation.

One of Washington's goals was to establish a sound financial system. Another was to resolve outstanding issues with Great Britain. His administration dealt with the nation's financial needs by guaranteeing payment of the interest on the national debt and establishing a national bank and system of taxation. It addressed relations with Britain by negotiating the Jay Treaty, which fostered trade between the two nations and provided for the arbitration of boundary disputes with Canada. There was an outpouring of opposition to the Jay Treaty, because it did not meet some of the American demands, but Washington's public esteem enabled him to carry the day.

In 1792 war erupted between revolutionary France and Great Britain. There was pressure from Federalists to support Britain and from Republicans to side with France. Washington refused to involve the fledgling nation in an overseas military conflict, however, and he issued a proclamation declaring the United States neutral. In 1794 residents of the Pennsylvania frontier refused to pay a federal tax on distilled spirits. Washington dispatched troops to put down the Whiskey Rebellion and personally led the first stage of the advance. The insurrection evaporated as the federal government demonstrated it had the power to enforce its laws.

No president made as much of a difference as Washington. No one else in the new nation had his capacity to legitimize the nation. It once was held that Washington was indispensable for who he was but not for what he did. It is now recognized that he was fully in charge of his presidency, although his influence was not always visible because he exercised it through intermediaries, such as Rep. James Madison and Secretary of the Treasury Alexander Hamilton. Without Washington as president, there might not be a United States of America today.

JOHN ADAMS: ABSENTEE PRESIDENT

It would be difficult to imagine two more different presidents than George Washington and John Adams. Washington radiated authority, even in his commanding appearance. Adams was unimposing. He was short, pudgy, and susceptible to seemingly unprovoked rages. Adams has been called "self-righteous," "irritable," and "contentious." Benjamin Franklin described him as "always an honest man, often a wise one, but sometimes, and in some things, absolutely out of his senses."

John Adams was one of the nation's most politically inept presidents. One of his errors was retaining the cabinet he inherited from Washington; he was seemingly unaware that three of its members were secretly taking signals from his political enemy, Alexander Hamilton. Another was removing himself from the capital for extended periods. Adams spent more than one-third of his presidency at his home in Massachusetts or on his way to or from it. His absences from the capital made it necessary for members of his cabinet to go their own ways, which they sometimes did, often in different directions.

The overriding concern of the Adams presidency was an undeclared naval war between the United States and France, which was an offshoot of the larger war between France and Great Britain. At the time Adams took office, the

French had begun seizing U.S. ships to prevent them from supplying Britain. Adams asked Congress to vote funds for a military buildup, but he also dispatched a peace delegation to France. In March 1798, the delegation reported that France had refused to receive it. Moreover, the delegation had been approached by French agents who requested a bribe to arrange a meeting with the French foreign minister, a demand the outraged Americans rejected. Adams forwarded the report to Congress, substituting the letters *XYZ* for the names of the French agents.

The XYZ Affair triggered an outpouring of patriotic indignation. Adams was showered with messages of public support to which he replied with such assertions as "Providence may intend [war] for our good, and we must submit. That is a less evil than national dishonor." His rhetoric led many to conclude that he was preparing the nation for war. Early in 1799 Adams stunned the political community by announcing without prior warning that he intended to resume peace negotiations with France. Adams then departed for a seven-month stay in Massachusetts. On his return, he dispatched a peace mission to France, and in September 1800 the mission reached an agreement with the French that ended the conflict. Before word crossed the Atlantic, Adams had been defeated for reelection by Thomas Jefferson.

The stubbornly impolitic John Adams provides an example of an incumbent who was psychologically ill suited for the presidency. Adams's presidential performance suffered from a contentiousness that made him difficult to work with, a failure to control his cabinet, and a propensity to remove himself from the seat of government. He was the first, but far from the last, chief executive whose cognitive strengths were undermined by his emotional weaknesses.

By the time Adams became president, the new American nation was solidly institutionalized. That would not have been the case if the illness that afflicted Washington in his second month as president had been fatal and Adams had succeeded him in the early months of the new political system. If that had occurred, it is uncertain whether the United States would have survived.

THOMAS JEFFERSON AND THE ART OF GOVERNANCE

Thomas Jefferson was a complex and contradictory figure. He was an advocate of economy who spent lavishly on personal luxuries. He also was an eloquent spokesman for the equality of man but owned many slaves. And as secretary of state in the Washington administration, he subsidized an anti-administration newspaper but denied it. Jefferson also was an inventor, architect, Enlightenment thinker, and republican theorist. One might expect to find little in the way of political skill on the part of a chief executive who was steeped in the life of the mind, but Jefferson was a gifted politician, especially under the favorable circumstances of his first term.

In contrast to Adams, Jefferson appointed a loyal, well-qualified cabinet. He was also an able practitioner of personal politics, who entertained members of Congress at small dinners where he plied them with fine wine and food and urbane conversation to win them over. Jefferson's political skill helped him bridge the separation of powers. His public stance was that he did not involve himself in the business of the legislative branch, but he exercised great behind-the-scenes influence on Capitol Hill, even drafting bills and arranging for members of Congress to introduce them but telling them not to reveal that he was their author.

Jefferson's political skills enabled his administration to achieve an ambitious first-term agenda that included eliminating domestic taxes and reducing the federal debt and the size of the armed forces. Jefferson's crowning achievement was buying the huge Louisiana Territory from France, an acquisition that doubled the size of the nation. Because he believed in a strict construction of the Constitution, Jefferson considered calling for a constitutional amendment to authorize such a purchase. But when it became evident that Napoleon's offer might not wait, he dismissed his ideological scruples as "metaphysical subtleties" and signed off on the politically popular purchase.

Jefferson's second term was vastly different from his triumphant first term. After an interlude of peace, war broke out again between Britain and France. Each of the great powers sought to prevent the United States from supplying the other. In addition, the British boarded U.S. ships to remove alleged deserters from the Royal Navy and force them back into service. This practice rankled Americans, but the British viewed it as necessary to prevent a hemorrhage of trained seamen in a time of war.

Jefferson's republican ideology, which had led him to reduce the size of the armed forces, also led him to oppose war as an instrument of statecraft. As a result, he responded to the attacks on American shipping by instituting the embargo of 1807, which confined American vessels to port. Jefferson was convinced that if Britain were denied trade with the United States, it would alter its policies. The main effect of the embargo, however, was to damage the U.S. economy, especially in areas that relied on trade. Although the embargo was politically costly for Jefferson, he persisted in it, enforcing it with repressive measures that were inconsistent with his values.

Entire books have been written on Jefferson's enigmatic personality. This much is certain: he was a gifted political pragmatist *when he chose to be.* But he had a darker and less pliable side. Jefferson's flexibility was evident when he put aside his constitutional scruples in order to acquire the Louisiana Territory. The other side of his psyche manifested itself in his rigid adherence to a counterproductive embargo. His political skill made his first-term successes possible, and his ideological blinders contributed to his second-term failures.

THE POLITICAL INCOMPETENCE OF JOHN QUINCY ADAMS

John Quincy Adams's public service began at age fourteen, when he served as an aide to the American minister in Russia. It ended at age eighty, when he died after suffering a stroke on the floor of Congress. During the course of his career, Adams was minister to the Netherlands, Prussia, Russia, and Great Britain; helped negotiate the end of the War of 1812; was secretary of state; and capped his career with seventeen years of post-presidential service in the House of Representatives. Adams has been widely praised for his courage in advancing unpopular views as a member of Congress and for his effectiveness as a diplomat, but he was one of the least effective presidents in U.S. history.

Adams brought many of his presidential difficulties upon himself. He became chief executive in 1824 after running second to Andrew Jackson in an election that had to be resolved in the House of Representatives, because none of its four candidates had a majority of the electoral vote. The necessary votes to make him the winner were supplied by Speaker of the House Henry Clay. Adams then took the politically disastrous action of naming Clay as his secretary of state. Jackson charged that there had been a "corrupt bargain" with Adams, firing the opening salvo in the next presidential campaign. From then on, Jackson's supporters did what they could to deny Adams a record of accomplishment.

In his first message to Congress, Adams proposed an array of policy departures that would have been visionary for a landslide winner, never mind a minority president who had finished a distant second in the popular vote. Included was a program of public improvements; a national bankruptcy law; and the establishment of a department of the interior, a national university, and an astronomical observatory. Adams's ambitious program might have been taken seriously a century later in the period of positive government, but it was widely held in his time that the best government is the least government.

Adams's program was met with a mixture of indifference and opposition. A politically able president might have moderated his proposals, established priorities, and set about building support for the measures he deemed most important. It was not in Adams's character, however, to make such adjustments. In 1826 Jackson's supporters won control of Congress. In 1828 Adams's opponents compounded his difficulties by enacting a prohibitively high tariff. Adams was aware that the measure would embarrass him politically, but he signed it on the principle that the veto should only be used to strike down legislation on constitutional grounds. Adams was also handicapped by his refusal to cultivate political support and to discharge members of his administration who were working against him.

John Quincy Adams resembled his father in being ill suited for leadership in a democracy. But he differed from the senior Adams in that he was marked by rigidity rather than passivity. The younger Adams was an archetypical political purist who lacked the capacity to bend to political realities and do what was called for to get results.

ANDREW JACKSON: FORCE OF NATURE

Andrew Jackson was a barely educated frontier general who nevertheless succeeded in redefining the role of the chief executive. Jackson established a precedent for conceiving of the presidency as a policy-making institution rather than an office principally responsible for carrying out the will of Congress. He also anticipated the modern practice of making extensive use of advisers and aides. And he transformed the veto from a rarely used instrument for negating unconstitutional measures to a means of influencing public policy, vetoing more bills than his predecessors combined.

The defining episodes of Jackson's presidency were the nullification crisis and the bank war. The nullification crisis was triggered by the claim of southerners that states have the right to declare federal laws null and void within their boundaries. In 1832 a South Carolina convention voted to invalidate a pair of tariffs that had an adverse economic effect on the South and to secede from the Union rather than allow them to be enforced in the state. Jackson responded with a combination of threat and conciliation. He signed a bill that authorized him to use military power to enforce the collection of tariffs, but he also assented to a measure that provided for tariff reduction. South Carolina repealed its nullification of the tariffs.

The Bank of the United States was originally created as part of the financial reforms of the Washington administration. Jackson's confrontation with it was slow in developing, but by its conclusion the United States no longer had a central banking system and would not have one until the passage of the Federal Reserve Act in 1913. Jackson had a frontiersman's distrust of banks and credit.

In January 1832, the bank's strong-willed president, Nicholas Biddle, requested that its charter be renewed even though it had four more years to run. Biddle and his congressional allies reasoned that Jackson would not dare attack a perceived pillar of the economy in an election year.

Congress granted Biddle's request, but Jackson vetoed the action, denouncing the bank in a blistering veto message. His veto was sustained. Jackson then withdrew the government's funds from the Bank of the United States, which went bankrupt before long. Jackson once declared that the bank was trying to kill him, but that he would kill it. In doing so, he destroyed an institution that in the view of many economic historians played a constructive part in stabilizing the economy.

Like George Washington, Andrew Jackson brought exceptional force of character to the conduct of the presidency, although he often lacked our first president's sense of political prudence. He fought a war against the national bank that many of his close advisers had counseled against as being far too risky. Had a Democrat like Martin Van Buren been in office, there almost certainly would have been no bank war. Jackson's uncompromising stance against nullification played better with the New England opposition than it did with his own Democratic constituency, but Jackson persevered nonetheless.

Throughout his presidency, Old Hickory plunged without hesitation into the political fray, foreshadowing the presidencies of the twentieth and twenty-first centuries in which the chief executive is the central political actor in the nation.

THE PRESIDENTIAL DIFFERENCE

The American presidency has been described as a chameleon that takes its color from the personality of the president. The observation is particularly apt for the presidency in its infancy, when incumbents were painting on a largely empty canvas. Faced with the ambiguities of the Constitution, these men imposed their personal proclivities on their jobs.

Some of the early presidents—most notably Washington, Jefferson, and Jackson—had personal qualities that were conducive to placing their stamp on the nation's policies and politics. Others—especially John Adams and John Quincy Adams—were ill suited for the demands of presidential leadership. Presidential success and failure have many causes, but among the most important are the skills, judgment, temperament, and other personal qualities the chief executive brings to the office.

NOTES

INTRO

1. James David Barber, *The Presidential Character: Predicting Performance in the White House* (Englewood Cliffs, NJ: Prentice-Hall, 1972).
2. Stephen Skowronek, *The Politics Presidents Make: Leadership from John Adams to George Bush* (Cambridge, MA: Belknap Harvard Press, 1993).
3. Fred I. Greenstein, *The Presidential Difference: Leadership Style from FDR to Barack Obama,* 3rd ed. (Princeton, NJ: Princeton University Press, 2009).

CON

4. For more elaboration, see Fred I. Greenstein, *Inventing the Job of President: Leadership Style from George Washington to Andrew Jackson* (Princeton, NJ: Princeton University Press, 2009).

RESOLVED, Presidential power is (still) the power to persuade

PRO: Matthew J. Dickinson

CON: George C. Edwards III

The first sentence of Article II of the Constitution says, "The executive Power shall be vested in a President of the United States of America." Sounds impressive, doesn't it? In 1793 Secretary of the Treasury Alexander Hamilton made it sound even more so when he waged a newspaper debate with Rep. James Madison of Virginia about whether President George Washington had the power to declare that the United States would remain neutral in the war between Great Britain and France. Hamilton argued that "the executive Power" extended beyond the list of enumerated powers spelled out in the Constitution, such as the power to veto legislation and nominate federal judges.

The idea that the presidency is an office of great power gained momentum at the outset of the twentieth century, during the Progressive Era. Watching President Theodore Roosevelt wield influence persuaded political scientist and Princeton University president Woodrow Wilson that "The President is at liberty, both in law and conscience, to be as big a man as he can. His capacity will set the limit." Roosevelt agreed. Writing to a British friend in 1908, the last year of his presidency, Roosevelt suggested that "there inheres in the presidency more power than in any other office in any great republic or constitutional monarchy of modern times." For progressives such as Wilson and Roosevelt the president's unrivaled power was rooted not only in the formal powers of Article II but in the president's ability to rally the people and thereby compel Congress to do his (and the people's) bidding.

During the next half century, presidential power seemed to grow in leaps and bounds along with the growth of the federal government. By 1960, in the midst of the Cold War, some scholars celebrated presidential power and others lamented it, but few of them doubted the premise that the office is powerful. When Richard E. Neustadt published a book that year called *Presidential Power,* most people assumed that it would be another work chronicling the puissance of the presidency. They were in for a surprise.

When Neustadt, who worked for seven years in the Truman administration, started teaching at Columbia University in 1954, he discovered that scholarship on the presidency "seemed to be very remote from what I had experienced." One reason he wrote *Presidential Power* was "to fill the gap between the academic literature that existed in the middle '50s on the presidency and my experience of it."

Neustadt argued that far from being a powerful office, the presidency is essentially an empty vessel—a glorified "clerkship" that at any given moment takes the shape of the person who fills it. Whether it is filled ineptly or skillfully was, for him, the vital question. What marked successful modern (that is, post–Franklin D. Roosevelt) presidents was their understanding that "presidential power is the power to persuade," not command. Appeals to reason, to duty, or to loyalty were not what Neustadt meant by persuasion. Instead, he wrote, "the power to persuade is the power to bargain"—to trade favors or the promise of favors—so that other powerful Washington figures become convinced that "*what he wants of them is what their own appraisal of their own responsibilities requires them to do in their own interest, not his.*" The italics were Neustadt's—he really meant it.

Matthew J. Dickinson maintains that "presidential power is (still) the power to persuade" because the constitutional system of "separated institutions sharing powers" has not changed. Presidents still have to bargain with members of Congress in order to persuade them to align their votes with presidential intentions. George C. Edwards III argues that neither Congress nor the American people are open to persuasion in great numbers and that real presidential leadership consists of riding the tide of "opportunities already present in their environments."

PRO: Matthew J. Dickinson

"Presidential power," political scientist Richard Neustadt proclaimed in his classic eponymous work, "is the power to persuade." That statement remains as true today as when Neustadt first made it more than half a century ago, and for a simple reason: presidents continue to operate in what Neustadt famously describes as a constitutionally based "government of separated institutions *sharing* power." Because the sharing of powers across institutions creates relationships of "mutual dependence" between the president and other governmental actors, a president's effective influence is primarily derived from persuasion and not command. In Neustadt's words, "Their vantage points confront his own; their power tempers his."[1] Barring a substantial alteration to this system of shared powers, persuasion is likely to remain at the core of presidential power for the foreseeable future.

By "persuasion," however, Neustadt does not mean that presidents rely on "charm or reasoned argument" to convince others to adopt his or her point of view. With rare exceptions, presidential power is *not* the power to change minds. Instead, presidents must induce others "to believe that what he wants of them is what their own appraisal of their own responsibilities requires them to do in their interests, not his." That process of persuasion, Neustadt suggests, "is bound to be more like collective bargaining than like a reasoned argument among philosopher kings." In short, "the power to persuade is the power to bargain."[2]

Neustadt's definition of persuasion as bargaining rather than opinion change is an important and sometimes overlooked distinction.[3] Presidents are not powerful philosopher kings or queens who attract support through the strength of reasoned argument. Instead, their influence depends on enlisting the backing of actors who rarely share the president's bargaining vantage point. Thus, no matter how "logical [the president's] argument according to his lights, their judgment may not bring them to his view."[4] As a result, Neustadt concludes, presidents are not very powerful—an assessment that remains unchanged through five editions (1960, 1968, 1976, 1980, 1990) of his classic work.

PRESIDENTIAL POWER REVISITED

Although Neustadt updated *Presidential Power* to account for new research findings and real-world developments, he remained focused throughout each new edition on answering the central question that prompted him to write his classic work in the first place: How does a president gain and retain power? The answer, Neustadt advises, is to think prospectively. Presidents must continually ask how their choices today influence their sources of power down the road. By power, Neustadt means nothing more than a president's effective influence on government's processes and outcomes. That influence, Neustadt writes in an oft-quoted passage, is largely predicated on three related factors:

> [F]irst are the bargaining advantages inherent in his job with which to persuade other men that what he wants of them is what their own responsibilities require them to do. Second are the expectations of those

other men regarding his ability and will to use the various advantages
they think he has. Third are those men's estimates of how his public
views him and of how their publics may view them if they do what he
wants. In short, his power is the product of his vantage points in government, together with his reputation in the Washington community and
his prestige outside.[5]

In making this argument, Neustadt draws a critical and often overlooked
distinction between presidents' formal "powers" and their power.[6] Powers refer
to the constitutional, statutory, and traditional authority designated to the
president. These are the primary (but not exclusive) source of a president's
"vantage points" from which to bargain. In a system of shared powers, other
institutions and actors must cultivate presidential support in order to fulfill
their own responsibilities.[7] Formal powers, however, do not translate fully into
power—effective influence—because the president's bargaining audiences
view their exercise from dissimilar vantage points; they are separated institutions, responding to different constituencies and with different time frames
and operating incentives.[8]

If formal powers are no guarantee of bargaining success, they do ensure that
presidents will be locked into mutually dependent relations with other
"Washingtonians" (defined by interest in the president's action, not geography)—that they will at least be clerks, if not leaders. Of course, this dependence
yields advantages to the president. But to capitalize on these advantages, presidents must convert their provision of clerkship services for others into the
means through which they might obtain their own goals. Presidents' ability to
do so, however, depends in part on how well they cultivate two additional
sources of influence: their professional reputation and their public prestige.

By professional reputation, Neustadt means a president's "skill and will . . . to
use his advantages." Simply put, presidents develop a reputation through time for
the effectiveness (or lack thereof) with which they employ the powers of their
office to achieve desired ends. Presidents determine this reputation largely
through their own presidential actions, with first impressions weighted more
heavily than subsequent ones. Indeed, a president's reputation is not infinitely
pliable; once fixed in the minds of Washingtonians, it thereafter becomes difficult
(but not impossible) to change. Because Washingtonians use presidents' reputation to anticipate their likely behavior in the bargaining process, it becomes a
potential source of leverage. As Neustadt writes, "What other men expect of him
becomes a cardinal factor in the president's own power to persuade."[9]

A president's public prestige—his or her standing with Washingtonians'
various publics—provides a third source of influence. But prestige does not

refer to a president's overall public support as measured, for example, by monthly Gallup Polls. Rather, it signifies the president's standing in the "aggregate of the publics as diverse and overlapping as the claims Americans . . . press on Washington."[10] As such, prestige takes a subtler and more variable form, one not easily captured by opinion polling. It often changes depending on the bargaining audience and topic, and the "quality" of that prestige is as important, if not more so, than its quantity. That is, judgments regarding a president's prestige assess what he or she is liked for as well as how many people like him or her. Moreover, Neustadt suggests that prestige operates mostly in the political background, providing "leeway" regarding what a president might accomplish rather than directly determining bargaining outcomes.

As with reputation, presidents can influence their prestige, but in a much more limited manner. This is because prestige varies according to the public's changing conceptions of what they want from the presidency as an office, and those conceptions are based predominantly on events happening to them, in their lives. Presidents are rarely positioned to control these events; at best, they might interpret them in ways that redound to their bargaining advantage. This "teaching" is often more effectively accomplished by action rather than talk. But even then, a president's influence is limited by the public's willingness to listen and by the president's previous actions in that area, particularly if those actions contradict the lesson he or she is trying to teach.

Neustadt fine-tuned his analysis in subsequent editions of *Presidential Power* to address new political developments.[11] However, his central argument does not change from the first edition to the last: "Presidential weakness . . . remains my theme. It runs through the eight original chapters . . . and through five later ones that are meant to supplement, bring up to date, revise and reconsider, as befits a new edition. The doing has not brought a change of theme." Why is presidential weakness Neustadt's constant refrain? Because of the constitutionally mandated system of many separated institutions sharing powers. "To share is to limit; that is the heart of the matter, and everything this book explores stems from it."[12]

ASSESSING THE BARGAINING MODEL OF PRESIDENTIAL POWER

The core argument in *Presidential Power* is now more than half a century old, but it has aged well.[13] Indeed, despite the visible intellectual soul searching by a few presidency scholars regarding Neustadt's allegedly stultifying influence on the state of presidency research, his insights have stimulated some of the subfield's most significant and enduring research agendas.[14] For the most part, this research has largely substantiated Neustadt's claim of presidential weakness.[15] This is not to say, however, that his theory of power as persuasion is universally accepted. While space constraints prevent a full review of all the objections to his bargaining model, I examine five of the most commonly cited ones here.

One of the most pervasive critiques is that Neustadt's "personal" approach to studying the presidency, in which power appears contingent on the attributes of individual presidents, understates the growing role played by institutions and formal processes in the exercise of presidential power.[16] At the same time, a theory based on the personal characteristics of individual presidents is not likely to generate cumulative and generalizable findings. For this reason, rational choice scholars in particular have been critical of Neustadt's theory of presidential power.

However, these critiques reflect a misunderstanding of Neustadt's over-the-president's-shoulder analytic perspective. Although Neustadt discusses differences in presidents' sensitivity to their power prospects, *Presidential Power* is decidedly not a study of individual presidents. His generic advice regarding how to gain and retain power applies to all presidents, regardless of personality "type." This makes Neustadt's model entirely compatible with—indeed, it anticipates—rational choice approaches to studying the presidency.[17]

Similarly, although Neustadt writes from the president's vantage point, his is not a president-centered model of power. Instead, he recognizes that presidents' influence is conditioned by their having to operate in a system of shared powers, and that their behavior is increasingly affected by the institutionalization of specialized staff operating under organizational rules and processes.[18] However, Neustadt is less sanguine than others regarding whether the institutionalization of staff support make presidents more powerful. Presidential advisers, he cautions, are frequently "holier than the Pope"; they zealously serve the president without always fully comprehending the president's true bargaining interests. The combination of well-intentioned loyalty and the lack of a shared perspective can have disastrous consequences, as Neustadt illustrates through his discussion of the Reagan administration's Iran-Contra affair.[19]

This divergence in the bargaining perspectives of presidents and executive branch officials is the reason Neustadt took issue with a second major critique of his model: the notion that presidents can utilize administrative means, such as national security directives, executive orders, proclamations, and other "unilateral" instruments, to achieve policy objectives not through bargaining but with "the stroke of a pen."[20] Such administrative strategies, his critics suggest, are facilitated by appointing loyalists to senior positions in the executive branch, in addition to institutionalizing a large, White House–centered staff. Political appointees' loyalty to the president and sense of duty to the highest office in the land make them particularly responsive to these presidential commands.[21] The result is that Neustadt underestimates the president's formal powers, particularly in areas like foreign affairs where presidents' command authority seems greater than he acknowledges.[22]

It is true that presidents may gain advantages in speed and efficiency by using unilateral means, such as executive orders, to achieve policy objectives. However, these actions often lack durability because they are susceptible to reversal by subsequent presidents who may have different policy preferences.[23] Moreover, efforts by presidents to bypass other political institutions, particularly members of Congress, in the policy-making process often stimulate increased opposition to a president's subsequent bargaining efforts.

For all these reasons, Neustadt spends much of *Presidential Power* exposing the limits of presidents' efforts to exercise power without persuasion, even in foreign affairs. In his oft-cited reference regarding Harry S. Truman's warning to Dwight D. Eisenhower—"he'll say, 'Do this! Do that! And nothing will happen! Poor Ike . . .'"—Neustadt reminds readers that issuing commands is no guarantee of compliance by members of the executive branch. Indeed, he explicitly warns scholars not to succumb to "the illusion that administrative agencies comprise a single structure, 'the' executive branch, where presidential word is law. . . . Like our governmental structure as a whole, the executive establishment consists of separated institutions sharing powers," and thus is not impervious to the bargaining that characterizes politics elsewhere.[24] This applies both to the development of administrative directives as well as their implementation.

It thus would not surprise Neustadt that numerous case studies of "unilateral" action, from Roosevelt's decision to intern Japanese Americans during World War II[25] to Ronald Reagan's fight within his own administration to curtail federal spending[26] to Bill Clinton's failed 1993 effort to issue an executive order ending the ban on gays serving openly in the military, illustrate that policymaking via administrative action is often no less subject to bargaining and compromise than is policymaking through the legislative process.[27] The shift from legislative to administrative policymaking is not necessarily a shift between a "multilateral" to a "unilateral" process. Instead, it can be a shift in where and with whom presidents bargain. And even when presidents do appear to achieve a policy objective through administrative means, it may come at a substantial long-term cost in political influence.

There is a third major critique of Neustadt's theory: the claim by some scholars that "going public" has supplanted bargaining as the preferred mode of presidential influence because of what Samuel Kernell describes as a shift, beginning in the 1970s, from a political system of "institutionalized" pluralism composed of relatively durable coalitions of political elites to one of "individu-alized pluralism" constructed from more ephemeral and ideological-based coalitions of political activists. In this new political context, goes the argument, presidents increasingly favor communication strategies designed to enlarge and mobilize public support in lieu of inside-the-beltway bargaining. By bol-stering their public approval, presidents can use it as a resource to pressure Washingtonians to accede to their wishes.[28] According to Kernell, "the sensitiv-ity of self-reliant politicians to public opinion is their vulnerability and the key to [the president's] influence."[29]

Neustadt was not oblivious to the impact of the evolving relationship between presidents and the public on a president's power. In later editions of *Presidential Power*, he addressed this development, citing in particular how it made changes to presidents' prestige matter more to their professional reputa-tion, and vice versa.[30] But he rejected the idea that "going public" served as a growing alternative to bargaining or that the two strategies for securing influ-ence were as incompatible as Kernell suggested. Instead, Neustadt insisted that "public appeals are part of bargaining, albeit a changing part since prestige bulks far larger than before in reputation."[31]

One reason Neustadt doubted the efficacy of going public as an alternative to bargaining is that presidents cannot readily influence the events that deter-mine their popularity.[32] Neustadt's contention is supported by studies showing that approval ratings are largely governed by factors such as the state of the economy and whether the nation is at war, as mediated through individuals' partisan attachments and their degree of attentiveness to public events and as reported by the media.[33] Moreover, a president's efforts to "go public" must compete with alternative messages pushed by other political actors.[34] The situ-ation was further complicated in recent years by the balkanization of the media market through cable, the Internet, and social media, which has made presi-dential efforts to command a broad audience increasingly problematic. Rather than a single "public," there exists instead many smaller "publics" composed of viewers who select their preferred media outlet based in part on its perceived compatibility with their ideological leanings. As a result, presidents increas-ingly focus their media efforts on "narrowcasting" designed to mobilize select partisans rather than reaching out to presumably persuadable moderates, to say nothing of those in the opposing political camp.[35] The upshot, according to George Edwards, is that presidents' public appeals rarely move public opin-ion. Instead, using words that Neustadt might have written in 1960, Edwards advocates "staying private"—conducting "quiet negotiations" behind the scenes with interested parties.[36]

A fourth critique is that Neustadt's argument is dated. *Presidential Power,* of course, was first published in 1960, during a period Neustadt characterized as "emergencies in policies with politics as usual" and based largely on case studies of three presidents.[37] In an important work, Stephen Skowronek suggests this makes Neustadt's bargaining model of limited historical applicability. This is partly because Neustadt creates an artificial distinction between modern and premodern presidents.[38] In fact, Skowronek argues, the leadership dilemmas confronted by presidents that Neustadt classifies as modern are often quite similar to those faced by presidents serving in the premodern era. At the same time, Neustadt mistakenly assumes that the modern presidents confront similar operational problems. In truth, Skowronek claims, they often preside during quite different periods of "political" (as opposed to "secular") time, as judged by an existing political regime's resiliency and whether the president is affiliated with that regime.[39] Effective presidents, Skowronek believes, are those who understand the opportunities and constraints associated with their place in political time and act accordingly, often by trying to reshape the system they have inherited.

Upon closer inspection, however, one finds more overlap between the two leadership models than Skowronek acknowledges. Indeed, the apparent disagreement between the two regarding the substance of presidential influence may be largely because of their adopting different levels of analysis.[40] As a scholar surveying the sweep of presidential history, Skowronek looks more broadly at presidents' efforts to place themselves in political time and judges their effectiveness as presidents accordingly. Neustadt, standing behind presidents and looking over their shoulder, tries to understand how presidents might "make politics" on a strategic level, regardless of whether they are working to strengthen or to replace the existing regime. Indeed, Skowronek's wider focus on a president's place in history offers precious little in the way of concrete advice regarding how to turn an understanding of time and place into effective influence.[41] Instead, grasping the transformational possibilities that Skowronek suggests inhere in the presidency seems to depend on the skillful harnessing of the power sources specified by Neustadt.[42]

A final critique of the Neustadt model is that it is too instrumentalist; Neustadt counsels presidents on how to husband their power but provides few ethical guidelines for its exercise.[43] For Neustadt, the pursuit of power by a president serves objectives "far beyond his own"; it "contributes to the energy of government and to the viability of public policy."[44] However, in the foreword to the final edition, he acknowledges that he might have been too optimistic in his assumption that those who use his book as a governing manual would be "mostly experienced in government," and would possess the understanding of history to realize that presidents' power is supposed to be shared and that getting what they want is supposed to be hard. Nonetheless, Neustadt reiterated his belief that the "pursuit of presidential power . . . constitutionally conditioned, looking ahead, serves purposes far broader than a president's satisfaction. It is good for the country."[45]

CONCLUSION

Contrary to the expectations of some scholars, more than five decades of research have not relegated *Presidential Power* to the bookshelf of "classic period pieces."[46] Instead, as the editors of a volume assessing the state of presidency research at the turn of the century acknowledged, "Political scientists still consider *Presidential Power* as the seminal book on the American Presidency—the one that still influences not only their thinking and research about presidential power but also that of presidents and their advisers who have come to learn directly or indirectly about Neustadt's advice."[47] That assessment, I claim, holds true today.

Why does Neustadt's bargaining model retain its relevance? Why does it continue to serve as a major intellectual foil for presidency scholars? Because it is derived from the constitutional framework established by the framers more than two centuries ago. Presidents operate in a system of separated institutions sharing power, and therefore they must bargain to exercise influence. By focusing on the search for power, Neustadt's analysis cuts to the heart of what it means to be president in the American political system. The significance of that quest and the care with which Neustadt elucidates a strategy for achieving it makes *Presidential Power* a foundational work in the presidency subfield. In Chuck Jones's assessment, "No one had written a book like it then. No one has since."[48] Barring fundamental change to the Constitution and the authority structures that are derived from it, the persuasion-as-bargaining model will likely remain the key to understanding presidential leadership for some time to come.[49]

CON: George C. Edwards III

Persuasion refers to causing others to do something by reasoning, urging, or inducement. Influencing others is central to the conception of leadership of most political scientists. Scholars of the presidency want to know whether the chief executive can affect the output of government by influencing the actions and attitudes of others. In a democracy, we are particularly attuned to efforts to persuade, especially when most potentially significant policy changes require the assent of multiple power holders.

RICHARD NEUSTADT AND THE POWER TO PERSUADE

Perhaps the best-known dictum regarding the American presidency is that "presidential power is the power to persuade."[50] It is the wonderfully felicitous phrase that captures the essence of Richard Neustadt's argument in *Presidential Power*. For nearly three generations, scholars, students, and presidents have viewed the presidency through the lens of Neustadt's core premise.

Neustadt argued that the American political system is not a fertile field for the exercise of presidential leadership. Most political actors, from the average citizen to members of Congress, are free to choose whether to follow the chief executive's lead; the president cannot force them to act. At the same time, the sharing of powers established by the Constitution's checks and balances prevents the president from acting unilaterally on most important matters and gives other power holders different perspectives on issues and policy proposals. Thus the political system compels presidents to attempt to lead while inhibiting their ability to do so. They have to rely on persuasion.

Neustadt began with the premise that presidents would have to struggle to get their way. As he put it, "The power to persuade is the power to bargain."[51] Indeed, it was the inherent weakness of the presidency that made it necessary for presidents to understand how to use their resources most effectively. Not everyone has such a restrained view of leadership, however, and few are blessed with Neustadt's penetrating and nuanced understanding of the presidency. Many observers accepted the premise that presidents *could succeed* in persuading others. The view that presidents not only need to persuade but that they also can succeed at it has led scholars and other observers of the presidency to focus on the question of *how* presidents persuade rather than the more fundamental question of *whether they can do so*. As a result, for example, many scholars and other commentators on the presidency have fallen prey to an exaggerated concept of the potential for using the "bully pulpit" to go public. We should not *assume* the power to persuade.

The issue is *not* whether major policy changes that presidents desire occur. They do. The fundamental question is whether presidents have the potential to create opportunities for change by persuading others to follow them.

DO PRESIDENTS PERSUADE?

The tenacity with which many commentators embrace the persuasive potential of political leadership is striking. They routinely explain historic shifts in public policy, such as those in the 1930s, 1960s, and 1980s, in terms of the extraordinary persuasiveness of Franklin D. Roosevelt, Lyndon Johnson, and Ronald Reagan. Equally striking is the lack of evidence of the persuasive power of the presidency. Observers in both the press and the academy base their claims about the impact of such leadership on little or no systematic evidence. There is not a single systematic study that demonstrates that presidents can reliably move others to support them.

Leading the Public

Presidents invest heavily in leading the public in the hope of leveraging public support to win backing in Congress. Nevertheless, there is overwhelming evidence that presidents rarely move the public in their direction. Most observers view Ronald Reagan and Bill Clinton as excellent communicators. Nevertheless, pluralities and often majorities of the public opposed them on most of their policy initiatives. Moreover, public opinion typically moved away from rather than toward the positions they favored.[52]

Despite the favorable context of the national trauma resulting from the September 11 terrorist attacks, the long-term disdain of the public for Saddam Hussein, and the lack of organized opposition, George W. Bush made little headway in moving the public to support the war in Iraq, and once the war was over, the rally resulting from the quick U.S. victory quickly dissipated.[53] Despite his eloquence, Barack Obama could not obtain the public's support for his initiatives that were not already popular. For example, his health care reform lacked majority support even five years after it passed.[54]

Even Franklin D. Roosevelt, the president often viewed as the greatest politician of the twentieth century, faced constant frustration in his efforts to move the public to prepare for entry into World War II, and his failure to persuade the public regarding his plan to pack the Supreme Court effectively marked the end of the New Deal.[55] George Washington, who was better positioned than any of his successors to dominate American politics because of the widespread view of his possessing exceptional personal qualities, did not find the public particularly deferential.[56]

Presidents find it difficult to focus the public's attention on a policy because the White House must deal with so many issues and faces competition in agenda setting from Congress and the media. In addition, the White House finds it increasingly difficult to obtain an audience for its views—or even airtime on television to express them. Moreover, many people who do pay attention miss the president's points. Because the president rarely speaks directly to the American people as a whole, the White House is dependent on the press to transmit its messages, but the media are unlikely to adopt consistently either the White House's priorities or its framing of issues. Moreover, committed, well-organized, and well-funded opponents offer competing frames.

Predispositions

Presidents must overcome the public's predispositions if they are to change people's minds about their policies or their performance. However, most people seek out information confirming their preexisting opinions and ignore or reject arguments contrary to their predispositions. When exposed to competing arguments, they typically accept the confirming ones and dismiss or argue against the opposing ones.[57] Similarly, presidents are likely to be more credible to those predisposed to support them than to adherents of the opposition party.[58]

Partisan leanings significantly influence perceptions of and interpretations and responses to politics—and contribute to misperceptions. Even the most basic facts are often in contention between adherents of the parties, such as whether inflation, tax rates, or the budget deficit had risen or fallen or whether there were weapons of mass destruction in Iraq.[59] Partisan bias and the misperceptions it causes are often most prevalent among those who are generally well informed about politics. Political knowledge neither corrects nor mitigates partisan bias in perception of objective conditions. Instead, it enhances it.

Those who pay close attention to politics and policy are likely to have well-developed views and thus be less susceptible to persuasion. Better-informed citizens possess the information and sophistication necessary to identify the implications of presidential messages and reject communications inconsistent with their values. They are best able to construct counterarguments to evidence that they are emotionally inclined to resist. In the typical situation of competing views offered by elites, reinforcement and polarization of views are more likely than conversion among attentive citizens.[60]

Those with less interest and knowledge cannot resist presidential arguments if they do not possess information about the implications of those arguments for their values, interests, and other predispositions. However, these people are also less likely to be aware of the president's messages. To the extent that they do receive the messages, they will also hear from the opposition how the president's views are inconsistent with their predispositions. In addition, even if their predispositions make them sympathetic to the president's arguments, they may lack the understanding to make the connection between the president's arguments and their own underlying values.[61]

John Zaller argues that those in the public most susceptible to presidential influence are those attentive to public affairs (and thus who receive messages) but who lack strong views (and thus who are less likely to resist messages).[62] Such persons are a small portion of the population. In addition, these persons receive competing messages, and there is no basis for inferring that they will find the president's messages the most persuasive.

More broadly, public opinion usually moves contrary to the president's position. Because public officials have policy beliefs as well as an interest in reelection, they are not likely to calibrate their policy stances exactly to match those of the public. Thus a moderate public usually receives too much liberalism from Democrats and too much conservatism from Republicans.[63]

Misinformation and Misperceptions

In addition, people are frequently *misinformed* (as opposed to uninformed) about policy, and the less they know, the more confidence they have in their beliefs. Even when others present them with factual information, they resist changing their opinions.[64] Relying on media that share their beliefs makes it less likely people will encounter information that could correct their misperceptions.

Negations (e.g., "I am not a crook") often reinforce the perception they are intended to counter.[65] In addition, even if people initially accept corrections debunking a false statement, they may eventually fall victim to an "illusion of truth" effect in which people misremember false statements as true over time.[66] Finally, misleading statements about politics continue to influence people's beliefs even after they have been discredited.[67]

The media play a large role in creating misperceptions. The Internet, cable television, and talk radio facilitate selective exposure to information through "narrowcasting" to particular audiences. They create a distrust of information from other sources. Moreover, the highly charged nature of discourse on these venues magnifies the impression of partisan conflict, heightening viewers' and listeners' emotional engagement with politics and lessening the accuracy of their political perceptions.[68]

Loss Aversion

People have a broad predisposition to avoid loss[69] and place more emphasis on avoiding potential losses than on obtaining potential gains. In their decision making, they place more weight on information that has negative, as opposed to positive, implications for their interests. Similarly, when individuals form impressions of situations or other people, they weigh negative information more heavily than positive. Impressions formed on the basis of negative information, moreover, tend to be more lasting and more resistant to change.[70]

Risk and loss aversion and distrust of government make people wary of policy initiatives, especially when they are complex and their consequences are uncertain. Since uncertainty accompanies virtually every proposal for a major shift in public policy, it is not surprising that people are naturally inclined against change.[71] Further encouraging this predisposition is the media's focus on political conflict and strategy, which elevates the prominence of political wheeling-dealing in individuals' evaluations of political leaders and policy proposals. The resulting increase in public cynicism highlights the risk of altering the status quo.

Presidents proposing new directions in policy encounter a more formidable task than do advocates of the status quo. Those opposing change have a more modest task of emphasizing the negative to increase the public's uncertainty and anxiety to avoid risk.[72] In addition, fear and anger, which negative arguments presumably evoke, are among the strongest emotions and serve as readily available shortcuts for decision making when people evaluate an impending policy initiative.[73]

LEADING CONGRESS

Presidents invest an enormous amount of time trying to lead Congress. They know that their legacies are highly dependent on their proposals passing the legislature. Are presidents persuasive with senators and representatives? The best evidence is that presidential persuasion is effective only at the margins of congressional decision making. There is little relationship between presidential legislative leadership skills and success in winning votes. Even presidents who appeared to dominate Congress understood their own limitations and explicitly took advantage of opportunities in their environments. Working at the margins, they successfully guided legislation through Congress. When their opportunities lessened, they reverted to the more typical stalemate that usually characterizes presidential-congressional relations.[74]

We can illustrate this relationship by looking at three of the most famous periods of presidential success in Congress.[75]

The Hundred Days

Perhaps the twentieth century's most famous period of presidential-congressional relations was the Hundred Days of 1933, when Congress passed fifteen major pieces of legislation proposed by President Franklin D. Roosevelt. FDR won a clear electoral victory, and the Democrats gained large majorities in both houses of Congress. The day after his inauguration in 1933, FDR called a special session of Congress to deal with the economic crisis. All he planned to ask from Congress was to pass legislation to regulate the resumption of banking (he had closed the banks three days *after* taking office), amend the Volstead Act to legalize beer (a very popular policy), and cut the budget. He expected to reassemble the legislature when he was ready with permanent and more constructive legislation.

The first piece of legislation Roosevelt proposed was a bill regarding the resumption of banking. He found that he did not have to persuade anyone to support his bill, which passed unanimously in the House after only thirty-eight minutes of debate and without a roll call vote (although few members had seen the bill—there was only one copy for the chamber) and by a margin of seventy-three to seven in the Senate, which simply adopted the House bill while waiting for printed copies. An hour later, the bill arrived at the White House for the president's signature. The whole affair took less than eight hours.

Much to his surprise, the president found a situation ripe for change. The country was in such a state of desperation that it was eager to follow a leader who would try something new. Thus FDR decided to keep Congress in session and exploit the favorable environment by sending it the legislation that became known as the New Deal.

FDR went on to serve in the White House longer than anyone else, but most of these years were not legislatively productive. James MacGregor Burns entitles his discussion of presidential-congressional relations in the late 1930s "Deadlock on the Potomac." Either Roosevelt had lost his persuasive skills, which is not a reasonable proposition, or other factors were more significant in determining congressional support. By 1937, despite the president's great reelection victory, his coalition was falling apart.[76]

The Great Society

The next great period of legislative productivity for a president was Lyndon Johnson's success with the Eighty-ninth Congress in 1965 through 1966. The 1964 election occurred in the shadow of the traumatic national tragedy of the assassination of John F. Kennedy, and Johnson won a smashing victory. With it, opposition to his proposals melted. For the first and only time since the New Deal, liberals gained majorities in both houses of Congress.

Johnson did not have to convince these liberals to support policies that had been on their agenda for a generation. He even received substantial Republican support for some of his major initiatives. Civil rights was the most contentious issue of the time, and it was Johnson's political genius to realize that the time for change had arrived. He chose the moment when the civil rights movement was peaking in its appeal to the nation's conscience to pass the Voting Rights Act in 1965. This was a widely supported policy, however. Even some members of Congress from the Deep South supported it.

No one understood Congress better than LBJ, and he knew that his personal leadership could not sustain congressional support for his policies. He believed that he had a rare window of opportunity in Congress, and he pushed as much legislation as possible through Congress to exploit fully the favorable political environment. In the 1966 midterm elections, the Democrats lost forty-seven seats in the House and four in the Senate. Legislating became much more difficult as a result. Sixteen months later, in March 1968, the president declared that he would not seek reelection. Johnson had lost neither his leadership skills nor his passion for change. Instead, he had lost the opportunity to exploit a favorable environment.

The Reagan Revolution

It was the Republicans' turn in 1981. Ronald Reagan beat incumbent Jimmy Carter by 10 percentage points, and the Republicans won a majority in the Senate for the first time since the 1952 election. The unexpectedly large size of Reagan's victory and the equally surprising outcomes in the Senate elections created the perception of an electoral mandate. Reagan's victory placed a stigma on big government and exalted the unregulated marketplace and large defense budgets. He had won on much of his agenda before Congress took a single vote.

The new president also benefited from the nature of the times. Although 1981 was hardly a repeat of 1933, there was a definite sense of the need for immediate action to meet urgent problems. David Stockman, a principal architect and proponent of Reagan's budgeting and tax proposals, remembers that when the president announced his "Program for Economic Recovery" to a joint session of Congress in February 1981, "the plan already had momentum and few were standing in the way." Reagan was "speaking to an assembly of desperate politicians who . . . were predisposed to grant him extraordinary latitude in finding a new remedy for the nation's economic ills . . . not because they understood the plan or even accepted it, but because they had lost all faith in the remedies tried before."[77]

The president's advisers recognized immediately that they had a window of opportunity to effect major changes in public policy. Like LBJ, the White House knew it had to move quickly before the environment became less favorable. Thus the president was ready with legislation, even though it was complex and hastily written. Moreover, within a week of the March 30, 1981, assassination attempt on Reagan, his aide Michael Deaver convened a meeting of other high-ranking officials at the White House to determine how best to take advantage of the new political capital the shooting had created.

The Reagan administration also knew it lacked the political capital to pass a broad program. Thus it enforced a rigorous focus on the president's economic plan and defense spending, its priority legislation, and essentially ignored divisive social issues and tried to keep the issue of communist advances in Central America on the back burner. By focusing its political resources on its priorities, the administration succeeded in using the budget to pass sweeping changes in taxation and defense policy.

It was wise for Reagan to exploit his opportunities. The going was much tougher the next year as the United States suffered a severe recession, and for the rest of his tenure, commentators frequently described Reagan's budgets as DOA: Dead on Arrival.

Leadership of Congress in Perspective

Despite the prestige of their office, their position as party leader, their personal persuasiveness, and their strong personalities, presidents often meet resistance from members of Congress to their appeals for support. Personal appeals by themselves are useful but unreliable instruments for passing legislation. As a result, one-on-one lobbying by the president is the exception rather than the rule. The White House conserves appeals for obtaining the last few votes on issues of special significance to it, a recognition that presidents cannot personally persuade members of Congress with any frequency.

In his important work on pivotal politics, Keith Krehbiel examined votes to override presidential vetoes, focusing on those members of Congress who switched their votes from their original votes on the bill. He found that presidents attracted the support of 10 percent of those members who originally opposed the president's preferred position but lost 11 percent of those who originally supported the president's position. Those closest in ideology to the president were most likely to switch to his side, which may indicate they voted their true views, rather than responding to other interests, when it really counted. Even among those most likely to agree with the White House, the net swing was only one in eight. The majority of switchers were from the president's party, indicating that the desire to avoid a party embarrassment rather than presidential persuasiveness may have motivated their votes.[78]

Thus presidential legislative leadership is more useful in exploiting discrete opportunities than in creating broad possibilities for policy change. It operates in an environment largely beyond the president's control and must compete with other, more stable factors that affect voting in Congress in addition to party. These include ideology, personal views and commitments on specific policies, and the interests of constituencies. By the time a president tries to exercise influence on a vote, most members of Congress have made up their minds on the basis of these other factors.

As a result, a president's legislative leadership is likely to be critical only for those members of Congress who remain open to conversion after other influences have had their impact. Although the size and composition of this group varies from issue to issue, it will almost always be a minority in each chamber. Whatever the circumstances, the impact of persuasion on the outcome will usually be relatively modest. Therefore, conversion is likely to be at the margins of coalition building in Congress rather than at the core of policy change.

In sum, the most effective presidents do not create opportunities by reshaping the political landscape. Instead, they exploit opportunities already present in their environments to achieve significant changes in public policy.

CONCLUSION

Although it may be appealing to explain major policy changes in terms of persuasive personalities, public opinion is too biased, the political system is too complicated, power is too decentralized, and interests are too diverse for one person, no matter how extraordinary, to dominate. Recognizing and exploiting opportunities for change—rather than creating opportunities through persuasion—are the essential presidential leadership skills. To succeed, presidents have to evaluate the opportunities for change in their environments carefully and orchestrate existing and potential support skillfully. When the various streams of political resources converge to create opportunities for major change, presidents can be critical facilitators in engendering significant alterations in public policy. But while presidents' power to achieve policy change may hinge on presidents correctly sizing up their opportunities, it rarely if ever depends on the power to persuade.

NOTES

PRO

1. Richard E. Neustadt, *Presidential Power and the Modern Presidents: The Politics of Leadership from Roosevelt to Reagan* (New York: Free Press, 1990), 28–9, 31.
2. Ibid., 32, 40.
3. See, for example, George C. Edwards III, *The Strategic President* (Princeton, NJ: Princeton University Press, 2009).

4. Neustadt, *Presidential Power*, 38.

5. Ibid., 150.

6. Ibid., 29, endnote 1.

7. Chuck Jones takes Neustadt's insight a step further. In the American political system, Jones points out, separated institutions do not simply share powers. They actively *compete* for them. Charles O. Jones, *The Presidency in a Separated System* (Washington, DC: Brookings, 1994), 18.

8. As evidence regarding the weakness of formal powers, Neustadt presents three cases of command—Truman seizing the steel mills, Truman firing Gen. Douglas MacArthur, and Eisenhower integrating public schools in Little Rock, Arkansas. In each, a president is forced to utilize formal powers after persuasion fails. In so doing, however, they suffer significant damage to their sources of bargaining power.

9. Neustadt, *Presidential Power*, 52.

10. Ibid., 73.

11. Chapter 9, "Appraising a President," was initially published as an afterword to the 1968 French edition of *Presidential Power* and included in the American edition. Chapter 10, "Reappraising Power," grew out of lectures Neustadt gave in 1976 and primarily explores lessons he derives from Johnson and Nixon's presidencies. Chapter 11, "Hazards of Transition," is an expansion of Neustadt's 1979 Phi Beta Kappa lecture and focuses on the problems of transition and of the presidency more generally in light of Ford's and Carter's time in office. The 1990 edition includes a study of the Iran-Contra affair and two case studies of presidential successes: Kennedy's handling of the Cuban missile crisis in 1962 and Eisenhower's 1954 decision not to intervene at Dien Bien Phu.

12. Ibid., ix–x.

13. More than two decades after its last revision, *Presidential Power* continues to reach new audiences, including non-English-speaking ones; a Portuguese language version was published in 2008.

14. Of course, we should not overstate *Presidential Power*'s intellectual ascendancy within presidency research; the bargaining model of presidential leadership is not now and never was the only game in town. See Erwin Hargrove, *The President as Leader* (Lawrence: University Press of Kansas, 1998), 1–48; and Raymond Tatalovich and Thomas S. Engeman, *The Presidency and Political Science: Two Hundred Years of Constitutional Debate* (Baltimore: Johns Hopkins University Press, 2003).

15. For an expanded discussion of this point, see Matthew J. Dickinson, "We All Want a Revolution: Neustadt, New Institutionalism, and the Future of Presidency Research," *Presidential Studies Quarterly* 39, no. 4 (December 2009): 736–70.

16. Terry Moe, "Presidents, Institutions and Theory," in *Researching the Presidency: Vital Questions, New Approaches,* ed. George C. Edwards III, John H. Kessel, and Bert A. Rockman (Pittsburgh, PA: University of Pittsburgh Press, 1993); Terry Moe, "The Revolution in Presidency Studies," *Presidential Studies Quarterly* 39 no. 4 (December 2009): 701–24; Lyn Ragsdale, "Personal Power and Presidents," in *Presidential Power, Forging the Presidency for the 21st Century,* ed.

Robert Shapiro, Martha Joynt Kumar, and Larry Jacobs (New York: Columbia University Press, 2000).

17. In fact, consistent with the idea that Neustadt's work is compatible with a rational choice approach, President John F. Kennedy reportedly confided after reading *Presidential Power* that Neustadt "makes everything a President does seem too premeditated." Arthur M. Schlesinger Jr., *One Thousand Days* (Boston: Houghton-Mifflin, 1965), 678–79. Similarly, Neustadt often recounted how some colleagues worried that his work on the presidency drew too heavily on the "Rochester school"—a well-known center of rational choice research.

18. Neustadt, *Presidential Power,* 218–29.

19. Ibid., 269–94. See also Jane Mayer and Doyle McManus, *Landslide: The Unmaking of the President, 1984–1988* (Boston: Houghton-Mifflin, 1988).

20. Phillip J. Cooper, *By Order of the President: The Use and Abuse of Executive Direct Action* (Lawrence: University Press of Kansas, 2002); William G. Howell, *Power without Persuasion: The Politics of Direct Presidential Action* (Princeton, NJ: Princeton University Press, 2003); Kenneth R. Mayer, *With the Stroke of a Pen* (Princeton, NJ: Princeton University Press, 2001).

21. Peter Sperlich, "Bargaining and Overload: An Essay on Presidential Power," in *The Presidency,* ed. Aaron Wildavsky (Boston: Little, Brown, 1969), 168–92.

22. Richard M. Pious, *The American Presidency* (New York: Basic Books, 1979).

23. Matthew J. Dickinson and Jesse Gubb, "The Limits to Power without Persuasion," *Presidential Studies Quarterly* 46, no. 1 (March 2016): 48–72.

24. Neustadt, *Presidential Power,* 33–4.

25. Greg Robinson, *By Order of the President: FDR and the Internment of Japanese Americans* (Cambridge, MA: Harvard University Press, 2001).

26. David Stockman, *The Triumph of Politics: How the Reagan Revolution Failed* (New York: Harper & Row, 1986), 101–02.

27. Hugh Heclo, *A Government of Strangers: Executive Politics in Washington* (Washington, DC: Brookings, 1997); Richard P. Nathan, *The Administrative Presidency* (New York: John Wiley & Sons, 1983), 82–5; Richard Waterman, *Presidential Influence and the Administrative State* (Knoxville, TN: The University of Tennessee Press, 1989), 188–89.

28. Samuel Kernell, *Going Public: New Strategies of Presidential Leadership,* 4th ed. (Washington, DC: CQ Press, 2007); Theodore Lowi, *The Personal President* (Ithaca, NY: Cornell University Press, 1985).

29. Kernell, *Going Public,* 32.

30. Neustadt, *Presidential Power,* 264.

31. Ibid., xv.

32. Ibid., 81–3.

33. Paul Brace and Barbara Hinckley, *Follow the Leader: Opinion Polls and the Modern Presidents* (New York: Basic Books, 1992); Richard Brody, *Assessing the President: The Media, Elite Opinion, and Public Support* (Stanford, CA: Stanford University Press, 1991); Douglas A. Hibbs, *The American Political Economy: Macroeconomics*

and Electoral Politics (Cambridge, MA: Harvard University Press, 1987); Benjamin I. Page and Robert Y. Shapiro, *The Rational Public: Fifty Years of Trends in Americans' Policy Preferences* (Chicago, IL: University of Chicago Press, 1992).

34. George C. Edwards III, "Impediments to Presidential Leadership: The Limitations of the Permanent Campaign and Going Public Strategies," in *Presidential Leadership: The Vortex of Power,* ed. Bert A. Rockman and Richard W. Waterman (New York: Oxford University of Press, 2008), 163–66.

35. B. Dan Wood, *The Myth of Presidential Representation* (Cambridge, UK: Cambridge University Press, 2009).

36. George C. Edwards III, *On Deaf Ears: The Limits of the Bully Pulpit* (New Haven, CT: Yale University Press, 2003), 251–54; see also Cary R. Covington, "'Staying Private': Gaining Congressional Support for Unpublicized Presidential Preferences on Roll Call Votes," *The Journal of Politics* 49, no. 3 (August 1987): 737–55.

37. Neustadt, *Presidential Power,* 1990 ed. Because his empirical examples were drawn from a narrow band of presidents, Neustadt thought it prudent not to generalize beyond his data (xi; see also Charles O. Jones, "Richard Neustadt: Public Servant as Scholar," *Annual Review of Political Science* 6, no. 1 [2003], 19). But there is no reason why his bargaining model could not apply to "premodern" presidents.

38. Stephen Skowronek, *The Politics Presidents Make* (Cambridge, MA: Harvard University Press, 1993), 5.

39. Ibid., 36–45.

40. Robert C. Lieberman, "Political Time and Policy Coalitions," in Shapiro, Kumar, and Jacobs, eds., *Presidential Power,* 276.

41. Ibid., 301.

42. Russell Riley, "The Limits of the Transformational Presidency," in Shapiro, Kumar, and Jacobs, eds., *Presidential Power,* 435–36; Erwin Hargrove, "Presidential Power and Political Science," *Presidential Studies Quarterly* 31, no. 2 (June 2001): 251.

43. Richard M. Pious, *Why Presidents Fail: White House Decision Making from Eisenhower to Bush II* (Lanham, MD: Rowman and Littlefield, 2008), 263.

44. Neustadt, *Presidential Power,* 154.

45. Ibid., xix.

46. Stephen Skowronek, "Review of Jeffrey Tulis' 'The Rhetorical Presidency,'" *The Review of Politics* 49, no. 3 (Summer 1987): 430.

47. Shapiro, Kumar, and Jacobs, eds., *Presidential Power.*

48. Jones, "Richard Neustadt," 8.

49. Thanks to Danny Zhang for his editorial assistance. Portions of this chapter draw upon material in Dickinson, "We All Want a Revolution."

CON

50. Richard E. Neustadt, *Presidential Power and the Modern Presidents: The Politics of Leadership from Roosevelt to Reagan* (New York: Free Press, 1990), 11.

51. Ibid., 32.

52. George C. Edwards III, *On Deaf Ears: The Limits of the Bully Pulpit* (New Haven, CT: Yale University Press, 2003).

53. George C. Edwards III, *Governing by Campaigning: The Politics of the Bush Presidency*, 2nd ed. (New York: Longman, 2007).

54. George C. Edwards III, *Overreach: Leadership in the Obama Presidency* (Princeton, NJ: Princeton University Press, 2012); George C. Edwards III, *Predicting the Presidency: The Potential of Persuasive Leadership* (Princeton, NJ: Princeton University Press, 2016).

55. George C. Edwards III, *The Strategic President: Persuasion and Opportunity in Presidential Leadership* (Princeton, NJ: Princeton University Press, 2009); Edwards, *On Deaf Ears.*

56. Edwards, *On Deaf Ears*, chap. 5.

57. James N. Druckman, Jordan Fein, and Thomas J. Leeper, "A Source of Bias in Public Opinion Stability," *American Political Science Review* 106 (May 2012): 430–54; Rune Slothuus and Claes H. de Vreese, "Political Parties, Motivated Reasoning, and Issue Framing Effects," *Journal of Politics* (July 2010): 630–45; Charles S. Taber, Damon Cann, and Simona Kucsova, "The Motivated Processing of Political Arguments," *Political Behavior* 31 (June 2009): 137–55; Charles S. Taber and Milton Lodge, "Motivated Skepticism in the Evaluation of Political Beliefs," *American Journal of Political Science* 50 (July 2006): 755–69; John T. Jost, "The End of the End of Ideology," *American Psychologist* 61, no. 7 (2006): 651–70; Richard R. Lau and David P. Redlawsk, *How Voters Decide: Information Processing in Election Campaigns* (New York: Cambridge University Press, 2006); Milton Lodge and Charles S. Taber, "The Automaticity of Affect for Political Leaders, Groups, and Issues: An Experimental Test of the Hot Cognition Hypothesis," *Political Psychology* 26 (June 2005): 455–82; David P. Redlawsk, "Hot Cognition or Cool Consideration: Testing the Effects of Motivated Reasoning on Political Decision Making," *Journal of Politics* 64 (November 2002): 1021–044; Milton Lodge and Ruth Hamill, "A Partisan Schema for Political Information Processing," *American Political Science Review* 80 (June 1986): 505–19; Charles Lord, Lee Ross, and Mark R. Lepper, "Biased Assimilation and Attitude Polarization: The Effects of Prior Theories on Subsequently Considered Evidence," *Journal of Personality and Social Psychology* 37 (November 1979): 2098–109.

58. On the importance of source credibility, see James N. Druckman, "Using Credible Advice to Overcome Framing Effects," *Journal of Law, Economics, and Organization* 17, no. 1 (2001): 62–82; James N. Druckman, "On the Limits of Framing Effects: Who Can Frame?" *Journal of Politics* 63 (November 2001): 1041–66; Joanne M. Miller and Jon A. Krosnick, "News Media Impact on the Ingredients of Presidential Evaluations: Politically Knowledgeable Citizens Are Guided by a Trusted Source," *American Journal of Political Science* 44 (April 2000): 301–15.

59. See Howard Lavine, Christopher Johnston, and Marco Steenbergen, *The Ambivalent Partisan* (Oxford, UK: Oxford University Press 2012); Brendan Nyhan and Jason Reifler, *Misinformation and Fact-Checking: Research Findings from Social*

Science (New American Foundation, 2012); Alan S. Gerber and Gregory A. Huber, "Partisanship, Political Control, and Economic Assessments," *American Journal of Political Science* 54 (January 2010): 153–73; Paul Goren, Christopher M. Federico, and Miki Caul Kittilson, "Source Cues, Partisan Identities, and Political Value Expression," *American Journal of Political Science* 55 (October 2009): 805–20; Brian J. Gaines, James H. Kuklinski, Paul J. Quirk, Buddy Peyton, and Jay Verkuilen, "Same Facts, Different Interpretations: Partisan Motivation and Opinion on Iraq," *Journal of Politics* 69 (November 2007): 957–74; Edwards, *On Deaf Ears*, chap. 9; Larry Bartels, "Beyond the Running Tally: Partisan Bias in Political Perceptions," *Political Behavior* 24 (June 2002): 117–50; Christopher H. Achen and Larry M. Bartels, "It Feels Like We're Thinking: The Rationalizing Voter and Electoral Democracy," paper delivered at the Annual Meeting of the American Political Science Association, Philadelphia, 2006; Larry M. Bartels, *Unequal Democracy* (Princeton, NJ: Princeton University Press, 2008), chap. 5; Mathew J. Lebo and Daniel Cassino, "The Aggregated Consequences of Motivated Reasoning and the Dynamics of Partisan Presidential Approval," *Political Psychology* 28 (December 2007): 719–46; Gary C. Jacobson, *A Divider, Not a Uniter: George W. Bush and the American Public*, 3rd ed. (New York: Longman, 2011); Suzanna DeBoef and Paul M. Kellstedt, "The Political (and Economic) Origins of Consumer Confidence," *American Journal of Political Science* 48 (October 2004): 633–49; Steven Kull, Clay Ramsay, and Evan Lewis, "Misperceptions, the Media, and the Iraq War," *Political Science Quarterly* 118 (Winter 2003–2004): 569–98; Edwards, *Governing by Campaigning*, chap. 3; Paul D. Sweeney and Kathy L. Gruber, "Selective Exposure: Voter Information Preferences and the Watergate Affair," *Journal of Personality and Social Psychology* 46, no. 6 (1984): 1208–221; Mark Fischle, "Mass Response to the Lewinsky Scandal: Motivated Reasoning or Bayesian Updating?" *Political Psychology* 21 (March 2000): 135–59.

60. John R. Zaller, *The Nature and Origins of Mass Opinion* (New York: Cambridge University Press, 1992), 102–13; Danielle Shani, "Knowing Your Colors: Can Knowledge Correct for Partisan Bias in Political Perceptions?" Paper presented at the annual meeting of the Midwest Political Science Association, Chicago, 2006.

61. Zaller, *The Nature and Origins of Mass Opinion*, 48; William G. Jacoby, "The Sources of Liberal-Conservative Thinking: Education and Conceptualization," *Political Behavior* 10 (December 1988): 316–32; Robert C. Luskin, "Measuring Political Sophistication," *American Journal of Political Science* 31 (November 1987): 856–99; W. Russell Neuman, *The Paradox of Mass Politics: Knowledge and Opinion in the American Electorate* (Cambridge, MA: Harvard University Press, 1986); Edward G. Carmines and James A. Stimson, "The Two Faces of Issue Voting," *American Political Science Review* 74 (March 1980): 78–91; Philip E. Converse, "The Nature of Belief Systems in Mass Publics," in *Ideology and Discontent*, ed. David E. Apter (New York: Free Press, 1964).

62. John R. Zaller, "Elite Leadership of Mass Opinion: New Evidence from the Gulf War," in *Taken by Storm: The Media, Public Opinion, and U.S. Foreign Policy in the*

Gulf War, ed. W. Lance Bennett and David L. Paletz (Chicago, IL: University of Chicago Press, 1994); Zaller, *The Nature and Origins of Mass Opinion*.

63. Robert S. Erikson, Michael B. MacKuen, and James A. Stimson, *The Macro Polity* (New York: Cambridge University Press, 2002). See also Stuart N. Soroka and Christopher Wlezien, *Degrees of Democracy* (New York: Cambridge University Press, 2010).

64. James H. Kuklinski, Paul J. Quirk, Jennifer Jerit, David Schwieder, and Robert F. Rich, "Misinformation and the Currency of Democratic Citizenship," *Journal of Politics* 62 (August 2000): 790–816. See also Brendan Nyhan, "Why the 'Death Panel' Myth Wouldn't Die: Misinformation in the Health Care Reform Debate," *The Forum* 8, no. 1 (2010, www.bepress.com/forum/v018/iss1/art5); Brendan Nyhan and Jason Reifler, "When Corrections Fail: The Persistence of Political Misperceptions," *Political Behavior* 32 (June 2010): 303–30; David P. Redlawsk, Andrew J. W. Civettini, and Karen M. Emmerson, "The Affective Tipping Point: Do Motivated Reasoners Ever 'Get It'?" *Political Psychology* 31 (August 2010): 563–93.

65. Ruth Mayo, Yaacov Schul, and Eugene Burnstein, "'I Am Not Guilty' vs. 'I Am Innocent': Successful Negation May Depend on the Schema Used for Its Encoding," *Journal of Experimental Social Psychology* 40 (July 2004): 433–49.

66. Norbert Schwarz, Lawrence J. Sanna, Ian Skurnik, and Carolyn Yoon, "Metacognitive Experiences and the Intricacies of Setting People Straight: Implications for Debiasing and Public Information Campaigns," *Advances in Experimental Social Psychology* 39 (2007): 127–61; Ian Skurnik, Carolyn Yoon, Denise C. Park, and Norbert Schwarz, "How Warnings about False Claims Become Recommendations," *Journal of Consumer Research* 31 (March 2005): 713–24.

67. John Bullock, "Experiments on Partisanship and Public Opinion: Party Cues, False Beliefs, and Bayesian Updating," Ph.D. dissertation, Stanford University, 2007.

68. Robert Y. Shapiro and Lawrence R. Jacobs, "The Democratic Paradox: The Waning of Popular Sovereignty and the Pathologies of American Politics," in *The Oxford Handbook of American Public Opinion and the Media*, ed. Robert Y. Shapiro and Lawrence R. Jacobs (Oxford, UK: Oxford University Press, 2011).

69. David Kahneman and Amos Tversky, "Choices, Values, and Frames," *American Psychologist* 39 (April 1984): 341–50; David Kahneman and Amos Tversky, "Prospect Theory: An Analysis of Decision under Risk," *Econometrica* 47 (March 1979): 263–92.

70. Stuart N. Soroka, *Negativity in Democratic Politics* (New York: Cambridge University Press, 2014); Susan T. Fiske, "Attention and Weight in Person Perception: The Impact of Negative and Extreme Behavior," *Journal of Personality and Social Psychology* 38, no. 6 (1980): 889–906; David L. Hamilton and Mark P. Zanna, "Differential Weighting of Favorable and Unfavorable Attributes in Impressions of Personality," *Journal of Experimental Research in Personality* 6, nos. 2–3 (1972): 204–12.

71. Richard Lau, "Two Explanations for Negativity Effects in Political Behavior," *American Journal of Political Science* 29 (February 1985): 119–38; Kevin

Arceneaux, "Cognitive Biases and the Strength of Political Arguments," *American Journal of Political Science* 56 (April 2012): 271–85.

72. Michael D. Cobb and James H. Kuklinski, "Changing Minds: Political Arguments and Political Persuasion," *American Journal of Political Science* 41 (January 1997): 88–121; David W. Brady and Daniel P. Kessler, "Who Supports Health Reform?" *PS: Political Science and Politics* 43 (January 2010): 1–5.

73. See Joanne M. Miller, "Examining the Mediators of Agenda Setting: A New Experimental Paradigm Reveals the Role of Emotions," *Political Psychology* 28 (December 2007): 689–717; George E. Marcus, W. Russell Neuman, and Michael MacKuen, *Affective Intelligence and Political Judgment* (Chicago, IL: University of Chicago Press, 2000); George E. Marcus, *The Sentimental Citizen* (University Park: Pennsylvania State University Press, 2002); Michael MacKuen, Jennifer Wolak, Luke Keele, and George E. Marcus, "Civic Engagements: Resolute Partisanship or Reflective Deliberation," *American Journal of Political Science* 54 (April 2010): 440–58.

74. George C. Edwards III, *At the Margins: Presidential Leadership of Congress* (New Haven, CT: Yale University Press, 1989); Edwards, *The Strategic President;* Jon R. Bond and Richard Fleisher, *The President in the Legislative Arena* (Chicago, IL: University of Chicago Press, 1990), chap. 8; Richard Fleisher, Jon R. Bond, and B. Dan Wood, "Which Presidents Are Uncommonly Successful in Congress?" in *Presidential Leadership: The Vortex of Presidential Power,* ed. Bert Rockman and Richard W. Waterman (New York: Oxford University Press, 2007).

75. This discussion relies on Edwards, *The Strategic President,* chap. 4.

76. James MacGregor Burns, *Roosevelt: The Lion and the Fox* (New York: Harcourt, Brace and World, 1956), 310–15, 321, 337–52, 366–70.

77. David A. Stockman, *The Triumph of Politics* (New York: Harper & Row, 1986), 79–80, 120.

78. Keith Krehbiel, *Pivotal Politics: A Theory of U.S. Lawmaking* (Chicago, IL: University of Chicago Press, 1988). It is possible that there is selection bias in votes on veto overrides. Presidents do not veto the same number of bills, and some veto no bills at all. Moreover, presidents may often choose to veto bills on which they are likely to prevail. In addition, most override votes are not close, allowing members of Congress more flexibility in their voting. Whatever the case, Krehbiel's data do not provide a basis for inferring successful presidential persuasion.

RESOLVED, Congress should be required to vote up or down on legislation proposed by the president

PRO: William G. Howell and Terry M. Moe

CON: B. Dan Wood

What happens when a major league baseball player thinks he should be paid more than the ball club that employs him? He submits his proposed salary to an arbitrator, who also receives the team owner's proposed salary figure. Then, instead of splitting the difference, the arbitrator chooses one figure or the other. Each side's proposal is either raised up in its entirety or cast down; the arbitrator's decision is all or nothing. The incentive for both the player and the club, therefore, is to be so reasonable that the arbitrator will be persuaded.

In the realm of government, up-or-down decision making has been resorted to on occasion. Sometimes Congress has granted the president "fast-track" authority to submit trade agreements with other countries for an up-or-down vote, with no amendments permitted. Congress also authorized a special commission to submit a list of military bases to be closed, again for straight up-or-down consideration. The idea behind such measures is that otherwise the constituency interests of individual representatives and senators will be so strong as to prevent them from agreeing on anything.

Most conflicts in government, as in life, are resolved differently, through a process of give and take. That is certainly true of how Congress and the president interact to make laws. When presidents submit legislation to Congress, they seldom expect it to be approved exactly as written. Instead, they assume that even under the best of circumstances the House of Representatives and the Senate will make their own preferred modifications before voting on the bill. The presidential incentive, therefore, is to propose a bill much stronger than the one Congress is expected to pass.

However successful the process of presidents submitting and Congress amending legislation may have been in bygone days, William G. Howell and Terry Moe argue that it is no longer satisfactory. From climate change to mounting debt, many think the problems now facing the country are too critical for government as usual. Howell and Moe look at 230 years of institutional evolution under the Constitution and see that with the passage of time, the president has become a much more active player in the legislative process, often with the encouragement of Congress. They argue that empowering the president to submit bills that Congress must either take or leave will encourage the sort of comprehensive solutions to problems that only the president can devise.

B. Dan Wood sees much more value in the current process of congressional give and take and is distressed that Howell and Moe see "nothing to be gained from the deliberative process within Congress." Because Wood regards neither the president nor Congress as fully representative of the American people, he argues that the only way for the public to be represented accurately in the making of laws is through the clash of power centers at either end of Pennsylvania Avenue.

PRO: William G. Howell and Terry M. Moe

Systematic disenfranchisement of populations, debasement of moral and civic obligations, and pervasive waste and corruption all have provided the impetus for institutional reform at various times in American history. Today, there is another—and more foundational—cause for concern: namely, the incapacity of our democracy to solve social problems. This incapacity is the reason we need to enhance the president's proposal powers by requiring Congress to vote up or down on legislation proposed by the president. By expanding the president's ability to set the national agenda, we stand a better chance of addressing the critical social problems that have vexed even the best-intentioned members of Congress, and thereby of avoiding a fate in which today's problems are handed down, in magnified form, to our children and grandchildren.[1]

GENERATIONAL CHALLENGES

All elected officials face their share of problems. Here, however, we want to focus on a particular class of problems that we will call "generational challenges," which most people concede are the subject of legitimate government action. Generational challenges exhibit greater resilience than most problems. They require the mobilization of numerous competing and often conflicting constituencies, always domestically, sometimes internationally. Generational problems require solutions that are neither obvious nor free. Left unaddressed, generational problems worsen over time.

Lest we drift too far into abstraction, let us offer a particular example: the halting and episodic interbranch struggles over the national debt, which now hovers around $18 trillion. This amount is roughly three times what it was in 2000; as a percentage of GDP, it is higher than at any point in American history except during World War II. In the summer of 2011, Congress and the president attempted to negotiate a comprehensive solution to the twin challenges posed by mounting debt and a frustratingly slow economic recovery. With just hours left before the federal government would default on its loan commitments, a deal was brokered that charged a bipartisan committee of legislators with developing a long-term plan to curb the nation's debt. And then, to improve its chances of success, Congress required that the committee's recommendations be voted on up or down. Going one step further, Congress mandated across-the-board cuts should its members fail to enact the recommendations of the so-called Super Committee.

What followed? After meeting just a handful of times during the early fall, members of the not-so-super committee disbanded without so much as even offering the beginnings of a recommendation. Standard and Poor's promptly downgraded the U.S. credit rating, which, according to the Government Accountability Office, subsequently increased the government's borrowing costs by billions of dollars.[2] Congress proved incapable of making any headway on the debt problem. Indeed, to the extent that it showed any penchant for addressing the issue, it was by selectively backtracking on the across-the-board cuts. But even these efforts failed, the bulk of the cuts took effect, and "sequester" entered our political nomenclature. Meanwhile, significant portions of the federal bureaucracy have been unable to do any serious budget forecasting. For the foreseeable future, the budgetary process now lurches from one partisan showdown to the next.

But the case for institutional reform rides on a great deal more than this single issue. Indeed, the challenges presented by the national debt pale in comparison to those of another issue: climate change. Here, the outcomes may prove nothing less than catastrophic. According to the Special Report on Emissions Scenarios by the Intergovernmental Panel on Climate Change,[3] when temperatures increase by roughly one degree, significant risks of species extinction arise. Increases of two degrees are accompanied by heightened flood and storm damages. At three degrees, 30 percent of species become at risk of extinction. With each subsequent temperature jump, the consequences grow more and more dire. So what do we know about recent temperature trends? Since 1960, Alaska has warmed by fully three degrees. Villages in Alaska have begun sinking into the ground as permafrost in coastal regions thaws. According to the Army Corps of Engineers, relocation costs for the villagers will run into the tens of millions of dollars. The Alaskan sea lion population has declined over 50 percent. Between 1980 and 2000, the Arctic Circle area warmed almost two degrees. Roughly half of the ice thickness in the Arctic was lost between 1980 and 2008. At current rates of decline, Arctic Sea ice may disappear by the 2020s. Farther south, average temperatures in China have risen by more than a degree since 1980. And since 1970, average temperatures in New England have risen by 1.5 degrees. 2015 was the hottest year on record, beating 2014, which was the previous title-holder. October 2015 was the hottest October ever recorded.

The precise causes of these temperature changes, of course, remain the subject of some dispute. Solutions are fraught with uncertainty. But what, exactly, has Congress done to meet the basic challenges presented by these warming trends, the fact of which every reputable scientist now recognizes? The short answer is very little. Bills are introduced, hearings are held, but during the last half century no systematic, comprehensive effort to deal with climate change has gained traction on Capitol Hill. Instead, Congress has opted to support piecemeal efforts at mitigating the symptoms associated with a rapidly warming Earth.[4] And it has met Barack Obama's efforts to broker an international solution with skepticism and disinterest, in roughly equal measure.

The national debt and climate change exhibit all the qualities of generational challenges. They present complex scientific and social challenges; solutions, if they are to be reached, will require the coordination of many different political actors, interest groups, and nations; and, left unaddressed, they can be expected to metastasize. But the national debt and climate change hardly exhaust the class of generational challenges that we as a country face. Energy, immigration, persistent un- and underemployment, rising inequality, the unbelievably complex tax code, and a good deal more populate the ranks of pressing contemporary social problems. And as the federal government episodically responds with a strange mix of indifference and spastic self-righteousness, the need for institutional reform only grows more urgent.

WHERE ARE OUR LEADERS?

Where are we likely to find the leadership needed to address critical social problems? Who, within our politics, is best equipped to define the problems that the country faces, not merely in moments of crisis but in the more regular struggle for peace? Who can chart out meaningful, pragmatic solutions to these problems? Who can call upon the American public to make smaller sacrifices today so that more substantial sacrifices are not required tomorrow? And who will take stock of the full scope, both national and international, of these problems and the solutions they require?

To set some limits on possible answers, let us assume that we are going to continue to work within our current system of separated and federated powers. Rather than dream about altogether different political systems, as previous generations of institutional reforms have done, let us stipulate that we must work with what we have. Also, before we turn to competing considerations—as, eventually, we must—let us first reflect on what institutions are best equipped to meet generational challenges. Admittedly, discussions about government efficacy rest uneasily alongside, and sometimes sit unabashedly opposed to, a host of constitutional and philosophic commitments. Moreover, there are legitimate debates to be had about which problems warrant government action and which are best left to the private sphere. In this short essay, we cannot possibly sort through such matters, so let us agree, if only for now, that some form of government action is required to address at least some of the social problems identified above. And finally, let us set aside pragmatic concerns about the feasibility of implementing institutional reform. The preferred and the possible surely differ, but it is worth identifying the best available option before settling for some alternative.

So again, where is meaningful leadership to be found? Before offering an answer, we can rule out a handful of possibilities. The first lies in the spontaneous eruptions of public sentiment—in, that is, an informed and mobilized public that will not merely work around the gridlock within Washington, D.C., but will render it mute. Ah, but were the public so forceful an agent of change. Left to its own devices, the public has reliably demonstrated an extraordinary penchant for ignorance and rashness. The founders were well aware of the public's limitations, which goes some distance toward explaining the existence of the Electoral College, the eighteenth- and nineteenth-century practices of having state legislators rather than the broader public select senators, and the numerous checks and balances that define our system of governance. And since the Michigan School of Political Science cast forth a half century ago, a cottage industry of social scientists has devoted itself to documenting the shallow, unstructured character of political beliefs. To put your stock in an unfettered and undisciplined public is to deny the very need for leadership. Such a denial offers no remedy to the kinds of general challenges that we as a country face.

Perhaps what we need is simply a better, more committed batch of politicians. The problem, by this formulation, lies with the individuals currently in office and not the political framework in which they operate. So say the "I voted for the other one" bumper stickers that adorn the cars driven by the smug and indignant. But this argument is much too flippant, vacuous, and ahistorical to be of help. There are reasons why our elected officials so reliably equivocate, diminish, and deny. They face powerful incentives to behave the way they do, and these incentives have deep institutional origins. Until we attend to the institutional impediments to change, we cannot hope to make substantive headway on the challenges we face.

What, then, of Congress? The wishful thinking is that, through careful deliberation and a recommitment to basic norms of reciprocity, Congress may pave a way forward. But here again, there are ample reasons for skepticism. Truth be told, Congress is unlikely to provide the leadership needed to identify and design solutions for the nation's most vexing social problems. Its very character as a collective decision-making body nearly guarantees that it won't. Leadership is a scarce commodity among the 535 independently elected members who make up Congress, each with radically different views about what good policy looks like. Moreover, the overarching objective of each member is to get reelected, and the way you do this is to stand up for the parochial interests of your constituents. It should come as no surprise that the recent history of legislative activity is littered with bills that, in name, promise to confront challenges of national importance, but in fact constitute little more than disfigured conglomerations of sectional initiatives.[5]

Left to its own devices, Congress is not especially adept at solving problems. Rather, it holds two comparative advantages: first, in offering (and sometimes delivering) voice to the diverse and parochial concerns of the American public, and second, in qualifying, checking, and amending the policy positions of others. The first comparative advantage helps explain why lobbyists for Maine's fishing industries and Kansas wheat farmers make deeper inroads in Congress than any other branch of government. It is only in Congress, after all, that one finds a population of elected officials whose job security rides nearly exclusively on their ability to represent local interests. Meanwhile, because of its second comparative advantage, Congress most naturally assumes a reactive posture. When it must define and advance a national policy agenda, Congress predictably flails and founders. But when asked to deliberate, amend, and curtail policies that have been developed elsewhere, its members find their form. As a result, Congress plays a hugely important role in maintaining the health of a liberal democracy. It just cannot be counted on to provide leadership.

ANSWER: THE PRESIDENT

Where might we look for the leadership needed to address and solve the nation's most pressing social problems? By now, our answer should not surprise: in the president. Contemporary arguments for a stronger presidency have not exactly resonated politically, in large part because they have been tied to concerns about the waging of a largely clandestine war against terrorists, both suspected and confirmed. These concerns are legitimate—both for their immediate policy implications and for what they imply about the persistent need, which we discuss further below, for robust checks on executive leadership—and in no way do we want to soft-pedal them. But they are not the whole story.

What do we know about the American presidency? Here are some stylized facts that bear recognition when we think about the possibility, if not always the realization, of presidential leadership:

1. More than any other elected official, presidents represent the country as a whole. While we, as a nation, elect hundreds of thousands of people to local, state, and federal offices, we elect only one ticket (a president and vice president) that serves a distinctly national constituency.

2. Again, more than any other elected official, presidents care about their legacies—and legacies are ultimately defined not by public opinion today, the results of the latest congressional elections, or the clattering ephemera that preoccupy our fragmented and hyperventilating news sources, but rather by a demonstrated ability to craft lasting policy solutions to genuine problems.

3. Presidents are chief executives motivated and positioned to provide a coherent approach to the whole of government, whereas Congress can provide nothing of the sort. Its hundreds of members are mainly concerned about the various parts of government that matter to them as parochial politicians. Congress takes a piecemeal approach to the countless separate policies, programs, and agencies of government, while presidents care about the entire corpus of government and about making it work.

We are hardly the first to make these points. The Progressives of the late nineteenth and early twentieth centuries worried a great deal about the capacity of the federal government to respond to the profound challenges of industrialization, the influx of new immigrants from Europe, and the emergence of the United States onto the world stage. The answer, for them, lay not in constraining presidents who made the most of their Article II powers. Rather, it lay in "breaking through the constitutional form"[6] that does so much to undermine efforts at coordinated government action, and then, among other reforms, in rebuilding the larger political apparatus around an exalted presidency. As Woodrow Wilson wrote in the 1908 Blumenthal Lectures that he delivered at Columbia University, it is the president who "is the only national voice in affairs. . . . He is the representative of no constituency, but of the whole people."[7] And so when looking for leadership, Wilson reminds us, we must turn to the president.

Or recall the ruminations of people like Walter Lippmann, one of the most renowned journalists and social commentators of the twentieth century, who felt an acute anxiety over the "enfeeblement, verging on paralysis, of the capacity to govern" in Western liberal democracies. Lippmann vested little faith in either average citizens working alone or legislative majorities working directly on their behalf to solve generational challenges. For Lippmann, only the executive could rise above the sectionalism, self-interest, and parochialism that corroded the possibility of government action. Whereas the legislator keeps "close to the interest and sentiments of his constituents," the executive makes "fealty to the public interest . . . his virtue. And he must, at the very least, pay it the homage of hypocrisy."[8] Though legislators may occasionally perform like statesmen, "in the general run of mundane business" they vacillate between "defending local and personal rights" and promulgating "boss-ridden oligarchies." Even when legislators performed their duties with aplomb, Lippmann intoned, "representation must not be confused with governing." Governing, rightly understood, was the executive's province.

Not surprisingly, perhaps, Theodore Roosevelt offered the most fullthroated defense of a more expansive presidency. For Roosevelt, the president was uniquely equipped to articulate and advance the national interest—as embodied by his New Nationalism—and so it was he who stood the only real chance of meeting generational challenges. The president, Roosevelt famously recognized, held a distinct place in our political system as the only true "steward" of the American people.[9] Whereas Congress remain tethered to local interests, the president—and, among elected officials, the president alone—stood ready to guard and advance the nation's welfare in times both of crisis (as in his handling of the anthracite coal strikes) and relative calm (witness his wide-ranging conservation efforts).

Roosevelt believed that a president's national outlook and commitment to action established his unique credentials to meet generational challenges. But for all his grandiosity, Roosevelt was a pragmatist, and he recognized the dangers of vesting too much authority in any one individual. Roosevelt spent much of his time in office dismantling gross concentrations of corporate power within the marketplace, and in his writings Roosevelt recognized that presidents could demonstrate faults of character and conscience. As a result, Roosevelt admitted that meaningful checks—legislative, judicial, and electoral—must be preserved.[10] His was a project of emboldening and energizing the executive, not of erasing constitutional checks on executive authority.

A strong argument can be made that Theodore Roosevelt, more than any other president, laid the foundations of the modern presidency.[11] It is of some consequence, then, that the reform before us is broadly consistent with, and in some instances a good deal more moderate than, Roosevelt's institutional innovations in issuing public appeals, exercising unilateral powers, negotiating with Congress, and controlling the bureaucracy. Roosevelt certainly would have supported a reform that required Congress to vote on presidential initiatives. If anything, he may have lamented that it did not go far enough.

TO FACILITATE OR IMPEDE INSTITUTIONAL CHANGE?

It is no accident that the powers of the presidency over the last century have undergone such significant transformation. Since 1921, the president has had the responsibility of proposing a budget, which formally initiates the appropriations process. Nearly all major policy initiatives come at the behest of presidential—not congressional—initiative. The president's inaugural and State of the Union speeches, with rising frequency, set the legislative agenda and the terms under which it is debated. With fast-track authority, which Congress has intermittently granted and then withdrawn for decisions of international trade agreements, presidents can force the legislature to consider the terms of negotiated agreements on an up-or-down basis. This authority has worked, and worked well, for some forty years. Our proposal here is simply that this time-tested model of decision making be extended to cover all matters of public policy—enhancing the likelihood that government will be able to respond, and respond coherently and effectively, to pressing social problems.

We should conceive of the presidency as a work in progress. The presidency we have today is a far cry from the one the founders created, wherein few formal powers were explicitly granted (e.g., commander in chief, veto power, and responsibility to receive ambassadors), and the formal provisions that have proven over the years to be the foundations of presidential leadership—the vesting and take care clauses—were fraught with ambiguity. In a continual struggle to solve social problems, ours is a presidency made and remade. And it is no accident that through this process, the president's proposal powers have steadily expanded.

Should we now seek to curb these developments or build upon them? Given the challenges before us, we side with those who would build upon them— albeit purposefully, incrementally, and cautiously. Power should not be granted on a whim, motivated by some vague sense that the president can deliver where Congress and the courts cannot; hence, the kinds of new authority granted should match the president's specific comparative advantages. Change must not proceed from the fanciful imaginations of a cloistered institutional designer; hence, changes to the presidency must recognize the many interdependencies of successive generations of reformers. And finally, we must not lose sight of the ways in which presidents can make mistakes all of their own; hence, future grants of executive authority should be provisional, just as the exercise of future power remains contested. Having argued on behalf of institutional reform in one moment, we should not hesitate, in the next, in offering another should a corrective be needed.

That we should proceed purposefully, incrementally, and cautiously, however, is no excuse for not proceeding at all. Lest long-standing concerns about executive authority disrupt even the thoughtful consideration of continued institutional adaptation and reform, however, it is important to remember a basic fact about the proposal before us. This decidedly is not a proposition to increase the president's power generally or generically. It is about augmenting the president's proposal power and nothing more. Hence, it is perfectly legitimate to endorse an increase in this particular kind of presidential power, while also maintaining the view—as we do—that other dimensions of executive power ought to be curtailed.

It is of some consequence, moreover, that the institutional reform before us implicitly recognizes the comparative advantages of both the president and Congress. It does so first by putting the president at the front end of the legislation process, wherein problems are identified and solutions considered. Rather than tacking the president at the back end of the policy-making process—as the veto now accomplishes and as previous (and misguided) efforts to grant the president a line-item veto would have done in the 1990s—the proposal on offer here increases the chances that we will secure the unique sort of leadership that only the president can provide. It does so, however, without turning a blind eye to the mistakes that presidents can make or by denigrating the legitimate role that Congress plays in our system of checks and balances. Indeed, by requiring that members of Congress vote on a presidential initiative, this proposal encourages Congress to do the very things that Congress does best—namely, and as previously discussed, reacting, limiting, and amending solutions to generational challenges.

Rather than radically breaking from contemporary practice, the institutional reform under consideration would complement, extend, and rationalize institutional reforms long in the making. Rather than shunting Congress to the sidelines, this institutional reform would encourage members of Congress to actively debate the issues of the day. And rather than bemoaning the nagging persistence of generational challenges, this institutional reform would support the very kind of leadership needed to solve them. In turn, this institutional reform deserves our support as well.

CON: B. Dan Wood

The United States is governed by polarized, dysfunctional political institutions. Partisan obstruction and procedural roadblocks pose huge obstacles to coherent policymaking. And there is no sign that these obstructions and roadblocks will be removed anytime soon, despite a host of pressing national problems, including a massive federal debt, the need for immigration reform, gun violence, terrorism, and the war against ISIS. After 2012, Republicans in Congress were as determined as ever to block President Barack Obama's agenda. As former Nixon White House counsel John Dean observed shortly after the 2012 election, "Republican partisans (with whom I have spoken) are planning to continue their efforts to frustrate President Obama with ongoing obstructionism and increasingly shrill politics."[12] Having experienced this strategy over the subsequent four years, President Obama told Lee Cowan on *CBS Sunday Morning:* "The one thing that gnaws on me is the degree of continued polarization. It's gotten worse over the last several years."[13] Seemingly, polarization and gridlock will continue to hobble future presidents, whether Democratic or Republican.

Frustration with partisan polarization and gridlock in Washington has led some to call for institutional reform. Will Howell and Terry Moe have a radical idea: mandate that Congress be required to conduct an up-or-down vote on legislation proposed by the president. The assumption is that presidents, more than Congress, have the solution for most public problems. The president is assumed to have a coherent policy agenda that best reflects the national interest. Effectively, this proposal would greatly increase the legislative power of the president. It would give presidents and their parties greater agenda-setting power in Congress as well as move the nation closer to parliamentary government.

Before discussing the problems associated with this proposal, it is useful to understand its rationale and the problems it is intended to solve. The rationale for the proposal is to diminish congressional obstruction of presidential proposals. The modern Congress facilitates obstruction, not only of presidential proposals but also proposals by any legislator. It does so through formal and informal rules governing the procedures of the two chambers as well as the requirement for consensus between the two chambers and the president.

In both chambers, bills are almost always referred to committees before floor consideration. The majority party leadership in each chamber controls the assignment of bills to committees. Committees and subcommittees then typically vet bills before they come to the floor for debate and a vote. They "mark up" bills and in doing so can add amendments. Committee chairs typically decide whether and when to allow a bill to be reported from the committee. A positive committee vote is also needed for a bill to be considered by the full chamber.

In the House of Representatives, most bills must also flow through the House Rules Committee, which determines the rules to be used by the House when considering a bill on the floor. Closed rules allow no floor amendments; open rules allow them. Amendments can be a means of significantly altering or obstructing a bill. Of course, the rule under which a bill is considered in the House has important consequences for whether a bill ultimately passes. In the Senate, the threat of filibuster means that, realistically, passage cannot occur without a three-fifths vote to invoke cloture. In recent years, senators have also used a "hold" procedure to prevent bills from coming to the floor. If one or more senators object to a bill's movement to the floor, then it is held—that is, not placed on the Senate calendar (unless the majority party leadership disagrees). In both chambers, the majority party leadership controls what bills are placed on the calendar for debate and voting. However, under rare circumstances a bill can also be brought to the floor through a discharge petition signed by a simple majority of members. Discharge petitions are used more often in the House than Senate.[14]

Obviously, these complex procedures afford ample opportunity for members of Congress to alter or obstruct the president's proposals. A presidential proposal can be altered or obstructed through any of the following: by "hanging it out to dry" in committees or subcommittees, by amending it to death at the committee or floor level, by a single Senate member invoking a hold, by the absence of a three-fifths Senate majority for cloture, or by majority party leader opposition in either chamber. Furthermore, when different political parties control the two legislative chambers, then one chamber may take action while the other may prevent action. If one political party controls both legislative chambers, then it becomes easier to bring a measure to the floor in both houses. However, the obstacles are still considerable in the Senate, where members can invoke a hold or where there is not a three-fifths majority for cloture.

The proposal that Congress be required to conduct an up-or-down vote on legislation proposed by the president would short-circuit all of these procedures. The president's proposals would go to the chamber floor, avoiding committee and subcommittee deliberation, potential amendments, holds, the need for a three-fifths majority in the Senate, and agenda setting by party leaders. Of course, this change would greatly increase the legislative powers of the presidency. Presidents would be guaranteed a floor vote on anything they proposed. Under this scenario, Congress would merely affix a yes or no stamp to the president's proposals, contributing little to the interbranch deliberative process that has characterized the American republic for the past 227 years. Such a change in the legislative process would be a bad idea.

First, requiring Congress to take an up-or-down vote on presidential proposals assumes that there is nothing to be gained from the deliberative process within Congress. The president would not need to negotiate with the other party for a bill to be considered. Within Congress, the two political parties could not alter the language or content of the bill. There would be no bargain or compromise over the final form of the bill. The proposal assumes that the president is fully rational; has complete knowledge of what is best for the nation; and is the wisest of the wise, much like Plato's philosopher king. This view of the presidency is false. Virtually all presidential proposals can benefit from the vetting of the American legislative process.

Second, the proposal makes the normative assumption that presidents are wiser and less self-interested than legislative actors, and should therefore receive preferential treatment. A primary rationale behind giving the executive preferential treatment is that the president, as the sole elected representative of the entire nation, better reflects the national interest than does Congress. Certainly, the founders intended presidents to represent the national interest. Indeed, they abhorred the idea of partisanship and political parties and intended that all representatives would reflect the general interest of the nation. However, the founders failed to consider that what is in the national interest depends on one's political viewpoint. Early on, political parties developed competing visions of the national interest. Undoubtedly, modern partisans from both political parties also believe that their preferred policies are in the national interest.

Absent any objective definition of the national interest, various political scientists have argued that presidential ideology and policies should and do track the nation's median voter.[15] However, as I showed at length in *The Myth of Presidential Representation,* presidents and their policies do not usually reflect the median voter.[16] Rather, presidents are partisans who typically reflect the preferences of their own fellow partisans. That may or may not be in the national interest. Furthermore, recent research by Kriner and Reeves shows that presidents are also particularistic in their behavior and policies.[17] Like members of Congress, they target benefits toward those who can best get them or their party reelected. Thus presidents not only do not represent the national interest, but are self-interested actors who target benefits toward constituencies that can help them most. Presidents no more represent the national interest than Congress. Therefore, they should not be given preferential treatment in the legislative process.

Third, requiring Congress to conduct an up-or-down vote on unvetted presidential proposals will encourage presidents to be even more partisan than they currently are. Presidents are strategic actors. Under the current system, knowing that excessively partisan proposals have no chance of passing through the obstacle course of congressional procedures, they generally moderate their proposals to provide some chance of passage. Without the current deterrent to excessively partisan proposals, presidents would most likely propose what is consistent with their true preferences rather than what they think might pass. In short, if presidential proposals are not threatened by congressional winnowing, then they would undoubtedly become more extreme. Such a result would exacerbate polarization in the American system rather than resolve it.

Fourth, the proposal might actually weaken representation for Americans in a polarized system. In the current system, there is a representation gap in Washington. Presidents and the parties within Congress are more ideologically polarized and extreme than the average American.[18] However, extreme policies are seldom enacted because it is difficult to accomplish change in our system. There is a bias toward maintaining the status quo. Because the system favors maintaining the status quo, policies are more consistent with the preferences of the median voter. However, if the system facilitates change by making it easier for presidents to accomplish their partisan agendas, then the representation gap between political elites and the mass public will grow wider. With presidents and majority party legislators at the extremes, policies will move to the extremes. Citizens in the middle will be increasingly disenfranchised through the adoption of policies that do not reflect their views. The proposal would exacerbate this disenfranchisement by making it easier for extremists in Congress and the presidency to legislate extreme policies.

Fifth, the proposal to require Congress to hold an up-or-down vote on presidential proposals would not solve the problem it is intended to solve. The root of the problem faced by presidents is polarization and gridlock. The proposal would have no effect on polarization and, as noted above, might even exacerbate it. The proposal would only affect gridlock during periods of fully unified government, when the same political party controls the presidency and both houses of Congress. Currently during these periods, the opposing party can use procedural tools to obstruct the president's agenda. Under the proposal, these obstructions would be short-circuited. Of course, the proposal would have little effect during periods of divided government or a divided Congress. In a polarized system where party leaders maintain discipline, members of the opposing majority party would simply vote down the president's proposals.

Finally, the efficacy of requiring that presidential proposals be voted up or down by Congress depends on one's view of parliamentary versus republican government. Polarization and increased party cohesion have already moved the nation closer to a parliamentary-style system of party government.[19] Party leaders in Congress now successfully exercise discipline over their fellow partisans. Well over 90 percent of partisans vote with their own party in both chambers.[20] As a result, party-line voting is near its historical maximum. However, giving the president agenda-setting authority over Congress would increase this movement toward a parliamentary system. As partisan leaders, presidents would present a coherent party program and ensure its full consideration.

In a parliamentary system, policy changes sharply with each new government. Under liberal governments policy becomes more liberal; under conservative governments policy becomes more conservative. A key feature of such a system is that change is easier to accomplish. Accordingly, a parliamentary system is unstable in the sense that policy changes more, more readily, and more often. Furthermore, parliamentary systems provide little means for the minority party to achieve representation.

In contrast, republican government is biased toward stability and representation of minority interests. Through institutional checks and procedures, it becomes more difficult to accomplish change because the minority party often blocks it. The minority party holds in check efforts at change that are perceived as too ideological or inconsistent with its own view of the general interest. The legislative process imposes procedural roadblocks on presidential proposals for change for the explicit purpose of protecting the interests of the minority party. Said differently, under a republican system, there is a bias toward maintaining the status quo. Thus the efficacy of the proposal to require an up-or-down vote depends on one's view of whether the system should be parliamentary, in the sense that change should come easily, or republican, in the sense that change should be difficult.

Of course, the founders were very clear about their intention to establish a republican form of government that made change difficult and protected minority interests. Indeed, they were fearful and abhorrent of executive power of the kind that existed in the mother country. The entire purpose of a bicameral legislature with separate modes of representation was to make it more difficult for the majority to enact policies that would threaten minority interests. The original Congress had a nonelected Senate that reflected the interests of property owners (who were a minority) and a popularly elected House that reflected majority interests. An Electoral College was to select presidents, with electors chosen by the state legislatures, which generally consisted of property owners. Furthermore, the founders separated the executive and legislative branches so that neither would be able to dictate policy.

In conclusion, the system of shared legislative powers between Congress and the president has served the nation well over the last 227 years. While it may seem that we are currently in a decision-making crisis requiring institutional change, it would be unwise to alter the rules of the game permanently. The nation has passed through several periods of polarization and crisis, all of which were ultimately resolved. Furthermore, short-term solutions can have long-term consequences. For those who might favor the proposal to increase the president's agenda-setting power in Congress, remember that the opposing party will always return to power at some point in the future. In this case, the policies of the current president will be easier to overturn by a future president, but of course, the policies of the future president will also be easier to overturn. So the proposal cuts both ways for opposing partisans.

NOTES

PRO

1. For a longer discussion of this argument, and one that traces today's dysfunction to the Constitution, see William Howell and Terry Moe, *Relic: How Our Constitution Undermines Effective Government—And Why We Need a More Powerful Presidency* (New York: Basic Books, 2016).
2. Government Accountability Office, "Analysis of 2011–2012 Actions Taken and Effect of Delayed Increase on Borrowing Costs," GAO-12–701, July 2012.
3. IPCC Working Group III, *Emissions Scenarios: A Summary for Policymakers* (2000), http://www.ipcc.ch/pdf/special-reports/spm/sres-en.pdf

4. For a survey of existing climate change laws, see Robert Meltz, "Climate Change and Existing Law: A Survey of Legal Issues Past, Present, and Future," *Congressional Research Service Report,* 7–5700, May 25, 2013.

5. For a small subsample of recent lamentations on Congress, see Thomas Mann and Norman Ornstein, *The Broken Branch: How Congress Is Failing America and How to Get It Back* (New York: Oxford University Press, 2008); Thomas Mann and Norman Ornstein, *It's Even Worse than It Looks: How the American Constitutional System Collided with the New Politics of Extremism* (New York: Basic Books, 2012); Robert Draper, *Do Not Ask What Good We Do: Inside the U.S. House of Representatives* (New York: Free Press, 2012); Robert Kaiser, *Act of Congress: How America's Essential Institution Works, and How It Doesn't* (New York: Knopf, 2013).

6. Henry Jones Ford, *The Rise and Growth of American Politics* (New York: Macmillan, 1898), 292–93.

7. Woodrow Wilson, *Constitutional Government in the United States* (New Brunswick, NJ: Transaction Publishers, 2002 [1908]).

8. Walter Lippmann, *The Public Philosophy* (New York: The New American Library, 1956), 48.

9. These views are offered in their fullest detail in *Theodore Roosevelt: An Autobiography* (New York: Macmillan, 1913; New York: Da Capo Press, 1985). For a nice exposition of Roosevelt's evolving and at times inconsistent political thought, see Jean Yarbrough, *Theodore Roosevelt and the American Political Tradition* (Lawrence: University Press of Kansas, 2012).

10. For a longer discussion on such themes in a contemporary context, see William Howell, *Thinking about the Presidency: The Primacy of Power* (Princeton, NJ: Princeton University Press, 2013).

11. For more on this theme, see Sidney Milkis, *Theodore Roosevelt, the Progressive Party, and the Transformation of American Democracy* (Lawrence: University Press of Kansas, 2009).

CON

12. John W. Dean, "The Politics of Polarization and Obstructionism," *Verdict: Legal Analysis and Commentary from Justicia,* November 16, 2012.

13. Lee Cowan, "Barack Obama Interview with Lee Cowan," *CBS Sunday Morning,* January 24, 2016.

14. For more on the role of congressional procedures and norms in the policy process, see Walter J. Oleszek, *Congressional Procedures and the Policy Process* (Washington, DC: CQ Press, 2013).

15. See Robert S. Erikson, Michael B. MacKuen, and James A. Stimson, *The Macro Polity* (Boston: Cambridge University Press, 2002); and Brandice Canes-Wrone, *Who Leads Whom? Presidents, Policy, and the Public* (Chicago, IL: University of Chicago Press, 2006).

16. B. Dan Wood, *The Myth of Presidential Representation* (New York: Cambridge University Press, 2009).

17. Douglas K. Kriner and Andrew Reeves, *The Particularistic President: Executive Branch Politics and Political Inequality* (New York: Cambridge University Press, 2015).

18. See Alan I. Abramowitz, *The Disappearing Center: Engaged Citizens, Polarization, and American Democracy* (New Haven, CT: Yale University Press, 2010); and Morris P. Fiorina, Samuel J. Abrams, and Jeremy Pope, *Culture War? The Myth of a Polarized America*, 3rd ed. (New York: Longman, 2010).

19. See John H. Aldrich and David W. Rohde, "The Consequences of Party Organization in the House: The Role of the Majority and Minority Parties in Conditional Party Government," in *Polarized Politics: Congress and the President in a Partisan Era*, ed. Jon R. Bond and Richard Fleischer (Washington, DC: CQ Press, 2000); and John H. Aldrich and David W. Rohde, "The Logic of Conditional Party Government: Revisiting the Electoral Connection," in *Congress Reconsidered*, 7th ed., ed. Larry C. Dodd and Bruce I. Oppenheimer (Washington, DC: CQ Press, 2001).

20. Keith Poole and Howard Rosenthal, *Party Unity Scores*, February 8, 2013, http:// pooleandrosenthal.com/party_unity.htm

RESOLVED, Presidents have usurped the war power that rightfully belongs to Congress

PRO: Nancy Kassop

CON: Richard M. Pious

War transforms nations and governments. It centralizes power. It elevates state over society, the national government over local and regional governments, and the executive over the legislature. State building in Europe—in countries such as Great Britain, France, and Germany—was a direct result of war and the threat of war. Throughout much of its early history, the United States was blessedly free of the threat of war. Separated from the European powers by a vast ocean, the United States was able to maintain a relatively small military, a weak central government, and a limited executive.

The astute French observer Alexis de Tocqueville correctly diagnosed the political significance of America's isolation from the great powers of Europe.[1] Tocqueville understood that "it is chiefly in the realm of foreign relations that the executive power of a nation finds occasion to demonstrate its skill and strength." The United States that Tocqueville observed in 1831 had "an army that consists of six thousand soldiers" and a navy of "only a few vessels." The president was empowered by the Constitution to "direct the Union's dealings with foreign nations," but the nation had "no neighbors" and "no enemies." From Tocqueville's Eurocentric point of view, the United States was "separated from the rest of the world by the Atlantic Ocean." Rarely, he observed, "do its interests intersect with those of other nations of the globe." The result was that, although "the president of the United States possesses prerogatives that are almost royal in magnitude," the president has "no occasion to use" such powers, "and the powers that he has been able to use until now have been very circumscribed."

For Tocqueville, these observations underlined the need to look beyond formal powers and constitutional theories. "The law," he wrote, "allows [the president] to be strong, but circumstances keep him weak." Yet "if the existence of the Union were under constant threat, if its great interests were daily intertwined with those of other powerful nations, the executive power would take on increased importance in the public eye, because people would expect more of it, and it would do more." In other words, if and when circumstances changed to diminish the importance of the Atlantic Ocean as a barrier, then the chief executive of the United States would begin to look more like the strong executives of Europe. Executive power—along with the power of the central government as a whole—would grow. Not for the only time, Tocqueville was prescient.

Of course, the United States did have its wars in the nineteenth century, none more important than the Civil War. But during the Civil War and even during World War I, the growth in executive power and in the control exercised by the central government was followed by a period of reaction in which nearly all of the powers bestowed on the executive and the central government were dismantled. The executive powers exercised during these wars were justified as extraordinary measures necessitated by a national emergency. It was expected that after the threat passed, the political system would revert to its normal, more decentralized pattern of authority.

At first, it appeared that World War II would follow this venerable American tradition of wartime centralization and peacetime reaction. But the Cold War with the Soviet Union changed that pattern. War no longer seemed a temporary state but a permanent condition. Anxiety about the communist threat justified the accretion of executive power. After the Berlin Wall was torn down in 1989 and the Soviet Union collapsed in 1991, it appeared that the pendulum might swing back again. With the nation no longer under threat from communism, expansive executive power no longer seemed essential. Many scholars during the Bill Clinton years and the opening months of George W. Bush's presidency forecast a weakened presidency and a smaller central government. But the September 11, 2001, terrorist attacks on the United States changed all that. The Cold War was replaced by the "war on terror," which also seemed to have no clear beginning or end. Anxieties about the threats posed to the nation were again ubiquitous, and with these feelings of anxiety about the nation's safety came, as Tocqueville predicted, further expansion of executive power.

Whether enhanced executive power is good or bad and whether it is contrary to the intentions of the framers of the Constitution are among the subjects of the debate between Nancy Kassop and Richard M. Pious. Kassop laments that Americans have forgotten the wisdom of the framers, who placed the power to "declare war" in the hands of Congress. Pious, by contrast, sees the Constitution (in legal scholar Edward S. Corwin's famous phrase) as "an invitation to struggle" for control of foreign policy. In Pious's telling, it is not that the president has usurped the war power of Congress, but that Congress, with an assist from the courts, has handed power over to the president.

PRO: Nancy Kassop

"The Constitution . . . is an invitation to struggle for the privilege of directing American foreign policy."[2] So wrote the constitutional scholar Edward S. Corwin in 1957. But the words of the framers of the Constitution are actually clear and unambiguous, leaving little over which to struggle. Article I gives Congress the power to declare war, along with the power to provide for and maintain an army and a navy. Article II designates the president as commander in chief, whose authority, according to Alexander Hamilton in *Federalist* No. 69, "would amount to nothing more than the supreme command and direction of the military and naval forces, as first general and admiral of the Confederacy; while that of the British king extends to the *declaring* of war and to the *raising* and *regulating* of fleets and armies—all which, by the Constitution under consideration, would appertain to the legislature."[3] Thus, as with most of the other shared powers in the Constitution, the lines of authority delineated by the framers are clear.

Article II, Section 2, of the Constitution reads: "The President shall be Commander in Chief of the Army and Navy of the United States, and of the Militia of the several States, when called into the actual Service of the United States." That provision gives the president a title, *commander in chief,* but no specific list of powers that can be exercised in that capacity. It also suggests that the president is not "Commander in Chief" all of the time but only "when called into the actual Service of the United States." As Hamilton wrote, also in *Federalist* No. 69, "The President will have only the occasional command of such part of the militia of the nation as by legislative provision may be called into the actual service of the nation."[4] Further evidence of Hamilton's understanding that the president's power was to be limited is found in his proposal to the Constitutional Convention (he was a delegate from New York) that the president "have the direction of war when authorized or begun."[5] It is Congress, then, that calls the president into service as commander in chief when it declares war or authorizes the use of force by statute. The framers could not have been clearer: the decision to go to war belongs to the deliberative branch of government, because declaring war is a political decision to move the nation from a state of peace to a state of war. Only then does the president command the troops and conduct military operations.[6] As law professor Louis Henkin has noted, "Generals and admirals, even when they are 'first,' do not determine the political purposes for which troops are to be used; they command them in the execution of policy made by others."[7]

The framers, however, were not blind to the possibility that emergency or exigent situations could arise. Notes from the Constitutional Convention confirm that the delegates' change in wording of Article I—from the power "to make war" to the power "to declare war"—indicated their intention to give the president "the power to repel sudden attacks" without specific statutory authorization from Congress.[8] But this sole exception makes the rule all the more plain: presidents can act on their own *only* in defensive circumstances. Any offensive military action, regardless of size, duration, or purpose, must be authorized by Congress. Offensive versus defensive was the crucial distinction for the framers. However, enforcement of that distinction, at least since the middle of the twentieth century, has been sorely lacking. No delegate at the Constitutional Convention, not even Hamilton, would recognize the power to use military force that presidents have wielded in the international arena since World War II.

At a bare minimum, the Constitution requires the following:

1. All offensive uses of military force must be authorized by Congress, either through a formal declaration of war or by specific statutory authorization. Joint action by both branches is required—that is, passage by both houses of Congress and signing by the president.

2. Any independent constitutional authority the president may have to direct the use of military force without Congress's approval must be defensive in purpose—"to repel sudden attacks."

3. The president's status as commander in chief is confined to the authority to conduct military operations when Congress determines, through the mechanisms of a declaration of war or specific statutory authorization, that such operations are warranted.

4. The president's status as commander in chief confers on the president, subject to Congress's authorization, the power to conduct military operations after Congress has identified the location, purpose, scope,

and to the extent possible, anticipated duration of hostilities. Status as commander in chief does not confer a "blanket" or open-ended authority to direct domestic policy, unless Congress has delegated specific emergency powers to the president in connection with the use of military force it has previously approved.

5. In order for Congress to make effective judgments about whether to authorize the use of military force in any situation, the president and other executive branch officials must make good-faith efforts to supply the legislature with accurate and complete information in a timely manner. The decisions Congress makes are only as good as the information it receives.

6. The constitutional requirement that Congress approve the use of military force is not satisfied by the approval of other international bodies, such as the North Atlantic Treaty Organization (NATO) or the United Nations Security Council. When an international body calls for the deployment of U.S. military forces, Congress must still give its approval.

Each of these constitutional requirements has been violated by presidents, with increasing impunity, since the mid–twentieth century. Some presidents have violated more than one of these requirements in a single decision. President Harry S. Truman's decision to send U.S. troops to Korea in December 1950 is the most-cited example of a president ordering troops into combat on the basis of inherent executive authority without any participation by Congress. Truman's action violated all of the items just listed. He sent troops to Korea without either a declaration of war by Congress or specific statutory authorization (No. 1). The purpose of the action was not to repel an attack against the United States but rather to protect U.S. interests by defending an ally against communist aggression (No. 2). Truman based his decision to employ U.S. forces on his commander in chief authority alone, without any participation by Congress (No. 3). He issued an executive order in April 1952 directing the secretary of commerce to seize privately owned steel mills and operate them under government control, arguing, partly on the basis of his status as commander in chief, that averting a strike and continuing production of steel were essential for the war effort (No. 4). He did not consult with or inform Congress about his ordering of U.S. troops to Korea before announcing his decision to the American public (No. 5). And he cited a United Nations Security Council resolution as justification for sending U.S. forces to Korea (No. 6).[9]

Truman's actions established a precedent for presidents to ignore and bypass what had previously been understood and honored, more or less, as baseline constitutional requirements. Previous presidents had, at times, acted on their own authority. For example, Franklin D. Roosevelt made a destroyers-for-bases deal with Great Britain in 1940, and in the spring and summer of 1941 sent American forces to Greenland and Iceland. He also ordered U.S. naval ships in the North Atlantic to "shoot on sight" any German and Italian submarines west of the twenty-sixth meridian.[10] Although Roosevelt ordered these actions without congressional authorization, historian Arthur M. Schlesinger Jr. has shown that the president conducted "extensive and vigilant consultation—within the executive branch, between the executive and legislative branches, among leaders of both parties and with the press."[11] Schlesinger concedes that Roosevelt's prewar actions skirted the edge of the president's constitutional authority but notes that FDR displayed "a lurking sensitivity to constitutional issues," that he "made no general claims to inherent presidential power," and that he "did not assert . . . that there was no need to consider Congress because his role as commander in chief gave him all the authority he needed."[12]

Thus the shift in constitutional approach from Roosevelt in 1940 to Truman in 1950 was significant, if not tectonic. Most important, it signaled a new interpretation of the commander in chief clause as a source of executive authority independent of Congress. Such power, once seized without effective challenge, is unlikely to be returned. Congress's efforts since 1950 to remedy its loss of constitutional authority to the president have been few and ineffective.[13]

JUSTIFYING THE EXPANSION OF PRESIDENTIAL AUTHORITY

To understand how this expansive interpretation of presidential authority was justified, one need look no further than a 1966 memo written in defense of the Vietnam War by State Department legal adviser Leonard Meeker.[14] Acknowledging that the president's authority to commit U.S. forces to Vietnam did not depend on constitutional sources alone, because Congress and the SEATO (Southeast Asia Treaty Organization) Treaty had supplemented that authority, Meeker nevertheless offered a sweeping, absolutist view of presidential power based on the commander in chief clause. "Under the Constitution," he wrote, "the President, in addition to being Chief Executive, is Commander in Chief of the Army and Navy. He holds the prime responsibility for the conduct of United States foreign relations. These duties carry very broad powers, including the power to deploy American forces abroad and commit them to military operations when the President deems such action necessary to maintain the security and defense of the United States."[15]

Meeker's argument misrepresents what the framers intended the commander in chief clause to mean. The framers attached no substantive powers to that title, other than to direct the military once Congress had commanded the president to do so. Only to repel a sudden attack could the commander in chief initiate military action.

Meeker's counterargument is that "in 1787 the world was a far larger place, and the framers probably had in mind attacks upon the United States. In the twentieth century, the world has grown smaller. An attack on a country far from our shores can impinge directly on the nation's security. . . . The Constitution leaves to the president the judgment to determine whether the circumstances of a particular armed attack are so urgent and the potential consequences so threatening to the security of the United States that he should act without formally consulting Congress."[16] Even if one accepts Meeker's "smaller world theory," it does not justify the transfer of constitutional power from Congress to the president. An assertion that the power to make war has in fact been shifted to the president does not make that power legitimate or constitutional.

THE FAILURE TO REASSERT CONGRESSIONAL AUTHORITY

Just how far presidents have strayed from the Constitution can be measured in the futile efforts by Congress to rein in rapacious executives and to reassert "first principles." Those efforts found a voice in the National Commitments Resolution of 1969, a nonbinding "sense of the Senate" resolution expressing that, henceforth, "a national commitment by the United States results only from the affirmative action taken by the executive and legislative branches of the United States Government by means of a treaty, statute or concurrent resolution of both Houses of Congress specifically providing for such commitment."[17] This first attempt by the Senate, at the height of the Vietnam War, to reassert its authority was buttressed by a report of the Committee on Foreign Relations that offered an extensive history and analysis of war making, identifying an unmistakable change after World War II that, by 1969, had reached "the point at which the real power to commit the country to war is now in the hands of the president. The trend which began in the early 20th century has been consummated and the intent of the framers of the Constitution as to the war power substantially negated."[18] The report explained that although the country still believed that Congress had the sole power to declare war, it was also widely believed, or at least conceded, that the President in his capacity as Commander in Chief had the authority to use the Armed Forces in any way he saw fit. Noting that the President has in fact exercised power over the Armed Forces we have come to assume that he is entitled to do so. The actual possession of a power has given rise to a belief in its constitutional legitimacy. The fact that Congress has acquiesced in, or at the very least has failed to challenge, the transfer of the war power from itself to the executive, is probably the most important single fact accounting for the speed and virtual completeness of the transfer.[19]

Four years later, Congress passed the War Powers Resolution (WPR) over President Richard Nixon's veto. That joint resolution, which has the force of law, imposed procedural requirements on presidents when they decide to send U.S. military forces into hostilities. Its lofty purpose was "to fulfill the intent of the framers of the Constitution of the United States and insure that the collective judgment of both the Congress and the President will apply to the introduction of United States Armed Forces into hostilities."[20] Thus this resolution enacted into law the "commitment" that the Senate had urged in its report four years earlier. Today, however, after more than forty years of experience with presidents refusing to comply strictly with its requirements, many scholars and commentators have concluded that this effort, though well-meaning, has failed.[21] It has simply added another set of legal requirements that presidents ignore or evade.[22]

Courts have done little or nothing to restrain the presidential power grab. At best, they have treated these issues as nonjusticiable, and, at worst, they have supported presidential usurpation of war powers.[23] The only serious judicial effort to restrain a president's usurpation of Congress's war power was *Dellums v. Bush* (1990), in which a federal district court refused to accept President George H. W. Bush's claim that the president alone had the authority to distinguish between military actions that constitute war, requiring congressional authorization, and those that are "only an offensive military attack," short of war, thereby needing no congressional approval.[24] Judge Harold Greene called such a claim "far too sweeping to be accepted by the courts. If the Executive had the sole power to determine that any particular offensive military operation, no matter how vast, does not constitute war-making but only an offensive military attack, the congressional power to declare war will be at the mercy of a semantic decision by the Executive. Such an 'interpretation' would evade the plain language of the Constitution, and it cannot stand."[25] If that was not enough to demonstrate the court's willingness to protect Congress's power, then a comment further into the opinion should suffice: "To put it another way: the Court is not prepared to read out of the Constitution the clause granting to Congress, and to it alone, the authority to declare war."[26] Unfortunately, Judge Greene never decided the merits of the issue in that case, and so the decision stands as a rare pronouncement of judicial resolve, but without any practical consequence flowing from it.

PRESIDENTIAL WAR POWERS IN THE BUSH YEARS

Constitutional interpretations of the commander in chief clause took on renewed prominence during the George W. Bush administration. In the aftermath of the September 11, 2001, terrorist attacks on the United States, President Bush proceeded on two fronts: (1) he asked Congress to approve an authorization for the use of military force (AUMF), and (2) he tasked a select group of executive branch lawyers to provide an interpretation of the commander in chief clause to guide the president during a "war on terror."

On September 18, 2001, Congress passed S.J. Res. 23, a joint resolution authorizing the president "to use all necessary and appropriate force against those nations, organizations, or persons he determines planned, authorized, committed, or aided the terrorist attacks that occurred on September 11, 2001, or harbored such organizations or persons, in order to prevent any future acts of international terrorism against the United States by such nations, organizations or persons."[27] At the same time, lawyers from the offices of the Counsel to the President and the Counsel to the Vice President worked secretly with handpicked lawyers in the Office of Legal Counsel in the Department of Justice to produce a series of legal opinions that determined that the president had inherent authority under the commander in chief clause to take whatever actions deemed necessary to protect the nation during wartime. The opinions gave the president a green light to "override" or brush aside acts of Congress, treaties and other international legal agreements, and constitutional guarantees that stood in the way of the president's counterterrorism policy preferences.[28] President Bush relied on both the AUMF and his commander in chief authority to justify a wide array of controversial counterterrorism policies: indefinite detention of terrorist suspects at Guantánamo Bay, trial by military commission, interrogation techniques that amounted to torture, domestic surveillance without a warrant, and domestic use of the military for law enforcement purposes.[29] Congress intended the AUMF to provide specific statutory authorization for the deployment of the U.S. military into Afghanistan in pursuit of al-Qaeda and the Taliban, but the Bush administration interpreted it as congressional acknowledgement of the president's inherent constitutional authority to take *any* action, military or nonmilitary, in Afghanistan or anywhere else (including within the United States), to forestall any future terrorist attacks. This interpretation claimed that the president had independent and unlimited authority—as commander in chief—to take these actions, even without the AUMF.[30]

In October 2002 President Bush again asked Congress for authorization to use military force, this time against the regime of Saddam Hussein, who the administration believed to be hiding weapons of mass destruction in Iraq. Congress obliged by passing the Authorization for Use of Military Force against Iraq Resolution,[31] and on March 20, 2003, Bush ordered the start of U.S. air strikes against Iraq. By May 1, 2003, President Bush stood on the deck of the aircraft carrier *Abraham Lincoln* under a "Mission Accomplished" banner and proclaimed the end of the military phase of the effort to remove Hussein from power. No weapons of mass destruction were ever found, leading critics to claim that the administration had misled Congress and that it was a "war of choice" rather than a war of necessity.

The Bush administration increased presidential power in the national security realm to an unprecedented extent by relying on an untenably expansive interpretation of the commander in chief clause as well as on an overly broad reading of the powers authorized by Congress under the 2001 and 2002 AUMFs.[32] The administration's legacy was a dramatic enhancement of the powers of the president during wartime. Most significant was the administration's insistence that "the battlefield" of an amorphous "global war on terror" had no geographic limits. The president claimed that his power to conduct foreign and military policy extended to *any* actions, at home or abroad, military or otherwise. And because the president asserted an exclusive responsibility to keep the country safe, he rejected claims to authority by Congress or the courts to intervene in or oversee executive branch actions when national security was at stake. Such an interpretation is fundamentally at odds with the principles lain down by the Constitution's framers, but in the Bush administration's view, two-hundred-year-old expectations were incompatible with twenty-first-century realities. The result was a "changed" Constitution, one that had effectively transferred power from Congress to the president, without formally amending the document.

PRESIDENTIAL WAR POWERS IN THE OBAMA YEARS

President Barack Obama came into office in January 2009 having pledged to end the Iraq War; to commit sufficient resources to the long-neglected war effort in Afghanistan so that it, too, could be brought to a close; and to roll back the excesses of the Bush administration's national security policies. Specifically, Obama promised to ban the use of torture by U.S. personnel, to end the use of

CIA "black sites," and to close the military prison at Guantánamo Bay within a year. During his first year in office, Obama reversed some of the Bush administration's policies (e.g., regarding torture) and continued others (e.g., detention at Guantánamo and domestic warrantless surveillance), but a perceptible shift in rhetoric occurred. Gone was a reliance on the inherent war powers of the president—and the commander in chief clause specifically—as the source of authority for the administration's policies. State Department Legal Adviser Harold Koh noted in a March 2010 speech that the Obama administration differed from the Bush administration in its legal approach. "[A]s a matter of *domestic law,*" Koh explained, "the Obama administration has not based its claim of authority to detain those at GITMO and Bagram on the President's Article II authority as Commander-in-Chief. Instead, we have relied on legislative authority expressly granted to the President by Congress in the 2001 AUMF."[33]

But the administration's shift away from reliance on the commander in chief clause was short-lived. In the spring of 2011, President Obama relied on the clause in defending his authority to order the U.S. military to carry out air strikes on Libya.[34] He also invoked United Nations Security Council Resolution 1973 to justify imposing a no-fly zone over Libya. When Obama notified Congress on March 21 that he had ordered the U.S. military to begin operations against Libya, there had been no authorization from Congress for this engagement. Congress became involved only when it notified the president in June 2011 that the military operations were about to exceed the ninety-day clock under the WPR, requiring him either to terminate the mission or to obtain statutory authorization from Congress to extend it. The president did neither, prompting a contentious debate over whether this requirement applied to these specific circumstances. Administration lawyers from the State Department and the White House Counsel's office argued that the WPR did not apply here because (1) there were no longer "hostilities" (the operative word in the WPR) involving U.S. forces since the early April hand-off to NATO troops; (2) U.S. operations in Libya at this point were of "limited nature, scope and duration"; (3) there were no U.S. ground forces under serious threat; and (4) the WPR was not intended to apply in circumstances short of "hostilities."[35] Lawyers from the Office of Legal Counsel and from the Department of Defense disagreed with this interpretation but lost out to their counterparts in the White House and the State Department.[36]

In May 2013 perhaps the most controversial issue of all erupted when President Obama publicly acknowledged that the United States had engaged in a policy of targeted killings of specific categories of terrorist suspects abroad, including American citizens, when it is not possible to capture them.[37]

Admitting such a policy—and asserting a legal justification for it—poses an exceptionally troubling and legally dubious expansion of presidential authority to use military force without the consent of Congress. In his remarks, President Obama drew on the 2001 AUMF as the source of authority for this policy, while also noting his *position* "as commander in chief," though not explicitly referring to any powers he derived from that position.

This example shows, as do many during the Bush administration, that even when Congress acts in its constitutional role of authorizing military action, the restrictive purpose of such statutes can be undermined, either by (1) overly broad or ambiguous statutory wording (often the price of passage in Congress), or (2) presidents who stretch or bend the meaning of the statute's words so as to authorize actions the statute was never intended to cover. Congress has a long history of authorizing the use of military force in circumstances that amount to less than "war." The challenge is to craft statutory language that permits executive discretion in those cases that Congress intended while preventing presidents from using it in cases that Congress did not intend. Unless Congress makes its authorizations more precise and time limited, presidents will continue to thwart congressional intent and thereby usurp congressional war powers and aggrandize their own.

Moreover, the five-year civil war in Syria that began in March 2011 and its tangled connection to the U.S. effort to drive Islamic State forces out of Iraq and Syria are the most recent—and most vexing—examples of the complex dance between Congress and the president over control of the use of military force. In neither circumstance has Congress acted definitively to formally authorize U.S. forces, despite fitful, intermittent, and inconsistent efforts from both branches to produce congressional authorizations. With the Islamic State, President Obama has claimed that (1) he would welcome formal congressional approval for military force, but that (2) he is, nevertheless, able to rely upon the 2001 AUMF passed in the wake of the September 11 attacks and, possibly, also on the 2002 AUMF on Iraq to serve as congressional approval for the limited number of special operations forces he has sent to battle the Islamic State in Iraq and Syria. Legal scholars are critical of this argument, noting that a fifteen-year-old AUMF written for a different time and a different enemy cannot plausibly serve to authorize the conflict with the Islamic State.

CONCLUSION

Although the most extreme and strained interpretations of the commander in chief clause advanced by the Bush administration have been scaled back under the Obama administration, the president's war powers, whether based on the commander in chief clause or on executive branch construction of language in statutory authorizations, remain far beyond anything envisioned by the founders. Some scholars insist that this only underscores that the Constitution's allocation of war powers is an eighteenth-century anachronism that no longer makes sense in the twenty-first century.[38] But the framers' reasons for separating the power to declare war from the power to conduct it are just as relevant today as they were in 1787. Indeed, their "deep-seated fear of unilateral executive power and . . . commitment to collective decision-making in foreign affairs" is more relevant than ever, since the consequences of war in the twenty-first century are more terrible than ever before.[39] It has never been more important than it is today to ensure that the decision to engage in a war is made by more than one person—and more than one branch—and through a deliberative process resulting in an agreed understanding by both Congress and the president of the terms of military engagement.

CON: Richard M. Pious

The Constitution is silent or ambiguous on many issues, and nowhere is this more of a problem than on the question of how war powers are to be exercised. The debates at the 1787 Constitutional Convention did not settle the issue. The framers had before them a proposal that gave Congress the power "to make war." Delegate Charles Pinckney proposed instead giving the power to the Senate, because it would be "more acquainted with foreign affairs" and smaller in size than the House of Representatives. Fellow South Carolinian Pierce Butler suggested vesting the war power in the president, "who will have all the requisite qualities, and will not make war but when the nation will support it." George Mason of Virginia spoke against "giving the power of war to the executive, because [the executive is] not safely to be trusted with it." Fellow Virginian James Madison and Elbridge Gerry of Massachusetts moved to insert "declare" instead of "make," thereby leaving the executive "the power to repel sudden attacks." That change was agreed to by seven states, with two opposed and one absent. Delegates from all ten states present voted down a proposal by Butler to give the legislature "the power of peace, as they were to have that of war." The president was to be "Commander in Chief of the Army and Navy of the United States, and of the Militia of the several States, when called into the actual Service of the United States." George Washington of Virginia, Alexander Hamilton of New York, and Gouverneur Morris of Pennsylvania preferred to leave language incomplete or ambiguous, with presidential powers underdefined, because once in office they intended to exploit the silences and ambiguities of the Constitution in order to expand those powers.[40]

What can one conclude from the debates at the convention? Only that Congress has the power to declare war and thus can turn a state of peace into a state of belligerency with another nation. But because presidents can repel invasion on their own authority, the power to "make" war or otherwise make use of the armed forces is not reserved to Congress alone but is a concurrent responsibility of the president and Congress. Beyond these principles nothing is clear. Some commentators argue that no language in the Constitution prevents the president from using force and making war and that many framers would have approved of presidential war making. Others argue that the intent of the framers was to have Congress participate in all decisions involving the use of force. Trying to parse meaning from the literal language of the constitutional text and the statements made by delegates in 1787 will not resolve the debate. A better way is to consider the precedents in American history: How have presidents exercised war powers without a congressional declaration of war? And how have Congress and the federal courts responded?

WAR POWERS: THE LIVING CONSTITUTION

Of the more than two hundred occasions on which the United States has committed armed forces abroad, Congress has declared war only in five: the War of 1812, the Mexican-American War in 1846, the Spanish-American War in 1898, World War I in 1917, and World War II in 1941. Of the early presidents, George Washington used forces without any congressional declaration to clear the Ohio Valley of American Indians; John Adams ordered the navy into action under congressional prodding in an "undeclared" naval war against the French; and Thomas Jefferson used the navy and Marine Corps against pirates harassing American shipping in the Mediterranean Sea. Later presidents used the military to intervene on behalf of American settlers in Florida, Texas, California, and Hawaii. Once America became a world power, armed forces were used to defeat insurgents in the Philippines.

When presidents used force to topple regimes (Grenada in 1982, Iraq in 2003) or safeguard them from being toppled by others (South Korea in the 1950s, South Vietnam in the 1960s), no declaration of war was made by Congress. Since the start of the Cold War in the 1950s, Congress has not declared war in any of the major hostilities that have seen the involvement of hundreds of thousands of U.S. troops. Presidents made the decision for peace or war, and Congress used its powers of appropriation, its power to draft or otherwise raise the armed forces, and its other war powers to back the executive, a pattern of behavior known to the courts as "joint concord."

Congress can even express its support retroactively. For example, at the beginning of the Civil War Abraham Lincoln did not call Congress into session (it was not scheduled to meet until December 1861), and he took many actions on his own prerogative, including raising military forces, calling state militias into federal service, sending funds from the Treasury to encourage western Virginia to secede from the Confederacy, and sending naval forces south to enforce federal law. Lincoln then called Congress into special session and informed it that the actions he had taken did not go beyond the scope of the war powers of the national government. This formulation begged the question of whether he had gone beyond the powers assigned to the executive by the Constitution. The congressional response was neither to repudiate his actions nor to impeach him for overreaching. Instead, Congress passed an appropriations act that retroactively legitimized all the actions he had taken in the war. In the *Prize Cases* (1863), the Supreme Court considered whether Lincoln's proclamation ordering a blockade of southern ports had been legal before Congress met and "ratified" it.[41] The Court ruled that no declaration of war was required in a civil conflict. The justices held that any decision to use force in a civil conflict could be made by the president and that federal courts would be governed by his decision. Finally, the Court observed that even if the president had erred in acting alone, the act passed by Congress ratifying his actions would "cure the defect."

Presidents Grover Cleveland and Theodore Roosevelt extended presidential war powers to include "international police powers." They argued that the president's duty to "take care that the laws be faithfully executed" extended to the treaty obligations of nations and the canons of international law. Harry S. Truman extended the police powers and fused the president's powers as commander in chief with the new U.S. obligation to enforce the United Nations Charter's provisions against aggression. Article 51 of the charter recognizes the right of self-defense against aggression and the right of collective security. Article 53 permits regional security pacts and organizations to repel aggression. When Truman sent troops to South Korea in the summer of 1950 to repel an attack from the North, the State Department claimed that a UN Security Council resolution calling on nations to repel the aggression was an obligation to be met by the president without any need for a declaration of war by Congress. In taking these actions, Truman ignored the United Nations Participation Act of 1946, which requires congressional approval of U.S. collective security efforts under the UN. But instead of protesting, Congress acquiesced, though in this instance it was clear that Truman went beyond its intent and that of the framers.

Presidents also have argued that the North Atlantic Treaty Organization (NATO), Southeast Asia Treaty Organization (SEATO), and Organization of American States (OAS) collective security treaties are self-executing and give the president the right to use the armed forces to protect allies. By contrast, Congress interprets treaty provisions that every nation will act "in accordance with its constitutional processes" to mean that a declaration of war would be required. In consenting to these treaties, the Senate has "agreed to disagree" with the president's interpretation, leaving the president with a free hand to act.

During the Cold War, Congress signaled support for presidential use of armed forces in two different ways. In the confrontations in 1955 with communist China in the Formosa Strait, in 1962 with the Soviet Union in the Cuban missile crisis, and in 1964 with North Vietnam in the Gulf of Tonkin incident, Congress passed resolutions in which it would "approve" and "support" possible presidential military actions. In the two more recent conflicts with Iraq, the Persian Gulf War of 1991 and the Iraq War of 2003, Congress went much further, passing joint resolutions (with the force of law) that specifically authorized the president to use armed forces against Iraq. For all intents and purposes, these resolutions were the functional equivalent of declarations of war. Why, then, were they not declarations? Because Congress, in passing them, hoped to send a final signal to Iraq that it must agree to a diplomatic resolution of the crisis or else hostilities would ensue. If the intent of the framers was to require that the president obtain advance congressional consent to a decision to authorize hostilities, then in both conflicts with Iraq the president complied with that obligation.

WAR POWERS AND THE JUDICIARY

Through much of American history, the federal courts did not shy away from ruling on the merits of war powers cases and occasionally checking presidential prerogative. During and after the Vietnam War, however, the federal courts invoked a series of procedural hurdles in order to evade decisions on the substantive issues, thereby leaving the president with a free hand to take military actions without congressional assent.

In *Luftig v. McNamara* (1967), a draftee argued that the secretary of defense, Robert McNamara, had no legal authority to send him to Vietnam because Congress had not declared war.[42] The district court held that judges were precluded "from overseeing the conduct of foreign policy or the use and disposition of military power: these matters are plainly the exclusive province of Congress and the executive." However, in *Berk v. Laird* (1970), although the government argued that absent a declaration of war the president possessed all war powers, a federal appeals court rejected that claim because it would reduce the congressional power to declare war to "an antique formality."[43]

The court held that joint action by Congress and the executive was required. In *Orlando v. Laird* (1971), a court of appeals dealt with the question of whether there must be a declaration of war to satisfy the joint concord standard.[44] Salvatore Orlando, an enlisted soldier, argued that the president had placed Congress in an impossible position because once the war escalated, Congress could hardly refuse appropriations or draft legislation. The court disagreed, finding that "[t]he Congress and the executive have taken mutual and joint action" in prosecuting the Vietnam War from the very beginning. It pointed to the Gulf of Tonkin Resolution whose "broad language . . . clearly showed the state of mind of the Congress and its intention fully to implement and support the military and naval activities" of the president. In *Massachusetts v. Laird* (1971), an appeals court found that Congress had amply participated in the Vietnam War in the form of appropriations and selective service extensions.[45] Although the court held that the Constitution requires the "joint participation of Congress in determining the scale and duration of hostilities," it rejected the argument that a declaration of war was required to satisfy the joint concord standard, observing that no language in the Constitution says that Congress must declare war before supporting war. Most important, the court held that it would not decide which institution had what war power but rather would accept the legality of war powers exercised by the national government when the president and Congress were held to be acting in joint concord.

Even after Congress repealed the Gulf of Tonkin Resolution (thereby ending joint concord in prosecuting the Vietnam War), a federal appeals court ruled in *Da Costa v. Laird* (1971) that the repeal did not change the fact that when the war began Congress had acquiesced in executive actions and had supported them.[46] "It was not the intent of Congress in passing the repeal amendment to bring all military operations in Vietnam to an abrupt halt," the court held. Instead, the court saw repeal as part of the process of Vietnamization of the war that had been started by the president, and it claimed that the war involved "mutual action by the legislative and executive branches." This claim was quite a stretch, considering that the Nixon administration had opposed the repeal measure. Nevertheless, the court ruled that Congress and the president, not the courts, would decide how the war would wind down. Then it added a bit of dicta (language not needed for the decision), observing that "if the executive were now escalating the prolonged struggle instead of decreasing it, additional supporting action by the legislative branch over what is presently afforded might well be required." Yet in 1973, after the president escalated the war to put pressure on the North Vietnamese to negotiate an end to the war, the court did not find that the escalation required any "additional supporting action" by Congress. The court backed down from its earlier holding in *Da Costa* about escalation, and now it claimed that there was a "lack of discoverable and manageable judicial standards" and that "judges, deficient in military knowledge[,]" could not make decisions about whether a specific military operation constituted an escalation of the war.[47] By the end of the Vietnam conflict, the practical effect of judicial rulings on war powers cases was to provide the executive with great flexibility in the exercise of war powers.

THE FAILURE OF THE WAR POWERS RESOLUTION

In response to these court decisions, Congress passed the 1973 War Powers Resolution (WPR) over President Nixon's veto. The WPR required the president to consult Congress before sending armed forces into either hostilities or a situation in which hostilities might be imminent; he was to report to Congress within forty-eight hours of doing so and every six months thereafter. It also required the president to withdraw forces if within sixty days he had not received from Congress a declaration of war, specific authorization, or an extension of the sixty-day period. He also was to withdraw forces if Congress, by concurrent resolution, required him to withdraw them. In such instances, he was given thirty days to execute the withdrawals.

Every president from Nixon to George W. Bush denied that the WPR is constitutional. President Barack Obama sidestepped the question of the constitutionality of the WPR by arguing that the WPR didn't apply to the administration's bombing campaign in Libya in 2011 because it was not the sort of "hostilities" envisioned by the architects of the WPR, since the Libya air war did "not involve sustained fighting or active exchanges of fire with hostile forces." Presidents have routinely sabotaged the WPR by failing to consult with Congress prior to the introduction of forces (they provide briefings instead) and by issuing one- or two-page "reports" that they say are consistent with the WPR but not in compliance with it. For example, in 1982 Ronald Reagan signed a measure Congress had passed extending his time period under the WPR, but in his signing statement he insisted that the legislature could not set conditions on his use of the armed forces. Congress, for its part, has turned a blind eye to case after case of presidential nonfeasance or misfeasance involving the WPR. In 1987, in the midst of a crisis with Iran over American-flagged Kuwaiti shipping in the Persian Gulf, Congress gave up entirely on trying to make the WPR a vehicle for joint decision making and instead used the more traditional authorization after the fact. During the crisis, 110 unhappy members of the U.S. House of Representatives contended that the Reagan administration had ignored the reporting requirements of the WPR by using U.S. naval vessels to escort the Kuwaiti tankers and engage in combat with Iranian mine-laying vessels. They then asked a federal court to rule that a report had been required months before. The judge not only refused to rule on the suit but also observed that the constitutionality of the WPR could not be assumed.

In both wars against Iraq and in the intervening hostilities in the Balkans, the war powers of Presidents Clinton and both Bushes were left unscathed after judicial challenges. In *Dellums v. Bush* (1990), fifty-three members of the House and one senator sought a court order prohibiting George H. W. Bush from using armed forces for a war against Iraq in 1990.[48] In that case, Judge Harold Greene used a new procedural dodge to avoid making a decision: the court could not rule because the case was not "ripe" for decision. "It would be both premature and presumptuous for the court to render a decision . . . ," he said, "when the Congress itself has provided no indication whether it deems such a declaration either necessary on the one hand or imprudent on the other." Greene would not take choices out of Congress's hands or use judicial injunctive relief absent a showing that it was what Congress itself required under the WPR. The intent of the WPR was that congressional inaction would lead within sixty days to the withdrawal of U.S. forces. But after the *Dellums* decision, it was clear that in the face of congressional inaction the courts would excuse themselves from enforcing the WPR, enabling the president to ignore it.

Even with this latitude, there have been few instances in which a president has engaged in war making without congressional support. President Obama's 2011 air war in Libya is one instance. A second was in 1995, when President Clinton ordered the bombing of Serbian forces fighting in Bosnia without seeking or obtaining congressional authorization. Instead, Clinton relied on NATO's establishment of a no-fly zone. Clinton also did not seek advance congressional approval when he bombed Serbia in 1999 to end war crimes in Kosovo.[49]

In conducting hostilities against Iraq, neither Presidents George H. W. Bush nor George W. Bush acted contrary to the intent of the framers. The elder Bush secured congressional authorization, but he also indicated in a news conference that he reserved the right to act in defense of U.S. interests based on his own prerogatives. Similarly, the younger Bush claimed that a 1998 congressional resolution calling for "regime change" in Iraq could be combined with a 2002 resolution authorizing the use of force against Iraq as a form of joint concord. In both wars, after receiving congressional authorization, the final decision to attack was made unilaterally by presidents without consulting with or reporting to Congress. Once the fighting began, Congress supported both presidents. In the second Iraq conflict, Congress, by overwhelming bipartisan votes, passed a resolution supporting the troops, and within three weeks it appropriated some $80 billion, in a clear demonstration of joint concord.

Once again the federal courts refused the invitation to get involved. In *Doe v. Bush* (2003), active-duty service personnel, their parents, and some members of the House sought a preliminary injunction to prevent Bush from initiating war against Iraq.[50] They argued that, by passing the resolution, Congress had unconstitutionally delegated to the president its power to declare war. The court, however, declined to rule, claiming that the issue was a political question and therefore nonjusticiable. It also held that there was evidence of joint concord because Congress had called for regime change and had authorized hostilities.

CONCLUSION

Since the nation's earliest years, presidents have used the military on their own prerogative, making decisions to use force unilaterally and obtaining congressional support after the fact. For their part, since the start of the Cold War the courts have been reluctant to rule on "boundary questions" between the president and Congress, preferring to find evidence of joint concord. Any attempt to try to hold the president to an ambiguous (perhaps nonexistent) constitutional standard is ultimately to engage in fruitless speculation about whether a presidential use of force goes beyond the framers' intent. The real issue is not that presidents have made war without the consent of Congress—for the most part, they have obtained that consent either before or after using the armed forces in major hostilities—but rather that Congress has failed to insist that presidents follow the collaborative mechanisms of the War Powers Resolution before making these decisions, and that judicial decisions have left presidents free to do so.

In the final analysis, the issues in debates over presidential war making do not really involve legitimacy—such as whether the president followed proper procedures or made a decision that was lawful and constitutional—although they are often presented that way by critics. Criticisms of the president's war power usually stem from disagreements with a particular presidential action. These questions about the viability or wisdom of the policy, rather than attempts to parse original intent from limited debates and vague constitutional clauses, are the ones that really matter.

NOTES

INTRO

1. Alexis de Tocqueville, *Democracy in America,* trans. Arthur Goldhammer (New York: Library of America, 2004).

PRO

2. Edward S. Corwin, *The President: Office and Powers* (New York: New York University Press, 1957), 201.
3. Alexander Hamilton, James Madison, and John Jay, *The Federalist Papers* (New York: New American Library, 1961), 418 (emphasis in original).
4. Ibid., 417.
5. Max Farrand, ed., *The Records of the Federal Convention of 1787,* 4 vols. (New Haven, CT: Yale University Press, 1937), 1:292.
6. That same concept was included in an early federal court case, *U.S. v. Smith* (27 Fed. Cas. 1192 [No. 16,342] [C.C.N.Y. 1806] at 1230), in which the court said that "it is the exclusive province of congress to change a state of peace into a state of war."
7. Louis Henkin, *Foreign Affairs and the Constitution* (Mineola, NY: Foundation Press, 1972), 50–51.
8. Farrand, *Records of the Federal Convention of 1787,* 2:318.
9. The April 1952 executive order was declared unconstitutional by the Supreme Court in *Youngstown Sheet & Tube Co. v. Sawyer,* 343 U.S. 579 (1952). For an analysis of Truman's decision to send U.S. forces to Korea in 1950, see Louis Fisher, *Presidential War Power* (Lawrence: University Press of Kansas, 1995), 84–90; Louis Fisher, "The Korean War: On What Legal Basis Did Truman Act?" *American Journal of International Law* 89 (1995): 21; and Glenn D. Paige, *The Korean Decision: June 24–30, 1950* (New York: Free Press, 1968).
10. Senate Committee on Foreign Relations, S. Rep. no. 91-129 (1969), as reprinted in Peter M. Shane and Harold H. Bruff, eds., *Separation of Powers Law: Cases and Materials* (Durham, NC: Carolina Academic Press, 1996), 777–91.
11. Arthur M. Schlesinger Jr., *The Imperial Presidency* (Boston: Houghton Mifflin, 1973), 108. Congress effectively ratified the bases deal retroactively in April 1941.
12. Ibid., 113.
13. There is no better description of this circumstance than Justice Robert Jackson's pointed as well as prescient warning to Congress in his *Youngstown* concurrence: "We may say that power to legislate for emergencies belongs in the hands of Congress, but only Congress itself can prevent power from slipping through its fingers," 343 U.S. at 654.
14. Leonard Meeker, "The Legality of United States Participation in the Defense of Viet-Nam," *Department of State Bulletin* 54 (1966): 474, as reprinted in Shane and Bruff, *Separation of Powers Law: Cases and Materials,* 771–76.
15. Ibid., 772.

16. Ibid.

17. S. Res. 85, *Congressional Record* no. 91-115 (June 25, 1969): S 7153.

18. Senate Committee, S. Rep. 129, in Shane and Bruff, *Separation of Powers Law,* 781.

19. Ibid., 781–82.

20. Public Law 93–148, *U.S. Statutes at Large* 555 (1973).

21. Some scholars, such as Louis Fisher and David Gray Adler, would go further, arguing that the existence of the resolution has actually lulled Congress into even greater complacency by discouraging it from using the constitutional tools over the war powers it already—and always—had, such as the appropriations power, the legislative power, and, ultimately, the impeachment power. See Louis Fisher and David Gray Adler, "The War Powers Resolution: Time to Say Goodbye," *Political Science Quarterly* 113 (Spring 1998): 1.

22. Since 1973, presidents routinely notify Congress when they order the use of military force but decline to report pursuant to the specific requirement of Section 4 of the War Powers Resolution. Instead, they insist that they are reporting "consistent with" that resolution. The difference in language is more than semantic. The choice in words signals that presidents refuse to be legally bound by the explicit requirements of the War Powers Resolution, while conceding that it is politically expedient for them to inform Congress when they take military action.

23. The record of cases challenging the constitutionality of the Vietnam War that the federal courts refused to decide on the merits demonstrates how unwilling the judiciary is to challenge a sitting president during wartime. See, for example, *Mora v. McNamara,* 386 U.S. 934 (1967); *Mitchell v. Laird,* 488 F.2d 611 (D.C. Cir. 1973); *Orlando v. Laird,* 443 F.2d 1039 (2d Cir. 1971); and *Berk v. Laird,* 429 F.2d 302 (2d Cir. 1970).

24. *Dellums v. Bush,* 752 F. Supp. 1141 (D.D.C. 1990).

25. Ibid.

26. Ibid.

27. Authorization for the Use of Military Force, 2001. P.L. 107-40, 115 Stat. 224 (September 18, 2001), http://www.gpo.gov/fdsys/pkg/PLAW-107publ40/html/PLAW-107publ40.htm

28. See, for example, John C. Yoo, "Memorandum Opinion for the Deputy Counsel to the President: The President's Constitutional Authority to Conduct Military Operations against Terrorists and Nations Supporting Them," U.S. Department of Justice, Washington, D.C., September 25, 2001, https://www.justice.gov/sites/default/files/olc/opinions/2001/09/31/op-olc-v025-p0188_0.pdf

29. In judicial decisions challenging some of these policies, the Supreme Court produced mixed responses. For example, in *Hamdi v. Rumsfeld,* 124 S. Ct. 2633 (2004), the Court determined that the president could validly detain terrorist suspects during wartime. The decision was based on the AUMF and never reached the question of authority under Article II, commander in chief, but the Court also ruled that citizen-detainees must be afforded "a fair opportunity to rebut the Government's factual assertions before a neutral decisionmaker." In

two later cases, the Court ruled against the government, declaring unconstitutional in *Hamdan v. Rumsfeld*, 548 U.S. 557 (2006), the military commissions that President Bush authorized in his November 2001 military order and deciding in *Boumediene v. Bush*, 128 S. Ct. 2229 (2008), that the process established by the administration for determining whether Guantánamo detainees were illegal enemy combatants was an insufficient substitute for the traditional privilege of habeas corpus.

30. See, for example, Alberto Gonzales, "Legal Authorities Supporting the Activities of the National Security Agency Described by the President," U.S. Department of Justice, Washington, D.C., January 19, 2006, https://www.justice.gov/sites/default/files/olc/opinions/attachments/2015/05/29/op-olc-v030-p0001.pdf. See also http://www.justice.gov/olc/olc-foia1.htm for links to Office of Legal Counsel memos from 2001–2009 that proclaimed the president's unlimited and exclusive power to act in wartime. Absent in these memos was any suggestion (1) that there is a robust debate over whether the commander in chief clause is, in fact, "a substantive grant of authority" or, instead, a title that permits the president to exercise a set of functions after Congress has authorized the chief executive to do so; and (2) that the "broad" scope of the president's authority knows any limits.

31. P.L. 107-243, 116 Stat. 1498 (October 16, 2002), https://www.gpo.gov/fdsys/pkg/PLAW-107publ243/html/PLAW-107publ243.htm

32. In May 2013 the Senate Armed Services Committee held a hearing on whether the 2001 AUMF should be revised or repealed. One question was whether this statute had been used by both Presidents Bush and Obama to authorize activities far beyond the expectations of the Congress members who had voted for it, more than a decade earlier. Sen. Dick Durbin, D-Ill., commented that "None of us, not one who voted for it, could have envisioned we were voting for the longest war in American history or that we were about to give future presidents the authority to fight terrorism as far flung as Yemen and Somalia." Quoted in John Bresnahan, "Senators Discuss Revising 9/11 Resolution," *Politico*, May 7, 2013.

33. Harold Hongju Koh, "The Obama Administration and International Law," speech delivered at the Annual Meeting of the American Society of International Law, Washington, D.C., March 25, 2010, http://www.state.gov/s/l/releases/remarks/139119.htm; emphasis in original.

34. "Letter from the President Regarding the Commencement of Operations in Libya," March 21, 2011, http://www.whitehouse.gov/the-press-office/2011/03/21/letter-president-regarding-commencement-operations-libya

35. Harold Hongju Koh, "Libya and War Powers," Testimony Before the Senate Foreign Relations Committee, June 28, 2011, http://www.state.gov/s/l/releases/remarks/167250.htm; "United States Activities in Libya," report submitted to Congress by the Obama administration, June 15, 2011, http://www.washingtonpost.com/wp-srv/politics/documents/united-states-activities-libya.html

36. Charlie Savage and Mark Landler, "White House Defends Continuing U.S. Role in Libya Operation," *New York Times*, June 15, 2011; Charlie Savage, "Two Top

Lawyers Lost to Obama in Libya War Policy Debate," *New York Times,* June 17, 2011; "United States Activities in Libya," report submitted to Congress June 15, 2011, http://www.washingtonpost.com/wp-srv/politics/documents/united-states-activities-libya.html

37. White House, http://www.whitehouse.gov/the-press-office/2013/05/23/remarks-president-national-defense-university

38. David Mervin, "The Demise of the War Clause," *Presidential Studies Quarterly* 30 (December 2000): 767–73.

39. David Gray Adler, "The Virtues of the War Clause," *Presidential Studies Quarterly* 30 (December 2000): 777–82.

CON

40. All quotations are taken from *Notes of Debates on the Federal Convention of 1787* (Athens: Ohio University Press, 1966), 475–77.

41. *Prize Cases,* 67 U.S. 635 (1863).

42. *Luftig v. McNamara,* 373 F.2d 664 (1967).

43. *Berk v. Laird,* 429 F.2d 302 (Calif. 2 1970).

44. *Orlando v. Laird,* 443 F.2d 1039 (2d Cir. 1971).

45. *Massachusetts v. Laird,* 451 F.2d 26 (1st Cir. 1971).

46. *Da Costa v. Laird I,* 448 F.2d 368 (2d Cir. 1971).

47. *Da Costa v. Laird II,* 471 F.2d 1146 (2d Cir. 1973).

48. *Dellums v. Bush,* 752 F. Supp. 1141 (D.D.C. 1990).

49. Members of Congress tried to challenge the legality of Clinton's Serbian bombing campaign, but a district court concluded that the members of Congress did not have standing (*Campbell v. Clinton,* 52 F. Supp. 2d 34 [D.D.C. 1999]). Congress itself had sent contradictory messages. At first, it voted down a proposed declaration of war against Serbia. It also cast a tie vote in the House on authorizing air strikes, and so the measure failed to pass. But it then voted to fund the bombing and voted down a proposed funding cutoff. Because of this inconsistent congressional activity—part endorsement and part attempted check—the court held that "the President here did not claim to be acting pursuant to the defeated declaration of war or a statutory authorization, but instead 'pursuant to [his] constitutional authority to conduct U.S. foreign relations and as Commander-in-Chief and Chief Executive.'" Ironically, then, because Clinton relied on his own claim of war powers rather than on an action by Congress, the legislators were held to lack standing.

50. *Doe v. Bush,* 322 F.3d 109 (2003).

RESOLVED, Presidential signing statements threaten the rule of law and the separation of powers

PRO: Peter M. Shane

CON: Nelson Lund

When the colonists drew up their list of grievances against King George in the Declaration of Independence, their first complaint was that he "refused his Assent to Laws, the most wholesome and necessary for the public good." Yet a decade later, when drawing up the new constitution in Philadelphia, the framers decided to give a veto power to the president, albeit in a qualified form. Only a few delegates—Alexander Hamilton, James Wilson, Gouverneur Morris—favored granting the president an absolute veto, but the convention very nearly required a vote of three-quarters of both houses to override a presidential veto. Only in the Constitutional Convention's final days, by a narrow 6–4 vote, did the delegates consent to lower the override threshold from three-quarters to two-thirds.

James Madison (as well as George Washington) had been among the delegates who objected to this late change. Madison insisted that a three-quarters override would be necessary to "check legislative injustice and encroachments." The diminutive Virginian shared Wilson's fear that the gravest threat to the new American government would come not from executive aggrandizement but from the "legislature swallowing up all the other powers." Madison and his allies may have lost the battle, but they won the war. Since the Constitution's ratification 225 years ago, Congress has succeeded in overriding a president's veto on only 110 occasions. That is, only about 7 percent of the nearly 1,500 presidential regular vetoes have been overridden. And that leaves out of the equation the more than 1,000 pocket vetoes that presidents have issued in the nation's history—which Congress cannot override.

At first, the veto was used sparingly. Washington vetoed only two bills, and Adams and Jefferson none at all. In the nation's first half century the regular veto was exercised on only thirteen occasions and the pocket veto ten times— with Andrew Jackson accounting for about half of these vetoes. Since the Civil War, however, every president except James Garfield and Warren G. Harding, neither of whom served even a single full term, has issued at least as many vetoes as Jackson did.

As use of the veto increased, so too did legislative efforts to override the president's veto. John Tyler, dubbed "His Accidency" by detractors, was the first president to have a veto overridden. Congress roughed up the ineffective Franklin Pierce, overriding five of his nine vetoes. But that was kid-glove treatment compared with what Congress handed out to Andrew Johnson, whose twenty-one vetoes were overridden an astounding fifteen times. Pierce and especially Johnson were anomalies, however. For the rest of the nineteenth and twentieth centuries, presidents fared very well in sustaining their many vetoes. Only one president who served during this 130-year time span had a success rate of less than 75 percent: Richard Nixon, whose twenty-six regular vetoes were overridden on seven occasions, or 27 percent of the time.

The twentieth-century pattern of many vetoes and few overrides came to an end with George W. Bush's presidency. During his first term, Bush never vetoed a bill, not a regular veto or even a pocket veto. In his second term, particularly after 2006 when Democrats gained control of the Senate and the House of Representatives, Bush began to wield the veto more often, but at the end of his two terms Bush had used the pocket veto only once and the regular veto on only eleven occasions—four of which (36 percent) were overridden by Congress. One has to go all the way back to Warren G. Harding, who served for only two-and-a-half years, to find a president who issued fewer vetoes than Bush.

Perhaps part of the reason why Bush relied less on the veto is that he discovered an alternative to the veto: the presidential signing statement. During his eight years in office, Bush issued about 160 signing statements that challenged the legality of well over 1,000 statutory provisions; nearly 70 percent of these signing statements came in his first term. It should be noted that President Barack Obama has also issued few vetoes (twelve as of October 2016) but been decidedly more restrained in his use of signing statements; as of October 2016 he had issued thirty-six signing statements, only nineteen of which registered constitutional objections or concerns about the statute he was signing.

The Constitution calls upon the president to explain a veto, but it is silent about what a president should do when signing a bill; it neither requires nor forbids a president from issuing a signing statement. The origins of this practice can be traced all the way back to the early nineteenth century, but it was only in the Reagan administration that signing statements began to be seen as a way for the president to shape the way the law would be interpreted, at least by executive officials if not judges. Not until George W. Bush's administration, however, did this practice generate widespread public comment, including a sharply critical 2006 report by an American Bar Association (ABA) task force that concluded that signing statements posed "a serious threat to the rule of law."

Nelson Lund and Peter M. Shane agree that Bush made unprecedented use of the signing statement, not in absolute numbers—Lyndon Johnson, Richard Nixon, Jimmy Carter, Ronald Reagan, George H. W. Bush, and Bill Clinton all penned more signing statements than George W. Bush—but in the manner and the extent to which the statements were used to challenge laws. The almost 1,200 statutory provisions challenged by George W. Bush are roughly double the number challenged by the previous forty-one presidents combined.[1] Lund and Shane differ radically, though, on whether this development is healthy or pernicious for American democracy. Lund takes to task the ABA task force report for its faulty constitutional analysis and insists that signing statements, properly understood, are neither unconstitutional nor dangerous. Shane, in contrast, like the ABA, views heavy reliance on signing statements as bad for both representative democracy and the rule of law.

PRO: Peter M. Shane

The framers of the U.S. Constitution bequeathed Americans a national system of checks and balances, but each branch of the federal government is vested with powers that are difficult for other branches to control. This feature of the constitutional design may seem ironic, but without some capacity for each branch to act all but autonomously, it would be hard to imagine how checks and balances could work. For example, if it were easy for Congress to override presidential vetoes, the veto power would not be much of a check on Congress. The resulting system, however, institutionalizes a significant degree of risk. Any branch's insistence on using its autonomous powers too ambitiously can threaten important constitutional values and undo the institutional equilibrium that makes governance possible.

We can see this truth clearly in the history of presidential signing statements—formal statements in which a president, while signing an enacted bill into law, nonetheless indicates doubts about the constitutionality of particular provisions of the newly enacted statutes the president is signing. In such cases, presidents typically state that they will implement or interpret the statutory provisions in question to minimize the perceived constitutional difficulties. In some instances, presidents even say they will simply ignore the statutory provisions they take to be unconstitutional. By one scholarly count, the total number of statutory provisions to which presidents objected on constitutional grounds between the administration of James Monroe and the beginning of the first Reagan administration was 101.[2] The practice, however, dramatically accelerated from the second Reagan administration through the second George W. Bush administration. Bush's abuse of the signing statement power demonstrates the threat that signing statements can pose to the rule of law and prompted the near-abandonment of the practice by the Obama administration.

To appreciate fully Bush's anomalous enthusiasm for signing statements, some context is necessary. Presidents are constitutionally required to provide written statements on proposed legislation only when they veto it. The Constitution obliges the president—as long as Congress or its clerks are available to receive presidential messages—to return that legislation "to that House in which it shall have originated" along "with his Objections."[3] In contrast, when presidents sign proposed legislation into law, they are not required to say anything. The only constitutionally compelled presidential expression is a signature. Presidents, however, commonly do speak about legislation they are approving. Until recent decades, it was all but certain that these messages would simply tout the benefits that the approved legislation was projected to achieve. Such statements are of no legal significance and not much importance otherwise.

The advent of the Reagan administration, however, marked a significant increase in the frequency of signing statements objecting to the legislation being enacted, plus a dramatic departure in their intended institutional significance. Attorney General Edwin Meese persuaded the company that publishes new laws also to publish the president's signing statements. The signing statements were intended to become, as one report explained, "a strategic weapon in a campaign to influence the way legislation was interpreted by the courts and Executive agencies."[4]

Over the course of two administrations, President Reagan, through his signing statements, objected to or unilaterally reinterpreted 71 statutory provisions. In a single term, President George H. W. Bush objected to 146. Most of the objections involved the president's asserted foreign policy powers, although many reflected the administration's full embrace of unitary executive theory and some of the more expansive claims of presidentialist constitutionalism. President Bill Clinton used the signing statement device as well; his objections to 105 statutory provisions exceeded the record of President Reagan, though they were more modest than the record of President George H. W. Bush.[5] In terms of robust presidentialism, however, none of these three presidents can compete with the record of the George W. Bush administration. With regard to laws enacted between 2001 and 2009, President Bush objected to approximately 1,070 provisions embodied in 127 statutes. Objections to a number of these provisions were stated on multiple grounds. If one counts as an "objection" each precise ground on which the president registered concern about a provision of law, then the 1,070 or so provisions at issue elicited 1,496 objections.[6]

The threat to the rule of law that such excess poses comes in two forms, one fairly mechanical and one more subtle but far more critical. The mechanical problem is straightforward: when presidential signing statements proliferate to this degree, they become utterly unmanageable as a source of legal guidance. First, it is a fair guess that government lawyers rarely consult signing statements in deciding what a statute means, since they have no clear legal status. Their relevance is likely to be episodic, if not wholly random. Second, because they are frequently conclusory, even cryptic, they hardly provide a source of legal reasoning from which separation of powers law can emerge in any orderly way. They typically offer no actual legal argument or reference to legal authority for the claims being asserted. Finally, many signing statements are quite obviously inflected with the political philosophy of a particular president rather than law.

As a presidential candidate, then-senator Barack Obama had been critical of the Bush administration's signing statement practice. "The problem," he said, with the Bush administration "is that it has attached signing statements to legislation in an effort to change the meaning of the legislation, to avoid enforcing certain provisions of the legislation that the President does not like, and to raise implausible or dubious constitutional objections to the legislation."[7] It was therefore unsurprising that, soon upon taking office, President Obama issued a memorandum on signing statements promising to "act with caution and restraint, based only on interpretations of the Constitution that are well-founded."[8] His memorandum directed executive agencies as follows:

> To ensure that all signing statements previously issued are fol-
> lowed only when consistent with [the] principles [stated in this
> memorandum], executive branch departments and agencies are
> directed to seek the advice of the Attorney General before relying
> on signing statements issued prior to the date of this memoran-
> dum as the basis for disregarding, or otherwise refusing to comply
> with, any provision of a statute.

In other words, President Obama effectively told agencies: don't act on the basis of my predecessors' constitutional qualms without approval by the attorney general. But what would have happened if President Obama had replicated Bush's pattern of signing statements? Could agencies act upon Obama signing statements *without* having to consult the attorney general? And if President Obama should have a Republican successor, might that president issue their own order directing agencies to treat President Bush's statements as well as their own as authoritative, but not to implement President Obama's (or per-haps those of any Democratic president) without consultation? A system of legal pronouncements that presumptively alters with every change in the party identification of the incumbent president would not be a system of law at all.

Putting aside that signing statements could become a largely unmanageable mass of obscure, politicized, and conclusory quasi-legal objections to legisla-tion, the second way in which signing statements threaten the rule of law runs much deeper. And to see this point, it must be recognized that the efflorescence of signing statements during George W. Bush's administration was no accident. Despite what the sheer volume of Bush's signing statements might imply, it is really not plausible that, between 2001 and 2009, Congress acted in constitu-tionally offensive ways three times more often than all the Congresses that came before, put together. Nor, for the most part, was President Bush facing a hostile Congress. For President Bush's first two years in office, Republicans held a majority in the House of Representatives and were only one vote short of control in the Senate. From 2003 through 2007, Republicans controlled both houses of Congress. Thus from 2001 to 2007, when the overwhelming majority of Bush signing statements appeared, President Bush was not pushing back against any genuine threat to his party's exercise of executive power.

Instead, the Bush administration sought to take advantage of the fact that there is virtually no formal legal or other institutional check on the content of signing statements. The president and his lawyers used signing statements in order to fabricate a body of official documents that might lend credence to an audacious and largely unsupportable theory of expansive executive power. No president wants to appear to claim to be above the law. The president's lawyers want to have some text to hold up as authoritative legal support for any claim of executive authority. Constitutional text, statutes, and judicial opinions are the pieces of paper that usually serve this kind of function. Unfortunately for our most aggressive supporters of presidential authority, the Constitution is ambiguous, at best, on the nature of executive power. Congress enacts very few statutes that embody anything like congressional ratification for the executive branch's most prodigious ambitions. There are few judicial opinions support-ing what I call the "presidentialist" view of the Constitution because separation of powers disputes are rarely litigated, and the courts have not been receptive to extreme presidentialist claims of executive authority. There were thus no cases to cite with anything like strong support for many of President Bush's most frequently asserted claims, and there was frequently strong contrary authority. There was thus a pressing need for the executive branch to manufac-ture its own legitimating documents, formal pieces of paper that seemed to sanction the president's expansive assertions of unilateral power.

Two examples crystallize just how bizarre were some of Bush's claims. Con-sider first the president's signing statement for the 2006 Postal Accountability and Enhancement Act.[9] That act amends the law describing an agency called the Postal Regulatory Commission. As amended, this rather undramatic law now reads as follows:

> The Postal Regulatory Commission is composed of 5 Commis-sioners, appointed by the President, by and with the advice and consent of the Senate. The Commissioners shall be chosen solely on the basis of their technical qualifications, professional stand-ing, and demonstrated expertise in economics, accounting, law, or public administration, and may be removed by the President only for cause. Each individual appointed to the Commission shall have the qualifications and expertise necessary to carry out the enhanced responsibilities accorded Commissioners under the Postal Accountability and Enhancement Act. Not more than 3 of the Commissioners may be adherents of the same political party.[10]

In signing the act, the president objected to this provision as one of two in the act that "purport to limit the qualifications of the pool of persons from whom the president may select appointees in a manner that rules out a large portion of those persons best qualified by experience and knowledge to fill the positions." He then went on to state that the executive branch would construe these provisions "in a manner consistent with the Appointments Clause of the

Constitution."[11] In other words, President Bush wanted to go on record as objecting to this innocuous statute as a violation of his power to nominate and appoint officers of the United States and said he would read the law in some unspecified manner that would be consistent with his authority.

Putting aside constitutional issues for a moment, what exactly could the president be thinking here? The statute invites the president to nominate new commission members "on the basis of their technical qualifications, professional standing, and demonstrated expertise in economics, accounting, law, or public administration." What "large portion of those persons best qualified by experience and knowledge" could possibly be excluded by this requirement? Because Congress's specifications are so broad and commonsensical, there is no plausible objection to be made that Congress's new version of the law compromises the public interest.

The strangeness of the president's insistence is all the more apparent, however, if one considers the institutional context we are discussing. The statutory qualifications for postal rate commissioners are legally unenforceable. If the president fails to nominate someone meeting the statutory standards, no one can sue the president. Senators might decline to confirm a nominee they believe falls short of the statutory standard, but senators are entitled to vote "no" on any nominee for any reason they want, so this hardly leaves the president worse off. Objecting to a statutory specification of qualifications in this context amounted to nothing but pointless swagger. It was really to say to Congress, "I, the President of the United States, am offended, constitutionally speaking, that you think I even have to listen to you with regard to the qualifications of potential office holders. It is irrelevant that this office operates directly to fulfill Congress's constitutionally vested authorities with regard to interstate commerce and the post."

Many of President Bush's constitutional objections fell within areas about which presidents are typically protective. Of the nearly 1,500 objections lodged in signing statements between 2001 and 2009, 88 mentioned potential interference with commander-in-chief powers; 152 mentioned interference with the president's constitutional authorities regarding diplomacy and foreign affairs; and another 199 pointed to alleged violations of the president's constitutional authorities to withhold or control access to information to protect foreign relations or national security, sometimes mentioning also the president's power to protect executive branch deliberative processes or the performance of the executive's constitutional duties.[12]

Even in these traditional contexts, however, the substance of the president's objections was often extreme and hypertechnical. My second example of presidential bizarreness is this: a statutory provision Bush thought in conflict with his commander-in-chief powers put limits on the number of Defense

Department civilian and military personnel who could be assigned to the Pentagon's Legislative Affairs office.[13] According to the president, Congress "cannot constitutionally restrict the authority of the President to control the activities of members of the armed forces, including whether and how many members of the Armed Forces assigned to the office of the Chairman of the Joint Chiefs of Staff, the combatant commands, or any other element of the Department of Defense shall perform legislative affairs or legislative liaison functions."[14] In other words, putting to one side the highly debatable proposition that the president is beyond congressional regulation in the use of the armed forces for bona fide military purposes—Article I explicitly authorizes Congress "to make Rules for the Government and Regulation of the land and naval Forces"—President Bush would actually have had Americans believe that presidents have unlimited authority to determine how many soldiers and sailors it takes to lobby Congress.

Going beyond these somewhat astonishing claims in areas of traditional presidential concern, there are hundreds in wholly novel areas. For example, the president objected to 219 legally imposed reporting requirements as interfering with his constitutional authority to recommend measures to Congress.[15] Apparently, President Bush believed that the entitlement of presidents to speak their minds to Congress entails a prohibition on Congress demanding any other reports or recommendations from the executive branch. This is a historically baseless argument. Our original secretary of the Treasury, Alexander Hamilton—the most pro-executive of the framers—did not complain about finding himself as responsible for filing reports with Congress as to the president.[16] Any constitutional infirmity in the requirement of executive reports to Congress is entirely a figment of the contemporary presidentialist imagination.

President George W. Bush also lodged 380 objections based on Congress's alleged interference with the president's control over the "unitary executive."[17] Many of these assertions seem to be merely "piling on" with regard to other, narrower objections. But others were distinctively rooted in an imagined presidential authority to direct personally the discretionary activity of every member of the executive branch on any subject, regardless of what the law prescribes. For example, one statutory provision to which the president objected on "unitary executive grounds" is Section 115 of a 2002 Act to Provide for Improvement of Federal Education Research, Statistics, Evaluation, Information, and Dissemination and for Other Purposes.[18] The act creates an Institute of Education Sciences within the Department of Education, to be run by a director and a board. Section 115 requires the director to propose institute priorities for board approval. The president of the United States, of course, has no inherent constitutional power over education. Yet executive branch lawyers seem to imagine that it somehow violates the separation of powers either to allow the director to recommend priorities or for the board to decide on those priorities, without presidential intervention. In a similar vein is a "unitary executive" objection to a statutory provision requiring the secretary of agriculture to consider, in preparing the department's annual budget, the recommendations of an advisory committee on specialty crops.[19] Although the law does not require the secretary actually to implement those recommendations but merely to take them into account, the president implicitly believes that the chief executive has inherent authority to forbid subordinates from giving any weight whatever to public policy input from any source other than the White House.[20]

The point here is not just that the content of these statements is legally insupportable. The very proliferation of such statements threatens the rule of law because they embody a kind of unchecked institutional ambition that feeds on itself. So extreme an outpouring of presidential signing statements is both a reflection of and encouragement to a psychology of constitutional entitlement within the executive branch. Such statements are intended as a form of discipline within the executive branch, signaling that, to be a part of the president's team, all administrators must subscribe to the theory that our Constitution envisions a presidency answerable, in large measure, to no one. There is thus a direct link between signing statements on topics as mundane as specialty crops and the dangerously irresponsible lawyering that attended the Bush administration's handling of Guantánamo and warrantless wiretapping. Official declarations of the theory of unilateral authority that fuels the president's stance on obscure matters helps to maintain the attitudes—the norms of governance— that lead to other, more consequential claims of unilateral executive authority. An important function of Bush's signing statements was that they served as reminders to administration members and especially to administration lawyers of how the president wanted the administration to behave: claim maximum power, concede minimum authority to the other branches. This is not the rule of law but its opposite.

To his credit, President Obama promised—and largely delivered—a return to earlier norms regarding signing statements. As noted above, in only his second month in office, he issued a memorandum promising to limit the use of signing statements to exceptional circumstances.[21] As of September 2016, with roughly four months left in his second term, he had issued only eighteen statements containing constitutional objections or reservations with regard to statutes he was signing into law.[22] All told, these statements contain ninety-six objections to roughly eighty-one enumerated provisions of law; it is hard to be more precise because a number of statements lodge objections to "certain provisions" or "numerous provisions,"[23] without citing them more specifically. In general, however, the close correspondence between the number of provisions challenged and the number of objections made suggests that President Obama, unlike President Bush, preferred not to make multiple objections to any single provision of law.

Intriguingly, President Obama's resort to signing statements to communicate his constitutional views would look even more modest if we exclude from the total his first signing statement making constitutional objections. Although that text appeared two days after President Obama released his general memorandum on signing statements, it was presumably prepared earlier and, in both tone and substance, bears closer kinship to the style of the previous administration than to his only newly pledged policy. The statement includes, for example, the following opaque utterance:

> Sections 714(1) and 714(2) in Division D prohibit the use of appropriations to pay the salary of any Federal officer or employee who interferes with or prohibits certain communications between Federal employees and Members of Congress. I do not interpret this provision to detract from my authority to direct the heads of executive departments to supervise, control, and correct employees' communications with the Congress in cases where such communications would be unlawful or would reveal information that is properly privileged or otherwise confidential.[24]

It is entirely obscure what operational significance the president's second sentence has or what effective communicative purpose it has with regard to any intended audience. The signing statement including this objection accounts for nine of President Obama's ninety-six protests and may simply not reflect the philosophy regarding signing statements that he expressed in his March 9, 2009, order.

In any event, no single president's memorandum or record of restraint can guarantee that past abuses will not be repeated. The only reform possible—and one we desperately need—is an enduring change in executive branch legal culture that cuts against gratuitous assertions of hypothetical presidential authorities. The repeated utterance, as during George W. Bush's administration, of the president's imagined immunity to both important and obscure forms of congressional regulation cannot help but shape executive branch behavior by inducing allegiance to norms of hostility to external accountability. Unless confined to relatively rare instances where presidents are standing up for bedrock, well-established principles of executive authority, signing statements embody both a disregard for the institutional authorities of the other branches—especially Congress—and too often a disregard for the necessity to ground legal claims in plausible law. President Obama's successors should follow his lead in curbing the use of signing statements.

CON: Nelson Lund

In 2006 a task force of the American Bar Association (ABA) declared that presidential signing statements—especially those issued by George W. Bush—threaten "the rule of law and our constitutional system of separation of powers."[25] Although the ABA report was signed by several prestigious members of the elite legal establishment, its position is analytically untenable and irresponsibly hyperbolic.

The key conclusion in the ABA report is that presidents violate the Constitution when they announce that they regard some provision in a bill they sign as unconstitutional and unenforceable or interpret the provision in a manner inconsistent with what the report calls "the will of Congress."

The dominating error in the ABA report is the notion that the president has a "constitutional obligation to veto any bill that he believes violates the Constitution in whole or in part" and that the chief executive therefore must either veto a bill or enforce all of its provisions. How does the Constitution impose this choice on the president? The ABA report offers two answers, based on different provisions of the Constitution. Neither answer can withstand scrutiny.

PRESENTMENT CLAUSE

The Constitution specifies how a bill may become a law:

> Every Bill which shall have passed the House of Representatives and the Senate, shall, before it becomes a Law, be presented to the President of the United States; If he approve he shall sign it, but if not he shall return it, with his Objections to that House in which it shall have originated [and the veto may be overridden by a two-thirds vote of each House]. If any Bill shall not be returned by the President within ten Days (Sundays excepted) after it shall have been presented to him, the same shall be a

> Law, in like manner as if he had signed it, unless the Congress
> by their Adjournment prevent its Return, in which Case it shall
> not be a Law.

This presentment clause offers no support for the ABA's claim that the president has a "constitutional obligation to veto any bill that he believes violates the Constitution in whole or in part." The presentment clause simply gives the president the option of returning a bill with objections (of whatever nature they may be) for reconsideration, which may result in an override of the veto. The chief executive also has two other options: sign the bill or do nothing, which has the same effect as signing except when the so-called pocket veto provision is applicable. The presentment clause does not tell the president which bills to veto. Nor does it say anything at all about the existence, scope, or nature of a president's obligations with respect to the enforcement of enacted statutes (whether they were enacted during the current administration or at some earlier time).

The ABA, however, claims that a president's refusal to enforce unconstitutional provisions after signing the bill in which they appeared is actually an illegal line-item veto—that is, a decision by the president to veto part of a bill while signing the rest of the bill into law. The report is correct that the president has no authority to exercise a line-item veto. Similarly, the president is not permitted to repeal statutes unilaterally. But an announcement that the president is not bound by a provision that the president regards as unconstitutional is not the same as a veto.

Perhaps of most practical significance, other legal actors (including the courts and future presidents) may disagree with the president's interpretation of the Constitution. They will then treat the provision as valid and enforce it. This cannot happen with a bill that the president has vetoed (unless, of course, the president's veto was overridden by Congress). For the same reason, a president's refusal to enforce statutes that the president believes are unconstitutional is not the same as repealing them.

TAKE CARE CLAUSE

The ABA's second effort to justify its denunciation of signing statements is based on the constitutional provision requiring the president to "take Care that the Laws be faithfully executed." According to the ABA, "[b]ecause the 'take care' obligation of the President requires him to faithfully execute all laws, his obligation is to veto bills he believes are unconstitutional."

Once again, the ABA has confused questions about the obligation of presidents to execute the laws with the question of whether they are obligated to veto bills they believe are unconstitutional. The take care clause says nothing at all about an obligation of the president to veto any bill. In addition, the ABA fails to recognize that the Constitution itself is one of the "Laws" that the president is obliged to execute. The take care clause does not purport to determine what the president should do when one law (such as a statute) conflicts with another (such as the Constitution). That is an important question, but it is not answered by the take care clause.

THE PRESIDENT AND THE COURTS

For these reasons, the ABA is wrong to claim that the Constitution imposes a rule requiring the president to "veto any bill he believes would violate the Constitution in any respect." Not only is this rule absent from the Constitution, it is absurd. And the ABA seems to realize that it is unworkable. In a somewhat confusing passage, the report acknowledges that there may be exceptions to the ABA's rule. One example mentioned in the report is a bill that contains "insignificant [though unconstitutional] provisions in omnibus emergency-relief or military-funding measures, enacted as Congress recesses or adjourns, [that] would seem not to merit a veto."

Another exception that shows the unworkability of the ABA's rule involves the persistent inclusion by Congress of unconstitutional provisions in its bills. The report admits that Congress includes unconstitutional provisions in many bills and suggests that presidents may be free to sign some of these bills and treat the unconstitutional provisions as nullities. The report, however, confines this departure from its "veto or enforce" rule to a narrow class of unconstitutional provisions, namely those that the courts have already said are unconstitutional.

Some such exception would certainly be necessary to salvage the ABA's rule from unworkability. But why should this exception apply only in cases where the courts have already declared a certain type of statute unconstitutional? Or, in other words, why should presidents be obliged to enforce unconstitutional statutes that have not yet been litigated? The report explains: "Definitive constitutional interpretations are entrusted to an independent and impartial Supreme Court, not a partisan and interested President. That is the meaning of *Marbury v. Madison.*"

Perhaps because of a touching faith in judges, the ABA is extremely offended by the thought that the president might have what the report calls "the last word" on which statutes will go unenforced because they are unconstitutional. But whatever the reason for the report's statement, it is wrong.

First, the Constitution nowhere says that "[d]efinitive constitutional interpretations" are entrusted to the Supreme Court, and the Constitution nowhere says that the Supreme Court must always get "the last word" about the meaning of the Constitution. Furthermore, there is no reason at all to assume that judges are more impartial and disinterested than presidents when it comes to deciding how much power they think the Constitution gives them. If anything, the self-evident fact is that Supreme Court justices are *not* impartial angels incapable of overreaching with respect to their own power. Like presidents, judges may sometimes be able to get away with exercising powers the Constitution does not give them. But the mere fact that some people claim that the Constitution gives them final authority doesn't make it so. That goes for judges, just as it does for presidents.

In addition, the ABA is wrong about the famous Supreme Court decision in *Marbury v. Madison* (1803), which nowhere made the sweeping claim to judicial supremacy attributed to it by the report. If anything, *Marbury* actually undermines the ABA's attack on presidential signing statements. That case held that the Supreme Court is authorized to refuse to enforce unconstitutional statutes. The most logically powerful argument in *Marbury* for that conclusion is this: faced with a conflict between the Constitution and a statute, courts have no choice except to give effect to the more authoritative of the two laws, namely the Constitution. That logic applies to the president every bit as much as it does to the Supreme Court.

Significantly, however, nobody on the Supreme Court has ever actually accepted all the implications of *Marbury*'s logic. Any justice who did so would have to conclude that conflicts between the Constitution and judicial precedent must always be resolved by giving effect to the Constitution, not the precedent. After all, if statutes enacted by the people's representatives are always trumped by the Constitution, it would seem to follow by inexorable logic that mere judicial opinions must also be trumped by the Constitution. According to the Constitution itself, the "supreme Law of the Land" includes the Constitution, statutes enacted pursuant to the Constitution, and treaties. Conspicuously absent from the list is any mention of judicial opinions.

In practice, the Supreme Court has developed a very complex and flexible approach to the exercise of constitutional review. There is almost nobody who would seriously maintain today that courts are obliged by the Constitution to enforce unconstitutional statutes. But it is also true that very few would seriously maintain that courts are *always* obliged to strike down statutes they think are unconstitutional, even in the face of thoroughly settled judicial precedent.

Presidents take the same general approach that the Supreme Court has taken, and properly so. In principle, presidents always have the option of refusing to enforce or comply with statutes they consider unconstitutional. But they are not obliged to ignore or defy *every* such statute. And the same goes for Congress. The Constitution nowhere imposes on the legislature an obligation to relentlessly impose its own constitutional views on other branches of government.

POLITICAL SELF-RESTRAINT

One might think that leaving the president, the Supreme Court, and the Congress with concurrent authority to decide on the meaning of the Constitution is an invitation to constitutional crises and ultimately to chaos. History demonstrates that this is not so. With respect to who gets "the last word" on the meaning of the Constitution and other laws, the simple fact is that each branch of government sometimes gets the last word and sometimes does not.

The Supreme Court, for example, has all kinds of devices by which it avoids trying to become the last word on all constitutional questions. These include doctrines under which the justices frequently decline to issue any decision at all as well as countless rulings that give the so-called political branches broad discretion to interpret their own constitutional powers.

Like the courts, presidents have also sought to minimize conflicts with the other branches. Over the years, for example, the president's legal advisers in the Justice Department have developed an elaborate internal jurisprudence that largely adheres to Supreme Court precedents. That jurisprudence displays some independence from the views of the judiciary, especially with respect to matters directly touching on the president's institutional interests, such as the scope of executive authority. But the jurisprudence is memorialized in written legal opinions that take judicial decisions very seriously and treat them as dispositive on many issues. In addition, the interpretive techniques—such as the practice of interpreting statutes so as to avoid constitutional difficulties—whose use has sometimes generated controversy, both in these Justice Department opinions and in presidential signing statements, are generally borrowed directly from the Supreme Court.

It is important to keep in mind that these Justice Department legal opinions are purely advisory so far as the president is concerned. The president is free to ignore or overrule them, and presidents sometimes do just that. Perhaps most important, presidents have not felt compelled to exercise every right they believe they have or that the Justice Department tells them they have. There is a fundamentally important distinction between claiming the authority to do something and actually doing it.

George W. Bush himself grasped the difference, perhaps better than his supposedly more sophisticated critics. That much, at least, is suggested by the following extemporaneous comment during a public press conference at which he was asked about one of his most controversial signing statements:

> I signed the appropriations bill with the McCain [antitorture] amendment attached on because that's the way it is. I know some have said, well, why did he put a qualifier in [the signing statement]? And one reason why presidents put qualifiers in is to protect the prerogative of the executive branch. You see, what we're always doing is making sure that we make it clear that the executive branch has got certain responsibilities. Conducting war is a responsibility in the executive branch, not the legislative branch. But make no mistake about it, the McCain amendment is an amendment we strongly support and will make sure it's fully effective.

We all need to keep President Bush's commonsense point in mind when evaluating alarmist rhetoric like that found in the ABA report. Bush did use his signing statements to *articulate* a relatively expansive view of presidential power somewhat more aggressively and systematically than his predecessors did, especially in connection with national security matters. But how much of this was limited to expressing his administration's constitutional views, and how much of it led to actual defiance of statutes? When I did a detailed study of the George H. W. Bush administration's jurisprudence of presidential power, I found that the first Bush had been quite aggressive in publicly claiming constitutional authority and extremely *timid* about actually exercising the powers he claimed to have.[26] Could the same thing have been true of his son, George W. Bush?

After the Democrats took control of Congress in 2007, they directed the Government Accountability Office (GAO) to conduct a study of the Bush administration's treatment of statutory provisions to which the president had objected in his signing statements. The most striking result of this research project was the GAO's inability to find evidence that the Bush administration failed to comply with even a single statutory provision as a result of objections articulated in a presidential signing statement.[27]

Like many others who study the Supreme Court, I think it has often misinterpreted the Constitution, sometimes badly and even inexcusably. I also disagree with a number of interpretations of the Constitution set forth in Justice Department opinions and presidential signing statements. And I believe that

Congress has passed more than a few unconstitutional statutes, some of which have been signed by presidents and upheld by the Supreme Court. There is lots of room for reasonable debate about these issues and about such questions as how much deference each branch of government should give to constitutional decisions reached by the others. But such debates are not usefully advanced either by the ABA report's shoddy legal analysis or by its hysterical claim that President Bush's signing statements constituted a threat to "the rule of law and our constitutional system of separation of powers."

Suppose that a president really did abuse the power of the office by systematically using dishonest legal interpretations as a fig leaf for efforts to approximate the exercise of an unconstitutional line-item veto or to suspend valid existing statutes by executive fiat. That might trigger a truly serious constitutional confrontation, and if it did there can be little doubt about which branch would have the last word. Congress, after all, still has the power of impeachment.

In fact, Congress has been very cautious about using this power to enforce its interpretations of the Constitution, and the impeachment of Andrew Johnson suggests why. He was accused of violating the Constitution by refusing to comply with a statute that interfered with his control over the military. Many decades later, in *Myers v. United States* (1926), the Supreme Court decided (correctly, I believe) that the statute was an unconstitutional infringement on the president's legitimate executive authority. Johnson's trial in the Senate may also serve as a useful reminder of what a real constitutional crisis looks like. Had he been convicted and removed from office, what the ABA calls "our constitutional system of separation of powers" might indeed have been profoundly altered.

THE FUTURE OF SIGNING STATEMENTS

Those who endorsed the ABA report were highly offended by President Bush's signing statements, and they no doubt strongly disagreed with his policies on national security and other matters. But offending your political opponents or an organized interest group like the ABA is not quite the same as threatening the rule of law and the separation of powers. Even if one assumes that Bush was wrong about some of the specific statutory provisions that he claimed were unconstitutional, it does not follow that these mistakes posed any real danger to the republic.

Barack Obama also denounced Bush's use of signing statements during his 2008 campaign. Shortly after assuming office, however, President Obama began issuing signing statements that were indistinguishable from Bush's statements about similarly worded statutory provisions. On March 9, 2009, the new president announced that signing statements "serve a legitimate function in our system, at least when based on well-founded constitutional objections." Two days later, he issued a signing statement objecting to numerous provisions in an appropriations bill and declaring that he would either ignore them or interpret them to be consistent with his own views of his constitutional authority.

President Obama has continued to issue signing statements with constitutional objections just like the ones Bush was excoriated for raising. The ABA, however, has not issued any reports castigating Obama as a threat to "the rule of law and our constitutional system of separation of powers." Why not? Was its attack on Bush nothing but a partisan smear? Because the ABA's report offered nothing but transparently defective legal analysis, it is hard to avoid that conclusion.

If the ABA's overwrought attack on signing statements has any significance at all, perhaps it is this: by crying wolf about President Bush, the ABA and the prestigious authors of its report have made it less likely that they will be taken seriously if they ever have occasion to warn the nation about a genuine threat to the constitutional order.

President Obama has issued fewer signing statements than his predecessor.[28] Obama, however, has gone far beyond Bush in actually defying Congress. Consider just a few examples. A statute enacted in 2003 required the State Department to honor requests from U.S. citizens born in Jerusalem to record Israel as the place of birth on their passports. The Obama administration refused to comply. While the Senate was holding formal sessions in 2012, President Obama made three "recess appointments," which are permitted by the Constitution only when the Senate is not in session. In 2011 the Obama administration continued to bomb Libya after a federal statute (the War Powers Resolution) required it to withdraw from hostilities. When Congress rejected President Obama's proposal to grant amnesty and work permits to millions of illegal aliens, he unilaterally implemented his program without congressional authorization.

In some cases President Obama may have been within his constitutional rights, and in some cases perhaps he was not.[29] Under the ABA's legal theory, however, these *actual violations* of "the congressional will" must be much graver threats to "the rule of law and our constitutional system of separation of powers" than President Bush's *mere statements* about his constitutional rights. The ABA, however, has not called Obama a threat to the constitutional order, which confirms that its legally nonsensical denunciation of Bush was just a politically motivated canard.

NOTES

INTRO

1. William G. Howell with David Milton Brent, *Thinking about the Presidency: The Primacy of Power* (Princeton, NJ: Princeton University Press, 2013), 42, 45.

PRO

2. Christopher N. May, *Presidential Defiance of "Unconstitutional" Laws: Reviving the Royal Prerogative* (Westport, CT: Greenwood Press, 1998), 76.
3. U.S. Constitution, Article I, Section 7, par. 2.
4. American Bar Association, "Report of the American Bar Association Task Force on Presidential Signing Statements and the Separation of Powers Doctrine," August 2006, 10, www.abanet.org/op/signingstatements/aba_final_signing_statements_recommendation-report_7–24–06.pdf
5. T. J. Halstead, "Presidential Signing Statements: Constitutional and Institutional Implications," *Congressional Research Service Report for Congress* (Washington, DC: Congressional Research Service, September 26, 2006), 3, 5, 6.
6. Neil J. Kinkopf and Peter M. Shane, "Signed under Protest: A Database of Presidential Signing Statements, 2001–2009," *Social Science Research Network*, October 8, 2009, http://papers.ssrn.com/s013/papers.cfm?abstract_id=1485715
7. Charlie Savage, "Barack Obama's Q&A," *Boston Globe*, December 27, 2007, http://www.boston.com/news/politics/2008/specials/CandidateQA/ObamaQA/
8. "Presidential Memorandum for the Heads of Executive Departments and Agencies Re: Presidential Signing Statements," *Federal Register* 74, no. 46 (March 11, 2009): 10669.
9. *Postal Accountability and Enhancement Act*, Public Law 109–435, *U.S. Statutes at Large* 120 (2006): 3198.
10. *U.S. Code*, title 39, sec. 502.
11. "Statement on Signing the Postal Accountability and Enhancement Act," *Weekly Compilation of Press Documents* 42 (2006): 2196.
12. Kinkopf and Shane, "Signed under Protest," 7.
13. *Department of Defense Appropriations Act*, 2002, Pub. L. No. 107–117, sec. 8098, *U.S. Statutes at Large* 115 (2002): 2230, 2268.
14. "Statement on Signing the Department of Defense and Emergency Supplemental Appropriations for Recovery from and Response to Terrorist Attacks on the United States Act, 2002," *Weekly Compilation of Press Documents* 38 (2002): 46.
15. Kinkopf and Shane, "Signed under Protest."
16. Gerhard Casper, "An Essay in Separation of Powers: Some Early Versions and Practices," *William and Mary Law Review* 30 (211, 240–242); Jerry L. Mashaw, "Recovering American Administrative Law: Federalist Foundations," *Yale Law Journal* 115 (2006): 1256, 1284–87.
17. Kinkopf and Shane, "Signed under Protest."

18. "Statement on Signing Legislation to Provide for Improvement of Federal Education Research, Statistics, Evaluation, Information, Dissemination and for Other Purposes," *Weekly Compilation of Press Documents* 38 (2002): 1995.

19. *Specialty Crops Competitiveness Act of 2004*, Pub. L. No. 108–465, sec. 1408A(d), U.S. Statutes at Large 118 (2004): 3882, 3886.

20. "Statement by President George W. Bush upon Signing H.R. 3242," *Weekly Compilation of Press Documents* 40 (2004): 3009.

21. "Presidential Memorandum for the Heads of Executive Departments and Agencies Re: Presidential Signing Statements," *Federal Register* 74, no. 46 (March 11, 2009): 10669.

22. In identifying President Obama's signing statements, I have benefitted from the work of attorney Joyce Green, who maintains a running list of signing statements—including signing statements that make no objections to the laws in question, http://www.coherentbabble.com

23. Two of the eighteen statements include objections to "numerous provisions" of the respective statutes that amount to legislative veto provisions of the kind held unconstitutional in *Immigration and Naturalization Service v. Chadha*, 462 U.S. 919 (1983).

24. "Statement by the President on Signing H.R. 1105, The Omnibus Appropriations Act of 2009," http://www.whitehouse.gov/the_press_office/Statement-from-the-President-on-the-signing-of-HR-1105/

CON

25. American Bar Association, "Report of the American Bar Association Task Force on Presidential Signing Statements and the Separation of Powers Doctrine," August 2006, www.abanet.org/op/signingstatements/aba_final_signing_statements_recommendation-report_7–24–06.pdf

26. Nelson Lund, "Lawyers and the Defense of the Presidency," *Brigham Young University Law Review* (1995): 17.

27. See "Presidential Signing Statements Accompanying the Fiscal Year 2006 Appropriations Acts" (memo no. B-308603 from the U.S. Government Accountability Office to Sen. Robert C. Byrd and Rep. John Conyers Jr., June 18, 2007), www.gao.gov/decisions/appro/308603.pdf. For my analysis of the memo's findings, see Nelson Lund, "Presidential Signing Statements in Perspective," *William and Mary Bill of Rights Journal* (2007): 95.

28. See Todd Garvey, "Presidential Signing Statements: Constitutional and Institutional Implications," *Congressional Research Service Report*, RL33667 (January 4, 2012), http://www.fas.org/sgp/crs/natsec/RL33667.pdf

29. A divided Supreme Court upheld Obama's position on passports, and unanimously rejected his position on recess appointments. See *Zivotofsky v. Kerry* (2015); *NLRB v. Noel Canning* (2014). The Court has not ruled on the Libya bombing or immigration issues.

12

RESOLVED, Executive orders and other unilateral presidential directives undermine democracy

PRO: Gene Healy

CON: Andrew Rudalevige

"Stroke of the pen, law of the land. Kind of cool." That is how Clinton aide Paul Begala, in 1998, memorably described the appeal of executive orders and other unilateral presidential directives, such as proclamations, national security directives, and presidential memoranda. These unilateral orders are especially cool if you are a second-term president facing a recalcitrant Congress controlled by the other party, as Bill Clinton did. And Barack Obama too.

At the outset of his second term, Obama pledged that "When Congress isn't acting, I'll act on my own." And he did. In 2014, for instance, Obama issued Executive Order 13658, which raised the minimum wage of employees of government contractors by almost 40 percent, to $10.10 an hour. Republicans howled in protest. "Mr. President we are a nation of laws & we are supposed to follow our #Constitution," tweeted Kentucky senator Rand Paul. "You do not get to 'act alone.'"

Obama's defenders countered that the president was not behaving any differently than his predecessors. One of the earliest of George W. Bush's nearly three hundred executive orders included an order (Executive Order 13202) prohibiting federal dollars from going to construction projects in which a contractor had signed a "project labor agreement" with a labor union. This sort of executive unilateralism is hardly a recent invention. Back in 1840, Martin Van Buren sought to secure working class political support by issuing an executive order mandating that those laboring on federal public works could not be made to work more than ten hours a day.

Pointing out that the other side does it too or that it's been done before is hardly a satisfactory answer, however, to the question of whether or when presidents are justified in acting alone. Those who believe that executive orders undermine American democracy appeal to Montesquieu's famous precept that "there can be no liberty where the legislative and executive powers are united in the same person." If presidential directives involve an exercise of legislative power, then they indeed seem to subvert the separation of powers. On the other hand, if executive orders are directed at federal officials and agencies, as they typically are, then the directives would seem to be an unobjectionable exercise of executive power.

But does the U.S. constitutional system really establish a separation of powers, or is it instead, in Richard Neustadt's famous formulation, a system of "separated institutions sharing powers"? If the latter, then do executive orders undermine American democracy? After all, nothing in Obama's or Bush's or Van Buren's directive prevented Congress from enacting a law that overrode the order. Had these directives been concealed from Congress, then there might be a strong case for constitutional subversion. But all executive orders are required by law to be published. And in the case of Obama's minimum-wage order it was announced in the most public way possible: in a State of the Union message.

There is also the question of just how unilateral these directives really are. Notwithstanding Obama's pledge to act on his own when Congress failed to act, he did not in fact claim to be acting alone when he issued Executive Order 13658. Yes, his order began by invoking "the authority vested in me as President by the Constitution," but it also invoked the authority he derived from a specific statute: the Federal Property and Administrative Services Act, the same statute that George W. Bush cited in justifying his Executive Order 13202 (and that Obama cited in repealing Bush's order). In fact, most executive orders involving contested domestic policies invoke the authority of a legislative statute. Perhaps, though, invoking statutory authority is merely a strategic effort to cloak unilateralism. That presidents can appeal to the same statute and draw diametrically opposed conclusions would indicate that statutes may do little to constrain presidents who are intent on taking actions that fit their ideological predilections.

Of course, nobody thinks that every executive order is a threat to democracy. Even the most vigilant critic would strain to see a danger in the president giving federal workers a half-day off on Christmas Eve, as Obama did by executive order in December 2015. However, Gene Healy argues that the increasing trend toward governing by executive fiat in a broad range of contentious public policy domains, including immigration, education, and environmental regulation, poses a grave threat to the future of American democracy. Andrew Rudalevige is more skeptical. He suggests that presidential directives are often more multilateral than unilateral, and that in any event presidential directives to the bureaucracy bolster democracy by enhancing both accountability and responsiveness to the executive branch's sole elected leader.

PRO: Gene Healy

Every president from George Washington onward has issued unilateral directives.[1] It's hard to see how any president could do the job without them. Even in 1789, the federal chief executive couldn't execute the laws all by himself; to perform that core function, and simply to manage the executive branch in general, the president needs to issue instructions.[2]

No sensible person would argue that *all* such directives "undermine democracy." When carried out pursuant to genuine legislative or constitutional authority, unilateral presidential directives are unobjectionable—even trivial, as a perusal of the *Federal Register*'s "executive order disposition tables" makes clear. It would take a lurid imagination to spy the glimmerings of tyranny in, say, Executive Order 13713's proclamation of a half-day closing for federal workers on Christmas Eve or EO 13571's aspirational provisions for "Streamlining Service Delivery and Improving Customer Service in the Federal Government."[3]

And yet, other presidential directives aren't quite so innocuous. When presidents can, as they increasingly have, call new agencies into being, shield government operations behind a veil of secrecy, and issue commands unsupported by legal authority but indistinguishable from law, we have reason to worry about the health of our democracy.

THE PRESIDENTIAL ORDERS THAT LED TO MASS SPYING

Consider: Starting in the summer of 2013, courtesy of a former National Security Agency (NSA) contractor named Edward Snowden, Americans learned, in unsettling detail, about the vast surveillance machine the federal government had secretly constructed after 9/11. The dangers of dragnet data collection are, by now, fairly well understood: the digital trails we leave are a window into our private lives. They can be used to ferret out the sort of information that authoritarian governments have historically used to blackmail and control dissenters: who's leaking to reporters, how political opponents are organizing, who's sleeping with whom. In the NSA's quest to "collect it all," the agency had built what Sen. Ron Wyden, D-Ore., has described as a massive "human relations database," ripe for abuse—or, as Snowden himself termed it, a "turnkey tyranny."

What's less well appreciated, perhaps, is the fact that the burgeoning surveillance state Snowden exposed rests on a foundation built from unilateral presidential directives and executive orders.

Among the most important of those directives was a "presidential authorization" issued by President George W. Bush on October 4, 2001, that secretly— and illegally—allowed the NSA to evade the Foreign Intelligence Surveillance Act (FISA) Congress passed in 1978 to rein in domestic spying. The public has never been allowed to see a copy of Bush's order, but according to a secret draft report by the NSA's inspector general—also leaked by Snowden—it "allowed NSA to intercept the content of any communication, including those to, from, or exclusively within the United States" without a FISA warrant.[4] That purported "authorization" spawned a program code-named "Stellarwind," which involved, among other activities, targeted acquisition of the content of Americans' international phone calls and wholesale collection of their phone and e-mail records.

"I welcome this debate and I think it's healthy for our democracy," President Obama declared in June 2013, shortly after the Snowden leaks revealed the existence of the bulk collection programs: "it's a sign of maturity," because just a few years ago, "we might not have been having this debate." Which was true enough: if you've been deliberately kept in the dark about your government's surveillance policies, it's hard to get a proper debate going. But now, armed with better information, surely fixing the problem was just a matter of petitioning our elected representatives to address our grievances.

In early 2014 John Napier Tye, then a State Department official with a top-secret security clearance, prepared a speech making that very point: if citizens objected to mass data mining, "they have the opportunity to change the policy through our democratic process." But when Tye sent the draft over to the White House Counsel's office for approval, the president's lawyers told him to take out that line: it just wasn't true. Even after Snowden's disclosures, Tye later explained in an op-ed for the *Washington Post*, "some intelligence practices remain so secret, even from members of Congress, there is no opportunity for our democracy to change them."[5]

Thanks to another presidential directive, Tye hinted, some of those practices go beyond "metadata" and involve bulk collection of the *content* of citizens' personal communications. Tye pointed to Executive Order 12333, a Reagan administration directive that loosened restrictions on U.S. intelligence activities. "If the contents of a U.S. person's communications are 'incidentally' collected . . . in the course of a lawful overseas foreign intelligence investigation," Tye explained, "then Section 2.3(c) of the executive order explicitly authorizes their retention." Vast amounts of Americans' private communications—e-mail content, text messages, Skype chats, and Facebook messages—can now be funneled through that loophole and onto the NSA's servers; from there, that information can be legally shared with the Drug Enforcement Administration, the Federal Bureau of Investigation, and other law enforcement agencies, without judicial or congressional oversight.[6] Choosing his words carefully to avoid potential liability for revealing classified information, Tye writes that "Americans deserve an honest answer to the simple question: What kind of data is the NSA collecting on millions, or hundreds of millions, of Americans?"

"DEMOCRACY," THICK AND THIN

Did the presidential directives that led us to this pass "undermine democracy"? Unless one embraces the narrowest possible conception of the term—"yeah, but still: those guys were *elected*"—it's hard to see how they didn't.

At its most basic, etymological roots, "democracy" means rule (*kratos*) of the people (*demos*), as distinguished from "autocracy": ruling by oneself. A bare-bones definition of a democratic system might be: one in which, at regular intervals, leaders are chosen by elections. But in common parlance, "democracy" means more than that: it speaks to what those leaders are allowed to do once elected, and what we the people are allowed to know about what they're doing.[7]

"For almost a century in the West," Fareed Zakaria writes, "democracy has meant *liberal* democracy—a political system marked not only by free and fair elections, but also by the rule of law, a separation of powers, and the protection of basic liberties."[8] Accordingly, scholars who rank regimes on their democratic health tend to use robust criteria. The widely used Polity IV database puts democracy and autocracy at opposite ends of its scale, and weighs "constraints on the chief executive" most heavily among its criteria.[9] The annual Freedom House ranking grades regimes broadly on civil liberties and political rights, including whether "citizens have the legal right and practical ability to obtain information about government operations and the means to petition government agencies for it[.]"[10] And the Economist Intelligence Unit's *Democracy Index* tracks, among other indicators, whether the regime is "open and transparent, with sufficient public access to information?"; "is the legislature the supreme political body, with a clear supremacy over other branches of government?"; and "is there an effective system of checks and balances on the exercise of government authority?"[11]

Again, not all unilateral presidential directives threaten the rule of law, the public's right to know, our system of checks and balances, or other essential features of democracy, properly understood. But many clearly do. As presidents' responsibilities expanded throughout the twentieth century, their powers to make law by executive fiat expanded accordingly, in ways that undermine the representative system of government our Constitution's architects designed.

THE ORIGINAL DESIGN

Governments derive their just powers from the consent of the governed, the Declaration of Independence insists, a sentiment echoed by James Madison in *Federalist* No. 49: "the people are the only legitimate fountain of power." The Framers of our Constitution didn't believe in direct democracy, viewing it as unworkable in an extended republic and dangerous to minority rights. What their efforts produced was the basis for a *representative* democracy.

In such a system, the power to make law is properly lodged in the members of the legislative department: "the nature of their public trust implies a personal influence among the people," Madison wrote, and, compared to the chief executive or the judiciary, members of the legislative branch "are more immediately the confidential guardians of the rights and liberties of the people." Accordingly, in Article I, Section 1, the first sentence following its Preamble, the Constitution declares that "all legislative Powers herein granted shall be vested in a Congress of the United States."

The first sentence of Article II vests "The executive Power" in the president. At its core, that power consists of the authority to carry into execution the laws that Congress makes—a point underscored in Article II, Section 3, which imposes a number of duties on the president, among them that the chief executive "shall take Care that the Laws be faithfully executed."

Justice Hugo Black summed that framework up nicely in a 1952 Supreme Court opinion: "the President's power to see that the laws are faithfully executed refutes the idea that he is to be a lawmaker. The Constitution limits his functions in the lawmaking process to the recommending of laws he thinks wise and the vetoing of laws he thinks bad. And the Constitution is neither silent nor equivocal about who shall make laws which the President is to execute."[12]

LAWMAKER IN CHIEF

That case, of course, was *Youngstown Sheet & Tube Co. v. Sawyer*, which arose out of a labor dispute in the U.S. steel industry during the Korean War. Facing down a nationwide steelworkers' strike, President Harry S. Truman issued Executive Order 10340, "Directing the Secretary of Commerce to Take Possession of and Operate the Plants and Facilities of Certain Steel Companies." That directive rested on the theory that in times of (self-proclaimed) emergency, the president's powers were essentially unlimited. When asked by a reporter whether the president could also lawfully "seize the newspapers and/or the radio stations," Truman would say only that "under similar circumstances, the President of the United States has to act for whatever is for the best of the country."

The Supreme Court, however, disagreed with the proposition that the Constitution granted unlimited power to the chief executive, holding the seizure invalid by a 6–3 vote. Yet *Youngstown* turned out to be the vanishingly rare case in which the courts rebuked a president for overreaching with a unilateral directive, even as the president's unilateral powers continued to expand.

Where most of the executive orders during the 1920s related to administrative matters such as civil service rules, with no more than 10 percent "policy-specific," by the 1960s, executive orders making national policy "reached 50% and never declined."[13] Though Black's majority opinion rejected the notion of president-as-lawmaker, in the years after *Youngstown*, more and more presidential directives took on the character of legal commands.[14]

Our constitutional structure of separated powers rests on the Madisonian belief that "when the legislative and executive powers are united in the same person or body . . . there can be no liberty." The most infamous unilateral directive in our history—Executive Order 9066, through which President Franklin D. Roosevelt authorized the mass internment of over 110,000 innocent Japanese Americans—seemed to justify those fears.

A less notorious directive, but one that did lasting damage, was Truman's 1951 Executive Order 10290, which greatly expanded federal officials' ability to classify information they deemed "necessary . . . to protect the security of the United States." "One could say that the 'national security president' was born on paper at 10:57 a.m., September 26, 1951," Robert M. Pallitto and William G. Weaver write in *Presidential Secrecy and the Law*, "when E.O. 10290 was submitted for publication in the *Federal Register*."[15] Where before classification authority had rarely extended to nonmilitary departments, Truman's order gave secrecy powers to all civilian federal agencies and did not limit its exercise to wartime.[16] State secrecy was largely a presidential creation, Pallitto and

Weaver explain: by the late twentieth century, "less than two percent of all classification [was] made pursuant to statute; the rest is classified in accordance with executive orders and administrative guidelines."[17]

In *Federalist* No. 69, Alexander Hamilton undertook an extended comparison of the president's powers with those of the British monarch, the better "to place in a strong light the unfairness of the representations which have been made" against the proposed Constitution. There is obviously "a great inferiority in the power of the President," he insisted, when one considers that the British king "not only appoints to all offices, but can *create offices*." By the mid–twentieth century, the difference was no longer so stark, given the modern president's power to summon whole agencies into being with the proverbial "stroke of a pen."

Many of the most important agencies listed in the *United States Government Manual* were "immaculately" conceived by presidents, without the mess and bother the democratic process entails. Among the agencies established by presidential decree are the NSA (via a top-secret directive issued by President Truman in 1952), the Federal Emergency Management Agency (EO 12148), and the Drug Enforcement Administration (EO 11727). "Since the end of World War II," William G. Howell and David E. Lewis note, "presidents have unilaterally created over half of all administrative agencies in the United States," using executive orders and other unilateral directives to spawn new governmental bodies "that would never have been created through legislative action, [and] design[ing] these agencies in ways that maximize their control over them."[18]

Acting alone, a president can reshape the governmental landscape, presenting the people's elected representatives with a *fait accompli* and daring them to destroy what the chief executive has made. A good example of that dynamic can be found in President John F. Kennedy's creation of the Peace Corps in 1961, despite the failure of multiple bills aimed at establishing the agency. Via Executive Order 10924, JFK simply bypassed congressional opposition to what Republicans had called "a juvenile experiment," set up the program with contingency funds from the foreign-aid budget, and appointed his brother-in-law, Sargent Shriver, to head it. When the time came for Congress to actually vote on the program, the Peace Corps already had hundreds of employees and volunteers worldwide, and legislators balked at defunding an agency that could never command a majority in the first instance.[19] "Presidents create more agencies when Congress is relatively weak," Howell and Lewis explain. "By strategically employing these unilateral powers, presidents have managed to create a broad array of administrative agencies that perform functions that congressional majorities oppose."[20]

Modern presidents regularly use "the power of the pen" to take what legislative majorities won't willingly grant. Though the literature on "strategic timing" of presidential directives varies, one recent study finds that "presidents issue many more policy executive orders" when their ideological preferences differ significantly from those of congressional majorities, "suggesting that presidents are attempting to circumvent an ideologically hostile Congress."[21] One person makes national policy and then, should legislators object, it is up to them to change the law.

That process turns the Constitution on its head. Under Article I, a law must meet with the approval of the representatives of three different constituencies: the House, the Senate, and the president. But when the executive branch makes the law unilaterally, those constitutional hurdles then obstruct legislative efforts to repeal it. "Congressional repeals of executive orders are relatively rare in modern times," the Congressional Research Service reports, "primarily because such legislation could run counter to the President's interests and therefore may require a congressional override of a presidential veto."[22] One review of significant executive orders from 1936 to 2001 finds that fewer than 4 percent have been successfully modified or terminated via legislation;[23] another that only twice since 1970 has Congress managed to "explicitly invalidat[e] an executive order of any substance."[24] Nor are the courts a reliable bulwark against executive overreach. Between 1943 and 1997—a period that saw some four thousand EOs—presidents lost only fourteen times in federal court challenges to those orders.[25]

Of course, checks and balances are utterly unavailing when presidential lawmaking is done in the dark, as so much of it is today, via secret rulemaking, classified legal opinions, and national security directives. Such instruments often affect Americans' rights directly, setting out the procedures under which American citizens can be spied upon or even targeted for assassination abroad. Yet, as Howell explains, "unlike other tools presidents have for unilateral action, such as proclamations or executive orders, national security directives are not subject to the Freedom of Information Act. They are not published in the National Register, and indeed their very existence often remains unknown," even to Congress.[26] Ours is supposed to be a system based on "the consent of the governed," but knowledge has to precede consent. On fundamental questions of national policy, we're increasingly becoming a "democracy in the dark."[27]

UNILATERAL DIRECTIVES IN THE BUSH/OBAMA ERA

As Aaron Wildavsky observed in his seminal 1966 article, "The Two Presidencies": "Presidents have had much greater success in controlling the nation's defense and foreign policies than in dominating its domestic policies."[28] What applied during the Cold War has largely held true during the War on Terror as well: both President Bush and President Obama found themselves freer to act unilaterally in the national security arena than in a purely domestic context.

But it's not as though the powers the president claims in the name of national security apply only outside U.S. borders, never disturbing our domestic tranquility. In the post-9/11 era, presidential unilateralism in the name of national security impacts the rule of law and civil liberties on the home front as well.

On October 8, 2001, for example, President Bush issued Executive Order 13228, creating the Office of Homeland Security and setting the stage for the establishment of what would become the cabinet-level Department of Homeland Security. A little over a month later, Bush issued a sweeping "military order" allowing for the arrest of noncitizens—even legal residents of the United States—and their trial before military commissions in cases where the president has "reason to believe" the suspect has connections to international terrorism.[29]

Nor are foreign policy crises the only occasions that enhance the chief executive's ability to govern without Congress, as the financial crisis of 2008 made clear. In December of that year, American automakers General Motors and Chrysler tottered on the brink of bankruptcy, while Congress debated legislation to provide some $15 billion to keep two of the "Big Three" alive. A week after the auto bailout bill failed to pass a key procedural vote in the Senate, President Bush announced that, despite the bill's failure, he had decided to lend the car companies $17.4 billion out of funds Congress had already approved for an entirely different purpose: taking toxic mortgage-backed securities off failing banks' asset sheets. White House spokesman Tony Fratto explained: "Congress lost its opportunity to be a partner because they couldn't get their job done."

President Obama vigorously exercised the new economic powers his predecessor had left him. After *Youngstown*, the president might not have been able to seize a steel mill, but he could summarily fire the CEO of a major American company, as became clear in March 2009, when President Obama's "car czar" summoned GM's CEO Rick Wagoner to his office to get pink slipped.

No crisis was necessary for President Obama to dramatically reshape American immigration law by executive fiat. He'd initially resisted the temptation, telling a panel of Latino journalists in 2011 that "This notion that somehow I can just change the laws unilaterally is just not true. . . . We live in a democracy." By 2012 he'd decided he could change the laws unilaterally after all, using a "Homeland Security Directive" to grant legal status to up to 1.7 million undocumented residents, a move that basically implemented the core of an immigration reform bill that had been stalled in Congress. As Obama prepared to further extend the program in 2014, he told his congressional critics that if they think he's "taking too many executive actions, the best solution to that is passing bills. Pass a bill; solve a problem." But there's little incentive to build legislative coalitions if presidents can effectively change the law on their own.

In his second term, boasting that "I've got a pen and I've got a phone," President Obama increasingly governed by unilateral directive in areas ranging from education policy, immigration, and environmental regulation at home to military action abroad. Even if you like the results, Obama won't be the last president to wield the expansive new powers he's forged.

A "LOADED WEAPON"

In discussions with his advisers, President Obama has been heard to worry about "leaving a loaded weapon lying around" for future presidents, as *Newsweek* reported just before the 2012 election in an article titled "Obama's Executive Power Grab."[30]

At this writing, as Election 2016 looms, Obama's possible successors seem eager to pick up that weapon. Democratic nominee Hillary Clinton said she'd go "as far as I can, even beyond President Obama," acting unilaterally on immigration and using presidential directives to stop corporations from headquartering abroad to avoid taxes.[31]

"I won't refuse them," Republican nominee Donald Trump said of executive orders. "I mean, [Obama] has led the way, to be honest with you." Not to worry, though: Trump made it clear that he'd wield the "power of the pen" to do the "right things."[32]

George Washington University law professor Jonathan Turley notes that those who've applauded Obama's efforts to govern by decree have ignored the "obvious danger that they could be planting a deeply unfortunate precedent . . . while the policies may not carry over to the next president, the powers will." Why couldn't a president with a different set of priorities "use his executive discretion to extend, perhaps indefinitely, the deadline for corporate income tax payments," or use Obama's broad theory of administrative waivers to amend national curriculum standards and create space for "creation science" in America's schools? And in the national security arena, where the president's unilateral powers are at their height, what's to stop future commanders in chief from going "even beyond" our two post-9/11 presidents, in ways that further infringe on Americans' privacy rights? "The problem with allowing a president to become a government unto himself," Turley concludes, "is that you cannot guarantee who the next president might be."[33]

If you introduce a gun in the first act, it needs to be fired in the second, the old dramatic principle goes. Unfortunately, we seem determined to play out that script.

CON: Andrew Rudalevige

"The President has been blatantly ignoring the will of the people throughout his Presidency and it's time to rein in his Administration," trumpeted Rep. Randy Weber in a March 2016 press release.[34] Weber's feelings on the matter had been clear for some time. As Barack Obama was about to deliver his 2014 State of the Union address, the Texas Republican tweeted that he was waiting for the "'Kommandant-In-Ch[i]ef' . . . the Socialistic dictator."[35]

What prompted such hostility? The release was in support of a House measure to file an amicus brief in a lawsuit opposing President Obama's initiatives in immigration policy. The tweet previewed Obama's promise that "a year of action" was in store, regardless of whether any of that action took place on Capitol Hill. As the president had already said, "I'm going to be working with Congress where I can, . . . but I'm also going to act on my own if Congress is deadlocked. I've got a pen to take executive actions where Congress won't."[36] Weber, and Obama's many other critics, argued that Obama was making law, rather than simply enforcing it, in violation of the Constitution and of democratic principles. A "brazen" Obama had revived the "imperial presidency," charged Sen. Ted Cruz, R-Tex. "Increasingly lawless," complained future House Speaker Rep. Paul Ryan, R-Wis.[37]

This essay argues instead that unilateral presidential directives do not undermine democracy but may in fact reinforce it. Administrative actions vary widely in their scope and import, but even at their most powerful they aim to shape the behavior of unelected and often uncoordinated bureaucratic actors consonant with the preferences of the only official chosen by the American people to represent the entire nation. To be sure, presidents sometimes overstep their branch's constitutional bounds. But "democracy" should not be glibly defined in a knee-jerk way as "congressional enactment": the framers of the Constitution did not glorify the legislative branch, and nor should we. Indeed, in some cases executive action may be democracy's last line of defense.

WHAT DO EXECUTIVE ACTIONS DO?

The very first sentence of Article II of the U.S. Constitution vests "the executive power . . . in a President of the United States." That power is not defined, and many (starting with Alexander Hamilton) have suggested the vesting clause gives the president residual authorities beyond those granted in the rest of the document. Even without making that claim, serving as "chief executive" clearly must include the power to manage the executive branch (given the hierarchy set up between presidents and their department heads in Article II, Section 2) through the control of personnel and policy implementation.

Executive actions flow directly from this authority. They proceed from statutory or constitutional authority—not personal whim—and apply to the president's initiatives as manager of a large and complex enterprise.

That also means, as a congressional committee put it, that "executive orders are generally directed to, and govern actions by, Government officials and agencies. They usually affect private individuals only indirectly."[38] An indirect impact can certainly be important; by changing how cost-benefit analysis is applied to regulatory review, or how antidiscrimination laws are enforced by government contractors, for instance, presidents can influence the private-sector economy. However, many orders deal with organizational issues or civil service rules—President Jimmy Carter issued five orders extending the retirement date of a single member of the Civil Aviation Board.[39] In 2009 President Obama prohibited texting while driving in federal vehicles. In 2016 he allowed the Peace Corps to come up with a new logo.[40] So it's clear that simply counting up executive orders, even broadly defined,[41] is a poor proxy for "dictatorship."

Relatedly, Obama's critics were fond of calling his use of administrative directives "unprecedented" or "unparalleled."[42] But every president has utilized these tools. Indeed, as political scientist Graham Dodds has documented, "early unilateral presidential directives were more numerous and more important than conventional wisdom holds."[43] From George Washington's 1793 neutrality proclamation onward, Americans recognized the need for, and legitimacy of, administrative instruments that would allow presidents to direct the function of executive branch subordinates. Indeed, in cases as early as 1795, the federal courts took presidential directives for granted.[44] Even when the Supreme Court disallowed the substance of an order a decade later, it affirmed the power of the president to issue that order, even "without any special authority for that purpose."[45]

The vast increase in the size and scope of the federal government has made executive management all the more crucial, and thus presidential action in this vein all the more necessary. As early as the 1920s, scholars were documenting what they called "administrative legislation" and "the ordinance-making powers of the president."[46] In the 1940s, the eminent scholar Edward Corwin observed that "executive interpretations of statutes flower—[in] . . . proclamations, orders, ordinances, rules, regulations, 'directives'. . . ."[47] In March 1961 John F. Kennedy himself noted that when it came to his civil rights priorities he had identified a "good deal of things we can do now in administering laws previously passed by the Congress, . . . and also by using the powers which the Constitution gives the President through Executive orders. . . . When I feel there is a necessity for congressional action, with a chance of getting that congressional action, then I will recommend it to the Congress."[48] And in the 1980s, former White House staffer Richard Nathan concluded that "in a complex, technologically advanced society in which the role of government is pervasive, much of what we would define as policymaking is done through the execution of laws in the management process."[49]

The rhetoric greeting Obama's actions is not new either. Kennedy received so much correspondence charging him with seizing "absolute power" through a series of executive orders setting up emergency planning processes that the White House developed a form letter to keep up. Reagan received similar fan mail—in 1981, a Mississippi voter wrote that one order made him "think the CFR [Council on Foreign Relations] owns R. R., smile and all. . . . Wouldn't it be healthy if all E.O.'s were revoked?"[50]

But the administrations' responses reinforce the purpose of executive action noted above. The Kennedy White House (using language drafted by the Justice Department) wrote that "it appears . . . that [people] are under the impression that the President can enhance his powers simply by issuing an Executive Order. That, of course, is a misconception. . . . [Such] documents having the effect of law, are issued only pursuant to, or in conformity with, powers vested in the President by the statutes or the Constitution of the United States, or both" and do not directly apply to private citizens. The Reagan administration noted likewise: "Executive Orders are a part of the management prerogative exercised by the President. They provide him with a facility for dealing with a range of governmental concerns." (Whether President Reagan's smile was leased from the CFR was, alas, not addressed.) [51]

BUREAUCRACY AND DEMOCRACY

Let's turn, then, to the field where executive orders play out—the bureaucracy. It's worth noting that the rise of the administrative state—driven by programmatic expansion under the New Deal, World War II, the Cold War, the Great

Society, and the 1970s explosion of regulation—reflects the aggregation of congressional choices about governmental functions over time.

In so doing, legislators directly delegated a wide range of administrative power to the president and also created a wide range of imprecise statutory provisions. Maneuvering a bill through Congress nearly always requires some degree of ambiguity, so each side can claim its demands were met. In the No Child Left Behind Act, for instance, how was the broad notion of educational "accountability" to be defined in practice? In the Affordable Care Act, what insurance plans would comply with the law? These details were not in the statutes themselves. It is difficult to anticipate every possible outcome in legislative language. Thus executive departments and agencies are routinely delegated power to promulgate regulations specifying how a given law will work in practice. Statutes also frequently grant waiver authority, allowing the suspension of parts of the law under certain conditions.

Who should exercise this power? Should it be the millions of unelected civil servants—the "fourth branch" of government—who make up the permanent bureaucracy? It seems far more democratic for presidents, elected nationally, to influence executive preferences. As an academic, Woodrow Wilson posited a difference between "politics" and "administration," handing over implementation to the bureaus, but he changed his mind when he became president.[52] The Supreme Court has held that "the discretion to be exercised is that of the President in determining the national public interest and in directing the action to be taken by his executive subordinates to protect it."[53] Presidential executive action thus helps ensure that executive branch behavior is in tune with the popular will.

Presidential appointments are surely one way of trying to shape how executive branch employees behave.[54] But very few of the 2.5 million civilians working for the federal government are chosen by the president. In the Department of Agriculture, just 60 or so of a staff of over 95,000—less than one-tenth of 1 percent—are politically appointed. It is hard to imagine that provides much in the way of direct supervision.

Furthermore, the executive branch is hopelessly fragmented—in 2015 one senator claimed it contained 430 departments, agencies, and subagencies.[55] And the same governmental function—for environmental protection or trade policy, for instance—may be spread across the overlapping jurisdictions of multiple agencies. At least fifteen bureaus have a say in food safety. "Chickens are regulated one way, but when the egg emerges, it's another agency's problem," *Politico* reported in 2016. "Crack the egg and you're off in a new direction."[56]

Presidents have long understood their responsibility for ensuring coordination and accountability. Only the president can referee this jockeying over turf (and potential chaos) and, again, rein in the bureaucratic autonomy it helps shield. Many executive orders and memoranda are devoted to creating interagency committees—deadly dull on their face, but with the important role of merging multiple departmental jurisdictions into a decision-making process that produces a unified policy, one that in turn can be assessed by the electorate.

Those policy decisions, and the directives sent to the bureaucracy to implement them, will of course reflect the president's preferences. Some point to the constitutional command to "take care that the law be faithfully executed" to suggest that any presidential interpretation of the law is by definition problematic. But note that presidential decisions of this sort, though usually termed unilateral, are rarely that. Presidents almost always take into account the effect their directives will have on the public and on other political actors, including Congress and the courts, and adjust their actions according to the anticipated reactions they predict.[57] Furthermore, presidential directives are normally arrived at by a process of bargaining across the multitude of actors contained within the executive branch, prior to their issuance.[58] Thus many interests have the chance to make their voices heard in the process of "unilateralism."

It's certainly true that presidents are at times tempted to substitute their preferences for the plain meaning of the text. But more often there is no plain meaning of the text. As noted above, for good reasons and bad Congress often passes vague laws that contradict other statutes already on the books. And rarely do legislators provide sufficient resources to fully enforce the penalties they demand. For example, federal statute requires all persons in the United States without citizenship or legal residence to be deported—which would mean deporting something like 11 million people. By contrast, Congress has typically provided enough money to deport 400,000 people a year.[59] Thus it would take more than twenty-seven years to deport everyone, even if none of those deported ever returned and if no new people ever crossed the border. In such circumstances, presidents must use their prosecutorial discretion and set priorities for how the law will be enforced.

Congress can specifically prohibit a given action or set of priorities in law. But when legislators fail to do so it is hard to say that inaction, even gridlock, is always the outcome most in tune with public opinion. And when they *do* grant discretion it is more, not less, democratic for presidents to utilize that discretion to reflect the preferences of the electoral majority that brought them into office. Certainly, it is more representative than allowing bureaucrats to ride herd according to their own desires.[60] And indeed, should we be so eager to argue that congressional preferences are themselves "democratic"?

THE "WHOLE GROUND": IS *CONGRESS* DEMOCRATIC?

In the 2012 congressional elections, Republican candidates for the House received 47.6 percent of the national vote, losing to Democratic candidates by some 1.4 million votes in aggregate. Their reward for this defeat? A strong majority comprising 54 percent of the House.

One standard response to presidential directives is that they overturn the will of the people—which usually means the will of Congress. (Leaders of the House, for their part, rarely go a full day without referring to their chamber as "the People's House.") Yet in that 2012 election, President Barack Obama received a clear majority of the national popular vote; despite the existence of the Electoral College, the candidate winning the popular vote has failed to become president only three times.[61] In 1834 Andrew Jackson bluntly told Congress that legislators had no right to judge him, since "the President is the direct representative of the American people."[62] Or as George H. W. Bush less truculently observed, "Consider the president's role. Thomas Jefferson once noted that a President commands a view of the whole ground, while Congress necessarily adopts the views of its constituents. The President and Vice President are the only officials elected to serve the entire Nation."[63]

This is a simple matter of institutional design. Legislators are a product of parochial geography, their election and reelection determined by voters in a specific corner of a single state. As a result, it has been said that Congress understands the national interest only when it is spoken in a local dialect.[64] If each district were a representative slice of the United States, that might not matter, but this is not the case; furthermore, House districts are skillfully gerrymandered to *prevent* just that sort of ideological diversity, making sure that members of Congress largely preach to—and are preached to by—a very loyal and homogenous choir. Even when a majority in the House or Senate could claim in aggregate to represent the country as a whole, the legislature's internal rules or polarized bickering frequently prevent it from acting. The filibuster in the Senate is designed to protect minorities from anything short of supermajority consensus. Likewise, the House Rules Committee served for many years as a mechanism allowing an entrenched vanguard of white Southern Democrats to fend off desegregation—in short, to save their region from majority rule. The 113th and 114th Congresses have been the least productive in modern history, and the public has taken notice. In 2015 Gallup found that about a third of Americans had confidence in the institution of the presidency. For Congress, the figure was 8 percent.[65]

As Ruth Morgan concluded in her book on executive orders, "legislating is preeminently a representative function. The President, as well as Congress, represents the nation. Each is popularly elected and must return periodically to the voters. . . . Each has its own constituency, the President a national one and the Congress a state and local one. Each affords interest groups access to the policy-making process, and frequently groups that have no access to one process will enjoy privileged access to the other."[66] In this sense executive action provides an outlet for national majorities thwarted by local factions that favor the status quo.

EXECUTIVE ACTION AND DEMOCRACY

I have argued here that executive action is anticipated in the Constitution—and that such action is necessary to make government work, now more than ever given the growth of governmental dysfunction. Most executive orders direct administrative behavior and have little impact on the public, except in coordinating governmental policy to allow that public to hold the president responsible for that policy. Presidential direction of the bureaucracy thus aids both accountability and responsiveness. As Alexander Hamilton noted long ago, "it may be laid down as a general rule that [the people's] confidence in and obedience to a government will commonly be proportioned to the goodness or badness of its administration." And "a government ill executed, whatever it may be in theory, must be, in practice, a bad government."[67] It would lack energy; it "must always savor of weakness, sometimes border upon anarchy." And it was anarchy, not government, that posed the greatest threat to democracy at the time of the founding. The "energy" of government was therefore something worth protecting.[68] So it remains today.

None of this is to deny that the president's actions must flow from constitutional or statutory authority. Presidents must obey the letter of the law—which means that Congress must step to the plate and legislate clearly. "Faithful execution" can be gauged, and often is, by the court system. But it would be better for all concerned—including the public—if the legislative and executive branches were to work together to forge policy, rather than to reflexively choose rancor and gridlock. As it stands, presidents arguably gain politically by acting aggressively—and even illegally.[69]

This might be especially true in the arena of foreign policy and national security. War powers receive little attention in this chapter, but represent an arena where Congress has too often backed away from its constitutional duties.

Legislative lawsuits are a poor substitute for the hard work of deliberation and oversight.

Still, foreign policy is not the worst place to consider the role of executive action in its broadest context. As Abraham Lincoln famously observed, "my oath to preserve the constitution to the best of my ability, imposed upon me the duty of preserving, by every indispensable means, that government—that nation—of which that constitution was the organic law." He argued it was not "possible to lose the nation, and yet preserve the constitution."[70] Executive action might be necessary to save the very system of American democracy. A nation cannot meet crises, or even the day-to-day needs of governing, with 535 chief executives or commanders in chief.

So does executive action undermine democracy? No—and even less in the context of the American system of separated powers. If it is not, by some definitions, "democratic," it is certainly "republican." And a democratic republic is what the Constitution's framers bequeathed us.

NOTES

PRO

1. Since 1789, presidents have "inscribe[d] upon a sheet of paper words establishing new policy, decreeing the commencement or cessation of some action, or ordaining that notice be given to some declaration. Dated and signed by the Chief Executive, the result was a presidential directive." Harold C. Relyea, "Presidential Directives: Background and Overview," *Congressional Research Service Report for Congress*, November 26, 2008, 2, https://www.fas.org/sgp/crs/misc/98-611.pdf

2. See ibid. for a partial taxonomy of the instruments presidents have used.

3. "Executive Orders Disposition Tables Index," http://www.archives.gov/federal-register/executive-orders/disposition.html

4. Charlie Savage, "Government Releases Once-Secret Report on Post-9/11 Surveillance," *New York Times*, April 24, 2015. (NSA didn't do it domestically.)

5. John Napier Tye, "Meet Executive Order 12333: The Reagan Rule That Lets the NSA Spy on Americans," *Washington Post*, July 18, 2014.

6. Ryan Gallagher, "The Surveillance Engine: How the NSA Built Its Own Secret Google," *The Intercept*, August 25, 2014, https://theintercept.com/2014/08/25/icreach-nsa-cia-secret-google-crisscross-proton/. This too was the result of another executive order, modifications to 12,333 issued by President George W. Bush in 2008 that allowed the NSA to share "incidentally" collected "signals intelligence" on American citizens with other agencies. *See* Charlie Savage, *Power Wars: Inside Obama's Post-9/11 Presidency* (New York: Little, Brown & Co., 2015), 217–18.

7. See, generally, Bernard Crick, *Democracy: A Very Short Introduction* (Oxford, UK: Oxford University Press, 2002).

8. Fareed Zakaria, "The Rise of Illiberal Democracy," *Foreign Affairs*, November 6, 1997.

9. Monty G. Marshall and Benjamin R. Cole, *Global Report 2014: Conflict, Governance and State Fragility* (Vienna, VA: Center for Systemic Peace, 2014).

10. "Methodology," *Freedom in the World 2016,* https://freedomhouse.org/report/freedom-world-2016/methodology

11. Economist Intelligence Unit, *Democracy Index 2015: Democracy in an Age of Anxiety*, 48–58.

12. *Youngstown Sheet & Tube Co. v. Sawyer,* 343 U.S. 579, 587 (1952).

13. Lyn Ragsdale and John J. Theis III, "The Institutionalization of the American Presidency, 1924–92," *American Journal of Political Science* 41, no. 4 (October 1997): 1288–90.

14. "Since 1949, about 15 percent of executive orders have involved significant policy changes." Kenneth B. Mayer, "Executive Orders," in Joseph M. Bessette and Jeffrey K. Tulis, *The Constitutional Presidency* (Baltimore: Johns Hopkins University Press, 2009), 154. "The proportion of substantively significant orders tripled from the 1950s to the 1990s." Andrew Rudalevige, *The New Imperial Presidency: Renewing Presidential Power after Watergate.* (Ann Arbor: University of Michigan Press, 2005), 171–72.

15. Robert M. Pallitto and William G. Weaver, *Presidential Secrecy and the Law* (Baltimore: Johns Hopkins University Press, 2007) (Kindle Locations 1021–1022).

16. Arvin S. Quist, "Security Classification of Information, Vol. 1: Introduction, History, and Adverse Impacts," September 20, 2002, http://www.fas.org/sgp/ library/quist/index.html

17. Pallitto and Weaver, *Presidential Secrecy and the Law* (Kindle Locations 959–960).

18. William G. Howell and David E. Lewis, "Agencies by Presidential Design," *Journal of Politics* 64, no. 4 (November 2002): 1096, 1099. "Presidents also were less likely [than Congress] to create agencies governed by independent boards or commissions . . . agencies created through executive action almost always reported directly to the president."

19. William G. Howell, "Unilateral Powers: A Brief Overview," *Presidential Studies Quarterly* 35 (2005): 428. "Peace Corps Set Up for AID Abroad," in *CQ Almanac 1961*, 17th ed. (Washington, DC: Congressional Quarterly, 1961), 324–28, http://library.cqpress.com/cqalmanac/cqal61-1373293

20. Howell and Lewis, "Agencies by Presidential Design," 1113.

21. Jeffrey A. Fine and Adam L. Warber, "Circumventing Adversity: Executive Orders and Divided Government," *Presidential Studies Quarterly* 41, no. 2 (June 2012), 272.

22. Vivian S. Chu and Todd Garvey, "Executive Orders: Issuance, Modification, and Revocation," *CRS Report for Congress,* April 16, 2014, 9, https://www.fas.org/sgp/crs/misc/RS20846.pdf

23. Adam L. Warber, *Executive Orders and the Modern Presidency* (Boulder, CO: Lynne Rienner, 2006), 118–120.

24. Kenneth B. Mayer, *With the Stroke of a Pen: Executive Orders and Presidential Power* (Princeton, NJ: Princeton University Press (2001); Mayer, "Executive Orders," 163.

25. Howell, *Power without Persuasion,* 199–201.

26. William G. Howell, *Thinking about the Presidency: The Primacy of Power* (Princeton, NJ: Princeton University Press, 2013), 29. See also Robert Knowles, "National Security Rulemaking," *Florida State University Law Review* 41 (2014).

27. Frederick A. O. Schwarz Jr., *Democracy in the Dark: The Seduction of Government Secrecy* (New York: New Press, 2015).

28. Aaron Wildavsky, "The Two Presidencies," *Trans-Action,* December 1966.

29. Military Order—Detention, Treatment, and Trial of Certain Non-Citizens in the War against Terrorism, November 13, 2001.

30. Andrew Romano, "President Obama's Executive Power Grab," *Newsweek,* October 22, 2012, http://www.newsweek.com/president-obamas-executive-power-grab-65287

31. Laura Meckler and Richard Rubin, "Hillary Clinton Talks Tough on Executive Action," *Wall Street Journal,* December 9, 2015.

32. Transcript, "Meet the Press," NBC News, January 10, 2016, http://www.nbcnews.com/meet-the-press/meet-press-january-10-2016-n493596

33. Jonathan Turley, "How Obama's Power Plays Set the Stage for Trump," *Washington Post,* December 13, 2015.

CON

34. "Weber Supports Amicus Brief to Defend Congress's Article I Power," Office of U.S. Rep. Randy Weber, http://weber.house.gov/media-center/press-releases/weber-supports-amicus-brief-to-defend-congress-article-i-power

35. The full tweet read: "On floor of house waitin on 'Kommandant-In-Chef' [sic] ... the Socialistic dictator who's been feeding US a line or is it 'A-Lying?'" The original message may be found at https://twitter.com/TXRandy14/status/428334051595132928

36. Barack Obama, "Remarks of the President and First Lady at the College Opportunity Summit," Office of the White House Press Secretary (January 16, 2014), http://www.whitehouse.gov/the-press-office/2014/01/16/remarks-president-and-first-lady-college-opportunity-summit

37. Quoted in Andrew Rudalevige, "Old Laws, New Meanings: Obama's Brand of Presidential 'Imperialism,'" *Syracuse Law Review* 66, no. 1 (2016): 3.

38. House Committee on Government Operations, 85th Cong., 1st Sess., *Executive Orders and Proclamations: A Study of a Use of Presidential Powers* (committee print, 1957), 1.

39. These were issued on behalf of G. Joseph Minetti. See Executive Orders 12006, 12011, 12016, 12037, and 12056.

40. Gregory Korte, "Obama's Executive Orders You Never Hear About," *USA Today,* April 11, 2016.

41. The term *executive order* actually refers to a specific type of directive issued by the president and published in the *Federal Register*. But the term is often used in the press and even by political actors to refer to a wide range of presidential orders and decision-making documents that include presidential proclamations, formal findings, guidance documents, designations, letters, memoranda, and a wide range of national security orders. A 2008 Congressional Research Service report listed twenty-seven types of such directives. See Harold Relyea, "Presidential Directives: Background and Overview," *Congressional Research Service Report,* 98-611 (updated November 26. 2008).

42. See Rep. Jim Gerlach, D-Pa., in Rudalevige, "Old Laws, New Meanings," 3; Ted Cruz, "The Imperial Presidency of Barack Obama," *Wall Street Journal* (January 28, 2014). The next year Senator Cruz piled on: "This administration has been the most lawless administration we have ever seen," RealClear Politics, http://www .realclearpolitics.com/video/2015/09/01/ted_cruz_barack_obama_has_become_ the_president_nixon_wished_he_could_be.html

43. Graham G. Dodds, *Take Up Your Pen: Unilateral Presidential Directives in American Politics* (Philadelphia: University of Pennsylvania Press, 2013), 26.

44. Ibid., 57, 84–85; see also Glendon Schubert Jr., *The Presidency in the Courts* (Minneapolis: University of Minnesota Press, 1957).

45. *Little v. Barreme,* 2 Cranch 170 (1804).

46. John A. Fairlie, "Administrative Legislation," *Michigan Law Review* 18 (January 1920): 181–200; James Hart, *The Ordinance Making Powers of the President of the United States* (Baltimore: Johns Hopkins University Studies in Historical and Political Science, Vol. XLIII, 1925).

47. Edward Corwin, *The President: Office and Powers* (New York: New York University Press, 1948), 149.

48. Ruth Morgan, *The President and Civil Rights: Policy-Making by Executive Order* (New York: St. Martin's Press, 1970), 46–7.

49. Richard Nathan, *The Administrative Presidency* (New York: Macmillan, 1983), 82.

50. Lee White to Rep. Dominick Daniels, letter of November 18, 1963, and related materials, White House Central Files: Subject File, Box 100, Folder [FE 4-1: Presidential Powers: General], John F. Kennedy Library; Jonna Lynn Cullen to Thad Cochran, letter of January 5, 1982, and related materials, White House Office of Records Management Subject Files, Box 7, folder [FE003 (039870-069999)], Record 043653, Ronald Reagan Library.

51. Ibid.

52. Woodrow Wilson, "The Study of Administration," *Political Science Quarterly* 2 (1887): 197–222.

53. *Myers v. United States,* 272 U.S. 52 (1926).

54. See, e.g., David E. Lewis, *The Politics of Presidential Appointments* (Princeton, NJ: Princeton University Press, 2008).

55. Prepared statement by Sen. Charles Grassley, R-Iowa, Senate Judiciary Committee Hearing on "Examining the Federal Regulatory System to Improve Accountability, Transparency and Integrity" (June 10, 2015), http://www.judiciary.senate .gov/imo/media/doc/06-10-15%20Grassley%20Statement.pdf. The *Federal Register* lists a still-unwieldy 257 such entities in its index: https://www.federalregister.gov/index/2015

56. Christina Aminashaun, "Who Regulates Your Egg?," *Politico* (March 16, 2016), http://www.politico.com/agenda/story/2016/03/crazy-us-chicken-egg-regulation-graphic-000077. See also the work of the U.S. Governmental Accountability Office (GAO) on this topic, for instance its *2016 Annual Report: Additional Opportunities to Reduce Fragmentation, Overlap, and Duplication and Achieve Other Financial Benefits*, GAO Report 16-375SP (April 13, 2016).

57. See, e.g., William Howell, *Power without Persuasion* (Princeton, NJ: Princeton University Press, 2003).

58. Andrew Rudalevige, "Executive Branch Management and Unilateralism," *Congress and the Presidency* 42 (2015): 342–65.

59. David Rogers, "At Stake in Immigration Debate: Billions of Dollars," *Politico* (February 10, 2015), http://www.politico.com/story/2015/02/immigration-debate-price-115050

60. For how these might be derived, see Anthony Downs, *Inside Bureaucracy* (Prospect Heights, IL: Waveland Press, 1967); and James Q. Wilson, *Bureaucracy* (New York: Basic Books, 1989).

61. In 1824, 1888, and 2000. This excludes 1876, but that electoral process was so corrupted that it is hard to know who properly won the popular vote. Even including 1824 is somewhat generous, since at that time not every state linked the popular vote to its votes in the Electoral College.

62. Jackson's "Protest" to the Senate, quoted in Sidney M. Milkis and Michael Nelson, *The American Presidency: Origins and Development*, 6th ed. (Washington, DC: CQ Press, 2012), 133.

63. George H. W. Bush, "Remarks at Dedication Ceremony of the Social Sciences Complex at Princeton University," May 10, 1991, http://www.presidency.ucsb .edu/ws/?pid=19573. The "whole ground" comes from Jefferson's first inaugural address in 1801, though he does not mention Congress specifically. ("When right, I shall often be thought wrong by those whose positions will not command a view of the whole ground.")

64. Thanks to Morris Fiorina for this formulation.

65. Justin McCarthy, "Confidence in U.S. Branches of Government Remains Low," Gallup.com (June 15, 2015), http://www.gallup.com/poll/183605/confidence-branches-government-remains-low.aspx. Note that the figure for the Supreme Court was 32 percent.

66. Morgan, *President and Civil Rights*, 84.

67. See *Federalist* Nos. 27, 70, and 22, respectively. No. 70 famously lays out the need for "energy in the executive," while No. 22 warns against procedures that would destroy that energy and lead to "contemptible compromises of the public good."

68. Note that this notion is echoed by James Madison. In *Federalist* No. 37, Madison argued that "energy in government is essential to that security against external and internal danger, and to that prompt and salutary execution of the laws, which enter into the very definition of good government."

69. See, e.g., William G. Howell, with David Milton Brent, *Thinking about the Presidency: The Primacy of Power* (Princeton, NJ: Princeton University Press, 2013).

70. Lincoln's letter to Albert G. Hodges, April 4, 1864, http://www.abrahamlincolnonline .org/lincoln/speeches/hodges.htm

RESOLVED, The president has too much power in the selection of judges

PRO: David A. Yalof

CON: John Anthony Maltese

Few issues have engendered more controversy in Washington in recent years than the selection of federal judges. Republican president Ronald Reagan's nomination of Robert H. Bork to the Supreme Court in 1987 provoked a bitterly partisan debate between anti-Bork liberals and pro-Bork conservatives. In the end, the Democratic-controlled Senate voted Bork down. Reagan's Republican successor as president, George H. W. Bush, sparked an even fiercer firestorm when he nominated Clarence Thomas, a conservative, to the Court in 1991. Amid charges and countercharges about Thomas's alleged sexual harassment of law professor and former employee Anita Hill, the Senate confirmed him by the narrowest majority of any Supreme Court nominee in history, 52–48. When Bill Clinton, a Democrat, became president in 1993 and the GOP took control of Congress in 1995, Republican members of the Senate Judiciary Committee defeated many of Clinton's appellate court nominations by refusing to send them to the full Senate for a vote. Although Republican George W. Bush enjoyed a Republican Senate for most of his time as president, Democratic senators were able to defeat or delay several of his court of appeals nominees by threatening or launching filibusters. Bush managed to win Senate confirmation of two Supreme Court nominees, John G. Roberts Jr. and Samuel A. Alito Jr., only after succumbing to political pressure to withdraw the nomination of White House counsel Harriet Miers.

Like Bush, President Barack Obama benefitted during six of his eight years in office from having his party control the Senate, but that did not prevent ever longer delays in the confirmation of appellate and district court judges and, as the clock ran out on his presidency in 2016, of Supreme Court nominee Merrick Garland. According to a 2012 study, the average time between nomination and confirmation to the federal bench in Obama's first term was 224 days: that is, 50 days longer than under George W. Bush and more than twice as long as under Clinton.

With Democrats in control of the Senate, Obama did secure the appointments of both of his first-term Supreme Court nominees, Sonia Sotomayor and Elena Kagan, but neither justice received much support from across the aisle. Only five Republican senators voted to confirm Kagan, and nine voted for Sotomayor (twenty-two Democrats voted for Roberts, but only four for Alito).

The increasing rancor over judicial nominations stems in large part from the bitter ideological partisanship that characterizes contemporary politics, with conservative Republicans and liberal Democrats fighting fiercely about a whole range of issues. But the polarized judicial nomination process also reflects the willingness of the federal courts to wade into controversial issues such as abortion, affirmative action, gun rights, same-sex marriage, and campaign finance reform. In such a climate, seats on the Supreme Court and the thirteen federal courts of appeals are prizes worth fighting about.

The ultimate source of the fights over judgeships, however, reaches deep into the Constitution. Although the framers gave federal judges life tenure in order to remove them from partisan politics once they were on the bench, they entrusted the process by which these judges are appointed to intensely political actors. Specifically, the framers mandated that the president "shall nominate, and by and with the Advice and Consent of the Senate, shall appoint" judges to the federal courts. In other words, the power of judicial selection is a shared power that can be exercised only if both branches cooperate. The Senate cannot "nominate" anyone to serve on a federal court. Nor can the president give a nominee the constitutional "consent" necessary to make someone a judge.

Does the president have too much power in the selection of federal judges? Although David A. Yalof says yes and John Anthony Maltese says no, both agree that much hinges on the meaning of the other crucial word in the Constitution's judicial appointments clause: *advice*. Specifically, did the framers want the president to seek advice from the Senate before making a judicial nomination, or did they intend to restrict the Senate's advisory role to the post-nomination phase of the judicial selection process?

PRO: David A. Yalof

A s Judge Merrick Garland made his way up to the Rose Garden podium to accept his nomination to the U.S. Supreme Court, President Obama's Republican opponents were already brimming with confidence. Exactly one month earlier, on February 13, 2016, Justice Antonin Scalia's unexpected death had created a prized vacancy on the high court. Yet just hours after that shocking news became public, Senate Majority Leader Mitch McConnell, R-Ky., issued a statement declaring that the Senate would consider no replacement for Scalia until after the 2016 election. Then, in a matter of days, the entire Republican membership of the Senate Judiciary Committee lined up in support of their leader. As this harsh political reality quickly unfolded, President Obama appeared especially ill-suited to mount a sustained campaign for his nominee. During his first seven years in office, the young president had mostly failed in his promise to overcome partisan divisions and change the tenor of Washington. Nor had he excited the Democrats' core constituencies, most of whom longed for more progressive reforms than he could deliver. Moreover, even if Obama could have claimed the high approval ratings achieved by Presidents Ronald Reagan and Bill Clinton at similar points in their respective presidencies, what good would that do? Given the awkward timing of this vacancy in the midst of a presidential election year, such a nomination battle would have been an uphill fight for even the most popular of chief executives. Viewed in these terms, the nomination of Garland, a sixty-three-year-old moderate jurist, seemed all but doomed to fail, and Obama would be powerless to change that outcome. Certainly, that was the story gleeful Republicans were telling themselves as Garland began his remarks on that sunny morning in March.

Fortunately for Obama and the Democrats, the power dynamics at work in Supreme Court nominations lean strongly in favor of the presidency even when all indications run to the contrary. Consider that Justice Scalia's nomination fell unexpectedly into the lap of a president already resigned to spending the final year of his presidency mired in policy deadlock and legislative inaction. It was against this political background that Obama had taken unilateral action on other matters. During the previous year he had issued executive orders on gun control and immigration, much to the consternation of his political opponents. Now, this high court vacancy offered him yet another chance to take strong unilateral action, and this time with the balance of the Supreme Court at stake. Whether or not Garland's nomination culminated in a successful confirmation vote before the November elections,[1] it allowed the president to go on the offensive once again by acting presidential (he was, after all, fulfilling his Article II responsibilities), while at the same time relegating the Senate to one of three unfortunate options: (1) approve the nominee, and thus shift the balance of the Court in favor of the so-called "liberal bloc"; (2) hold hearings and reject the nominee (a difficult proposition, given Garland's relatively moderate judicial record); or (3) refuse even to hold hearings for the nominee, thus reinforcing the Republican majority's reputation for inaction and gridlock during the heat of a presidential election campaign. Indeed, by submitting the nomination of a judge who some leading Republicans (including Sen. Orrin Hatch, R-Utah) had praised, the White House could effectively frame the battle as yet another display of the Republicans' refusal to take action on important issues facing the country. Such a narrative could well influence more than just the looming presidential election, as Republicans at the time held twenty-four of the thirty-four Senate seats at stake in November 2016. Senators in New Hampshire, Illinois, Wisconsin, and other states won by Obama both in 2008 and 2012 were busy fighting for their political lives, and the Garland nomination would only make matters worse for them. On one hand, these endangered Republicans might invite conservative primary challenges if they bucked the party leadership; on the other, they would be hard-pressed to follow the Senate leadership to its extreme position of "no hearings" under any conditions.[2]

In the modern political system, presidential dominance remains business as usual when it comes to the process of selecting judges and justices for the federal bench. As the events of 2016 make clear, that premise holds even when a relatively weak lame-duck president is in charge. Up to and including President George W. Bush, chief executives tended to choose their high court nominees without giving most senators the privilege of even a cursory consultation beforehand.[3] Even leading senators from the president's own party often discover the name of the president's nominee only a short time before everyone else.

With its constitutional advice function a virtual dead letter, can the Senate simply fall back on its power to withhold consent for Supreme Court nominees? In theory, that power remains, and Senate Republicans went to extreme lengths to exercise that power against Judge Garland in 2016. Yet in practice it is only rarely exercised, and even then with mixed success. For all the attention given to the nomination debacles of Bork, Douglas Ginsburg, Clarence Thomas, and Harriet Miers, of those four failed nominees only Bork was actually rejected by a vote of the Senate (Ginsburg and Miers withdrew, and Thomas was confirmed). In fact, between 1932 and 2016 only three of forty-seven Supreme Court nominees were rejected in an actual Senate vote on the merits of the nomination.[4] Perhaps that explains why the Senate leadership was so determined to refuse hearings of any kind for Garland; experienced senators knew that once Garland appeared at an actual hearing before the public, the odds would shift dramatically in his favor, especially if he answered the senators' questions diplomatically and deferentially.[5]

Nor do senators find much consolation in the appointment process for the federal district and appeals courts, the context in which senatorial advice has traditionally received its due. The era in which senators confidently instructed the White House as to whom to nominate for federal judgeships in their home states is now a relic of the past. Recent presidents have dominated the lower-court selection process, reducing senators from their own party to the status of well-respected advisers, on a par with important interest groups and other significant presidential constituents. Despite this shift in practice, Senate resistance to all but the most objectionable nominees remains muted at best. Until the practice was eliminated in November 2013, the frequent resort by senators in the minority to filibuster lower-court nominees garnered considerable attention, as this effectively created a 60-vote minimum required for the approval of lower-court judges. Yet based on raw numbers, both presidents George W. Bush and Barack Obama largely got their way despite the procedural obstacles placed in their respective paths. Democrats outright blocked fewer than 20 of George W. Bush's 373 lower-court judicial nominees with a filibuster or negative vote. And after the parties' roles flipped starting in 2009, President Obama enjoyed similar success despite the increasing partisan deadlock in the Capitol. Up through August 2016, he had successfully appointed 55 of 62 court of appeals judges; add to that at least 270 additional Article III judges and the Democratic president had actually surpassed President George W. Bush's total of 324 confirmed judges during his own two terms in office. So much for fears that partisan deadlock would have the same effect on judicial nominations that it has had on so many other areas of domestic policy.

How did the presidency come to enjoy such a stranglehold over judicial selections? Some of the chief executive's increased leverage in this area mirrors the growth of presidential power as a whole during the twentieth century. Yet there is something especially disconcerting about the growth in the president's power to appoint judges. In foreign affairs, the nation, arguably, must speak with a unified voice. But lively dialogue between the nominating institution (the president) and the advising and consenting institution (the Senate) hurts no one, save those nominees whose credentials are so thin that they stand little chance of surviving more intense forms of review.

THE FOUNDERS AND THE JUDICIAL APPOINTMENT PROCESS

Judicial appointments were a hotly debated subject at the Constitutional Convention in 1787. The initial efforts to vest the appointment authority in the executive were soundly defeated. A proposal by James Madison, delegate from Virginia, to give the president the power to appoint judges "unless disagreed to" by two-thirds of the Senate was rejected, because it would tip the balance too far toward the executive. Proposals to have the Senate make all appointments enjoyed the support of a majority of delegates for nearly two months, but that plan was eventually discarded. In the end, the convention settled on a shared arrangement between the two branches. The final scheme of presidential appointment with the Senate's advice and consent was eventually approved as a way to create a mutually dependent process.

One noted scholar contends that by separating the act of nomination from the act of appointment (the Constitution says the president "shall nominate, and by and with the Advice and Consent of the Senate, shall appoint"), the framers meant to keep the Senate's advice and consent out of the nomination phase.[6] Such an interpretation would effectively merge the advice and consent functions into one: if the Senate must wait until after the president has submitted a nomination to advise, what difference is there between advising the president that a nominee will be rejected and actually rejecting the nominee with a formal vote? The framers would never have identified a separate advice function if they did not intend that function to have real influence in the nominating process.

The Constitution gives no specific criteria to guide the selection of justices, but this absence of criteria does not mean the president was expected to have unlimited authority over the selection process. Consider the views of New York delegate Alexander Hamilton, perhaps the foremost advocate among the founders of a strong executive. In *Federalist* No. 77, Hamilton argued that Senate influence over presidential appointments was intended to provide a formidable check on the chief executive: "If by influencing the President be meant restraining him, this is precisely what must have been intended." At the same time, in *Federalist* No. 76 Hamilton assumed that the Senate would only rarely reject a president's nominees—after all, why would the Senate routinely reject candidates who emerge from a process in which the Senate offers significant assistance in the first place?[7]

In the early years of the republic, the Senate quickly learned to practice what the founders preached. Although only one of President George Washington's nominees to the high court was rejected, that rejection was based on the Senate's *political* objections to the nominee, a clear rebuke to the notion that the Senate was intended to be merely a screening mechanism to ensure the minimal competence of judges. When, in 1795, Washington nominated John Rutledge of South Carolina to be chief justice, Rutledge's credentials were impressive, including previous service on the Supreme Court as an associate justice. But Rutledge had openly opposed ratification of the Jay Treaty with England, and he had urged Washington not to sign it. That stand put Rutledge squarely at odds with the Federalist majority in the Senate, which rejected his nomination. President Washington may have been disappointed by this turn of events, but he never openly challenged the Senate's power to reject his nominees on political grounds. Because he had acted as president of the Constitutional Convention, Washington knew firsthand that the appointment authority had been granted to two branches rather than one.

THE ADVICE FUNCTION

For much of U.S. history, presidents have sought senators' advice on judicial appointments, and not just because the words of the Constitution encouraged them to do so. Involving senators at an early stage in the process was smart politics—it invested senators in the appointment process, thereby creating critical allies for the confirmation stage. Many senators were also knowledgeable Washington insiders, and most presidents valued their advice. Thomas Jefferson even relied on House and Senate members to scout out potential Supreme Court nominees. When Associate Justice Alfred Moore of North Carolina retired in 1804, Jefferson looked to two members of the South Carolina congressional delegation, Sen. Thomas Sumter and Rep. Wade Hampton, to help him find a replacement. Presidential-Senate dialogue over judicial nominees continued into the early twentieth century. For example, in 1902 Republican senator Henry Cabot Lodge of Massachusetts championed Oliver Wendell Holmes for a seat on the Supreme Court.

By contrast, presidents today rarely seek senatorial advice on Supreme Court vacancies. Modern presidents tend to mobilize their administrations to identify and research prospective nominees behind the scenes, leaving senators to learn about the shortlist of nominees only at the tail end of the process, after presidents and their advisers have already performed the most critical vetting functions. On the rare occasion when the president publicly seeks legislators' advice, the process often entails meaningless consultations between presidential aides and senators about a decision that has already been made. For example, Chief of Staff Howard Baker insisted, even after Robert Bork became President Reagan's clear choice to fill a Court vacancy, that White House officials go through the charade of meeting with key senators and asking their advice about an artificial list of "potential nominees." Some observers believe that President Bill Clinton leaned heavily on key senators for advice before making his two Supreme Court nominations, but in fact they enjoyed no special insider status, learning the names of possible nominees at the same time as the public at large. Even Barack Obama, the first senator elected directly to the White House in nearly half a century, ultimately settled on a short list of high court nominees dominated by friends, cabinet members, and others he knew personally.

Even more dramatic changes have occurred in the lower-court appointment process, and once again senators have seen their opportunities to exert influence over such appointments sharply reduced. In the nineteenth century, such judgeships were mostly a matter of senatorial patronage. Well into the twentieth century, presidents continued to defer to senators—particularly those of the president's own party—on nominees to judgeships in their states. Indeed, that practice continued up until the 1970s. A president who violated this norm by nominating his own candidate over the objections of the home-state senator risked seeing that nomination permanently buried by the Senate Judiciary Committee. That was precisely the fate suffered by William B. Poff, President Gerald R. Ford's nominee for the federal district court in Virginia. Sen. William Scott, R-Va., preferred another candidate and made his views known to the president. When Ford boldly went ahead with Poff's nomination anyway, the Senate Judiciary Committee, though run by Democrats at the time, tabled the nomination in deference to their Senate colleague from the other party.[8]

Of course, no amount of deference to home-state senators would keep the White House from exercising free rein over all the seats on the U.S. Court of Appeals for the D.C. Circuit, now widely recognized to be the second most powerful court in America. Meanwhile, in the other lower courts, presidents during the last quarter century have been increasingly willing to disregard the preferences of home-state senators. President Reagan, for example, insisted that Republican senators identify three individuals for every judicial vacancy, and he required that those names meet his administration's stringent ideological criteria.[9] His successor in office, George H. W. Bush, continued this practice. At the end of the twentieth century, the rising use of "blue slips" by senators—a blue slip was in effect a veto over judicial appointments in a senator's state—allowed them to reassert some of their authority, but it did not result in a greater advisory role for the Senate.

In summary, today presidents control the choice of Supreme Court and D.C. Circuit Court nominees. For all other courts, senators play an active, if somewhat curtailed, role in the nominating process. The judicial appointment process now in place thus seems a far cry from the shared dialogue imagined by the framers.

THE CONSENT FUNCTION

While the senators' advisory function has been reduced substantially, the Senate can theoretically exert considerable leverage by withholding consent for the president's judicial nominees. In practice, however, the Senate only rarely exercises that right. In his award-winning book, *The Selling of Supreme Court Nominees,* my debate partner John Anthony Maltese speaks of the "increasingly contentious nature of recent confirmations."[10] Political scientist Mark Silverstein notes that in 1968 the politics of judicial confirmations underwent an abrupt transformation as "the presumption respecting presidential control was honored more in the breach than in the observance."[11] Yet what has the Senate actually gained in this supposedly new era of relative parity between the branches? As noted earlier, since 1932 only three Supreme Court nominees have been rejected outright by the Senate, while thirty-nine have been confirmed (four others withdrew before the Senate voted, and Garland's nomination was still in limbo at the time this book went to press). Even counting Garland's nomination as a defeat, sixteen of the last twenty nominees have been confirmed in this highly contentious partisan era, and most of them were confirmed by comfortable margins.

Changes in the procedures for confirmation have contributed to Senate deference to the president. Nominees appeared at public confirmation hearings for the first time in 1925, but such appearances did not become routine until 1955.[12] Yet instead of clarifying matters for senators considering a possible challenge, public confirmation hearings have made evasion and obfuscation by nominees the norm. As Maltese notes, "Most nominees have refused to discuss cases with members of the Judiciary Committee."[13] Judge Antonin Scalia's refusal in 1986 even to comment on such a well-settled precedent as *Marbury v. Madison* made a near-mockery of the proceedings. The exception was Robert Bork in 1987, and by all accounts, his willingness to wrestle candidly with all the hot-button issues of the day contributed mightily to his appointment's undoing. Three years after the Bork fiasco, nominee David H. Souter deftly ducked pointed questions about his position on *Roe v. Wade;* in doing so, he denied potential conservative and liberal critics of his nomination any real ammunition with which to defeat him.

Even in an era of greater openness and transparency, nominees continue to obfuscate in their confirmation hearings with few or no repercussions. As a nominee for associate justice in January 2006, Samuel A. Alito Jr. was confronted with a "personal qualifications statement" he had submitted decades earlier when applying to be an assistant attorney general under President Ronald Reagan. Alito had forthrightly declared on the form that the Constitution "does not protect the right to abortion"; responding to outrage expressed by Sen. Charles E. Schumer, D-N.Y., and others, the nominee volunteered only that he would "respect *stare decisis*" and the "judicial process." Alito's willingness to fall back on such vague platitudes obviously did not derail his confirmation prospects. Fears that Barack Obama's initial Supreme Court nominee, Judge Sonia Sotomayor, would face intense resistance proved misguided as well. Sotomayor conceded to her Senate interrogators that remarks she made several years earlier that a "wise Latina" would more often than not reach a "better conclusion" than a white male amounted to a "bad attempt" at a rhetorical flourish.[14] In the end, few votes shifted either way, and she coasted to a 63–37 confirmation victory.

Another obstacle in the path of concerted Senate resistance to a president's judicial nominees has been the marked increase in partisan polarization. In the past, senators from the president's party would sometimes refuse to go along with a proposed Supreme Court nomination. More often than not, when Senate opposition takes on a bipartisan cast in such proceedings, controversial nominees can find their appointments in serious jeopardy. For example, six Senate Republicans joined fifty-two Senate Democrats to defeat Robert Bork's nomination for the Supreme Court in 1987. By contrast, just four years later, the only two Republican senators remaining from that sextet to oppose the controversial nomination of Clarence Thomas were Sen. Robert Packwood of Oregon and Sen. James M. Jeffords of Vermont, the latter of whom bolted the Republican Party once and for all in 2001. (Thomas was thus able to squeak out a 52–48 confirmation victory.) Senators from the president's party have learned that in this current era of hyperpartisanship, the political cost of voting against the president's nominee tends to be prohibitive. As a result, Supreme Court nominees tend to coast to victory if their appointing president enjoys majority support in the Senate. Consider that not one Republican senator voted against either of George W. Bush's two Supreme Court nominees, while a combined sixty-four votes were cast against them by Senate Democrats. President Obama did nearly as well up until his final year in office: Sen. Ben Nelson of Nebraska was responsible for the lone Democratic vote cast against either of Obama's first two Supreme Court nominees. So long as the political costs of defection appear so high, it will be a rare occasion indeed when senators choose to cross their own party leader in the White House.

On one occasion, senators from the president's own party *did* make themselves heard to a degree in the appointment process. In October 2005 some conservative Republican senators, including Sam Brownback, helped to convince President Bush of the need to withdraw his second nominee for the high court, Harriet Miers. Miers, they felt, lacked a reliably conservative track record and was creating a serious split within the president's conservative base of support. Yet those senators pressing for her withdrawal were hardly acting from a position of strength. Minority Leader Harry Reid had already offered his open support for Miers, and several Republican senators, including John Cornyn, still supported the controversial nominee at the time of her withdrawal. Thus Brownback and Miers's other detractors were most fearful that an up-or-down vote on Miers would go in her favor—certainly most headcounts of the Senate at that time indicated that a pro-Miers alliance between Democrats and moderate Republicans offered her more than enough votes to secure her confirmation. Most telling was the fact that key senators from President Bush's own party had been excluded from the decision-making process—how else can one explain their vocal frustration with Miers's candidacy? Thus while the president may occasionally confront resistance in the confirmation process, those rare flare-ups should not be confused with what the framers hoped would be a truly deliberative appointment process.

What about the lower courts, where senators once enjoyed the upper hand? During his first term in office, President Obama's lower-court nominees could count on a significant degree of support from the Democratic-controlled Senate. The upper chamber that convened during the 111th Congress included nearly sixty members allied with Obama's party; fifty-three senators then caucused with the Democrats during the 112th Congress that followed. Because Democratic senators rarely vote against Obama's nominees, the Senate filibuster quickly became the primary tool by which Senate Republicans could block judicial nominees, up until Senate leaders ended the practice in 2013. The need to resort to such extreme measures in order to block even the most ideologically extreme nominees illustrates just how desperate the legislature has become in this process. As was already noted, during his two terms as president, George W. Bush successfully made 324 appointments to the lower courts. His record of successful appointments is comparable to those of other recent presidents: the elder president Bush appointed 187 lower-court judges during his one term as president, and President Bill Clinton made 366 judicial appointments in eight years. During Obama's first term, even with the president and the Senate seemingly at loggerheads over the confirmation of federal judges, the wheels just kept turning, and the vast majority of nominees (171 out of 186) were eventually confirmed.

Though President Obama's second term proved even more contentious than his first, his judicial nominees continued to receive mostly favorable treatment. In fact, Obama's success continued well into his second term, even after the Democrats lost the Senate in 2014. By the late summer of 2016, the Democratic president had already surpassed the number of lower-court appointments made by his predecessor. Moreover, the lone Supreme Court nomination of his second term, rather than showing off the lame-duck president's weakness, only managed to highlight the fissures and frustrations of his partisan opposition in the months leading up to the 2016 presidential election. All of that is because in American politics today, presidents nominate judges for the federal judiciary, and with very few exceptions, the Senate obediently confirms those choices. So much for the framers' vision of a judiciary staffed by "shared arrangement" between the president and the U.S. Senate.

CON: John Anthony Maltese

What exactly does Article II, Section 2, of the Constitution mean when it says that the president "shall nominate, and by and with the Advice and Consent of the Senate, shall appoint . . . Judges of the supreme court"? (By law, the same procedure is used for appointing lower federal court judges.) Questions about this clause took on particular significance when, in the wake of the death of Justice Antonin Scalia on February 13, 2016, Senate Republicans announced that they would refuse to consider President Barack Obama's nomination of Merrick Garland to fill the vacancy (prior to that, Senate Majority Leader Mitch McConnell and other Republican leaders had urged Obama to withhold a nomination and to leave the choice to his successor). That led to the question: Does the advice and consent clause require the Senate to offer advice by casting an up-or-down vote on a nominee, or does the refusal to consider a nomination constitute a form of advice?

Before turning to that specific question, a review of the history of the advice and consent clause may be useful. The Constitutional Convention of 1787 considered and ultimately rejected several different methods of judicial appointment: by Congress as a whole, by the Senate alone, and by the president alone. New York delegate Alexander Hamilton was among the most articulate defenders of the final constitutional language, and his explanation of that language in *Federalist* No. 76 is worth considering.[15] Hamilton assumed that the Senate would rarely reject nominees put forth by the president. It is "not very probable," he wrote, that the Senate would often overrule the president's nomination. Only when there were "special and strong reasons for the refusal" would the Senate risk placing a "stigma" on a nominee through rejection and thereby call into question "the judgment of the chief magistrate."[16]

What might these "special and strong reasons" be? Could such a reason include a nominee's failure to comply with a "litmus test" of how he or she should vote on particular issues? Could the fact that a nomination arises in an election year—particularly when that is the president's final year in office—constitute such a reason? And is it reasonable for senators to expect presidents to withhold a nomination during their terminal year in office? Anyone seeking to answer such questions must look at the precise wording of the Constitution and consider the intent of those who framed it.

Clearly, nothing in the text of the Constitution precludes a president from nominating Supreme Court justices or any other officials in a presidential election year, even when it is the president's terminal year in office. Indeed, the precise language of the Constitution says that the president "*shall* nominate" (emphasis added). This strongly suggests that the nomination is a duty—not an optional exercise. The historical record reinforces this interpretation. Throughout our history, presidents have consistently and routinely nominated Supreme Court justices during their terminal year in office: fifteen times in the calendar year of the election of their successor (most recently Lyndon B. Johnson's nominations of Abe Fortas and Homer Thornberry in 1968), another six times in the calendar year prior to the election but within 365 days of the election of their successor (most recently Ronald Reagan's nomination of Anthony Kennedy in 1987), and—amazingly, from our current vantage point—another eleven times in the beginning of the lame-duck calendar year following the election but before the inauguration of the next president. The Senate confirmed eighteen of those thirty-two nominations (including two made by President Andrew Jackson on his last day in office).[17] The fact that vacancies seldom arise in an election year accounts for the relative rarity of presidents making such nominations in the twentieth century. Still, when vacancies arose, presidents nominated.

The nomination itself belongs exclusively to the president. As Hamilton put it in *Federalist* No. 76, the president exercises "his judgment alone" in the act of nomination.[18] Even George Mason of Virginia, who opposed executive appointment of judges, conceded as much in a letter to fellow Virginian James Monroe: "There is some thing remarkable in the Ar[r]angement of the Words: 'He shall nominate.' This gives the President *alone* the Right of *Nomination*."[19]

Hamilton argued in *Federalist* No. 76 that the president's power to nominate meant that the "person ultimately appointed must be the object of his preference."[20] Why? Because "one man of discernment is better fitted to analyze and estimate the peculiar qualities adapted to particular offices, than a body of men of equal or perhaps even of superior discernment."[21] This is so, Hamilton said, because "a single well directed man . . . cannot be distracted and warped by that diversity of views, feelings, and interests, which frequently distract and warp the resolutions of a collective body."[22]

The Constitutional Convention ultimately rejected the legislative appointment of judges largely because the delegates feared that legislative appointments would be subject to intrigue and corrupted by factions. The Virginia Plan had originally proposed that Congress as a whole choose federal judges. When the convention debated that proposal on June 5, 1787, James Wilson of Pennsylvania objected. Experience among the states showed "the impropriety of such appointments in numerous bodies," he said. "Intrigue, partiality, and concealment were the necessary consequences. A principal reason for unity in the Executive was the officers might be appointed by a single, responsible person."[23] On July 18, the convention considered appointment by the Senate alone. Nathaniel Gorham of Massachusetts argued that the Senate was still "too numerous, and too little personally responsible, to ensure a good choice."[24] He suggested a compromise: presidential appointment subject to the advice and consent of the Senate. James Madison of Virginia, who originally had been wary of executive appointment, conceded on July 21 that the executive would be more likely than any other branch "to select fit characters." He added that requiring Senate consent would check "any flagrant partiality or error" on the part of the president.[25] Madison's interpretation sheds light on what "advice and consent" means. It suggests that the Senate should withhold consent only in exceptional circumstances ("flagrant partiality or error" on the part of the president).

What, then, does the word *advice* in the appointments clause mean? Does it mean that the president must seek the advice of the Senate in advance of nomination? No. Although presidents are free to seek advice, this is not required by the Constitution. To suggest otherwise runs counter to Hamilton's position in *Federalist* No. 76 by presuming that the power to nominate is *not* one held solely by the president but rather is a power shared with the Senate.[26] Such a view conforms neither to a strict reading of the advice and consent clause nor to the intent of the framers. As legal scholar John O. McGinnis has persuasively argued:

> The very grammar of the clause is telling: the act of nomination is separated from the act of appointment by a comma and a conjunction. Only the latter act is qualified by the phrase "advice and consent." Furthermore, it is not at all anomalous to use the word

"advice" with respect to the action of the Senate in confirming an appointment. The Senate's consent is advisory because confirmation does not bind the President to commission and empower the confirmed nominee. Instead, after receiving the Senate's advice and consent, the President may deliberate again before appointing the nominee.[27]

In short, the Senate's proper role is limited to offering advice on the nominee presented by the president. But we are still left with a number of questions: Is the Senate's refusal to consider a nomination a valid form of withholding consent, or should advice and consent be communicated through a vote? On what grounds may the Senate withhold its consent? When is a nominee "an unfit character" unworthy of confirmation?

Once the president submits a nomination, it is the Senate's duty to offer advice on that nomination. Although nothing in the text of the Constitution commands a vote on the nominee by the Senate, the advice and consent clause clearly implies action. There may be instances when a nomination comes so late that there is not time for adequate consideration of a nominee, but that was hardly the case with the Garland nomination. That is why President Obama believed the Senate had an obligation to consider Garland's nomination by voting him up or down. The refusal to hold hearings or allow a vote on a nominee grinds the process to a halt and prevents the Senate from fulfilling its constitutional duty. Saying nothing at all is not a valid form of withholding consent because it leaves open the possibility of giving consent in the future. It also means that individual senators may evade going on the record for or against the nominee. The constitutional command to offer advice and consent not only implies senatorial action, it also demands closure. Either the Senate votes to confirm the nominee or it does not. The process is not complete until that vote takes place. To stall is to subvert the process.

Assuming that action is required, when is it appropriate to vote against a nominee? Hamilton, in *Federalist* No. 76, viewed the Senate's power to withhold consent as primarily "a check upon the spirit of favoritism in the President" designed to prevent individuals from being appointed because of "family connection" or "personal attachment."[28] This statement corresponds with Madison's notion that the check be used to prevent "flagrant partiality or error." Some scholars have argued that the Constitutional Convention viewed Senate confirmation as a way of preventing the president from making too many appointments from large states.[29]

The failure of a nominee to pass a "litmus test" imposed by senators who want him or her to rule in cases in certain ways does not rise to the level of "special and strong reasons" for rejection. For one thing, this notion runs counter to the ideal of judicial independence, which the framers took great pains to protect. Moreover, it opens the door to the intrigue and the threat of factions that the framers sought to avoid. As noted earlier, Hamilton argued that because the president is best fitted to analyze the qualities necessary for each judgeship to be filled, the person appointed "must be the object of his preference." For senators to reject a nomination on the basis of a litmus test is to substitute improperly their preferences for those of the president. Likewise, to suggest that the outcome of an election must guide the choice of nominee is to undermine the core principle of judicial independence.

Nonetheless, imposing litmus tests and engaging in blatantly obstructionist measures are precisely what senators of both parties have done at all levels of the federal judicial appointment process in recent years. Senate opposition led to the rejection or withdrawal of six out of twenty-three Supreme Court nominations from 1968 through 2010 when President Obama nominated Elena Kagan to serve on the Court (a failure rate of 26 percent).[30] If one omits the unsuccessful renominations of individuals already blocked by the Senate, the rate of failed Supreme Court nominations before 1968 was 17.1 percent (21 out of 123 nominations).[31] Many observers of the Court point to the Senate's rejection of President Ronald Reagan's nomination of Robert H. Bork in 1987 as a watershed event. After an intense fight against Bork led by a coalition of some three hundred liberal interest groups, the Democratic-controlled Senate rejected his nomination—not because of any improprieties or lack of qualifications, but because of how Bork might vote on the Court.

The Senate's refusal to consider the Garland nomination is part and parcel of the politicization of the process, which includes obstructionist measures used by both political parties to block or delay judicial nominees at all levels of the federal system. Obstruction and delay of lower federal court nominees became common during the administrations of Bill Clinton and George W. Bush and continued during the administration of Barack Obama. Among the procedural tactics used to obstruct nominations have been the use of the "blue-slip" procedure to block hearings of nominees, "holds" used by individual senators or groups of senators to block floor consideration of nominees, and the filibuster to block final votes on nominees.

The "blue-slip" procedure stems from the long-standing practice of presidents and fellow senators turning to the senators from the state where a lower-court vacancy occurs for advice on nominees (particularly before technological developments that led to easy communication, these home-state senators were thought to possess the best information about the qualifications and temperament of nominees from their own state). This evolved into the blue-slip procedure. Once the president nominates someone, the home-state senators receive a form on blue paper (hence the term *blue slip*). If they have no objection to the nominee, they return the blue slip. Failure to return the blue slip or returning it with a negative response effectively vetoes committee hearings. Currently, senators of both political parties can exercise their blue-slip power, though during some periods of time that power was limited to home-state senators from the party controlled by the White House.[32] In contrast, "holds" are requests by individual senators or groups of senators to their party leader asking for a delay in floor action. It is up to the majority leader to decide whether to honor a hold, and for how long.[33] In recent years, both parties have even resorted to filibusters of judicial nominees. However, a strong argument can be made that filibusters are not an appropriate tool for senators to use to block a judicial nominee.

The filibuster is not a power granted by the Constitution. As political scientists Sarah A. Binder and Steven S. Smith have noted, "Delegates to the convention did not write into the Constitution any procedural protections for Senate minorities."[34] The Senate's original rules are also instructive. Those rules did not allow for a filibuster. Instead, they allowed for a simple majority to close debate. A senator would make a "motion for the previous question," and an up-or-down majority vote would follow. Not until an 1806 rules change eliminated "previous question motions" was a filibuster even possible. Nonetheless, Binder and Smith point out that because previous question motions "had not been used as a means of limiting debate, its deletion could not have signaled a commitment to extended debate."[35] Lawyers Martin B. Gold and Dimple Gupta not only concur but also argue that the 1806 rules change that opened up the possibility of filibusters was "a sheer oversight."[36] Indeed, no filibusters occurred in the Senate until the late 1830s. In 1917 the Senate enacted a cloture rule for ending debate by a two-thirds vote, and in 1975 the Senate changed the rule to a three-fifths vote.

The use of filibusters in the Senate has skyrocketed since the 1960s.[37] Using them to block judicial nominees is a relatively recent phenomenon. A coalition of progressive Republicans and Democrats considered filibustering against President Herbert Hoover's nomination of Charles Evans Hughes to the position of chief justice in 1930, but they decided not to take that path because they did not have the votes to sustain the filibuster.[38] In 1968 Republicans mounted a successful filibuster against President Lyndon B. Johnson's nomination of Abe

Fortas for chief justice (the nomination was withdrawn).[39] But only since 2002 has the practice become commonplace. Senate Democrats used the filibuster to block ten of President George W. Bush's first-term appellate court nominees. In response, Republicans threatened to retaliate with the so-called nuclear option, a tactic that would prevent filibusters of judicial nominees. The Senate averted the nuclear option by agreeing to a compromise that allowed judicial filibusters only in "extraordinary circumstances" and put off until the future any formal changes to the filibuster rule. But with filibusters becoming more routine by the outset of Obama's second term, Senate Majority Leader Harry Reid revived the nuclear option.[40] He and his fellow Senate Democrats enacted a rules change in November 2013 to allow a simple majority of senators present and voting to end debate and proceed to a vote on most executive and judicial nominations (excluding, significantly, those to the U.S. Supreme Court).[41]

The combined effect of these various obstructionist tactics has been profound. Both President Bill Clinton and President George W. Bush declared "vacancy crises" as a result of the obstruction. A look back reveals how much more aggressive the Senate had become. A Democratic Senate blocked none of Republican Richard Nixon's lower-court nominations and confirmed 224 during his five-and-a-half years in office (1969–1974). In Ronald Reagan's eight years as president (1981–1989), the Senate blocked 43 lower-court nominees and confirmed 368.[42] In Clinton's eight years as president (1993–2000), the Senate blocked 114 of his lower-court nominations and confirmed 366.[43] During Obama's first term, the Senate confirmed 30 of his 42 courts of appeals nominees and 143 of his 173 district court nominees.[44]

The process also takes dramatically longer than it used to. According to a May 2013 report by the Congressional Research Service, the *median* length of time from nomination to confirmation for Obama's first-term courts of appeals nominees was 225.5 days (meaning that half of the nominees took longer than 225.5 days and half took less) and the median length of time for his district court nominees was 215 days. In comparison, the median length of time from nomination to confirmation under Ronald Reagan's first term was 28 days for both courts of appeals and district court nominees.[45] At the time of the Garland nomination in 2016, the Federal Bar Association reported that more than one-third of the 103 then-existing vacancies in the U.S. Courts of Appeals and District Courts had existed for at least 18 months, leading the Judicial Conference to deem them "judicial emergencies." As Chief Justice Roberts put it in his 2010 year-end report on the federal judiciary, "Each political party has found it easy to turn on a dime from decrying to defending the blocking of judicial nominations, depending on their changing political fortunes." This, he said, had created "acute difficulties" for the federal judiciary and "an urgent need for the political branches to find a long-term solution to this recurring problem."[46]

Polarized politics has made obstruction and delay by the Senate a routine part of confirmation politics. The cost is a confirmation mess. Helped (and spurred) by interest groups, opposition party senators now look for ways to disqualify nominees who do not meet their approval. The result, as law professor Stephen Carter puts it, is often a "bloodbath."[47] Public confirmation hearings and public relations campaigns are designed less to reveal nominees' knowledge and understanding of the law than to highlight their positions on policy issues and to expose embarrassing details of their past. Indeed, the confirmation gauntlet has become a political free-for-all. As the Twentieth Century Fund Task Force on Judicial Selection reported in 1988, the modern confirmation process has become "dangerously close to looking like the electoral process," with the use of "media campaigns, polling techniques, and political rhetoric that distract attention from, and sometimes completely distort, the legal qualifications of the nominee." The task force warned that "choosing candidates for anything other than their legal qualifications damages the public's perception of the institutional prestige of the judiciary and calls into question the high ideal of judicial independence."[48] The prospect of enduring the gauntlet may also discourage potential nominees from engaging in public service.

In light of this recent history, it is difficult to conclude that the president has too much power in the selection of judges. If anything, the pendulum has swung in the direction of the *Senate* exercising too much power. A "vacancy crisis," with senators misusing their power by obstructing the confirmation process for partisan and ideological reasons, is now the norm. That sounds a lot like what some of the framers sought to avoid: a process corrupted by factions and subject to intrigue.

NOTES

PRO

1. At the time this book went to press, the Senate had not yet scheduled hearings or a confirmation vote on Garland's nomination.
2. During the spring of 2016, at least two "blue-state" senators bucked their leadership and called for hearings on Garland's nomination: Sen. Mark Kirk, R-Ill., and Sen. Susan Collins, R-Maine.
3. By all accounts, President Barack Obama—the first chief executive with Senate experience in thirty-five years—bucked this trend by phoning every member of the Senate Judiciary Committee for committee members' personal advice prior to

choosing Sonia Sotomayor as his first Supreme Court nominee in May 2009. According to Sen. Charles Grassley, R-Iowa, a longtime member of the committee, it was "the first time I've ever been called by a president on a Supreme Court nomination, be it a Republican or a Democrat." If anything, Grassley's sentiment only serves to confirm just how alienated senators of both parties have been from actual judicial selections in recent decades.

4. That threesome does not include Abe Fortas, whose ill-fated bid for chief justice in 1968 was technically filibustered by the Senate, thereby preventing a formal vote on the merits of his nomination.

5. Indeed, that is precisely what happened in 2009. In the period leading up to Judge Sonia Sotomayor's confirmation hearings, senators from both sides of the political aisle braced for fireworks about her controversial vote in the recent affirmative action case of *Ricci v. DeStefano*, 264 Fed. Appx. 106 (2d Cir. 2008), *summary order withdrawn, aff'd*, 530 F.3d 87 (2d Cir. 2008), *reh'g en banc denied*, 530 F.3d 88 (2d Cir. 2008). Yet when asked about her vote to uphold the city of New Haven's decision to throw out a test that disfavored minority firefighters, Sotomayor defended her position as simply "following applicable precedent," and the vote became something of a nonissue for the remainder of the appointment process.

6. John O. McGinnis, "The President, the Senate, the Constitution, and the Confirmation Process: A Reply to Professors Strauss and Sunstein," *Texas Law Review* 71 (February 1993): 638–39.

7. Alexander Hamilton, James Madison, and John Jay, *The Federalist Papers* (New York: New American Library, 1961).

8. See Sheldon Goldman, *Picking Federal Judges: Lower Court Selection from Roosevelt through Reagan* (New Haven, CT: Yale University Press, 1997), 210.

9. Michael Gerhardt, *The Federal Appointments Process: A Constitutional and Historical Analysis* (Durham, NC: Duke University Press, 2000), 145.

10. John Anthony Maltese, *The Selling of Supreme Court Nominees* (Baltimore: Johns Hopkins University Press, 1995), 7.

11. Mark Silverstein, *Judicious Choices: The New Politics of Supreme Court Confirmations* (New York: Norton, 1994), 4.

12. Maltese, *Selling of Supreme Court Nominees*, 93–109.

13. Ibid., 110.

14. "Sotomayor Explains Wise Latina Comment," CBS News, July 22, 2009.

CON

15. Alexander Hamilton, James Madison, and John Jay, *The Federalist Papers* (New York: New American Library, 1961), 454–59.

16. Ibid., 457.

17. For a complete list of these nominations, see John Anthony Maltese, "The Long History of Presidents Nominating Supreme Court Justices in Presidential Election Years," *The Cook Political Report*, February 15, 2016, http://cookpolitical.com/story/9260

18. Hamilton, Madison, and Jay, *Federalist Papers*, 456.

19. George Mason to James Monroe, January 30, 1792, quoted in Michael J. Gerhardt, *The Federal Appointments Process: A Constitutional and Historical Analysis* (Durham, NC: Duke University Press, 2000), 346, 92n. James Wilson of Pennsylvania likewise argued that presidential nomination should be "unfettered and unsheltered by counselors" (31).

20. Hamilton, Madison, and Jay, *Federalist Papers*, 457.

21. Ibid., 455.

22. This sentence appeared in the original publication of *Federalist* No. 76 in the *New-York Packet* but was omitted in the so-called McLean edition (the first collected edition), which serves as the basis for the New American Library edition cited above. The McLean edition was published in 1788 and was corrected and edited by Hamilton and Jay but not by Madison. Most online sources of *Federalist* No. 76, however, include this sentence, including those based on the McLean edition.

23. Gerhardt, *Federal Appointments Process*, 21. Other positions were taken by different members of the convention. Some, such as John Rutledge of South Carolina, remained fearful of too much executive power.

24. Ibid., 22.

25. Ibid., 24. The convention originally rejected the compromise (which required a two-thirds vote of the Senate to confirm) and voted 6–3 in July to vest the appointment power in the Senate alone. In September, however, the convention unanimously agreed to the "advice and consent" language for federal judges that ended up in the Constitution (24–25).

26. For an articulation of this view, see, for example, David A. Strauss and Cass R. Sunstein, "The Senate, the Constitution, and the Confirmation Process," *Yale Law Journal* 101 (1992): 1491ff.

27. John O. McGinnis, "The President, the Senate, the Constitution, and the Confirmation Process: A Reply to Professors Strauss and Sunstein," *Texas Law Review* 71 (February 1993): 638–39 (footnotes omitted).

28. Hamilton, Madison, and Jay, *Federalist Papers*, 457.

29. James E. Gauch, "The Intended Role of the Senate in Supreme Court Appointments," *University of Chicago Law Review* 56 (1989): 347–48.

30. These numbers do not include Lyndon B. Johnson's nomination or withdrawal of Homer Thornberry in 1968 or George W. Bush's withdrawal of the nomination of John G. Roberts Jr. to fill Sandra Day O'Connor's associate justice seat in 2005. Thornberry's name was withdrawn only because the anticipated vacancy in Abe Fortas's associate justice seat failed to materialize. Roberts was withdrawn so that he could be nominated to fill the vacancy left by the death of Chief Justice William H. Rehnquist. The numbers do include Ronald Reagan's nomination and withdrawal of Douglas H. Ginsburg in 1987, even though his nomination was never formally submitted to the Senate. Harriet Miers's nomination was submitted to the Senate in 2005 but was withdrawn before her confirmation hearings.

31. President John Tyler renominated three "failed" nominees in 1844: John C. Spencer (after Senate rejection), Edward King (after the Senate blocked his confirmation by postponement), and Reuben H. Walworth (twice renominated—first after a Senate vote to postpone and then again after no action was taken by the Senate). The 123 total nominations before 1968 do not include consecutive resubmissions of the same nominee by the same president for the same vacancy; nor do they include the 7 nominees who declined. They do include Edwin M. Stanton (who was confirmed in 1869 but died before taking office) and Stanley Matthews (who was consecutively renominated by two different presidents in 1881). Confusion over how to count renominations has led to some disagreement about the precise number of Supreme Court nominees. The official U.S. Senate website lists eight consecutive resubmissions of nominations of the same person by the same president for the same seat (usually for merely technical reasons).

32. Barry J. McMillion, "President Obama's First-Term U.S. Circuit and District Court Nominations: An Analysis and Comparison with Presidents since Reagan," *Congressional Research Service Report*, May 2, 2013, http://www.fas.org/sgp/crs/misc/R43058.pdf

33. Walter J. Oleszek, "'Holds' in the Senate," *Congressional Research Service Report*, May 19, 2008, http://www.fas.org/sgp/crs/misc/98–712.pdf

34. Sarah A. Binder and Steven S. Smith, *Politics or Principle? Filibustering in the United States Senate* (Washington, DC: Brookings, 1997), 5.

35. Ibid., 33, 37.

36. Martin B. Gold and Dimple Gupta, "The Constitutional Option to Change Senate Rules and Procedures: A Majoritarian Means to Overcome the Filibuster," *Harvard Journal of Law and Public Policy,* 28 (Fall 2004): 216. Gold served as floor adviser to Senate Majority Leader Bill Frist in 2003–2004; Gupta served in the George W. Bush Justice Department.

37. See Figure 2-5 in Binder and Smith, *Politics or Principle?*, 48.

38. John Anthony Maltese, *The Selling of Supreme Court Nominees* (Baltimore: Johns Hopkins University Press, 1995), 55.

39. Ibid., 71.

40. Jeremy W. Peters, "Republican Drive to Block Cabinet Picks May Spur Change to Senate Rules," *New York Times,* May 16, 2013, http://www.nytimes.com/2013/05/17/us/politics/obama-appointees-fight-may-change-senaterules.html?_r=0

41. Zachary A. Goldfarb, "Senate's Filibuster Rule Change Should Help Obama Achieve Key Second-Term Priorities," *Washington Post,* November 21, 2013, http://www.washingtonpost.com/politics/senates-filibuster-rule-change-will-help-obama-achieve-key-second-term-priorities/2013/11/21/ccf43c4c-52dd11e3-9fe0-fd2ca728e67c_story.html

42. Statistics for Franklin D. Roosevelt through George W. Bush can be found in a chart accompanying Neil A. Lewis, "Bitter Senators Divided Anew on Judgeships," *New York Times,* November 15, 2003, sec. A. The Senate did reject two of Nixon's Supreme Court nominees.

43. Sheldon Goldman, Elliot Slotnick, Gerard Gryski, and Gary Zuk, "Clinton's Judges: Summing Up the Legacy," *Judicature* 84 (March–April 2001): Tables 3 and 6.

44. McMillion, "President Obama's First-Term U.S. Circuit and District Court Nominations," 4–5.

45. Ibid., 13–15. The *average* length of time from nomination to confirmation under Obama's first term was 240.2 days for courts of appeals nominees and 221.8 days for district court nominees, compared with 45.5 for courts of appeals nominees and 34.7 days for district court nominees during Reagan's first term.

46. Chief Justice John Roberts, "2010 Year-End Report on the Federal Judiciary," 7–8, http://www.supremecourt.gov/publicinfo/year-end/2010year-endreport.pdf

47. Stephen Carter, *The Confirmation Mess: Cleaning Up the Federal Appointments Process* (New York: Basic Books, 1994), 187.

48. *Judicial Roulette: Report of the Twentieth Century Fund Task Force on Judicial Selection* (New York: Priority Press, 1988), 4, 9.

RESOLVED, The vice presidency should be abolished

PRO: Douglas L. Kriner

CON: Joel K. Goldstein

The Constitutional Convention lasted 116 days, from May 25 to September 17, 1787. Not until September 4—day 103—were the words *vice president* recorded as being spoken on the convention floor. The constitutional duties that eventually would be granted to the vice president—presiding over the Senate and, in the event that the presidency became vacant, succeeding to that office—instead had been assigned to a senator chosen by the Senate to serve as its president.

How did the vice presidency come about? The short answer is: as a by-product of the delegates' late decision to create the Electoral College. To keep electors from voting exclusively for presidential candidates from their own states, the Constitution required that each elector vote for two candidates from two different states—for president. To make sure that electors cast both of their votes seriously, a consequence was attached to both. In addition to the candidate who received the largest majority of votes becoming president, the candidate who received the second-most votes would become vice president.

Off to a good start—the nation's first and second vice presidents, John Adams and Thomas Jefferson, became its second and third presidents—the vice presidency entered a steep downward spiral beginning with the enact-ment of the Twelfth Amendment in 1804. Under the amendment, instead of voting for two candidates for president, each elector would cast one vote for president and one for vice president. The result was that the vice president lost the status of being, in effect, the second-most-qualified person to be president. Never a powerful office, the vice presidency ceased to be a presti-gious one as well.

The decline in the prestige of the vice presidency triggered a century-long decline in the caliber of political leaders who were willing to seek the office: a series of has-beens and never-wases. Only with Theodore Roosevelt's election as vice president in 1900 and his succession to the presidency after William McKinley died in 1901 did the vice presidency begin to regain some of its lost prestige. TR was elected to a full term as president in 1904, a feat accomplished by none of the four nineteenth-century successor presidents (John Tyler, Millard Fillmore, Andrew Johnson, and Chester Arthur). After Roosevelt, however, every successor president but one was subsequently elected in his own right: Calvin Coolidge in 1924, Harry S. Truman in 1948, and Lyndon B. Johnson in 1964. Gerald R. Ford, who lost in 1976, came very close. As the vice presidency gained in stature, prominent political leaders became willing to leave positions such as Senate majority leader and Speaker of the House of Representatives to accept vice presidential nominations, bringing their personal prestige to the office.

Serious questions remain, however, about the vice presidency's usefulness as an institution. In May 1974, six months after Vice President Spiro T. Agnew resigned in disgrace from the office, Arthur M. Schlesinger Jr. published a widely read article in the *Atlantic Monthly,* "Is the Vice Presidency Necessary?" Schlesinger's answer to this question—a clear and decisive *no*—came to seem misplaced when, starting with Walter F. Mondale's tenure as vice president in the Carter administration, the office experienced a renaissance of responsibility and prominence that lasted through Al Gore's vice presidency during the Bill Clinton years.

No one doubted that Richard B. Cheney, Gore's successor, was a highly influential vice president in the administration of George W. Bush. Ironically, however, it was the power that Cheney exercised in the office on behalf of controversial policies, not the office's weakness, that set the stage for renewed consideration of whether the vice presidency should be abolished. In the debate that follows, Joel K. Goldstein defends the office, and Douglas L. Kriner attacks it.

PRO: Douglas L. Kriner

During the constitutional ratification debates, anti-Federalist leader George Clinton wrote that "the establishment of a vice-president is as unnecessary as it is dangerous."[1] For the first two hundred years of the office's existence,

Clinton's bombastic warning seemed nothing more than sensationalist hyperbole. Yet almost 220 years later, pundits and scholars alike have decried the rise of an "imperial" vice presidency.[2] If told that his office would one day be called "imperial," any prior denizen of the vice presidential mansion would most likely have been flabbergasted. Nevertheless, under Vice President Cheney, who exercised enormous power subject to little oversight or restraint and with little regard for public opinion, the description was apt. Although Cheney's unique blend of skill and ambition fueled his unprecedented power grab, his course of action was made possible by the constitutional structure of the office itself. While Vice President Joe Biden eschewed his predecessor's controversial constitutional claims concerning the office, according to many insiders he took the soft power of the office to even greater heights, becoming, in the assessment of some, "the most influential vice president in history."[3]

Two features of the vice presidency render it a dangerous and undemocratic institution that should be abolished. First, the mechanisms by which vice presidents are initially nominated and then elected sharply minimize the public's influence in choosing who sits a heartbeat away from the presidency. Second, because the vice presidency possesses direct constitutional roles in both the executive and legislative branches, it violates the separation of powers doctrine, blurs lines of accountability, and emboldens efforts by the vice presidential office to evade oversight from both the executive and legislative branches. Seen in this light, the stunning transformation of the vice presidency over the past four decades is far from an unequivocal good. Rather, the institutionalization of the vice presidency has vested considerable power in an office that is not fully accountable to either branch of government and whose occupants lack democratic legitimacy, as they do not contest for the position in their own right.

UNDEMOCRATIC MECHANISMS OF SELECTION AND ELECTION

Undoubtedly, the most important function of the vice presidency is to provide a capable and democratically legitimate successor should the president die or become incapacitated. To be sure, changes in the mechanics of vice presidential selection have encouraged recent nominees increasingly to value experience and competence when selecting a running mate, in most instances.[4] However, particularly on the question of democratic legitimacy, the contemporary vice presidency misses the mark.

When defending the vice presidency at the Virginia ratification convention, James Madison specifically emphasized the office's direct electoral tie to the

American people: "The consideration which recommends it to me is, that he will be the choice of the people at large."[5] Madison was referring to the original text of Article II, Section 1, which provided that each member of the Electoral College must vote for two persons for president, one of whom was not from the elector's home state. The individual with the largest number of votes, provided it was a majority, became president; the runner-up became the vice president. In theory, this selection procedure provided a direct link between the public and the vice presidency because the vice president was the people's second choice for president.

In practice, however, the early emergence of political parties quickly led to the creation of presidential tickets with both a candidate for president and for vice president. The Twelfth Amendment, which was ratified in the wake of the Electoral College tie between Thomas Jefferson and his vice presidential candidate Aaron Burr during the election of 1800, changed the process to reflect this new partisan reality. The parties would nominate one candidate for president and one for vice president, and electors would cast separate ballots for each office.

The public has virtually no influence in selecting the vice presidential nominees. For most of American history, vice presidential nominees were selected not because of their stellar leadership credentials or accomplishments in elected office but for more raw political purposes, such as bringing regional or ideological balance to the party ticket or soothing rival factions within the party base.[6] Theodore Roosevelt, for example, was famously placed on the Republican ticket in 1900 to remove him from the New York governor's mansion, where he had aggressively combated the state's machine politics, and to place him in an office where party bosses believed he could do less harm. Since 1940, presidential candidates themselves have selected their running mates; however, for most of this period the single best predictor of an individual's prospects of selection was nothing more significant than the size of the vice presidential hopeful's home state.[7] To this day, the general public has no direct influence over the identities of the vice presidential candidates on the ballot in November.

Perhaps even more alarming is the very limited direct role of popular judgments in selecting who ultimately becomes vice president. Of course, Americans do elect the vice president, yet they do so only indirectly by voting for their preferred party ticket. In making this choice, Americans could give great weight to the various options for vice president; however, almost every study of American voting behavior suggests that the public makes its decision primarily based on who is at the top of the ticket. Although every four years media pundits reliably fill the airwaves with speculation about how a vice presidential candidate may help a ticket in a certain state or among a given demographic group, the bulk of the empirical evidence shows that the candidates for vice president have minimal influence on most Americans' electoral decisions.[8] Consequently, vice presidents gain their office on the coattails of the president without ever winning the public's sanction in their own right. The result is that the electoral linkage between the vice president and the public is far weaker than Madison anticipated in 1788.

That the public has such little direct say about who holds the vice presidency in and of itself is troubling. Yet the ramifications of this state of affairs become even more disconcerting when we remember that nine vice presidents, including five of the eighteen presidents who served during the twentieth century, have succeeded to the presidency upon the death or resignation of their predecessors. Each of these men was nominated through a process insulated from public input and based in large part on raw political calculations. Each gained office without independently contesting it. Each became president and served out the full remainder of his predecessor's term without ever having won a national election in his own right. In denouncing the role of the Electoral College in selecting the nation's chief magistrate, George Clinton, himself a future vice president, wrote: "It is a maxim in republics that the representative of the people should be of their immediate choice."[9] Considered in this light, vice presidential succession involves perhaps the clearest possible violation of this principle.

The troubling normative consequences of vice presidential selection and election do not arise only in cases of succession. In contemporary politics the vice presidency has proved an invaluable stepping-stone to the presidency. Although somewhat obscured by the recent decisions of both Vice Presidents Cheney and Biden not to seek their respective party's nomination, it is important to remember that since 1960 every vice president save one who sought his party's nomination received it.[10] The emergence of our current nominating system dominated by media primaries and caucuses has only further intensified the advantages vice presidents enjoy when seeking the presidency. Today, early contests are critically important because they provide the winners with momentum that carries them forward into subsequent primaries.[11] The candidates poised to do well in Iowa and New Hampshire are those who have the name recognition and requisite financial resources to stand out in a crowded field. On both counts, holding the office of the vice presidency gives its occupant significant advantages over any other candidate. Simply put, vice presidents are perfectly positioned to dominate the invisible primary during which the field is winnowed by elites before voters even have a chance to enter the nomination process.[12] As a result, our system fundamentally limits the presidential choices available to the general electorate by granting considerable, and sometimes almost insurmountable, advantages to an individual by virtue of that person's holding an office that was not achieved through an independently contested national election. In this way, the vice presidential office is doubly undemocratic.

VIOLATION OF SEPARATION OF POWERS

It might seem absurd to suggest that the structure of the vice presidency opens the door to constitutional mischief. The Constitution grants the office neither specific enumerated powers such as those entrusted to Congress nor a general grant of power such as that given the president through the vesting clause of Article II. However, the meager constitutional clauses dealing with the vice presidency do share one feature with those that have enabled other political actors to advance occasionally fantastic claims of implied power: *ambiguity.*

Ironically, the office of the vice presidency first appears not in Article II of the Constitution, which lays out the powers of the executive branch, but in Article I, which deals with the legislative power. Indeed, the only specific, enumerated power granted to the vice presidency appears in Article I, Section 3: "The Vice President of the United States shall be President of the Senate, but shall have no Vote, unless they be equally divided." Critics of the vice presidency were quick to declare this a stark violation of the separation of powers doctrine. At the Virginia ratification convention, George Mason expanded on Clinton's fear: "Mr. Chairman, the Vice President appears to me to be not only an unnecessary but dangerous officer. He is, contrary to the usual course of parliamentary proceedings, to be president of the Senate . . . the legislative and executive are hereby mixed and incorporated together."[13] During the Constitutional Convention itself, Massachusetts delegate Elbridge Gerry critiqued the provision even more sharply, lamenting that it "might as well put the President himself at the head of the legislature."[14]

Gerry's cries can be easily dismissed as a hyperbolic jeremiad. However, by making the vice president the presiding officer of the Senate, Article I, Section 3 did give the vice presidential office institutional roles in both the legislative and executive branches. George Mason speculated in 1787 that this failure to keep the two institutions of government separate could sow the seed for subsequent abuse. "I cannot, at this distance of time, foresee the consequences," Mason prophetically warned, "but I think that, in the course of human affairs, he will be made a tool of in order to bring about his own interest, and aid in overturning the liberties of his country."[15]

Throughout American history, a number of vice presidents have sought to leverage their constitutional role as president of the Senate into a position of greater legislative leadership. The nation's first vice president, John Adams, frequently presided over the Senate, addressed its members from the chair, and used his parliamentary skills to influence a number of major issues pending before the chamber. Indeed, in his writings Adams described the role of the vice president as fundamentally legislative in function.[16] Even as late as 1961, former Senate majority leader Lyndon B. Johnson attempted—albeit unsuccessfully—to retain his position as head of the Senate Democratic Conference after his election as vice president. This separation continued until Vice President Cheney succeeded in muscling his way into weekly Senate Republican caucus meetings during his tenure in the 2000s. When some senators objected that Cheney's presence was an inappropriate incursion of the executive branch into legislative affairs, Cheney retorted that he was the president of the chamber and paid by the Senate. Cheney carried the day.[17]

Cheney's would-be successor, Alaska governor Sarah Palin, also advanced the claim that the vice presidency's position as the constitutional presiding officer over the Senate gives it an important source of leverage vis-à-vis the upper chamber. In the 2008 vice presidential debate, Governor Palin plainly interpreted Article I, Section 3 as granting the office considerable legislative power: "I'm thankful the Constitution would allow a bit more authority given to the vice president if that vice president so chose to exert it in working with the Senate and making sure that we are supportive of the president's policies." Palin's statement generated some controversy, yet the governor stood by her position. Palin reiterated the vice presidency's constitutional responsibility "to oversee the Senate" and argued "that alone provides a tremendous amount of flexibility and authority if that vice president so chose to use it."[18] Such an interpretation plainly opens the door for usurpations of legislative authority by the executive branch.

Perhaps even more troubling, however, is an innovative line of constitutional reasoning advanced by Vice President Cheney exploiting the ambiguity in the constitutional treatment of the vice presidency to insulate it from oversight by the other branches. Shortly after the outset of the Iraq War in March 2003, President Bush signed Executive Order 13292, which overhauled the system for classifying and declassifying information and, among other things, dramatically expanded the power of the vice president to classify information. As a safeguard, the order also required all classification actions to be reported annually to the Information Security Oversight Office (ISOO) for review. Vice

President Cheney, however, refused to comply with the reporting requirement on the grounds that his office was not an "entity within the executive branch" and therefore not subject to the terms of the order.[19] In June 2006, Cheney's office rebuffed a request by the National Archives and Records Administration to conduct an on-site security inspection to ensure the protection and preservation of classified documents pursuant to Executive Order 12958. Cheney's refusal again rested on his assertion that the vice presidency was not an executive branch entity, despite having previously asserted his right as an executive officer to confidentiality with his advisers when he refused to reveal details of his energy task force to public interest groups and congressional committees.[20] When the head of the ISOO appealed to the attorney general to force Cheney and his office to comply, Cheney and his staff advocated the elimination of the ISOO via executive order.[21]

The implications of this novel constitutional interpretation go beyond the case of preserving classified records. In a government publication known colloquially as the "Plum Book," Cheney's counsel argued: "The vice presidency is a unique office that is neither a part of the executive branch nor a part of the legislative branch." Cheney's staff repeatedly used this logic to support claims that the office of the vice president was exempt from oversight provisions governing both branches.[22]

As a result, the violation of the separation of powers doctrine created by the vice presidency's very structure is not merely of philosophical consequence; rather, it also has bolstered attempts to evade both executive and legislative oversight, and it has raised the specter of future attempts to centralize even more legislative power within the executive branch.

GROWING DANGER IN AN ERA OF VICE PRESIDENTIAL POWER

Both of these institutional defects take on greater significance in the contemporary era of expanded vice presidential power. The dramatic growth in influence and governing authority of the vice presidency during the past forty years only heightens concerns that the officeholder is selected and elected with little input by the American people. From a purely empirical perspective, the institutional transformation of the vice presidency from an office derided by Franklin D. Roosevelt's first vice president, John Nance Garner, as "not worth a warm bucket of spit" to a position of genuine authority during the latter decades of the twentieth century is an impressive accomplishment. Beginning with Richard Nixon's tenure, vice presidents gradually assumed increasing levels of governing responsibility, culminating in Walter Mondale's transformation of the office into something akin to a general partnership in governing with the president.[23] However, from a normative perspective this development has entrusted growing authority to an official with meager direct electoral ties to the public.

Moreover, as the vice presidency has grown more powerful, the institutional quirks that loosen the bounds of accountability become more problematic. In many respects, the evolution of the office has been positive. As expectations for the office have grown among both politicians and the public, the caliber of those seeking the vice presidency has improved, and nominees have felt increased pressure to select running mates who appear "presidential." As a result, the stature and the authority of the office have increased. However, the eight tumultuous years of the Cheney vice presidency make plain how much power a modern vice president can wield and how insufficient are the checks on this exercise of authority.

Vice President Cheney's unparalleled assertions of power were perhaps most prevalent in the realm of foreign affairs. After September 11, 2001, the vice president short-circuited the standard decision-making process to secure quick presidential approval of the November 2001 military order that denied terror suspects access to civilian and military courts and created a system of military tribunals to try them if and when the administration saw fit.[24] Cheney's clandestine exercise of power was so swift and absolute that Secretary of State Colin Powell and National Security Adviser Condoleezza Rice learned of the decision only after the order had been signed. The vice president led the fight to bypass the legal strictures of the Foreign Intelligence and Surveillance Act and to authorize the National Security Agency to wiretap the international communications of U.S. citizens without warrants; Cheney did so without even informing the White House's ranking national security lawyer. Cheney and his advisers played a pivotal role in legalizing "enhanced interrogation techniques" for terror suspects, again without the approval or even knowledge of other key players within the administration, including the secretary of state and national security adviser. Finally, the vice president's office spearheaded the effort to silence critics of the Iraq War, a campaign that publicly culminated in the conviction of Cheney's chief of staff, I. Lewis "Scooter" Libby, for leaking the identity of Central Intelligence Agency operative Valerie Plame Wilson to the press. Moreover, Cheney's unprecedented influence was not limited to the conduct of the war on terror. On a range of domestic issues the vice president frequently played a pivotal role in shaping presidential priorities and proposals from energy initiatives to tax policy to environmental policy.[25]

In each of these areas, Vice President Cheney wielded extraordinary power unprecedented in American history, and he did so with virtually no constraints on its exercise.

Vice President Biden's tenure was not marred by the same types of controversial policy blunders. However, he often exerted influence across a wide range of issues through similar means. "I literally get to be the last guy in the room with the president," Biden explained. "That's our arrangement."[26]

Other executive branch officials whose names never appear on a ballot can also amass considerable power and exercise great influence on politics and policymaking. Two factors, however, set the vice presidency apart. First, most top-ranking cabinet and agency officials require Senate confirmation; vice presidents, by contrast, are essentially selected by the president alone, with little opportunity for public influence on the choice.[27] Second, and more important, executive branch officials serve at the pleasure of the president; by contrast, vice presidents can be removed only by impeachment or by a reelection-seeking president willing to drop the incumbent vice president from the ticket. As a result, congressional and public outrage has frequently been enough to force the resignation of executive officials such as President Bush's attorney general, Alberto Gonzalez, who are perceived to have abused their power. Vice presidents, by contrast, are all but immune from such pressures. For example, despite approval ratings dipping below 30 percent, no amount of public pressure or congressional opprobrium could force Cheney from office.

Defenders of the vice presidency argue that the Cheney years are likely anomalous; future presidents will be loath to devolve so much power to their vice presidential subordinates. This may well be true, though the seeming consensus of pundits and politicos hailing Vice President Biden as wielding as much if not more power than Cheney certainly suggests that an empowered vice presidency is here to stay. However, this obscures the more important point: Mason's admonition about the unpredictability of the future consequences that may result from defects in the office's constitutional design.[28] The lessons of Cheney's tenure stand as important warnings of what may occur again given the office's insulation from direct popular election, murky constitutional status straddling two branches of government, and the dearth of institutional checks on potential abuses of power.

ABOLISHING THE VICE PRESIDENCY

In theory, some of these criticisms of the office could be redressed through institutional reform. A constitutional amendment, for example, could address the separation of powers concern and establish that the vice presidency is an executive office subject to oversight by both the executive and legislative branches accordingly. However, the problems caused by the mechanisms of vice presidential selection and election are more intractable. Returning to the system before the Twelfth Amendment could well replicate the result of the election of 1796 and give us a rival president and vice president from competing factions or parties. Such a result clearly undermines coherence and energy in executive governance. In short, there is no simple way to create a vice president who is genuinely elected directly and personally by the public but who is also committed to the president's program.

The easiest remedy is to abolish the vice presidency. The Constitution should be amended to provide for a caretaker president—perhaps the secretary of state or secretary of defense, who might be best positioned to protect America from any foreign threats until a new president is elected—in the event of the president's death or incapacitation in office. Special elections should then follow within a short, predetermined period of time. A number of potential remedies—all of which do not involve the dangerous mixing of executive and legislative powers inherent in the current system—could be adopted to break a tie in the Senate. Finally, to replace the valuable advisory role that a number of contemporary vice presidents have provided, the president could simply create additional special assistants within the White House staff.

CON: Joel K. Goldstein

The vice presidency should be retained because it fills vital needs in our system of government in a manner superior to any readily imaginable substitute. The remarkable development of the vice presidency in recent times has made it a constructive, contributing governmental office and stands in marked, and welcome, contrast to the course of many other institutions. Our government would be weaker without the vice presidency, not only because it would lose the benefits the modern office now provides but also because alternative solutions would create new problems.

Three related, but often ignored, points should govern discussions of whether the vice presidency should be abolished. First, the test is not whether the vice presidency is imperfect—all political institutions are—or whether those who seek or hold the office sometimes act in an objectionable manner, a measure that would not differentiate the office from other governmental positions that presumably are not in jeopardy. Rather, the question should turn on how the office can reasonably be expected to perform.

Second, those arguing for abolition must show that some better alternative exists to perform the important functions the vice presidency serves without damaging other aspects of American government.

Finally, it is important to discuss the vice presidency as it now exists, not its frail ancestor that was lampooned for most of American history. The modern incarnation of the office bears virtually no resemblance to the vice presidency of the nineteenth century and most of the twentieth. Especially since the tenure of Walter F. Mondale (1977–1981), the vice presidency has been transformed into a robust institution that contributes significantly to American government.

The vice presidency became more important in the twentieth century because of changes in other institutions of government. As the role of the national government and the presidency grew during the twentieth century, especially from the New Deal on, the vice presidency was pulled into the presidential orbit. Around 1940, presidential candidates began to wrest control of the selection of their running mates from party leaders, which changed the relationship between president and vice president. After the New Deal and in the nuclear age, expectations of national government generally, and of the president specifically, increased dramatically. Whereas previously vice presidents had devoted much time to presiding over the Senate, beginning in the 1950s that constitutionally prescribed role ceased to engage their attention as vice presidents, starting with Richard M. Nixon (1953–1961), migrated to the executive branch. Nixon and his five immediate successors—Lyndon B. Johnson (1961–1963), Hubert H. Humphrey (1965–1969), Spiro T. Agnew (1969–1973), Gerald R. Ford (1973–1974), and Nelson A. Rockefeller (1974–1977)—took on a standard set of executive duties delegated to them by their presidents—emissary on diplomatic missions, commission head, legislative liaison, administrative spokesperson, political surrogate.[29] These vice presidents were busier in public activities than their predecessors had been but generally remained peripheral to high-level presidential decision making.

That changed during the Mondale vice presidency, when the office made its most significant—and enduring—institutional advance. Mondale pioneered a new vision of the vice president as a senior adviser to, and troubleshooter for, the president. He obtained important resources for the office, including a White House office; a weekly private meeting with President Jimmy Carter; access to the documents that went to the president, including those relating to national security; and the right to attend meetings on Carter's schedule or to see him when he had something to share. Carter and Mondale implemented that vision faithfully and skillfully. Mondale's service demonstrated that the vice president could make important, ongoing contributions in the executive branch as an integral part of the White House.

Carter and Mondale created the White House vice presidency with its occupant expected to perform in central advising and operational capacities with the resources to make such roles possible. With some variations, their first five successors covering three Republican and two Democratic administrations imitated the model.[30] George H. W. Bush (1981–1989), for instance, embraced Mondale's vision of the vice president as a generalist. He inherited Mondale's West Wing office, lunched privately with President Ronald Reagan each week, and often joined him for meetings. Bush encouraged Dan Quayle (1989–1993) to follow the same pattern. He gave Quayle the same resources and named him chair of the Council on Competitiveness and of the Space Council. Al Gore (1993–2001) and Bill Clinton established an easy rapport. Gore became an important voice during the transition and, once in office, acted as Clinton's principal general adviser and assumed significant ongoing responsibilities. Dick Cheney (2001–2009) probably exercised even more influence than had any of his predecessors, at least during President George W. Bush's first term. Bush delegated broad authority to him and relied on Cheney to shape options in many areas for the president's decision. Joe Biden played a highly substantive role in the Barack Obama administration, which he sustained throughout his two terms in office. He met with the president regularly, made important trips abroad, and assumed responsibility in crucial areas.

The White House vice presidency makes three important contributions to American government. First, it provides a qualified presidential successor who has been chosen in an acceptable manner. Second, it makes available to the president as a senior adviser an experienced political figure who is well positioned to view the full range of issues facing the president from a perspective similar to the president's. Finally, it provides the president with a senior constitutional officer to discharge important governmental missions that must be handled at the highest levels, thereby relieving the president of some burdens.

The successor role, though contingent, is critical. As Michael Nelson put it, "The office is most significant, of course, when cocoonlike, it empties itself to provide a successor to the presidency."[31] The Constitution provides that if the president dies, resigns, or is removed from office, the vice president becomes president; if the president is unable to discharge the powers and duties of the office, the vice president acts as president until the disability ends.[32] Nine presidents have died in, or resigned from, office before finishing their terms. Moreover, presidents, including James Garfield, Woodrow Wilson, Dwight D.

Eisenhower, and Ronald Reagan, have suffered periods of disability, ranging from a few days to many months.[33] Reagan and the second Bush have transferred power briefly to their vice presidents when they underwent surgery under anesthesia, and others were prepared to do so.[34]

The successor office must be suited to respond to the different contingencies that might create the need for a permanent or temporary transfer of power. Although the contingency of presidential death, which creates a permanent vacancy, more often requires an unanticipated transfer of power, the successor office must also be able to handle the somewhat different and vexing challenges that presidential inability presents when the need for a transfer of power may be temporary and may be disputed. Effective government continuity depends on the availability of an able and accepted successor who can assume the presidency without delay, and who shares the general outlook of the administration.

The other two roles, as senior presidential adviser and troubleshooter, involve the vice president on an ongoing basis as a highly significant contributing member of the administration. Presidential decision making depends heavily on the availability of informed and candid counsel from advisers with technical expertise and with political experience and judgment. Yet the president's ability to obtain good advice is often compromised. There is a tendency to shield the president from critical assessments or unwelcome news. Moreover, many presidents surround themselves with people who have technical proficiency in particular substantive areas but lack the political knowledge and skill that long experience in electoral politics may foster. Even those cabinet officers with political sensitivity tend to become consumed with, and committed to, their departmental priorities and programs. Accordingly, they lack the time and the independent perspective to counsel the president more generally. The vice president is uniquely equipped to provide the president with candid advice by a fellow politician whose perspective and political interests resemble those of the president.

The modern presidency receives more demands for intervention at the highest official level than one human can meet. The president needs someone of stature and skill to help handle a range of such assignments—conferring with foreign leaders on international trips, meeting with key legislators to win support for priority measures, refereeing interdepartmental disputes, and negotiating agreements with parties to disagreements with public implications, for example.

The modern vice presidency has become successful in attracting able political leaders to discharge these critical roles of presidential successor, adviser, and troubleshooter. Since 1953, most vice presidents have been highly skilled and accomplished political figures.[35] Of the twelve men who have served as vice president from Nixon to Biden, ten were clearly presidential timber by virtue of their prior or subsequent public service.[36] Four became president and four suffered the narrowest of defeats.[37] Of the twelve vice presidents, seven later won their party's presidential nomination ten times.[38] Five had been legislative leaders in the Senate or House of Representatives.[39]

The selection process as it has evolved during the past seventy-six years has increased the likelihood that presidents and vice presidents will be compatible. The presidential candidate, not the party leaders, now selects the running mate and accordingly is better able to choose a compatible partner. In turn, the vice president has reason to be loyal to the person who made the elevation to the vice presidency possible. Unlike many of their predecessors, vice presidents beginning with Mondale generally have established good working relationships with their presidents and most other key administration officials, which they have sustained for most of the administration.

Additional features of the selection process give presidential candidates incentive to choose able national figures as running mates. Presidential nominations now are generally secured months before the convention. The presidential candidates accordingly have time to consider their choice of a running mate in a deliberate and rational way. The selection process presents an important test of the presidential candidates as decision makers. Presidential candidates hope the vice presidential selection will reflect well on them, and they generally choose accordingly.[40]

Of course, voters cannot vote separately for vice president. The benefits the office provides depend on tying the election of the vice president to that of the president. The method of vice presidential selection and election that has evolved promotes compatibility and mutual dependence between the president and vice president. Yet it is a mistake to conclude that the lack of a separate election deprives the vice president of democratic legitimacy. The vice presidential candidates participate actively in the presidential campaign in a very visible way. Some vice presidential candidates have affected the outcome. Johnson's presence on the 1960 ticket was crucial to John F. Kennedy's victory, Mondale surely helped Carter prevail in 1976, and Gore gave Clinton an important boost in 1992. Polls suggested that widespread misgivings about the fitness of Gov. Sarah Palin to be vice president or president hurt the prospects of Sen. John McCain.[41]

When modern vice presidential candidates do not affect the outcome, it is generally because one of two situations exists. Few voters will weigh the running mates heavily when both presidential candidates choose able and broadly acceptable running mates who are generally compatible ideologically with their ticket partners. This situation occurred, for instance, in 1980 (Mondale versus Bush) and 1996 (Gore versus Kemp). Alternatively, when potential swing voters have serious misgivings about a presidential candidate, they are unlikely to support that candidate simply because they view the running mate positively. The difficulty occurs on the rare occasions when an otherwise preferred presidential candidate chooses a running mate whom the public disfavors.

Changes in presidential campaigns have created new political institutions and practices that should reduce the occasions when an unqualified vice presidential candidate is chosen. The longer, more visible process of vice presidential selection is one such feature that directs greater attention to the office and the candidates vying for it. Presidential candidates now usually stage a public announcement of their running mates before their party's national convention to focus attention on that person. Vice presidential debates in every presidential campaign but one since 1976 also have placed the second candidates in the national spotlight. These new but apparently permanent features of presidential campaigns encourage presidential candidates to choose impressive running mates. McCain surely paid a price for choosing Palin, a lesson that will not be lost on future candidates.

Once in office, modern vice presidents have performed important roles rather than retreating to oblivion, as once was the pattern. Every vice president since Rockefeller has had a weekly private meeting with the president. Those since Mondale have had a West Wing office only steps from the Oval Office and sandwiched between the offices of the chief of staff and that of the national security adviser. This proximity fosters involvement. Mondale and his successors have spent considerable amounts of time with the president and his other principal advisers, and have exercised significant influence. They have often been "the last person in the room."

Vice presidents have assumed significant troubleshooting and, in some cases, operational responsibilities. Mondale, for instance, took important substantive foreign missions to China, the Middle East, and Europe, and helped secure ratification of the Panama Canal treaties and passage of legislation creating the Department of Education. George H. W. Bush was a skillful and frequent foreign emissary during the Reagan presidency. Quayle performed ably as a legislative contact; ran the Council on Competitiveness, which incubated some important domestic proposals of the first President Bush's administration; and made diplomatic trips, especially to Latin America and Asia. Gore took charge of Bill Clinton's Reinventing Government initiative; helped direct the administration's environmental and telecommunications programs; and cochaired commissions with leaders of Russia, South Africa, and Egypt, among other involvements. Cheney exercised widespread influence, especially in matters relating to national security, economic and tax policy, energy, and various regulatory matters. He was an architect of the war against Iraq and the administration's antiterror policies. Biden handled an array of highly consequential assignments for Obama, including implementing the Recovery Act, overseeing American involvement with Iraq, managing the Middle Class Task Force, negotiating various budget and tax deals with Republican legislative leaders, and engaging in diplomacy through foreign travel and frequent office or telephone conferences with world leaders.[42]

The developments described above, and especially those during the last four decades, provide reasons to expect future vice presidents to have political skill and stature, to be generally compatible with the president, and to be engaged in the administration's work once in office. These features make the vice president well suited to contribute to American government as adviser, troubleshooter, and successor.

The vice presidency provides a good solution to the problem of presidential succession and inability. The office provides a well-qualified successor who is knowledgeable regarding administration policies and personnel and who generally shares the president's political disposition. The vice presidency provides substantial assurance of continuity in case of permanent vacancy and makes a transfer of power more likely in response to presidential inability. The vice presidential candidate's participation in the electoral campaign lends legitimacy to the vice president's role as first successor.

The vice president offers several advantages as a senior adviser. The vice president is likely to be an experienced political leader who can offer the perspective of an elected official. Because the vice president generally has no specific agency to run, the vice president largely shares the president's perspective and can see the entire range of issues facing the administration without departmental bias. Moreover, the vice president often adds a perspective that supplements that of the president. Five of our most recent presidents—Carter, Reagan, Bill Clinton, George W. Bush, and Obama—came to the White House with little or no experience in the federal government.[43] In each case, their vice presidents had substantial experience in Washington. Mondale, George H. W. Bush, Quayle, Gore, Cheney, and Biden had all served in Congress, all but Bush for at least a decade. Bush and especially Cheney had held important positions in the executive branch.

Finally, the vice president can assume significant responsibilities, thereby relieving some demands on the president's time and allowing the government to address more problems that require attention at the highest levels. Recent vice presidents have helped the executive branch respond to the enormous demands that domestic and international issues place on the president.

The institutional changes in the vice presidency are interrelated. The changes in the selection process and election campaigns increase the likelihood that vice presidents will be able people of stature who are compatible with the chief executive. Those attributes raise the probability that vice presidents will be put to work after they are in office. Similarly, the enhanced substantive role of the office makes it appealing to talented officials.

There is reason to expect the vice presidency to continue to do a good job in its three-part role of providing a presidential successor, senior adviser, and troubleshooter. The changes in selection, election, and vice presidential role appear to have been institutionalized. The pattern of high-level vice presidential involvement since Mondale has created public expectations for the office that encourage presidential candidates to choose capable running mates who can help them govern. In 1984 Paul Light wisely anticipated that each repetition of the then-recent practices that enabled vice presidents to play a more robust advisory role would make it more difficult for a future president to reverse the trend,[44] and more than three decades later the patterns and resources of the White House vice presidency seem even more firmly entrenched.[45]

The case for retaining the vice presidency is further enhanced by the absence of any appealing alternative. A frequently suggested reform would abolish the vice presidency and have some other officer serve in the interim, pending a special election. This reform would cause more harm than good. Several problems would accompany such a change:

- It would deprive the president of the advice of an experienced political figure who largely shares the president's interest.

- It would divest the president of the help of a high-level troubleshooter.

- The interim successor would lack prior exposure to the full range of issues the president faces.

- The interim successor would have only a remote connection to the most recent national election.

- Our political system is not adapted to holding special elections.

- A special election would impose the prospect of an election amid a period of national mourning, and an additional transition to a newly elected president above and beyond that caused by the unexpected vacancy.

Abolition of the vice presidency would damage, not enhance, our governmental system. Instead of such a draconian remedy, Michael Nelson's insight in 1988 that "civic education" presents "the greatest opportunities for continued improvement in the vice presidency"[46] remains true today.

To be sure, vice presidents will not always serve well. The same is true for presidents, cabinet members, senators, and Supreme Court justices, but that fact has not been thought to be an argument for abolishing those offices. The vice presidency now contributes in important ways to the effective operation of American government. Its recent development makes its retention imperative.

NOTES

PRO

1. Cato IV, *New York Journal,* November 8, 1787, in *Founding the American Presidency,* ed. Richard J. Ellis (Lanham, MD: Rowman & Littlefield, 1999), 263. Scholars have long attributed the Cato letters to Clinton; however, some scholars now argue that Clinton's political ally Abraham Yates may have penned the letters.

2. Bruce Montgomery, *Richard B. Cheney and the Rise of the Imperial Vice Presidency* (Westport, CT: Praeger, 2009); Sidney Blumenthal, "The Imperial Vice Presidency," Salon, June 28, 2007, www.salon.com/opinion/blumenthal/2007/06/28/cheney/

3. Michael Hirsh, "Joe Biden: The Most Influential Vice President in History?" *The Atlantic,* December 31, 2012, http://www.theatlantic.com/politics/archive/2012/12/joe-biden-the-most-influential-vice-president-in-history/266729/

4. See Mark Hiller and Douglas Kriner, "Dynamics of Vice Presidential Selection," *Presidential Studies Quarterly* 38 (2008): 401–21.

5. James Madison, "Virginia Ratification Debate," in *Federalists and Antifederalists: The Debate over the Ratification of the Constitution,* ed. John Kaminski and Richard Leffler (Lanham, MD: Madison House Publishers, Inc., 1998), 95.

6. Indeed, this was a major concern raised by opponents of the Twelfth Amendment who claimed that it would make the vice presidency nothing more than a political bargaining chip.

7. See Lee Sigelman and Paul J. Wahlbeck, "The 'Veepstakes': Strategic Choice in Presidential Running Mate Selection," *American Political Science Review* 91 (December 1997): 855–64. For changes in the importance of state size after the McGovern–Fraser reforms, see Hiller and Kriner, "Dynamics of Vice Presidential Selection."

8. Inter alia see Christopher Devine and Kyle Kopko, "Presidential versus Vice Presidential Home State Advantage: A Comparative Analysis of Electoral Significance, Causes, and Processes, 1884–2008," *Presidential Studies Quarterly* 43 (2013): 814–38; Thomas Holbrook, "The Behavioral Consequences of Vice Presidential Debates: Does the Undercard Have Any Punch?" *American Politics Quarterly* 22 (1994): 469–87; David Romero, "Requiem for a Lightweight: Vice Presidential Candidate Evaluations and the Presidential Vote," *Presidential Studies Quarterly* 31

(2001): 454–63. For a contrasting argument, see Martin Wattenberg, *The Decline of American Political Parties, 1952–1980* (Cambridge. MA: Harvard University Press, 1984); Martin Wattenberg, "The Role of Vice-Presidential Candidate Ratings in Presidential Voting Behavior," *American Politics Quarterly* 23 (1995): 504–14.

9. Cato IV, *New York Journal,* November 8, 1787, in Ellis, *Founding the American Presidency,* 263.

10. Richard Nixon in 1960, Hubert Humphrey in 1968, Walter Mondale in 1984, George H. W. Bush in 1988, and Al Gore in 2000 won their parties' nominations. Only Dan Quayle, who ended his 2000 run before the first primary ballot was cast, failed to become his party's nominee.

11. For the classic political science treatment of momentum in presidential primaries, see Larry Bartels, *Presidential Primaries and the Dynamics of Public Choice* (Princeton, NJ: Princeton University Press, 1988).

12. For an introduction to the "invisible primary" idea, see John Aldrich, "The Invisible Primary and Its Effects on Democratic Choice," *PS: Political Science and Politics* 42 (2009): 33–38. Of course, it could also be argued that the vice presidency is most dangerous precisely when the current occupant of the office has *no* intention of seeking the presidency. Such an incumbent is freed from the constraint of seeking the presidency and is empowered to expand aggressively the office's power base.

13. George Mason, "Virginia Ratification Debate," in *Federalists and Antifederalists: The Debate over the Ratification of the Constitution,* 2nd ed., ed. John Kaminski and Richard Leffler (Madison, WI: Madison House, 1998).

14. "The close intimacy that must subsist between the president & vice president," Gerry went on to argue, "makes it absolutely improper." See Mark O. Hatfield et al., Wendy Wolff, ed., *Vice Presidents of the United States, 1789–1993* (Washington, DC: U.S. Government Printing Office, 1997).

15. Mason, "Virginia Ratification Debate."

16. Adams wrote: "[The vice presidency] is totally detached from the executive authority and confined to the legislative." Hatfield et al., *Vice Presidents of the United States, 1789–1993,* 3–11.

17. Barton Gellman, *Angler: The Cheney Vice Presidency* (New York: Penguin Press), 56–57.

18. Imtiyaz Delawala and Z. Byron Wolf, "Palin Says Vice President 'In Charge of' Senate," ABC News.com, October 22, 2008, http://blogs.abcnews.com/politicalradar/2008/10/palin-says-vice.html

19. Mark Silva, "Cheney Keeps Classification Activity Secret," *Chicago Tribune,* May 27, 2006, http://articles.chicagotribune.com/2006-05-27/news/0605270039_1_government-secrecy-classification-decisions-national-archives-office

20. See *Cheney v. United States District Court,* 542 U.S. 367 (2004). To clarify, the initial request by the National Archives to inspect the vice presidential records was made in 2004. A June 2006 memo presented Cheney's justification for his office's repeated refusals to comply with Executive Order 12958. For a timeline and overview of the issues involved, see Henry A. Waxman, chair, Committee on Oversight and

Government Reform, U.S. House of Representatives (letter to Vice President Cheney, June 21, 2007), http://oversight.house.gov/documents/20070621093952.pdf

21. J. William Leonard to Alberto Gonzalez, January 9, 2007, http://www.fas.org/sgp/isoo/isoo-ag.pdf; Peter Baker, "Cheney Defiant on Classified Material," *Washington Post,* June 22, 2007, http://www.washingtonpost.com/wp-dyn/content/article/2007/06/21/AR2007062102309.html

22. For *United States Government Policy and Supporting Positions,* the so-called "Plum Book," with alternate issues published by the Senate and the House of Representatives, see www.gpoaccess.gov/plumbook/2004/p226_appendix5.pdf. For Cheney's efforts to use this doctrine to avoid both executive and legislative oversight, see Barton Gellman and Jo Becker, "A Different Understanding with the President," *Washington Post,* June 24, 2007, sec. A.

23. For an insightful and thorough analysis of the emergence of the modern vice presidency, see Joel Goldstein, *The Modern American Vice Presidency: The Transformation of a Political Institution* (Princeton, NJ: Princeton University Press, 1982); Joel Goldstein, "The Rising Power of the Modern Vice Presidency," *Presidential Studies Quarterly* 38 (2008): 374–89.

24. "Military Order of November 13, 2001," *Federal Register* 66, no. 222 (November 16, 2001): 57833–36.

25. For a thorough overview of Cheney's remarkably powerful tenure as vice president, see Barton Gellman, *Angler: The Cheney Vice Presidency* (New York: Penguin Press, 2008); see also James Pfiffner, *Power Play: The Bush Presidency and the Constitution* (Washington, DC: Brookings, 2008).

26. "Remarks by Vice President Joe Biden on Foreign Policy at a Campaign Event," April 26, 2012, https://www.whitehouse.gov/the-press-office/2012/04/26/remarks-vice-president-joe-biden-foreign-policy-camapaign-event

27. Most White House staff officials, including the chief of staff, do not require Senate confirmation.

28. Moreover, the Cheney years are not as anomalous as some protest. Previous vice presidents, most notably Walter Mondale and Al Gore, exerted considerable power and authority in office. Admittedly, they did so to a lesser extent than Cheney; however, these additional precedents speak to the potential for powerful vice presidents to arise again in the future.

CON

29. The argument in this paragraph is developed in greater detail in Joel K. Goldstein, *The Modern American Vice Presidency: The Transformation of a Political Institution* (Princeton. NJ: Princeton University Press, 1982).

30. See, generally, Joel K. Goldstein, *The White House Vice Presidency: The Path to Significance, Mondale to Biden* (Lawrence, KS: University Press of Kansas, 2016); Joel K. Goldstein, "The Rising Power of the Modern Vice Presidency," *Presidential Studies Quarterly* 38 (September 2008): 374–89.

31. Michael Nelson, "Background Paper," in *A Heartbeat Away: Report of the Twentieth Century Fund Task Force on the Vice Presidency* (New York: Priority Press, 1988), 22.

32. U.S. Constitution, Twenty-fifth Amendment. The Twenty-fifth Amendment supplanted in part and also supplemented Article II, Section 1, Clause 6.

33. See, generally, John D. Feerick, *From Failing Hands: The Story of Presidential Succession* (New York: Fordham University Press, 1966); John D. Feerick, *The Twenty-fifth Amendment: Its Complete History and Earliest Applications,* 3rd ed. (New York: Fordham University Press, 2014); Robert E. Gilbert, ed., *Managing Crisis: Presidential Disability and the 25th Amendment* (New York: Fordham University Press, 2000).

34. Goldstein, *The White House Vice Presidency,* 255–59, Feerick, *The Twenty-fifth Amendment,* 196–204.

35. For an argument that since the 1970s able people are chosen to run for vice president, see Mark Hiller and Douglas Kriner, "Institutional Change and the Dynamics of Vice Presidential Selection," *Presidential Studies Quarterly* 38 (September 2008): 401–21.

36. I would include on the list of "clearly presidential" Nixon, Johnson, Humphrey, Ford, Rockefeller, Mondale, George H. W. Bush, Gore, Cheney, and Biden. Agnew and Quayle are the other two. Quayle made important contributions as vice president and has been underestimated, in my view, but he had not been considered a leading presidential candidate when Bush chose him in 1988 and never later had success as a presidential candidate.

37. Nixon (1968), Johnson, Ford, and Bush became president; Nixon (1960), Humphrey, Ford, and Gore lost four of the closest elections of the twentieth century.

38. Nixon (1960, 1968, 1972), Johnson (1964), Humphrey (1968), Ford (1976), Mondale (1984), Bush (1988, 1992), and Gore (2000).

39. These leaders were Johnson (Senate majority leader), Humphrey (Senate majority whip), Ford (House minority leader), Cheney (House minority whip), Biden (chair of the Senate Judiciary Committee and the Senate Foreign Relations Committee).

40. Goldstein, *The White House Vice Presidency* 173–224.

41. Ibid. , 243, 247.

42. See, generally, ibid., 79–89, 109–13, 115–19, 122–27, 135–40, 143–47.

43. Carter, Reagan, Clinton, and George W. Bush had been governors and had never held office in the national government. Barack Obama had been a senator, but for fewer than four years. Of presidents elected between 1976 and 2012, only George H. W. Bush had had considerable experience in national government when first elected president.

44. Paul C. Light, *Vice-Presidential Power: Advice and Influence in the White House* (Baltimore: Johns Hopkins University Press, 1984), 268.

45. Goldstein, *The White House Vice Presidency,* 307–10.

46. Nelson, *A Heartbeat Away,* 100.